Bible Study with "Me" & The Cowboy

BIBLE STUDY WITH "ME" & THE COWBOY

BEA SERIOUS

Bible Study with Me and The Cowboy by Bea Serious

This book is written to provide information and motivation to readers. Its purpose is not to render any type of psychological, legal, religious, or professional advice of any kind. The content is the sole opinion and expression of the author, and not necessarily that of the publisher.

Copyright © 2022 Bea Serious

ISBN: 978-1-953115-74-4 (sc)
ISBN: 978-1-953115-73-7 (e)

All rights reserved.

No part of this book may be reproduced, stored, or transmitted by any means- whether auditory, graphic, mechanical, or electronic- without written permission of both publishers and author, except in the case of brief excerpts used in critical articles and reviews. Unauthorized reproduction of any part of this work is illegal and is punishable by law.

CONTENTS

BIBLE STUDY	10
THE OLD TESTAMENT	**11**
FREE – FREE FALL – FALLEN	13
GOD SPEAKS GENESIS TO REVELATION	16
I DID IT MY WAY, CAIN – "AM I MY BROTHERS KEEPER? GENESIS CHAPTER 4	19
"THE EIGHTH PERSON" – (2 PETER 2:5) GENESIS 5 – 9	21
A FRIEND OF GOD – ISAIAH 41:8	30
ONE STEP AHEAD	45
"HE, THAT GOD HATED" – GENESIS 25-33	55
I DID IT GOD'S WAY – GENESIS 37-50	58
THE FORTY MAN, MOSES EXODUS, LEVITICUS, AND NUMBERS	71
I DID IT MY WAY – THE HARD SOIL	102
WHO'S TO BLAME?	105
A MAN AFTER MY OWN HEART – DAVID	106
HEAVY HAIR – ABSALOM – 11 SAMUEL 13-19	124
THE WISEST "MAN" – SOLOMON	128
STRONG HAIR – SAMSON – JUDGES 13- 16	153
JOB	156
BLESSED BE THE NAME OF THE LORD – JOB 1-42	158
PSALM 151	163
PSALM 152	165
PROVERBS	166

WORDS, WHAT DO THEY MEAN?	170
DANIEL, "THE PROPHET" AND 'A MAN GREATLY BELOVED' BY GOD DANIEL 1-12	174
"MAD AS "SPIT," AT GOD? – JONAH 1-4	207
ONLY FORTY MORE DAYS	214

THE NEW TESTAMENT — 217

MY NAME IS JOHN – (LUKE 1-2)	219
HOW DO I GET TO HEAVEN FROM HERE? MATTHEW 19:16-22	231
HOW RICH WAS HE? – LUKE 16:19-31	234
HOW POOR WAS HE? – LUKE 16:19-31	237
THAT SON OF YOURS	240
LIVIN' AT HOME – LUKE 15:11-32	241
RIOTOUS LIVING	242
REALLY LIVING	243
BOB, WHAT ABOUT BOB?	244
WISE, OR FOOLISH? – MATTHEW 25:1-30	246
SET FREE – LUKE 8:1-2 – JOHN 20:1-20	250
LORD, LET'S KEEP OUR PRIORITIES STRAIGHT	254
JESUS WHERE ARE YOU? MARTHA, MARY, AND LAZARUS	255
THE THORN IN MY FLESH – 11 CORINTHIANS 12:2-10	260
BEFORE WE MARRY	264
IT'S ANOTHER GIRL	267
ME, MYSELF, AND I MUST DECREASE	269
"HE" MUST INCREASE	270
ONE WAY TO PRAY	272
ANOTHER WAY TO PRAY	273
WHAT'S YOUR SECRET	275

OH LORD, WHERE ARE YOU?	277
TIRED, SO TIRED	280
WHERE CAN YOU RUN?	282
WHAT DO YOU WANT ME TO DO?	284
MY LIFE	285
GOD'S WILL, MY CHOICE	287
JUST GIVE UP	289
"FEAR NOT, I WILL HELP YOU" - (ISAIAH 41:10)	290
WHAT IS IT LIKE TO BE YOKED TO JESUS?	293
HOW DEFEATED IS HE?	297
WHO'S RESPONSIBLE?	298
HOW DID I GET DOWN HERE IN HELL?	299
ALMOST PERSUADED	301
WHICH LIE, IS THE TRUTH?	303
FOOLISH STATEMENTS	305
THE RULES OF JESUS DAY	307
SOME RULES OF OUR OWN	308
YOUR LAST DAY	310
WORSHIP	311
THE WORSHIP SERVICE - MARK 4:31-32	312
ANOTHER WORSHIP SERVICE - MARK 4:31-32	314
WORDS TO USE IN CONVERSATION AT CHURCH	316
A CLEAN SWEEP	319
LUKEWARM	320
SEX IS SEX	322
WHY DO YOU DO WHAT YOU DO?	323
SEVEN TIMES SEVENTY	324
I DID IT MY WAY - MOST DESPISED MAN	326

JUST A BREATH AWAY	330
SOME THINGS YOU WOULD NEVER HEAR JESUS SAY	332
THINGS JESUS SAYS	333
QUESTIONS JESUS ASKED	335
I DID IT GOD'S WAY - JESUS (GENESIS 1:1 TO REVELATION 22:21)	337
BIBLE STUDY SO FAR	406

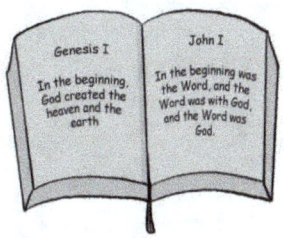

BIBLE STUDY

"I was wondering if we could have Bible Study together?"

"???????"

"You know, just the two of us."

"???????"

"We could start in Genesis or John, or maybe Nahum or Colossians."

"???????"

"Since it is just the two of us, we can start anywhere and go anywhere, and go as long as we want to."

"??????"

So, what do you think?"

"??????"

"So okay, I guess that means ok, RIGHT?"

THE OLD TESTAMENT

FREE

GENESIS 2

My beloved Eve,

"You are bone of my bones, and flesh of my flesh." (Gen. 2:23) You are my wife; 'of whom my soul loveth,' (Song of Solomon 1:7). You are the fairest of all that live and breathe. I want only to hear your "sweet voice speaking." Your beautiful eyes are deep and knowing, and your hair is most ravishing, your lips are perfect loveliness." (Song of Solomon)

Your body is clothed in the bright light of God's glory that glows with your every move, and I cannot take my eyes away from you all the daylong. You were given to me by God, "my garden," my friend, and my 'help meet' forever.

Your Darling,
Adam

*****

My God-Man Adam,

You are God's perfect creation. You came directly from God's loveliness to me. God fashioned me from one of your ribs; I am a part of you and I always want to be your helper, so that you will become all that God has planned for you now, and forevermore. You fill my days with meaning and delight. Your voice of song is so magnificent I can hardly breathe when you sing to the glory of God, and fill this garden with music.

God made me for you, and He put us together to enjoy Him and each other forever and ever.

This wonderful garden is heaven on earth as long as you are with me. "Every tree is pleasant to the sight and good for food" except one that you told me of. God has only restricted us from eating of 'one' Tree in the center of the garden, the "tree of knowledge of good and evil." (Gen 2:16-17) God is with us everywhere and listens to our every question and concern; we are content to be alive and together forever and ever with Him.

May you always know how much I love you, and how much I respect your devotion to me, and to God? God has put His great glory and strength in you, and we will be forever happy here with one another.

God is always with you to bless you with happiness and with His great love.

Your Help Mate,

Eve

FREE FALL

GENESIS 3

"WHAT'S GOING ON HERE ADAM? WHY ARE YOU WEARING FIG LEAVES?"

"Well, God, you know, my wife… I mean, that woman you gave me; it was 'all' her idea."

"EEEEVE!"

"God, I know this looks sort of funny, but the serpent…it…it starting talking to me about things. I know snakes don't usually talk, but God the serpent is very subtle, you know, and the 'smartest beast of the field' that "You" made to live with us here in the garden.

"Anyway, I mean… I know that You know all this because You made serpents extra smart. He, the snake, got to talking to me and confusing me, and after all Adam told me what You had said, and it was all secondhand and this serpent he kept interrupting me and he did 'beguile' me, and somehow or another I was over at the tree holding the fruit and before I knew it... it was in my mouth and I was chewing. Boy was it good too! You said we shouldn't try it, but I don't see why You would want to keep this luscious fruit from us God!

"I mean… You know how it is with people, we're only 'human' You know."

GENESIS 3

"Now we've been cast out of that beautiful garden, and it's 'ALL YOU'RE FAULT!"

"MEEEE?"

"Yes, YOU! 'YOU' talked me into it with your conniving ways and those fluttering eyelashes!"

MEEE? Who came over of his own free will and started picking, and eating, and laughing, and dancing?"

"Well…. 'YOU' were doing it too."

"Okay… But the bottom line is we didn't hurt anybody but ourselves. No one will ever have to know what happened here. Besides, if anything ever comes up, I'm sticking with the snake story."

GOD SPEAKS

GENESIS TO REVELATION

MY BREATH OF LIFE ADAM,

I CREATED THE HEAVEN AND THE EARTH AND ALL THE BEAUTY THEREIN. I CREATED ALL THE FISH AND ALL THE BIRDS AND ALL THE ANIMALS IN ALL THEIR DIVERSITY AS A GIFT JUST FOR YOU, MY MAN-CHILD.

I MADE YOU FROM THE GOLD DUST OF THE EARTH AS MOST GLORIOUS CREATION, MADE IN MY IMAGE AND LIKENESS, SO THAT I MIGHT BLESS YOU FOREVER AND EVER WITH ALL THAT I AM AND ALL THAT I HAVE AND ALL THAT I HAVE TO GIVE. (GENESIS 1:27 GENESIS 2:27)

I GAVE YOU EVE AS YOUR HELP MEET, TO SHOW YOU MORE OF MY ENDLESS LOVE AND CONCERN FOR YOUR EVERY DESIRE OR WISH. (Gen 2:21)

YOU NEED ONLY TO CALL MY NAME AND I AM INSTANTLY AT YOUR SIDE. IF EVER YOU COULD IMAGINE ANYTHING THAT YOU DIDN'T HAVE, I WOULD ALWAYS "SUPPLY IT ACCORDING TO MY RICHES IN GLORY BY CHRIST JESUS." (MY SON) (PHILIPPIANS 4:19)

ONE DAY I CALLED TO YOU AND YOU WERE HIDING FROM ME. I ASKED YOU "WHY?" AND YOU SAID THAT IT WAS BECAUSE YOU WERE NAKED. I ASKED YOU, WHO TOLD YOU THIS? (Gen 9:11) YOU ONLY GAVE ME EXCUSES AND BLAME, AND A LIE. I HAD TO SEND YOU OUT OF THE BEAUTIFUL GARDEN OF EDEN THAT I MADE JUST FOR YOU, SO THAT YOU COULD NOT 'PUT FORTH YOUR HAND AND TAKE ALSO FROM THE TREE OF LIFE, AND EAT,' AND LIVE FOREVER IN YOUR DISOBEDIENCE TO ME. (Genesis 3:22)

I KNEW WHEN I GAVE YOU MY CHOICE YOU WOULD SOMEDAY USE IT TO SEPARATE US. I KNOW EVERYTHING ABOUT YOU AND

YOUR EVERY THOUGHT BEFORE YOU EVER THINK IT, BUT IT IS NO LESS PAINFUL THAT I AM NO LONGER THE CENTER OF YOUR LIFE.

NOW YOU HAVE LET ANOTHER VOICE COME INTO YOUR THINKING, AND UNLESS YOU TURN FROM IT BACK TO ME, IT WILL CONSUME YOU DAY AND NIGHT. YOU KNOW NOW WHAT DEATH IS, BECAUSE YOU WATCHED ME AS I MADE YOU "COATS OF SKINS" FROM AN INNOCENT LAMB THAT HAD TO DIE TO COVER WHAT YOU BELIEVE IS YOUR NAKEDNESS, AND YOUR SHAME. (Genesis 3:21)

I CURSED THE SERPENT AND GAVE YOU A PROMISE THAT ONE WOULD BE "BORN OF A WOMAN" THAT WOULD DEFEAT THE SERPENT BY BRUISING HIS HEAD, AND THE SERPENT WOULD ONLY BE ABLE TO STRIKE AT THIS 'BLAME LESS' ONE'S HEEL,' YOU BELIEVE NOW THAT THIS "SAVIOR" WILL BE YOUR SON, BUT IT IS MY "BELOVED SON, MY ONLY BEGOTTEN SON." (Genesis 3:15)

I TOLD YOU YOUR FUTURE LIFE WOULD BE LIVED IN PAIN AND SORROW, HARD WORK, SWEAT, AND TEARS, JUST TO HAVE FOOD TO EAT AND CLOTHES TO WEAR, YOU AND YOUR WIFE WILL HAVE STRIFE BETWEEN YOU; AND, NOW, SHE WILL WANT TO RULE OVER "YOU." (Genesis 3:18-19)

ONE DAY, YOUR BODY WILL RETURN UNTO COMMON DUST. (Genesis 3:19) YOU WERE NEVER MADE TO DIE AND BE DUST AGAIN, BUT YOU MUST, TO BREAK THE CURSE OF DISOBEDIENCE.

MY PLAN AND PURPOSE FOR YOU IS AS I PLANNED IT BEFORE THE FOUNDATIONS OF THE EARTH, (Ephesians 1:4) AND IT WILL BE FULFILLED IN MY TIME. OUR RELATIONSHIP HAS BEEN CLOUDED, BUT NEVER WILL YOU OR ANY MAN HAVE TO BE SEPARATED FROM ME IN HELL, BECAUSE I HAVE PROVIDED ANOTHER INNOCENT "SACRIFICIAL LAMB" THAT WILL PAY THE HIGH PRICE OF YOUR SIN, AND RESTORE YOU TO ME BY TAKING YOUR JUDGEMENT, SO THAT YOU AND ALL THOSE WHO COME AFTER YOU CAN BE CALLED THE 'RIGHTEOUSNESS OF GOD' AND BE "CALLED BY 'MY NAME."

YOU WILL ALWAYS BE MY LOVELY CHILD. NOTHING CAN QUENCH "MY" ETERNAL, INFINITE LOVE FOR YOU.

YOUR CREATOR AND HEAVENLY FATHER,

GOD

I DID IT MY WAY, CAIN
"AM I MY BROTHER'S KEEPER?"
GENESIS CHAPTER 4

Sure, I killed my brother. He was so smug with his animal sacrifices I didn't see why my offering of the best "fruit of the ground "wasn't just as good as his animals. I brought almost the best of my harvest, after all.

Abel, my brother, kept sheep so of course, he could make an animal sacrifice to God. What was I supposed to do? God asked me why I was angry? Why not! God went on to warn me that "sin was crouching at the door" and He told me that 'I must subdue it and be its master.' (Genesis 4:7 NLB) No way, when God Himself accepted Abel but not me. Abel offered his sacrifice in faith: well, I had faith in my offerings too!

The day came when I could take it no longer, so I killed Abel and buried him in the ground when no one saw me. God came to me and asked me, "WHERE IS ABEL THY BROTHER?" I said, 'I know not; am I my brother's keeper?' (Genesis 4:9)

Of course, I lied; I was not going to be blamed for this. Abel deserved everything he got. God told me that I would be a "fugitive and a vagabond" in the earth. (Genesis 4:12) I said this was 'greater than I could bear.' I saw no reason to ask for mercy.

God put a sign on me so that no one would kill me. This satisfied me, so I left the presence of the Lord and went to the land of Nod and took a wife from among my relatives that lived there. I had a son that I named Enoch, and I built a city in his name. (Genesis 4:17) So this was my life.

"THE EIGHTH PERSON" (2 PETER 2:5)
GENESIS 5-9

My grandfather was Methuselah; my father was Lamech. I am Noah. Methuselah was Enoch's son. This Enoch is my Great Grandfather; (this is not Cain's son, that he named a city after); Jared was this Enoch's father. After Enoch had Methuselah "he walked with God, and when he was 365 years old, he walked into heaven; for God took him." Genesis 5:21-24 Enoch was one of the men in the Bible that did not die. The other man that did not die was Elijah, for he went to heaven in a whirlwind riding in a chariot of fire, pulled by horses of fire. (11 Kings 2:11) Methuselah lived to be 969 yrs. old, which was the oldest man that ever lived. (Methuselah's name means: "When he is dead, it shall be sent" McGee) The number of his years played a big part in my life and in the history of the world, because when he died the flood came. The people of my time knew what his name meant, but still, they did not believe that God would send a flood to cover the earth.

As you know, I was born before the "flood" that God sent to "Destroy man from the face of the earth. (Genesis 6:7) God saw that the wickedness of man was great in the earth, and that every imagination of the thoughts of his heart was only evil continually. (Genesis 6:5) God looked upon the earth, and, behold it was corrupt; for all flesh had corrupted his way upon the earth. The earth was filled with violence. (Genesis 6:11-12) God was grieved in His heart that He had made man." (Genesis 6:6)

I Noah, "found grace in the eyes of the Lord because I was a just man, and I walked with him." (Genesis 6:8-9) God spoke to me and I wanted to obey Him in all that He told me to do.

The Lord told me that "man" had only 120 more years to repent of his ways, and to live on the earth. He told me all flesh was filled with violence because of man's corruption, and He, God, was going to destroy all flesh with the earth.' (Genesis 6:3, 6:18) This meant, "He would destroy man, and beast, and the creeping thing, and the fowls of the air." What a terrible judgment was coming for mankind, and all the animals of the earth.

Because I had found grace in the eyes of the Lord, He told me that He would save me and my family from the terrible destruction to come. He told me to "make an ark of gopher wood; with rooms in the ark, and to pitch it within and without with pitch. He said to make the ark 450 feet long, (about as long as a football field) 75 feet wide and 45 feet high. I was to put a window at the top of the ark and there were to be three decks inside the ark; a bottom, middle and an upper deck, and there was to be one door in the side." (Genesis 6:14-16) Many ships that sail in the 21st century have been patterned after the ark.

God told me He was going to cover the earth with a flood, but He would save my family along with "every living thing of flesh," He said I must 'bring two of every kind of animal and bird and reptile, male and female, so they could reproduce after their own kind' when the carnage was over. I was to bring "seven pairs of all animals that God chose for food," and those that He chose to be used as a sacrifice to Him, after the flood was over. God also wanted me to take seven pairs of birds, and sufficient food for my family and food enough for all the animals. (Genesis 6:19-20)

God told me these things, about the flood, when I was 480 years old. The bible states that when I was 500 years old, I had three sons, Shem, Ham, and Japeth. There has been much speculation, over the centuries, that my sons were triplets, but it is not clear in the Bible that they were. In Genesis chapter 11, verse 10 it says; "These are the generations of Shem: Shem was a hundred years old, and begat Arphaxad two years after the flood." He should have been 102 or 103 years old two years after the flood if my sons were triplets, because I was 600 years old when I entered the ark, and it has been stated that I was 500 years old when I had my three sons. These mysteries will be revealed to you when and 'if' you go to Heaven to live with the Lord someday. You know that not all of you will be with God in Heaven when you die. You must accept Jesus as your Lord and Savior, and believe He died on the cross to redeem you from your sin. ("Believe on the Lord Jesus Christ and thou shall be saved, and thy house." Acts 16:31)

When God gave me His command to build the ark, I was very anxious to do all that he had said. Living on the earth at this time were millions and billions of people as it is in the 21st century. God's people were intermarried with unbelievers so that they all thought very highly of themselves, and they did not regard God as "God" ('they were outstanding individuals that believed that they had "arrived," and they believed they were greater than they really were'); they did not honor God or need Him in their lives, which is why God said "I (Noah) was the only truly righteous man living on the earth." (McGee)

Many of you may believe that the ark was some sort of crude flat-bottomed tub of a boat with animals hanging out of the windows as you have seen in children's books. The whole experience would be only distasteful, because the animals would be very smelly and noisy, and that my sons and I would only have time to pitch hay all day long. It would be a time of great endurance until the flood subsided and we could get outside again.

You may also believe that it took me 120 years to complete the ark. One hundred twenty years to make some sort of crude dwelling that only God could keep miraculously afloat in the flood time.

There is a passage in the bible that reads: 1 Peter 3:20 "…When once the long suffering of God waited in the days of Noah, while the Ark was preparing, wherein few, that is eight souls were saved by water." It sounds like I was pounding on the ark for 120 years while God waited patiently for me, because I was so slow and this was a very hard task; I must have just got it done in the nick of time when the animals came and we all got on board.

Actually, it only makes sense that the ark would be finished in a few years, so more could be made if people believed God, and wanted to be saved along with me and my family. I employed the finest minds, engineers, mathematicians, and laborers so a ship could be made that would be seaworthy, and one that would keep us afloat for a long period of time, and according to God's instructions. Many were willing to help me with this project because it offered them a job and an income. You know that no one wanted to get on board this vessel, however, once it was done.

During the 120 years I was preaching and preparing the people to know what was coming, as God had presented it to me. The Lord said,"

"MY SPIRIT SHALL NOT ALWAYS STRIVE WITH MAN, FOR THAT HE ALSO IS FLESH: YET HIS DAYS SHALL BE ONE HUNDRED AND TWENTY YEARS." Genesis 6:3 God' saw that the wickedness of man was great in the earth, and that every imagination of thoughts of his heart was only evil continually.' (Genesis 6:5) I told people over and over again what God was going to do at the end of the 120 years; torrents of rain would fall, and "water" would fill the earth. The people believed, if this did happen, climbing the highest mountain would save them because they could seek shelter there. (McGee)

Most only laughed and told me I was just trying to scare them with this kind of talk. But I was not deterred, because the Holy Spirit filled me with a Christ-likeness that made me bold to speak to their disobedience. (1 Peter 3:18) "For Christ also hath once suffered for sins, the just for the unjust, that He might bring us to God, being put to death in the flesh, but quickened by the Spirit. By which also He went and preached unto the spirits in prison: Which sometime were disobedient, when once the longsuffering of God waited in the days of Noah, while the ark was preparing…) (McGee)

I was the object of ridicule and much discussion, because, you see, there were no oceans or large bodies of water at this time, and no rain. We had no huge ships or vessels because none were needed; a mist watered the earth so people did not envision rain, or a flood. Once the ark was formed for all to see it became only speculation on how it would float on dry land.

Let me take you to another passage in scripture in Matthew 24:37-39, when Jesus told His Disciples the signs of the events that would signal His return to the earth. One sign He mentioned was: "Before the flood the world was at ease; banquets and parties and weddings abounded, just as in the days of Noah before the sudden coming of the flood;" people would not believe what was going to happen (to them) until the flood actually arrived and took them all away."

Now, ask yourself if these events sound like your day? Do you have much elaborate banquets and parties? And many well planned out weddings? Do you not have a food channel on your TV, and do you not have a channel that shows a wedding planned from the falling in love, by the couple, to the actual day of the wedding, and the reception (banquet) that follows? How many weddings have you been to in your lifetime? Do some of the couple's divorce and still send you an invitation to the next wedding, which is even more elaborate than the first? Jesus explained in Matthew 24 and Luke 21, and in Revelation, and other places in the Bible, what would take place before His coming back to the earth. Please understand your times, and prepare yourselves for what is coming; do not believe that nothing bad could ever happen to you, or to the United States.

God told me to make rooms in the ark (Genesis 6:14) These rooms were for my family and me, and for anyone who wanted to join us. They were self-contained with all the luxuries of my day. Each one was furnished with all the latest technology, and all the beauty that God had to offer to us. Yes, we had much technology as you do today. Man lived for hundreds of years, so he had time to study and create many self-saving devices, and to make many advances in the environment, in science, in physics, and in mathematics. It was these inventions, and much studying, that took the heart of man away from God. Man believed in his own power more than the power of God.

These rooms had luxurious linens, carpets, running water, and bathrooms with heat control and pure air, soft lighting for evening, and bright lighting for reading. We had insulation to close out the world beneath us and lovely music piped into every room to calm our spirits. We had voice carriers to communicate with each other without leaving our room. We had places to store clothing and personal items, and we had a way to fix food rapidly and get it to a room quickly.

This was no barbaric tub. The Lord wanted people to be close to Him, an appealing place to be, not some kind of endurance test. Yes, there was work that needed to be done: cleaning and laundry, cooking and taking care of the animals, but we had all the latest conveniences to make the work go fast and efficiently. We also had a room where we could look up and see the stars and the sky above, and to worship God and thank Him for our salvation.

The ark was to represent Heaven: God the Father, Son, and Holy Spirit, a place of refuge. It also was a picture of man: body, soul, and spirit. It was a safe place to be saved from certain death. My family was willing to trust that I had heard from God. My sons, Shem, Ham, and Japheth each had a wife that would come on board with them. (McGee)

When I was 600 years old God told me to take my family into the ark, and then "the animals came by two, male and female," and they came unto me into the ark as God commanded them. 'And it came to pass after seven days that God shut the door, and then the waters of the flood filled the earth. At the beginning of this account of my life, I told you that Methuselah was my grandfather and he lived to be 969 years old, the oldest man as recorded in the Bible. I also told you that his life had an impact on history. When he died, God told me to go into the ark; the flood did not come until his death. (Remember his name meant: "When he is dead, it shall be sent")

We did not know when "God" would shut the door, but my faith did not waver. The news went out to all the earth that my family and I were on board the ark, at last. The news media showed the animals coming, by their own power, into the ark, and the people had time to take the fast transportation of my day, and reach the ark in time to be saved. But as you know, no one came. No one believed God would do what He said He would. The scoffers, and those that had ridiculed me for 120 years were about to see the power of God's Word come to pass.

The water just poured down from the sky, and every crevice of the earth seemed to pour water out like a fountain until the ark was lifted up on the water above the earth. The mountains were covered with water twenty-two feet above the highest peaks. Every living soul and everything that breathed was "blotted out" from off the face of the earth. It was a sad time for God and for my family and me; knowing what was going on below, but God did not forget us, and after forty days and forty nights the heavy rain and gushing water, stopped. (Genesis 7:9-11)

"After 150 days the ark came to rest upon the mountains of Ararat." Three months later more mountain peaks appeared. After another forty days, I opened the window and released a raven, but she did not return to the ark. I realized a raven could feast on dead meat, so I sent out a dove, because she needed vegetation for food, and she could only get it if there was dry land; but she returned to the ark, so I held out my hand and drew her back inside.

Seven days later I sent the dove out again, and this time she returned, in the evening with an olive leaf in her break. I knew, now, the water was almost gone, so I sent her out again in another seven days, and this time she did not return I waited another twenty-nine days and opened the door and saw the water was gone from the earth, God then told me that we could all go out into the sunshine, and release all the animals and birds and reptiles. (Genesis 8:10-13)

I then built an altar and sacrificed on it some of the animals and birds that God had set aside for this purpose. The Lord was pleased and said, "I WILL NEVER AGAIN CURSE THE EARTH AND DESTROY ALL LIVING THINGS, EVEN THOUGH MAN IS BENT TOWARD EVIL FROM HIS BIRTH. AS LONG AS THE EARTH REMAINS, THERE WILL BE SPRING TIME AND HARVEST, COLD AND HEAT, WINTER AND SUMMER, DAY AND NIGHT." (Genesis 8:22)

God then blessed me and my sons and said unto them, "BE FRUITFUL AND MULTIPLY, AND REPLENISH THE EARTH." I will establish my covenant with you; NEITHER SHALL ALL FLESH BE CUT OFF ANY MORE BY THE WATERS OF A FLOOD; NEITHER SHALL THERE ANY MORE BE A FLOOD TO DESTROY THE EARTH. And God said, "THIS IS A TOKEN OF THE COVENANT WHICH I MAKE BETWEEN ME AND YOU, AND EVERY LIVING CREATURE THAT IS WITH YOU, FOR PERPETUAL GENERATIONS: I DO SET MY BOW IN THE CLOUD, AND IT SHALL BE FOR A TOKEN OF A COVENANT BETWEEN ME AND THE EARTH." (Genesis 9:13)

This was such a wonderful promise from God for the entire world to see forever and ever. A "rainbow" in the sky every time it rains and the sun shines through the rain; a gorgeous bow of colors (red, orange, yellow, green, blue, and violet) would arch over the sky.

God told us to go forth: do not stay close to the ark and the past. My sons Shem, and Ham, and Japheth went out and 'of them the whole earth was overspread." (with people again). This was the answer to God's promise to us. (Genesis 9:19)

You would think that after all of this that had happened to me, I would worship God and honor Him only, but I planted a vineyard and made wine and drank of it until I was drunk. This was a disgrace to me as I lay naked in my tent. My son Ham saw me and told his two brothers about it. Shem and Japheth took a garment and laid it upon both their shoulders, and went backward, and covered my nakedness, (so they could not see me)." This was a dark time for me, and because of my drunkenness Canaan (Ham's son) received a curse because of the part he played in my folly. (Genesis 9:20-25) This account of my sin should teach you that 'the spirit is willing, but the flesh is weak.' A believer does not lose his salvation by sinning, if he believes that Jesus washed his sin clean by His blood. But know this. "Your sin will find you out" and you will not like the end result.

I lived after the flood another 350 years, so I lived 950 years in all. It was a long satisfying life with God. Please know that you too can have a life lived in God's grace and mercy, with the great joy of knowing the God of all Creation.

A FRIEND OF GOD
(ISAIAH 41:8)

When I was born, my father Terah called me Abram. You know me best as Abraham, because God changed my name from Abram, which means "high father, to Abraham, which means "father of a multitude." I am known more than any other person in the world because the three great religions of the world relate to me: Judaism, Islam, and Christianity. It was because of my name and its meaning, and the fact that God promised me a son that would be born to Sarai, my wife, later named, Sarah, by God, that I had so many twists and turns in my life. Also I should mention that Sarah was my half-sister. It was okay to marry one's sister at this time, but later it proved to be a stumbling point in my life.

God promised Sarah and me a son, but we had to wait twenty-five years for our son to be born. I'm getting ahead of the story of my life, so I will go back to my home of Ur, of the Chaldees (today's Iraq). It was here that God spoke to me and told me to leave "all my kindred" and all of my friends and my country and 'come into a land God would show me.' He said I could only take my wife and possessions with me, but no one or nothing else. (Acts 7:2 - 4)

The reason God wanted me out of Ur, was because it was a land of idolatry. (Joshua 24:2) When I told my family about this departure, they were incredulous that I could think of leaving my home to go off on a "wild goose chase" with God that they knew nothing of.

My father insisted he would come with us, and he also told my nephew Lot that he could come with us too. ("And Terah took Abram his son, and Lot the son of Haran, his son's son and Sarai his daughter in law, Abraham's wife, and they went forth with them from Ur. (Genesis 11:31) My brother, Haran, had died young leaving Lot his son, so my father felt obligated to take care of him.

I should have made it clear that I could take no one but Sarai with me, but I did not because I believed my father was old and needed me to take care of him. (I could have trusted God to do that in my absence) I thought it would make no difference as long as I was doing most of what God told me to do. I now realize partial obedience to God is not acceptable. God demands perfection. But God is the God of second chances, and I Thank him, the God of many chances.

Instead of going on to the land that God told me of, my father decided we should stop in Haran, in Syria so I stopped too, and we stayed there until my father's death, which turned out to be fifteen years later. I did not hear from God in all the time.

Now God gave me a threefold promise that is the "backbone of the bible." He said: "GET THEE OUT OF THY COUNTRY, AND FROM THY KINGDOM AND FROM THY FATHER'S HOUSE, UNTO A LAND THAT I WILL SHOW THEE: AND I WILL MAKE THEE A GREAT NATION, AND I WILL BE BLESS THEE, AND MAKE THY NAME GREAT: AND THOU SHALT BE A BLESSING: AND I WILL BLESS THEM THAT BLESS THEE, AND CURSE HIM THAT CURSETH THEE; AND IN THEE SHALL ALL FAMILIES OF THE EARTH BE BLESSED." (Genesis 12:2-3)

"Has God made good on His promise to me? Yes, God brought from me a great nation, and God has through me blessed all of mankind, but you all know my descendants' do not have all the land God gave to me. The boundaries should be the land east to the Euphrates River and all the way north as far as the Hittite nation was, and all the way south to the river of Egypt, which is a river in the Arabian Desert. At the zenith of Israel's occupation, they occupied 30,000 square miles but that is not all God gave to us, it is actually 300,000 square miles." (McGee)

So, did God lie to me about the amount of land he would give to me? No, "God will make good on His promise, on His terms, and on His time table, sometime in the future." In fact, He will fight for Israel Himself: "The Lord shall roar out of Zion, and utter His voice from Jerusalem; and the heavens and the earth shall shake: but the Lord will be the hope of His people, and the strength of the children of Israel. 'SO SHALL YE KNOW THAT I AM THE LORD YOUR GOD DWELLING IN ZION, MY HOLY MOUNTAIN: THEN SHALL JERUSALEM BE HOLY, AND THERE SHALL NO STRANGERS' PASS THOUGH HER ANY MORE. AND IT SHALL COME TO PASS IN THAT DAY THAT THE MOUNTAINS SHALL DROP DOWN NEW WINE AND THE HILLS SHALL FLOW WITH MILK AND HONEY, AND ALL THE RIVERS OF JUDAH SHALL FLOW WITH WATERS, AND A

FOUNTAIN SHALL COME FORTH OF THE HOUSE OF THE LORD, AND SHALL WATER THE VALLEY OF SHITTIM. EGYPT SHALL BE A DESOLATION, AND EDOM SHALL BE A DESOLATE WILDERNESS FOR THE VIOLENCE AGAINST THE CHILDREN OF JUDAH, BECAUSE THEY HAVE SHED INNOCENT BLOOD IN THEIR LAND. BUT JUDAH SHALL DWELL FOREVER, AND JERUSALEM FROM GENERATION TO GENERATION. FOR I WILL CLEANSE THEIR BLOOD THAT I HAVE NOT CLEANSED: FOR THE LORD DWELLETH IN ZION." (Joel 3:16-21)

So, again we departed for Canaan. I gathered up "Sarai, my wife, and Lot, my brother's son, and all our substance that we had gathered, and the people that we had gotten in Haran," and we started out. I was seventy-five years old and Sarai was sixty-five. (Genesis 12:4-5) I want to tell you a bit of trivia about the age of Sarah. There are only two women in the Bible that have their ages disclosed, one is Sarah and the other is Anna.

Again, I did not completely obey God because I took Lot with me. I figured I could not leave him now that we had been together for so long, and it must be okay, or God would have said something about it. I realize now that God says what He says, and expects to be obeyed. He does not keep repeating Himself. He just lets you have your own way, and eventually you will realize that they have made a big mistake in not obeying completely, but still God's will, will be done.

When we arrived in Canaan God appeared unto me and said: "UNTO THY SEED WILL I GIVE THIS LAND." I immediately built an altar to the Lord and worshiped Him. (Genesis 12:7)

"There was a famine in the land." So --- I took my family and possessions into Egypt to stay it out, because it was a very "grievous" time. (Genesis 12:10) God did not tell me to do this, but I thought it was the thing to do. God could have taken care of us in the land He had given us, but I didn't trust Him to do that.

Sarah was a very beautiful woman, so as we neared Egypt, I explained to her that the Egyptians would see her and want her, but because she was married, they would kill me and take her to wife. So, I asked her to say she was my sister, and they would spare my life. Since she was my half-sister, I figured this was not really a lie, but God did not see it that way.

When we arrived in Egypt it happened as I thought it would. Sarah was taken into Pharaoh's house to become his wife. She agreed to lie for my benefit. The Egyptians had a preparation time for a woman to be trained to be the wife of a ruler. (The Royalty of England, and other Royalty, should consider this before any person is allowed to marry the children of the King or Queen). Because of Sarah, Pharaoh gave us many sheep, oxen, donkeys, camels, and servants.

Then God plagued the household of Pharaoh with great plagues because Sarah was there. Pharaoh called me and said, "What have you done unto me? Why did you not tell me that Sarah was your wife? Why did you say she was your sister? Now take her and go thy way!" He commanded his men to escort us out of his country and to take all the possessions he had given to us and the ones we had brought with us, and go far away. (Genesis 12:12-20)

You can see what my disobedience and this lie had cost me so far, but this was only the beginning of what I would later realize it would cost me and my nephew, Lot, and all of mankind. Our sins go on forever in the minds of man, even though God forgives us, but the consequences are usually more than we want to bear.

When we got back into the land God promised me, I went to the altar that I had built between Bethel and Hai, and "called on the name of the Lord." (Genesis 13:4) God was willing to take me back into 'His' plan for me. (McGee)

It became apparent that the land could not support me and Lot, and all that we had accumulated from God and from Egypt. Our herdsmen were fighting over the best pasture for the cattle. The Canaanite and the Perizzite people, of the land, were watching all of this and our witness was tarnished because of the strife.

I said to Lot, "We must separate from one another, and I give you the first choice of the land that you may chose as your own. I will take what is left." (Genesis 13:6-9)

Lot was so impressed with the "fertile land in Egypt and he had seen the plain of Jordan, that was well watered everywhere," that he chose this place to settle. He did not consider the type of people that lived there, and what effect they would have on him, and his wife, and children, in the future, because, 'the men of Sodom were wicked sinners before the Lord.' (Genesis 13:10, 13)

Now that Lot was gone from me, the Lord spoke to me again and said, "LIFT UP THINE EYES, AND LOOK FROM THE PLACE WHERE THOU ARE NORTHWARD, AND SOUTHWARD, AND EASTWARD, AND WESTWARD FOR ALL THE LAND WHICH THOU SEEST, TO THEE WILL I GIVE IT, AND TO THY SEED FOREVER. AND I WILL MAKE THY SEED AS THE DUST OF THE EARTH: THEN SHALL THY SEED ALSO BE NUMBERED. ARISE, WALK THROUGH THE LAND IN THE LENGTH OF IT AND THE BREADTH OF IT; FOR I WILL GIVE IT UNTO YOU." (Genesis 13:14-17)

Again, God verifies that He is giving me this land and that "my seed would be as the dust of the earth", even though I had no son as yet. If there is any doubt in the minds of men today that the Jews are in their own land given to them by God, this passage should be referred to once again. The reason there is doubt, is because I had two sons, that claimed this land, but God considered only Sarah's son as my seed, or the one that my descendants (and God's promised Son) would come through, and the one He promised me. (Here I might mention that I had eight sons total, but again I am getting ahead of the story.)

There is no doubt that God wanted me, and all of my descendents, to have this land as our own. I stated before that God would make good on His promise to me, even though it has not come to pass yet, though we are into the 21st century.

"I did arise and walk through the land and took our tents and moved them to the pain of Mamre, which is in Hebron, and I built an altar there unto the Lord." (Genesis 13:18) Mamre means 'richness' and Hebron means "communion," so this was a perfect place to dwell and worship God. I built many altars to the Lord as a testimony to Him, so that the people of that land knew me as 'that Hebrew,' Remember your identity in God and claim it always. (McGee)

The next thing that happened in my life was a war in Sodom, and Lot, my nephew, was captured and all his goods. I went to his rescue and "recovered Lot and his goods and the women also, and the people." (Genesis 14:16) The King of Sodom tried to give me many goods, but I would not take anything, 'lest the King would say I have made Abram rich.' I owed all to God in Heaven and I needed nothing else from anyone.

I did believe that my men, who helped me recover Lot, "should have a portion of the booty," so it was given to them. (Genesis 14:21)

After all this happened in Sodom, "the word of the Lord came to me in a vision, saying, `FEAR NOT, I AM THY SHIELD, AND THY GREAT REWARD." (Genesis 15:1) I said to the Lord God, 'What will thou give me, seeing I go childless, and the steward of my house is this Eliezer of Damascus? Behold, to me thou have given no seed, and, lo, one born in my house is my heir.' (Genesis 15:2-3)

I pointed out to God that my head servant, who had an offspring, would inherit all of my goods if I did not have a son of my own. I could not seem to grasp that God had promised me an heir, over and over Again. Still my faith wavered because Sarah and I were getting on in years.

God continued to be gracious to me, so again He said to me, "ELIEZER'S SON SHALL NOT BE YOUR HEIR, BUT HE THAT SHALL COME FORTH OUT OF THINE OWN BOWELS SHALL BE THINE HEIR." And he brought me forth, and said, 'LOOK NOW TOWARD HEAVEN AND TELL THE STARS, IF THOU BE ABLE TO NUMBER THEM: and He said unto me, SO SHALL THY SEED BE.' (Genesis 15:4-5)

"So, now God told me that my offspring would be as numberless as the sand on the seashore, and now He tells me they will be a numberless as the stars in heaven. I would actually have two seeds, my physical son, which represents the nation Israel, and a spiritual seed, the Christian church, coming by faith through Jesus Christ." (McGee) (Galatians 3:29)

I believed the Lord, and He counted it to me for righteousness." (Genesis 15:6) He told me again that He was giving me the land to inherit it. I asked, 'How shall I know that I shall inherit it?' God told me to prepare a sacrifice. I was to get a heifer, a she goat, a ram and divide them down the middle and put one half on one side but I was not to divide them, but put one over there and one over here." (McGee)

"I then fell into a deep sleep and I was shown the future by God. The Hebrew people, my people, would be put out of their land three times. The first would be for four hundred years, and we would be afflicted during this time and then we would return only to go into Babylonian captivity for seventy years, and the third time we would be scattered." (McGee) Even in the 21st century, we have not fully returned from this one. 'And it came to pass, that when the sun went down and it was dark, behold a smoking furnace and a burning lamp that passed between those pieces.' (Genesis 15:17)

The furnace speaks of Jesus Christ to come and of judgment, and the lamp speaks of Jesus as the light of the world. God made me the promise and I only accepted it to be true. I did not need to do anything of myself, as I could not, I could only believe what God told me, and this is what you too must do, to be saved." (McGee)

The next thing that happened to us is something that I wish had never happened. This goes back to our time in Egypt and the lie and the disobedience I experienced there. Sin causes all kinds of grief. At the time it seems so right, but later one understands why God tells us not to sin by disobedience to Him; He tells us this out of His love for us, for our own safety and peace of mind.

While we were in Egypt Sarah acquired a handmaid named Hagar, as a gift from the Pharaoh. Sarah had the "bright idea" that since time was passing and we did not have a child, we should have one by Hagar. When the child was born, Sarah and I would claim the child as our own. This was the custom in Egypt and it seemed so right at the time. God made it plain that a man should have only one wife (Genesis 2:24), so I was going to disobey God once again and have a child by Hagar making her my wife.

After all the times that God assured me that Sarah and I would have a child, I did not question this decision to make Hagar our surrogate mother. I did not go to God and ask Him about it, I just went unto Hagar and she conceived. When Hagar realized that she was with child, she despised Sarah; Sarah realized this was a big mistake and blamed me for it. But I would not take the blame, so I told Sarah to deal with Hagar herself.

"Sarah dealt harshly with Hagar and Hagar fled from her presence. While she was out in the wilderness by a fountain of water, the angel of the Lord said to her, 'SARAI'S MAID, WHENCE COMEST THOU? AND WHITHER WILT THOU GO:' She said, "I flee from the face of my mistress Sarai." (Genesis 16:6)

The angel of the Lord said to her, "I WILL MULTIPLY THY SEED EXCEEDINGLY, THAT IT SHALL NOT BE NUMBERED FOR THE

MULTITUDE, BEHOLD NOW, THOU ART WITH CHILD, AND SHALL BARE A SON, AND SHALL CALL HIS NAME ISHMAEL BECAUSE THE LORD HAS HEARD THY AFFLICTION. AND HE WILL BE A WILD MAN; HIS HAND WILL BE AGAINST EVERY MAN; AND EVERY MAN'S HAND AGAINST HIM. HE SHALL DWELL IN THE PRESENCE OF ALL HIS BRETHREN" Hagar returned to Sarah and bore her son, and his name was called Ishmael. I was 86 years old when this baby was born. (Genesis 16:7-16)

When I was ninety-nine years old, God spoke to me again and changed my name from Abram to Abraham, as I was to be the father of many nations. (Genesis 17:5) He said he would give to my descendants and me, all the land of Canaan, "for an everlasting possession and He would be our God." This name change is very important because God was giving me a new start, after I had been disobedient by taking Hagar to wife, and also the lies I told about Sarah being my sister, omitting that she was also my wife. Since the law had not been given, and Jesus had not come, God chose this way to change my heart and to forgive me. (McGee)

God said, "THIS IS MY COVENANT, WHICH YOU SHALL KEEP, BETWEEN ME AND YOU AND YOUR SEED AND YOUR SEED AFTER YOU: EVERY MAN CHILD AMONG YOU SHALL BE CIRCUMCISED. THE FLESH OF YOUR FORESKIN; SHALL BE TOKEN OF THE COVENANT BETWEEN ME AND YOU." (Genesis 17:9-11) The covenant is the promise God gave me concerning Isaac, the land, and my descendants. "We as Israelites do not circumcise ourselves, in order to become members of the covenant; we do this to show the world we are members of the covenant of God." (McGee) Today, a believer in Jesus Christ must circumcise his heart before God, that is; give God his ideas, his dreams, his plans, his time, and all that he is to God: then God will use him as He has designed a person to be in Christ. (McGee)

God, also at this time, changed Sarai's name to Sarah, and He said again that "Sarah would bare me a son and she would be a mother of nations; kings of people shall be of her." (Genesis 17:15-16) Sarah also had to have a name change, so she could bare the promised son.

I then tried to bargain with God that my son Ishmael should inherit the promise. God said, "NO!" SARAH WILL BEAR A SON AND YOU WILL CALL HIM ISAAC AND MY COVENANT IS WITH HIM AND HIS SEED

FOREVER." (Genesis 17:19)

I then took "Ishmael, my son, and all that were born in my house, and all that were brought with money, every male in my house; and circumcised the flesh of their foreskin that very same day, as God had said unto me." I was ninety-nine years old and Ishmael was thirteen years old. (Genesis 17:23-27)

Again, God reaffirmed his promise to me: I was sitting in the door of my tent when I saw three men coming toward me. I ran to meet them and bowed myself to them. I asked them to stay and told them that I would provide water to wash their feet while they sat in the shade of a tree. I told them I would make them a "morsel of bread to comfort their hearts." (Genesis 18:5)

They said they would accept my hospitality. I ran to Sarah and asked her to "measure out three portions of fine meal, knead it, and make cakes on the hearth. I also ran to the herd and found the best calf, and gave it to a young man and impressed him to cook the meat quickly. I also took butter and milk, along with the meat and bread, and spread this meal out before them, and they did eat." (Genesis 18:6-8)

When they had finished eating, they told Sarah and me that Sarah would have a son in a year's time. Sarah laughed that she would have a son at 90 years old. They asked why she laughed, and she lied that she had. She did not believe it was possible that she should have a son in her old age. I laughed too, but with delight that finally Sarah and I would have the promised son. (Genesis 18:9-150)

Next, two of the men went toward Sodom, but I stood talking with the Lord. He said, "THE SIN OF SODOM AND GOMORRAH IS GREAT, AND BECAUSE IT IS VERY GRIEVOUS IT WILL BE DESTROYED." I was incredulous that God would destroy these cities if there were righteous men living there. So, I asked the Lord if He would destroy the cities if fifty righteous men lived there. He said, NO, NOT FOR FIFTY." So I went on to 45. He said, "NO." So I went on down to 10. He said, "NO I WILL NOT DESTROY THE CITY IF TEN RIGHTOUS MEN LIVE THERE," I stopped at ten because there were ten in Lot's family, and I knew not if they were righteous or not. (McGee)

You may know what happened next. The two angels told Lot to get his family together and "escape to the mountains." Lot tried to get his sons-in-laws to leave the city with him, but they only 'mocked him.' The angels had to take Lot and his wife, and his two daughters by the hand, to pull them out of the city because they were reluctant to leave this wicked city. The angels told them not to look back, but Lot's wife did, and she immediately turned to a "pillar of salt." (Genesis 19:1-20)

When I arose in the morning "I looked toward Sodom and Gomorrah, and toward all the land of the plain, and beheld, and lo, the smoke of the country went up as the smoke of a furnace." (Genesis 19:27-28) My heart was very heavy for Lot and his family, but a person must honor God with his life and teach his children to fear God.

I must tell you of another time that I disobeyed God: I moved to a place between Kadesh and Shur in Gerrar; Sarah, now 90 years old, and still most beautiful, was taken by King Abimelech to be his wife. I again feared for my life, so I asked Sarah to lie and say she was my sister. You probably thought that I would have learned by now that God could not tolerate this sin in my life, and I would not repeat such an abominable thing again. I know now, that God had to deal with this sin, and I had to give it up to Him and never repeat it again, before Isaac our promised son could be born. (McGee)

You too, may be waiting on God to bring to pass something He has promised to do for you in your life. All the blessing of God is yours for the claiming, if you will repent of your sin and be obedient to God. The church of God has been talking of revival for many years, and Christians wonder why it has not yet come. Individuals must judge their own personal sin before God, and acknowledge it, confess it, and repent of it, or blessing cannot come. Please ask yourself what it is you are hanging onto, that you cannot face or give up, and trust God to take care of it for you. Are you into pornography, do you get angry easily, are you afraid of everything, do you condemn your Pastor and other church members, are Harry Potter books and movies more important to you than Jesus Christ? These kinds of sins can keep a congregation, or an individual, from moving forward in the plan that God has for them. (McGee)

Now, at last, as the Lord had said, our son Isaac was born at the "set time." I circumcised Isaac when he was eight days old, as God had commanded. Sarah and I were so very happy over Isaac's birth, and even his name means laughter. (Genesis 21:3-7)

Not everyone was delighted as we were over the birth of Isaac; Ishmael was mocking Sarah and Isaac, so Sarah told me I must "cast them out" of our home. I loved Ishmael and did not want to do this deed. But God being faithful to me, told me He would 'make a nation' (Genesis 21:13) from Ishmael, because he was my son. This helped me, so I did as I had to do, and "sent Hagar and Ishmael away with bread and a bottle of water." I could not send her with more, because thieves would attack and kill the two of them if they had anything of value with them. (McGee) I trusted God would help them as He had promised, and you know that God did keep His promise to Ishmael and his descendants; they are many, known to you as the Arabs.

I, by now—had learned that God is to be trusted and obeyed immediately when He speaks. The next test was the biggest of my life. God told me to "take my son, my only son Isaac, whom you love, and go into the land of Moriah; and offer him there for a burnt offering upon one of the mountains which I will tell thee of." (Genesis 22:2)

I spent no time questioning this command; I and Isaac rose up early and saddled a donkey and took two young men, wood for the burnt offering, and went to the place God told me of". (Genesis 22:3) When we got to the place for the burnt offering, Isaac and I went on alone. Isaac carried the wood on his back; I took fire, and a knife, Isaac asked, 'Where is the lamb for the burnt offering? 'I told him, "My son, God will provide himself a lamb for a burnt offering." (Genesis 22:7-8)

"When we arrived at the place which God told me of, I built an altar there and laid the wood in order." (Genesis 22:9) Isaac was now told that he was to be the sacrifice, but he was willing to let me use him as that sacrifice. 'I bound him, my son, and laid him on the altar upon the wood. 'Isaac was not a young boy; he was in his thirties, and he could have easily overpowered me and run away. (McGee)

"Next, "I stretched forth my hand, and took the knife to slay my son." And the angel of the Lord, called unto me out of heaven, and said, 'ABRAHAM, ABRAHAM:' and I said, "Here am I." And he said, 'LAY NOT YOUR HAND UPON THE LAD, NEITHER DO THOU ANY THING UNTO HIM: FOR NOW, I KNOW THAT THOU FEAREST GOD, SEEING THOU HAST NOT WITHHELD THY SON, THINE ONLY SON FROM ME.' (Genesis 22:10-12)

I then "lifted up my eyes, and looked, and behold behind me a ram was caught in a thicket by his horns: so, I went and took the ram, and offered him up for a burnt offering instead of my son." (Genesis 22:13)

This was most humbling to me, to know God is always faithful, and brings the most wonderful outcome to all things. Learn to trust Him in all your ways, and you will be free to live the "abundant life" He so willingly has given to you. It took me a lifetime to realize I could trust God in all things. Please learn from me and do not waste any more of your life trying to accomplish what only God can do, in you, and so willingly wants to do for you.

Why did I trust God in such a trial as this? I finally "Learned" that God could do anything, and that He could raise Isaac from the dead If necessary. You probably realize that this offering of Isaac was a picture of Jesus Christ, willingly giving His life on the cross for you. And you know that Jesus was resurrected after His death and burial; God does, and will raise all believers who die trusting in Christ. (McGee)

Again, God reaffirmed His promise to me that "He will bless me, and IN MULTIPLYING I WILL MULTIPLY THY SEED AS THE STARS OF THE HEAVEN, AND AS THE SAND WHICH IS UPON THE SEA SHORE; AND THY SEED SHALL POSSESS THE GATE OF HIS ENEMIES; AND IN THY SEED SHALL ALL THE NATIONS OF THE EARTH BE BLESSED; BECAUSE THOU HAST OBEYED MY VOICE." (Genesis 22:17-18)

When my beloved Sarah was 127 years old, she died in the land of Canaan. I was grief stricken, and I "mourned and wept for her." (Genesis 23:1-2) Isaac, too, was very sad at her passing. I purchased a sepulcher to bury her in. The people of Heth were generous to give me my choice of sepulchers; I paid "four hundred shekels of silver for a field and a cave;" Sarah and I, Isaac and Rebekah, and Jacob and Leah, are all buried at this spot. (Genesis 23:13-16)

Today, there is a Moslem Mosque built over our resting place. "We are buried in Israel, because our hope is to be raised from the dead, by God, in this land." (McGee)

With Sarah gone, and Isaac at the age of marriage, I had to secure a wife for him. I did not want him to marry one of the "Canaanites", so I sent my eldest servant to "my country, and to my kindred, to find a wife for my son Isaac.' (Genesis 24:4) After my servant "put his hand under my thigh, his master, and swore to me concerning this matter of a wife for Isaac, I sent him to Mesapotamia, unto the city of Nahor." (Genesis 24:9-10)

My servant took ten camels of mine, and gifts for the new bride, and her family. When he reached a well he prayed to God to reveal the right woman to him. "He asked that the damsel to whom I shall say, 'Let down thy pitcher. I pray thee, that I may drink,' and she shall say, "Drink, and I will give thy camels drink also." Let the same be she that thou hast appointed for thy servant Isaac; and thereby shall I know that thou hast showed kindness unto my master. '(Genesis 24:14)

Well, it turned out exactly as he had prayed. "Rebekah came out, who was born to Bethuel son of Milcah, the wife of Nahor, Abraham's brother, with her pitcher upon her shoulder. The damsel was very fair to look upon, a virgin neither had any man known her; and she went down to the well, and filled her pitcher, and came up. My servant ran to her and asked for a drink from her pitcher, and she said, "Drink my lord: and she hasted and let down her pitcher upon her hand, and gave him drink. The she said, "I will draw water for thy camels also, until they have done drinking. (Genesis 24:17-19) Rebekah invited him to her home, and my servant gave her a 'golden earring, and two bracelets of gold." (Genesis 24:22)

When my servant came into the house of Bethuel, Rebekah's brother, Laban, took care of the camels. Before my servant would eat a meal prepared for him, he told them of his errand. He said, "I am the servant of Abraham, who has been blessed greatly by the Lord. Abraham has sent me to take a wife for his son. The Lord has led me to Rebekah, and I wish to take her back with me as a bride for my master's son. "Both Rebekah's father and brother said I could take her and go. Rebekah's mother wanted her to stay ten days before she left, but my servant wanted to leave immediately. They called Rebekah and asked her I she would go with my servant, she said, 'I will go.' (Genesis 24:62-63)

When the caravan was close to our home in Cannan, Isaac saw them coming with Rebekah with them. Rebekah saw Isaac too and "lighted off her camel," and asked, 'What man is that, that walks in the field to meet us?' When she understood it was Isaac, she "took a veil, and covered herself," (Genesis 24:64-65)

My servant "told Isaac all that had been done and Isaac brought her into his mother Sarah's tent, and took Rebekah, and she became his wife: and he loved her: and Isaac was comforted after his mother's death,"

(Genesis 24:66-67) I was very pleased about all these events and with Isaac's wife Rebekah.

Since this chapter of my life was closed, I took a wife named Keturah. She bore me six sons, Zimran, and Jokshan, and Medan, and Median, and Ishbak, and Shuah. (Genesis 25: 1-2) I told you I had eight sons in all. When I was 175 I died, an "old man, full of years." My sons Isaac and Ishmael buried me in the cave of Machpelah, where Sarah was buried.

So this is the story of my life. God blessed me as He promised, and all my descendants. He will bless you and your descendants too, if you will give your life to Him. AMEN

ONE STEP AHEAD

GENESIS 25 - 46

As I Jacob, look back over my long life I see how God has blessed me. Before I was born God told my mother, Rebekah, that she was carrying twins. He told her that my brother Esau and I were warring within her because "Two nations were in her womb. The one people shall be stronger than the other people; and the elder shall serve the younger." This was to be the pattern of our lives together. When we were born Esau came out first, but I had a hold on his heel. We did not look much like twins because he was red and hairy and I was not. (Genesis 25:25-26)

My father Isaac loved Esau because he "did eat of his venison," and my mother Rebekah, loved me. (Genesis 25:28) I would rather stay in the house and do things there; I learned to cook. My brother Esau like to hunt and fish, and be outdoors all the time. He was a good hunter. As we grew up, I wanted to get the birthright away from Esau, after all, God said that 'the elder shall serve the younger,' so I figured I needed to get the birthright somehow. One day I saw my chance.

Getting the birthright would mean I would receive the first blessing from our father, and a great portion of the inherited money, and I would be the head of the household when our father died. One day I had made succulent lentil soup, and Esau came in from hunting, famished. He was very hungry and wanted some of the soup and bread that I had made. I said that I would feed him if he would give me his birthright for the soup. He said, "What good is a birthright if one is dead from hunger?" I could hardly believe it was so easy. (Genesis 25:29-32)

More years passed, and when our father was old and believed he was nearing death, (he was 60 years old when we were born) he called for Esau to go to the field and hunt for venison; he asked him to make him "savory" meat that he would eat, and then he would bless him, as the firstborn. He knew nothing of Esau's and my previous agreement over the lentil soup. (Genesis 27:1-8)

My mother was listening to the conversation between my father and Esau; she then came and told me that I must go in first and receive the blessing. She prepared meat from young goats that I killed and brought to her, and she had me put the skins of the goats on my hands and neck, then she had me put on a garment of Esau's so I would feel hairy like my brother, and smell like him. This was to fool my father into giving me the blessing, and I believed I would bring a curse upon myself and not a blessing. My mother assured me that any curse would be upon her, so I did as she said and went unto my father and told him I was back from the hunt, and that his meal was ready. (Genesis 27:12-17)

He wondered how I could do all this so quickly (unfortunately I brought the Lord's name unto it, by saying that God had brought it to me), and he didn't believe my voice to be Esau's. He asked me to come close so he could feel and smell me. The goats skin did the trick, because he believed I was his son Esau, and then blessed me as the first born (Genesis 18-27)

My father kissed me and gave me this blessing: "See, the smell of my son is as the smell of the field which the Lord hath blessed: Therefore, God give thee of the dew of heaven, and the fatness of the earth, and plenty of corn and wine: Let people serve thee, and nations bow down to thee: cursed be everyone that curseth thee, and blessed be he that blesseth thee." (Genesis 27:28-29)

My victory was short lived because Esau came in to be blessed just after I left, and he immediately found out what I had done. He pleaded with our father to be bless him too. His blessing was this "Behold, thy dwelling shall be the fatness of the earth, and of the dew of heaven from above; and by the sword shalt thou live, and shalt serve thy brother; and it shall come to pass when thou shalt have the dominion, that thou shalt break his yoke from off thy neck." Esau hated me because I received 'his' blessing (actually God gave "me" this blessing), and he vowed to kill me as soon as our father, Isaac, was dead. (Genesis 27:30-41)

My mother arranged for me to flee to her brother Laban's home for safety. She told my father that I should not take a wife from Canaan, but I should take a wife from my mother's relatives. She said that I would only have to stay until my brother "cooled off," then she would send for me.

My father again blessed me with God's blessing, that God would make me "fruitful and multiply me". In my lifetime God did do this for me. (Genesis 27:42 28:1-5)

This turned out to be the last time I saw my mother alive for I did not return home for twenty years, and she died during this time, but my father was still alive. Oh, what happened to me in those twenty years; that is another whole story? God was with me always, but I did not realize this or honor Him. I figured I had to take care of myself, as I had been doing. It never occurred to me that I was doing a terrible job of it. I continued to blunder along plotting and scheming, but I met my match in Uncle Laban.

My brother Esau had taken two wives from Canaan that pleased not our father Isaac. (Genesis 28:8) Now he took to himself a wife that was a daughter of Ishmael. Abraham's son by Hagar. (Genesis 28:9)

My first night out, when I lie down to sleep. I used the stones there for pillows. I dreamed that there was a ladder that stretched from earth to heaven and that there were angels of God "ascending and descending on it. "God said, I AM THE LORD GOD OF ABRAHAM THY FATHER, AND THE GOD OF ISAAC: THE LAND WHERE YOU LIE, I WILL GIVE TO YOU AND YOUR SEED: AND YOUR SEED SHALL BE AS THE DUST OF THE EARTH, AND THOU SHALL SPREAD ABROAD TO THE WEST, AND TO THE EAST, AND TO THE NORTH, AND TO THE SOUTH: AND IN THEE AND THY SEED SHALL ALL THE FAMILIES OF THE EARTH BE BLESSED. AND BEHOLD. I AM WITH THEE AND I WILL KEEP THEE IN ALL PLACES THAT YOU GO, AND I WILL BRING THEE AGAIN TO THIS LAND; FOR I WILL NOT LEAVE THEE, UNTIL I HAVE DONE THAT WHICH I HAVE SPOKEN TO THEE OF." (Genesis 28: 13-14)

I awoke and realized God was in this place with me, but I knew it not. I vowed that if God would keep me and give me food and clothes and bring me back to my father's house in peace, then I would honor Him as my God. This is the way I conducted myself with God without realizing that He had just promised me all that I asked of Him and more.

When I got to a well near my destination, I came upon those tending sheep. I inquired of them if they knew Laban. They said they knew him and that Rachel, his daughter, was coming with sheep, as we spoke. I went to Rachel and watered her sheep, kissed her, and wept with joy of seeing her and knowing that I was near her home. I told her that I was

Rebekah's son, and before I knew it she ran off to tell her father that I was there. (Genesis 29:11-12)

Laban, himself, ran out to meet me, and he embraced me, and kissed me and brought me into his house. After a month had passed, I told Laban I would work for him for seven years if he would give me Rachel, his younger daughter, for my wife, at the end of the seven years. He agreed, but his older daughter Leah was unmarried too, and it was the custom that the elder daughter be married before the younger. Rachel was a beauty, but Leah was not. I had no interest in Leah, but my love for Rachel was deep, so the seven years seemed like days to me, because I thought of none but Rachel and her beauty, and how she would soon be mine. (Genesis 29:15-20)

After I fulfilled the seven years, Uncle "Laban gathered the men of the place, and made me a feast." This was the first bachelor party recorded in the Bible. After we ate and 'drank' much. I went into the Bridal chamber to Rachel, or so I thought, in the morning, when I was sober. I found out that Laban had tricked me, and Leah was in my bed and not my lovely Rachel. I was furious with Laban, but he told me I could wait a week and He would give me Rachel as my wife. If I would work for him another seven years. (Genesis 29:23-28)

What could I do? I had to have Rachel as my own, so I agreed. God did not sanction a man having more than one wife, but this was an emergency. Now, my uncle was my father-in-law and my boss, and his two daughters, my first cousins, were my wives. Leah and Rachel immediately started a contest to see who could give me the most children, and to see whom I would love the most.

God knew that I did not love Leah, so he gave her children, but Rachel had none. After Leah had her son. She hoped I would love her - but still I did not care for her. She continued to have sons and with each one she prayed I would love her. The four boys she bore me - were Reuben, and then Simon, Levi, and Judah. Then, Leah did not have any more children for a while. Rachel still could not conceive so she blamed me for her barrenness --- she said that I must give her children or she would die. I was very angry with her for blaming "ME", was I God? (Genesis 30:1) Rachel decided that she must have a child, so I was to take her maid Bilhah, and have a child with her, and Rachel would then claim this child as her own. Bilhah did have a son, and Rachel called him Dan, because God heard her plea. Then Bilhah had another son, called Naphtali, which meant that Rachel had wrestled with her sister and prevailed.

Meantime, Leah was distressed to see Rachel have two boys by Bilhah, so she gave me her maid, Zilpah, so she could claim her children as her own. Zilpah bore two sons that Leah named, Gad and Asher. (Genesis 30:1-10)

Now I had four women in my life and all of them bearing me children. I never thought of God before I made these decisions to have children with the handmaids of my wives, but what could I do after all? I really only wanted my lovely Rachel, but now I had eight boys and the feuding was far from over.

Soon Leah and Rachel were fighting over some grapes (they were supposed to cause a woman to be fertile) that Reuben had brought to his mother, Leah. Rachel wanted them, so she told Leah if she would give them to her, she would let me sleep with her that night. Leah agreed and I went into her after work. God gave her a fifth son that she called Issachar, and God gave her a sixth son, named Zebulun. Now Leah had bore me six sons and she hoped I would live with her and love her. Later she bore a daughter and she called her Dinah.

Nothing had changed my love for Rachel. Finally, God opened her womb and she bore me a son, which she called Joseph. Now I had eleven sons, and they were a handful.

After Joseph was born, I went to Laban to ask him to let me take my wives and children and return to my country. Laban did not want to let me go, because he realized God had favored him because of me, so I stayed. We worked out an arrangement with the cattle, sheep, and goats. Laban tried to work it out so he would prosper and I would not, but I tricked him and my herd increased greatly.

This made Laban and his sons very angry, so God told me to return to "the land of my fathers, and my kindred." (Genesis 31:1) I had to call my wives; Leah and Rachel out to the field to talk to them so no one would overhear our conversation and tell Laban of our plans to leave.

I had been with Laban for twenty years and in all those years he "deceived me and changed my wages ten times." (Genesis 31:7) I had to work very hard for him. So, when Uncle Laban was shearing his sheep, we loaded up on camels, and took all our animals and possessions and left without looking back. (Genesis 31:17-19)

When I left home, I left quickly so Esau would not know I was leaving, and now I was leaving quickly so Laban would not know of my departure. However, on the third day of our departure Laban found out about it and he set out after us no doubt to capture us and drag us back to his home, or to do harm to me if I would not return.

After seven days he caught up to us, but God told him not to harm me. Laban said he wanted to kiss his daughters and their son's goodbye. He also said I had stolen his god's, or his idols and he wanted them back. I said we would search our camp, and when we found the one who had taken them, he would be killed. I did not know that my lovely Rachel had taken the idols herself. She managed to conceal them from her father, and thus to save her life.

Finally, Laban being satisfied went back home. But now I had to face my brother, Esau. I did not doubt that he was still furious with me and ready to kill me on sight. I prayed to God to spare my life. He told me: I "I WILL SURELY DO THEE GOOD, AND MAKE YOUR SEED AS THE SAND OF THE SEA WHICH CANNOT BE NUMBERED FOR MULTITUDE." Still I came up with a plan to give Esau a gift of, "200 she goats, 20 he goats, 200 ewes, 20 rams, 30 camels with their colts, 40 cows, 10 bulls, 20 donkeys, and 10 foals." I would send them on ahead of us in hopes that he would accept these gifts as a peace offering, and his anger would be turned away from me.

I sent my servants ahead with the animals in separate groups, one group at a time. Then in the night I sent my two wives and my two maidservants, my eleven sons, and all my possessions over the brook Jabbok, but I stayed behind. I ended up wrestling in prayer with the man of God (Jesus), until dawn. I refused to give in at first, so He touched me and my hip went out of place. I still would not surrender to Him until He blessed me. I ended up clinging to God: I realized I could do nothing without Him. He changed my name from Jacob to Israel (meaning: "A prince of God) I called this place 'Peniel which means, "I have seen God face to face, and my life is preserved." (Genesis 32:21-30)

God had always told me He was taking care of me and prospering me, but I could never trust Him. I still continued to live my life in my own strength.

I still wanted to be sure Esau wouldn't kill me, and my wives and children, so I put my handmaids and their children behind the gift of animals I was sending to Esau; then I sent Leah and her children and after them and my lovely Rachel and Joseph, last. Then I went out to meet Esau myself. Esau ran to me and hugged me and kissed me, and wept. I realized he was no longer mad at me.

Esau inquired as to all the animals and women and children and possessions I had with me. I told him the animals were a gift to him, and the women and children were those that God had so graciously given to me.

Esau did not want the gifts I gave him, because he said he had enough possessions of his own. But I insisted if I had found grace with him. It was because of God, and I wanted him to have all I had given him. He finally took it. (Genesis 33:10-11)

We settled in the land God had given to my father, and He again blessed me with these words: "Your name is Israel, I AM ALMIGHTY GOD, BE FRUITFUL AND MULTIPLY; A NATION AND A COMPANY OF NATIONS SHALL BE THY NAME." (Genesis 35:10)

The years passed, my lovely Rachel bore me one more son, Benjamin, but she then died in childbirth. Before she died, she called the baby "Ben-oni," which means 'son of my sorrow.' I changed his name to "Benjamin" which means 'son of my right hand." My heart was broken. Then my father (Isaac) died at 180 years old. My brother Esau and I, together, buried him.

My sons were jealous of Joseph because I favored him above the rest. I gave him a coat of many colors that set him apart from my other sons. I loved his mother so much. One day Joseph told his brothers and me of two dreams he had had. He said, "We were all binding sheaves in the field, when my sheaf arose and stood upright; behold your sheaves stood around it, and then bowed to my sheaf." Then he told another dream, "Behold the sun and the moon and the eleven stars bowed to me." (Genesis 37:7-9)

None of us knew what to think of these dreams, but his brothers hated him even more because of them. They waited their chance to get even with him, and one day while they were tending my flocks, I sent Joseph to check on how they were doing. Because they hated him so much, they decided to kill him and throw him into a pit, and tell me a wild animal had killed him. They stripped him of his coat of many colors and threw him into a pit; my fourth son Judah saw a caravan of Ishmaelite Traders coming, so he suggested that they should sell Joseph to the traders so that they would not have Josephs' blood on their hands. They all agreed.

They sold him for twenty pieces of silver, the price of a slave, and he was on his way to Egypt. They had to give me (Jacob) a plausible story, so they killed a goat and dipped Joseph's coat in the blood. They pretended they did not know it was Joseph's coat, but I deducted that a wild beast had killed him and they did not correct me. My heart was broken and I mourned Joseph for many days, after all he was my beloved Rachel's son. I knew I would never get over the loss of Joseph all the days of my life.

Many years passed and a "great famine came to the whole earth," but I heard that there was grain for sale in Egypt. I decided to send ten of my sons to Egypt. I would not let my youngest son Benjamin go with them because I was afraid that something could happen to him as it had to my Joseph; then I would have lost both sons that were born to my lovely Rachel. I could not let this happen.

The boys left and were gone many days, but when they returned they had the most fantastic story to tell me. Their brother Simeon had to stay in Egypt at the request of the governor of the land, and all the money they had taken as payment for the grain was now in the top of each sack of grain they had brought back with them. That was not all; they told me that Benjamin must go back with them to guarantee the release of Simeon, and to "prove that they were honorable men."

I immediately was panicky that I would lose three of my sons. I didn't trust God to work this all out as He had promised me. He told me He would be with me and help me all the days of my life; instead, I refused to let Benjamin go. Soon the grain was gone and I wanted the boys to go and buy more grain. Judah assured me that they could not go without Benjamin, and that he personally would take care of him and bring him back safely.

I was resigned that I must send Benjamin with them, so I sent double the money for the grain, and I also sent balm, honey, spices and myrrh, nuts, and almonds as a gift to the governor so he would be more apt to send my sons home again.

Again, many days passed before they returned. I was sure that they had come to a bad end, but then I saw them coming home again with many wagons of goods with them. They told me a most unbelievable story that I could not trust to be true at first. They said that my lost son Joseph was not dead, but alive, and he was the governor of Egypt that they had been dealing with the whole time. They finally convinced me as I inspected the many gifts Joseph had sent to us. I immediately wanted to go to Egypt and see Joseph myself and be united with him again.

The time came that we were ready to go to Egypt; the journey was long and slow, but we finally arrived and my most loved son Joseph met us at Goshen. We wept in each other's arms for a very long time. I said I could die happy now because I had seen my son Joseph again; he was not dead but very much alive.

When Joseph presented me to Pharaoh, Pharaoh asked me how old I was. I told him I was 130 years old and that I gave all the glory to God for my long and fruitful life. I blessed Pharaoh, and he graciously gave us the land of Goshen to live in; we lived there and prospered there for many years to come. I finally lived in faith; that God was my only source of life and help, and now I knew He had always been with me and that He, alone, had designed my life perfectly for me in His Divine will.

I lived another seventeen years in Egypt until my death at one hundred forty-seven years old. I had made Joseph promise that when I died, he would bury me in the land of Canaan with my people. I also blessed Joseph and his two sons and each of my other eleven sons in turn, and then I died. I now live in eternity with God, and with my people, and I thank God for it all. May we meet in eternity someday?

AMEN

HE, "THAT GOD HATED"

GENESIS 25 - 33

No twin brothers could be more different than Jacob and me. When I, Esau was born I was red and hairy all over; as I grew, I preferred to be outdoors hunting, or fishing, or just enjoying the fresh air and the world around me. Jacob, on the other hand stayed around home all the time. My mother, Rebekah, preferred and loved him over me, but my father Isaac, loved me more than my brother Jacob because he liked to eat the venison, I cooked for him.

Jacob was always sneaking around and I never knew what he was up to. When we were born his "hand took hold of my heel" and that is why his name was called Jacob, which means supplanter.

One day as I came home from hunting, famished; I passed Jacob's tent and smelled something cooking, so I went in to see what it was. He had prepared lentil stew and bread and it smelled and looked delicious. I asked him for a bowl. He said that he would give me some if I would sell him my birthright. I said, "I am at the point to die from hunger, so what good is my birthright to me?" (Genesis 25:32)

I saw nothing wrong with giving away my birthright because it didn't really mean anything. Even though Jacob made me "swear to him", no one heard our bargain. I figured no one could take my place as the firstborn son, but I was about to find out how deceived I was.

Time passed uneventfully until the day my father announced that he wanted to give his blessing to me before he died. He told me to go and kill a deer and fix the venison the way he liked it, and then bring it to him. He would then bestow the blessing on me, as the eldest, for my future as the head of the household.

I quickly took my bow and arrows and went out to the fields to find meat for my father. I thought of nothing else but fulfilling his request. When I returned with the meal I found that that "little sneak" of a brother of mine had already tricked my father into thinking he was me, and he had received my blessing before me. My father could not see well, with deceit he made himself hairy, and took my vest also, so he would smell like me too, and the deed was done before I could defend myself.

I was furious and wanted to kill Jacob on the spot, but vowed I would "slay him" after our father died. My father did give me a blessing after I begged him to do so. He said, "I would dwell in the fatness of the earth… and by the sword I would live, and I would serve my brother; but it would come to pass when I had the dominion, that I would break his yoke from off my neck." (Genesis 27:39-40)

Our mother and Jacob realized my wrath toward him, so Rebecca my mother, convinced Isaac that Jacob should be sent to her relatives to find a wife among them. He left the house immediately and went away to our uncle's home. I was even more distressed that Jacob had been sent away to find a wife. I had already taken two Canaanite women as my wives, but my parents did not approve of these marriages. I now took a daughter of Ishmael, my grandfather Abraham's son by Hagar, as my third wife. I hoped that my parents would approve of this marriage.

It would be twenty years before Jacob and I would meet again. By then God restrained me so I was glad to see Jacob, and I ran to him and kissed him and wept on his shoulder. Our father, Isaac, was still alive so we lived together in peace until his death and then we buried our father together.

I did things my way, but still I saw no reason why God would say… "ESAU, HAVE I HATED." (Romans 9:13) I am with J. Vernon McGee: He said that he could not understand why God would say, 'JACOB HAVE I LOVED.' (Romans 9:13)

Joseph

I DID IT GOD'S WAY

GENESIS 37-50

I am the eleventh son of Jacob my father. My younger brother is Benjamin, my mother is Rachel, and I am Joseph.

When I was seventeen years old, I was with my brothers, (those) born to my father's wives, Bilhah, and Zilpah. We were feeding the flock when I noticed their bad behavior, and reported it to my father. My father listened to me because I was 'his son of his old age,' and the first son of his beloved wife, Rachel, my mother. He showed his favor toward me when he made me a coat of many colors. (Genesis 37:2-3)

My brothers considered me a "tattletale," and they hated me because our father seemed to love me more than all my brothers together. They could not speak a good word toward me. (Genesis 37:4)

I then dreamed a dream and told it to my brothers, and this made them hate me all the more. I told them this is my dream: "Behold, we were binding sheaves in the field, and, lo, my sheaf arose, and also stood upright; and, behold, your sheaves stood round about, and made obeisance to my sheaf." They immediately took offense to this and challenged me that I might have dominion over them? (Genesis 37:7-8)

But this did not end my dreams; I had yet another and I again told it to my brothers. "Behold, I have dreamed that the sun and the moon and the eleven stars made obeisance to me." I then told my father this dream too. He rebuked me and said to me, 'what is this dream that thou have dreamed? Shall I, and your mother, and your brothers, indeed come to bow down ourselves to you? Obeisance means to 'show courtesy, reverence, or homage'. My brothers were all the more envious, but my father "pondered" what I had said. (Genesis 37:9-11)

My brothers were feeding our father's flock in Shechem, when my father sent me to check to see how they were doing. I could not find them but a man told me they had departed to Dothan, so I went there.

While I was still afar off they conspired to kill me. They said, "The dreamer comes; let us kill him and throw him into a pit. We will say that some wild beast has eaten him, and then what will become of his dreams?" (Genesis 37:16-20)

My oldest Brother, Reuben, listened to all this but asked my brothers not to kill me. He said that they could throw me into a pit, but they should not become murderers. He, Reuben, had the intention to return later alone, to the pit and fetch me back to our father.

When I reached my brothers, they immediately grabbed me and stripped off my coat of many colors. They then threw me into a dry empty pit nearby. Next they sat down to eat; while they were eating they saw a caravan of traders passing by, and immediately changed their plans; they decided to sell me to the traders as a slave for twenty pieces of silver. With the transaction completed I was on my way to Egypt. (Genesis 37:22-28)

Reuben was not with the others when I was sold as a slave, so when he returned and found that I was gone he was very distraught. My brothers then decided to kill a goat and dip my coat in the blood, and then tell our father that they found this coat and knew not if it was mine. My father recognizing my coat concluded that I was killed by a wild beast and torn to pieces. Jacob, my father, mourned for me, but he could not be comforted. (Genesis 37:32-35)

Meantime, I was sold to an Egyptian "officer of Pharaoh's and a captain of the guard, named Potiphar." (Genesis 37:36) This was such a time of change and betrayal for me. I would not let the dreams of God had given me leave me for a moment. I knew that God was with me and that He would keep me in all places that I would go, and would bring me again into my land: for He would never leave me until He had done all that He had spoken to me about. (Genesis 28:15) I was determined to cling to Him with much tenacity.

Because God was with me in Potiphar's home, I was made the overseer of the house, and all that he had was under my control. "The Lord blessed this Egyptian house for my sake; and the blessing of the

Lord was upon all that Potiphar had in the house, and in the field. Potiphar did not worry that I would do him harm." (Genesis 39:1-6)

I had full run of the home and everything in it, except Potiphar's wife. She "cast her eyes upon me," and she said, 'Lie with me'. She came to me everyday, day after day, and asked me to lie with her. I told her this, "There is none greater in this house than I; neither hath your husband kept back anything from me but thee, because thou art his wife: how then can I do this great wickedness, and sin against God?" (Genesis 39:7-9)

Most believe that I was unusually strong to resist this temptation; that I really wanted to lie with her, but that I had some sort of built-in constitution that made me different from other men. No, my courage came from God; I was serving God, I wanted to show honor and glory to Him in all that I did. To grieve Him in anyway would break His heart and mine. Those living in the 21st century and those living in my day have the same temptations, and we have the same God to strengthen us.

Once a choice is made, God will keep His own and see them through the trial and keep them with His power to the end. So, each day Potiphar's wife tried to entice me in new ways. "This one day I went to the house to do business: and there were no men inside." Potiphar's wife caught me by my garment, saying, 'Lie with me:' so "I fled the house leaving my garment in her hand."

She immediately called the men of the house, saying, "See, this Hebrew was brought here to mock us; he came in unto me to lie with me and I cried with a loud voice. When Joseph heard that I lifted up my voice and cried, he left his garment with me, and fled, and got out." (Genesis 39:11-16)

Potiphar's wife kept my garment with her until her husband arrived home. She immediately spoke to him, saying, "The Hebrew servant, which thou hast brought unto us, came in unto me to mock me: And it came to pass, as I lifted up my voice and cried that he left his garment with me and fled out." (Genesis 39:17-18)

Potiphar was very angry with me, and maybe with his wife, because the penalty for this crime was death; he had me put into prison instead. But the Lord was with me, and showed me mercy, and gave me favor in the sight of the keeper of the prison. The keeper of the prison committed all the prisoners to my hand. Because the Lord was with me everything I did prospered. (Genesis 39:21-23)

I refused to despair or to give up on God, so God's Spirit continued to bless me. Was it easy to live in the decay of the prison, "No," but the vision God had given me propelled me. One day the butler of the king of Egypt, and his baker, were thrown into the prison, where I was, because they had offended their lord the king of Egypt.

One night they each dreamed a dream; they dreamed according to their position with the king. In the morning I saw they were sad and asked them,"Why?" They said they had dreamed the night before and there was no interpreter for their dreams. I asked them, 'Do not interpretations belong to God? Tell me them, I pray you.' (Genesis 40:1-8)

The chief butler told his dream to me, and said, "In my dream, behold a vine was before me; and in the vine were three branches: and it was as though it budded and her blossoms shot forth; and the clusters thereof brought forth ripe grapes. Pharaoh's cup was in my hand: and I took the grapes, and pressed them into Pharaoh's cup and I gave the cup into Pharaoh's hand."

I said, 'This is the interpretation of it: The three branches are three days: yet within three days shall Pharaoh lift up thine head, and restore three unto thy place: and thou shall deliver Pharaoh's cup into his hand, after the former manner when thou was his butler.' (Genesis 40:9-13)

I then asked the chief butler, "To think on me when it shall be well with thee, and show kindness, I pray thee, unto me, and make mention of me unto Pharaoh and bring me out of this prison." I told him I was stolen away out of the land of the Hebrews: and here also have 'I done nothing that they should put me into this dungeon.' (Genesis 40:14-15) He promised to remember me to the king.

Now the chief baker, seeing the interpretation was good, asked me to interpret his dream also. He said, "I also was in my dream, and, behold, I had three white baskets on my head: and in the uppermost basket there was of all manner of bake meats for Pharaoh; and the birds did eat them out of the basket on my head."

I answered him and said, "This is the interpretation thereof: The three baskets are three days: yet within three days shall Pharaoh lift up thy head from off thee, and shall hang thee on a tree; and the birds shall eat thy flesh from off thee." (Genesis 40:18-19)

"It came to pass on the third day, which was Pharaoh's birthday, that he made a feast unto all his servants: and he lifted up the head of the chief butler, and of the chief baker among his servants. He restored the chief butler unto his butlership again; and he gave the cup into Pharaoh's hand:" but he hanged the chief baker: as I had (by God) interpreted to them. Yet, the chief butler did not remember me; he forgot me. (Genesis 40:20-23)

Two more years passed and then the Pharaoh had two dreams. In the first one he saw seven well fed, fat, cows come up out of the river, and then he saw seven very skinny cows come out of the river behind them. The lean cows ate-up the seven fat cows.

In the second dream he dreamed seven ears of corn came up on one stalk, very full and good. Then, behold, seven thin ears of corn sprung up on the east wind after them, and the thin ears devoured the full, good ears. The next morning Pharaoh was very troubled in his spirit; he sent and called for all the magicians of Egypt, and all the wise men thereof: and Pharaoh told them his dream; but here was none that could interpret them unto Pharaoh. (Genesis 41:1-8)

Now, the chief butler remembered me, and told Pharaoh that while he was in prison he dreamed a dream, and the chief baker, who was in prison too, dreamed a dream that same night. He said that a young Hebrew, a servant to the captain of the guard, interpreted both our dreams correctly. Pharaoh sent for me, and I was hastily brought out of the dungeon: I shaved, and changed my clothes, and was brought to Pharaoh. Pharaoh said to me, "I have dreamed a dream, and there is none that can interpret it: and I have heard say of thee, that thou can understand a dream to interpret it." (Genesis 41:9-15)

I answered Pharaoh saying, "it is not I: God shall give Pharaoh an answer of peace." Pharaoh then told me his dreams, and I said unto Pharaoh, 'The dream of Pharaoh is one: God hath showed Pharaoh what he is about to do. The seven good cows are seven years; and the seven good ears of corn are seven years. The seven thin cows that came after them are seven years; and the seven empty ears of corn blasted with the east wind shall be seven years of famine.'

"God is about to send seven years of great plenty throughout all the land of Egypt: and there shall arise after them seven years of famine; and all the plenty shall be forgotten in the land of Egypt; and the famine shall consume the land; and the plenty shall not be known in the land by reason of that famine following; for it shall be very grievous. This time of plenty and famine is established by God, and God will shortly bring it to pass." (Genesis 41:16-32)

I advised Pharaoh on how he should handle this information. I said "Pharaoh should set a man, discreet and wise over the land of Egypt. Let this man appoint officers over the land, and take up the fifth part of the land of Egypt in the seven plenteous years. Gather all the food of those good years, and keep it in the cities. This food shall be stored up to be used during the seven years of famine."

Pharaoh and his servants saw this as a good plan for the land of Egypt. Pharaoh said unto his servants, "Can we find such a one as this, a man in whom the spirit of God is?" Pharaoh said to me, 'As much as God has showed thee all this, there is none so discreet and wise as thou art: thou shall be over my house, and according unto thy word shall all my people be ruled: only in the throne will I be greater than thou. I now set you over all the land of Egypt.' (Genesis 41:33-41)

Pharaoh then took off his ring from his hand, and put it on my hand, and dressed me in fine linen, and put a gold chain about my neck. He then made me to ride in the second chariot that he had; and those that cried before me said: "Bow the knee."

Pharaoh said, as second to him, "Without me no man shall lift up his hand or foot in all the land of Egypt." He called me by the name of Zaphnath- paaneah; and he gave me a wife, Asenath the daughter of Potipherah priest of On. I was thirty years of age at this time, and I then went out from Pharaoh to oversee all the land of Egypt. (Genesis 41:42-46)

During the seven years of plenty, I saw to it that much food was put into the newly built storehouses in the cities. The food was stored in the cities because I wanted it to be close at hand and easily distributed to the people during the famine years. The amount of corn gathered was as the sand of the sea; so much of it that we gave up numbering the huge quantities. (Genesis 41:47-49)

Before the famine years started, two sons were born to me, my first-born was named Manasseh: For God, said, "He hath made me forget all my toil, and my father's entire house." My second son was called Ephraim: 'For God hath caused me to be fruitful in the land of my affliction.' (Genesis 41:50-52)

After the seven plenteous years, the seven drought years came as God had predicted through Pharaoh's dream. The famine was worldwide, but in Egypt there was bread. The people cried to Pharaoh for bread and he sent them to me. I opened all the storehouses, and "sold" grain unto the Egyptians. All the countries came to Egypt, and to me, to buy corn, because the famine was so bad in all lands. (Genesis 41:56-57)

"Now, God used me to preserve the race; I was about to see my family again, and I would help them to survive, also." (McGee) Because I was the governor over the land, my ten brethren, sent by my father to buy grain, came before me and bowed down before me with their faces to the earth.

When I first saw them, I knew them, but I did not want to reveal myself to them as yet. I spoke to them roughly saying, 'Whence come ye?' They answered me, "From the land of Canaan to buy food." (Genesis 41:6-8)

I immediately remembered the dreams, which God had given me, so many years before, picturing my family bowing low before me. I accused them saying, "You are spies; come to see the nakedness of the land." My brothers said that they came only to buy food, and they explained that they were one man's sons; 'Thy servants are twelve brethren, the sons of one man in the land of Canaan; and, behold, the youngest is this day with our father, and one is not.' (Genesis 42:9-13)

I continued to accuse them of being spies. I told them they must prove themselves to be telling the truth, by remaining captive until their younger brother came to Egypt. I intended to keep them all prisoners, save one to go and fetch their youngest brother. I then locked them up in the Bastille for three days. Then after three days I went to them and told them they may all go to their homeland with the food they came for, but one, that I would keep captive until they could return with their younger brother. I told them that if they did this they could live: '"for I fear God."' This should have been a hint that I knew their God, but they did not understand me. (Genesis 42:14-20)

They immediately started speaking in Hebrew, among themselves, saying that this was happening to them because they were guilty concerning their brother. They saw the anguish of his soul, when he asked them not to do their dastardly deed, but they would not hear. Reuben reminded them that he did not go along with their plans, and pleaded with them not to sin against the child. They did not know that I could understand their conversation concerning me.

I then turned away from them and wept. When I turned back to them, I took Simeon captive, and I had him bound before their eyes. Then I commanded that their sacks be filled with corn, and I put the money they had brought for payment at the top of each sack. They loaded their donkeys with the sacks and departed for home. (Genesis 42:21-25)

On the way home they realized that their money had been restored to them, and instead of being happy with this news, they were very upset thinking that they would be accused of stealing the money. When they got home, they told our father Jacob all that befell them; saying, "The man, who is the lord of the land spoke roughly to us, and took us for spies of the country. He told us that he would know that we were telling the truth if we would leave one of our brothers, take the food and bring our youngest brother unto him." (Genesis 42:29-34)

Jacob was very bereaved with this news, thinking, I, his son Joseph, and now Simeon, and soon Benjamin would be lost to him. He said he would not allow Benjamin to go with them on the next trip. My oldest brother Reuben spoke up to our father and said, that he would stake his two sons lives on the fact that he would make sure Benjamin would be brought back safely to him. (Genesis 32:37-38)

The famine only worsened, so when the grain my brothers had taken with them to their home ran out, our father said they must go again and buy food for them. Judah spoke to Jacob this time and said, the man did solemnly protest unto us, saying, "ye shall not see my face except your brother be with you." If thou will send our brother with us, we will go down and buy thee food: But if thou will not send him, we will not go down: for the man said unto us, 'ye shall not see my face except your brother be with you.' (Genesis 43:5)

My father Jacob, called Israel by God, said unto them: "Why did you tell him you had a brother at home?" They said that I had asked them plainly about any other kindred, and if our father was yet alive? Israel reluctantly gave in to my demands after Judah vowed, he would bring Benjamin back safely, or forever be blamed. Israel said that they must carry a present to be given to me: a little balm, and a little honey, spices, and myrrh, nuts, and almonds, and they must take double the money. (Genesis 43:1-12)

My father, then allowed my brother, Benjamin, to be brought to the land of Egypt, and so my brothers came before me. When I saw Benjamin with them, I had the ruler of my house invite them to my home for dinner. They were very afraid, but I wanted to speak to them privately. They were sure that I would harm them because of the money being returned to them.

I said to them, "Fear not: your God and the God of your father has given you treasure in your sacks." I then had Simeon brought in to join the rest of them. I sent them on ahead to my house, where they had their feet washed, were given water, and provision was made for their donkeys. When I arrived home, they gave me the gifts they had brought from our father. They again bowed down to me.

I inquired if their father was well and in good health. They said that he was, and then I looked and saw my full brother Benjamin standing before me. I asked if he was their younger brother that they had spoken of during their first journey? They said he was; I then had to enter my chamber to weep there because my heart went out to him. When I gained control of my emotions, I washed my face and returned to my brothers and asked that the meal be served to us. (McGee) I seated them, at the table, according to their birthright from the oldest to the youngest. They marveled at this. I had five times as much food served to Benjamin as the others: we drank and were merry together. (Genesis 43:13-34)

I told my steward to fill my brothers' sacks with food, as much as they could carry, and again to put every man's money in his own sack's mouth. I also had my silver cup put in the sack's mouth of the youngest, Benjamin, and his corn money too. As soon as the morning was light, the men were sent away, they and their donkeys. (Genesis 44:1-3)

When my brothers had been gone a short time, I sent my steward after them, and when he found them, he was to say, "Wherefore have ye rewarded evil for good?" Then he was to accuse them of stealing my silver cup. My brothers are, of course, speechless when the cup was found in Benjamin's sack; they tore their clothes as a gesture of extreme distress. (McGee) Before the search began, they spoke boldly saying, 'How could we steal out of thy lord's house silver or gold, when we returned the money that we found the first time in our sacks. If the cup is found in any of our sacks, let that man die and we also will be my lord's bondmen.' (Genesis 44:6-9)

I was testing them to see if they loved their brother Benjamin, and their father, and I wanted to see if the years had softened their hearts since they had sold me into slavery. Judah and his brothers came to my house again, and they fell before me on the ground. I said to them, "what deed have you done? The man in whose hand the cup is found, he shall be my servant; as for the rest of you, you may go in peace to your homeland and to your father." (Genesis 44 16-17)

Judah came near to me and asked that he might speak a word in my ears; he asked that my anger would not burn against Benjamin. He continued; "They had a father, an old man, who loves his youngest son, because he alone is left of his mother, after his brother surely was torn in pieces, and he had not seen him since. Our father did not want the lad to come with us, for he feared that something bad, like this, may happen to him, and our father would not want to live seeing that his life is bound up in the lad's life. I, Judah, told our father that I would bear the blame of his loss forever if Benjamin did not come home safely to him." Judah then pleaded with me saying, 'I pray thee, let thy servant abide instead of the lad, a bondman to my lord, and let the lad go up with his brethren. For how shall I go up to my father, and the lad be not with me, and see evil come on my father?' (Genesis 44:18-34)

I, Joseph, could not refrain myself before all them that stood by me; and I cried, "Let every man go out from me except my brothers,'" and then I wept aloud so that the Egyptians and the house of Pharaoh heard me.

I said unto my brothers, "I am Joseph: does my father yet live?" My brothers could not answer as they were so troubled by my presence. I asked my brothers to come near to me so I could reveal my identity, by showing them that I was circumcised. I said again, 'I am Joseph, your brother, whom ye sold into Egypt. Be not grieved, or angry with yourselves that ye sold me hither: for God did send me before you to preserve life. The famine has been in the land these two years: and there are five more years of drought and famine. God sent me before you to preserve you to prosper in the earth, and to save your lives by a great deliverance. So now it was not you that sent me here, but God; He has made me a father to Pharaoh, and lord of his entire house, and a ruler throughout all the land of Egypt. Haste ye, and go up to my father, and say unto him, "Thus saith thy son Joseph, God has made me lord of all Egypt: come down unto me, tarry not: and thou shall dwell in the land of Goshen, and thou, and thy children, and thy children's children, and thy flocks, and thy herds, and all that thou has: and there will I nourish thee; for yet there are five years of famine; lest thou, and thy household, and all that thou has, shall come to poverty.'" (Genesis 45:1-8)

Tell my father of all my glory in Egypt, and of all that ye have seen; and ye shall make haste and bring down my father at once. I fell on my brother Benjamin's neck, and wept; and Benjamin wept upon my neck. I then kissed all my brothers, and wept with them, and then we talked together. (Genesis 45:9-15)

Pharaoh heard that my brethren were with me, and he said to me, "Say unto your brethren, load your beasts and go to the land of Canaan: get your father and your households and come unto me: and I will give you the good of the land of Egypt. Take you wagons out of the land of Egypt for your little ones, and for your wives, and bring your father, and come." The children of Israel did so: and I gave them wagons, and each man changes of raiment; but to Benjamin I gave three hundred pieces of silver, and five changes of raiment. To my father I sent ten donkeys laden with the good things of Egypt, and ten donkeys laden with corn, and bread, and meat. (Genesis 45:17-22)

When my brothers told my father, Jacob, that I was still alive and governor over all the land of Egypt, his "heart fainted," for he believed them not. They told him all the words I had spoken, and showed him the wagons that I had sent to carry him back to Egypt; Jacob revived. Israel said, 'It is enough; Joseph my son is yet alive: I will go and see him before I die.' So my father took all the cattle, and goods, and all his seed, numbering seventy souls, and came unto Egypt and unto me. (Genesis 45:27-28) (Genesis 46:1-27)

When I heard Israel, my father was coming, I made ready my chariot, and went up to meet him in Goshen. I fell on his neck, and wept on his neck a good while. Israel said unto me, "Now let me die, since I have seen thy face, because thou art yet alive." My father dwelt in the land of Egypt seventeen years before his death, at one hundred forty-seven years. Just before his death I took my two sons Manasseh and Ephraim to my father for a blessing. Jacob said Ephraim would be greater than Manasseh, and Ephraim's seed shall become a multitude of nations, whereas Manasseh would be only a great people. (Genesis 46:29-30) (Genesis 48:17-19)

Now that our father was dead, my brothers thought I would take revenge on them, and do them evil. I wept at their repentance of selling me into slavery. I said unto them, "Fear not: for am I in the place of God? But as for you, ye thought evil against me; but God meant it unto good, to bring to pass, as it is this day to save much people alive. Now fear ye not: I will nourish you, and your little ones."

I comforted them, and I spoke kindly to them. We continued to live in Egypt as a family. I died when I was 110 years old, and during this time I was able to see my grandchildren and great grandchildren grow up around me. As you know my family stayed in Egypt for 400 years until they had to be delivered by God, through Moses. (Genesis 50:18-23)

My life has been compared to Jesus' life. We do have many comparisons that are the same: "Both Jesus and I had miraculous births: Both of us were beloved by our fathers: Both of us were set apart; me with a coat of may colors, Jesus was separate from sinners: I announced that I was to rule over the brethren, Jesus presented Himself as the Messiah: Both of us were ridiculed for this. Our father sent both of us to our brethren. Our brethren without a cause hated both of us." (McGee)

Was it easy for me to forgive my brothers of their injustice to me, "No," but I made a choice that God was in charge of my life, not people, and that He is faithful. Also, I did not want to hurt God; when I was alone in Egypt, I needed God to help me and encourage me. Put your loved ones into the hands of God, and let the hurts you have suffered from them go to God. God has a plan for your life that can only come to great good for you, and glory for Him. God said, 'Vengeance is mine, I will repay.' God always has a way that benefits you and those who have harmed you. Please, read my life and let it be a blessing to you. Amen!

THE FORTY MAN, MOSES

EXODUS, LEVITICUS, AND NUMBERS

You may believe that Charlton Heston and I, Moses, are the same person, and the movie, "The Ten Commandments" is an accurate portrayal of my life and me. Let me tell you the story of my life from the beginning.

When I was born, in Egypt, I was supposed to be killed immediately by being "cast into the Nile River," by any Egyptian. This decree had gone out from Pharaoh because he was fearful that the 'children of Israel' were "more mighty" than the Egyptians because there were many more of them. (Exodus 1:9)

The Israelites were in Egypt because three hundred and fifty years before my birth, Joseph, Jacobs's son, was sold into slavery by his brothers, but he had become overseer of Egypt by God's design and by the faithfulness of God. In order to save his family from famine (who lived in the land of Canaan), he had them move to Egypt. There they increased and became a mighty nation living among the Egyptians.

When Joseph died "there arose up a new king over Egypt, which knew not Joseph." (Exodus 1:8) The new king decided to make slaves of the Israelites so they would decrease in number. Instead 'they multiplied and grew.' So they were made to serve with "hard bondage making bricks and working in all manner of service in the field." None of this decreased their numbers; in fact, they only increased because God blessed them continually. (Exodus 1:14)

Next the king of Egypt spoke to the Hebrew midwives and told them to kill all the boy babies born, but they could let the "daughters" live. "But the midwives feared God, and did not as the king of Egypt commanded them, but saved the men children alive." When the King asked the women why they saved the boys too, the midwives told him that the

Hebrew women gave birth very quickly, and they did not have time to assist in the birth. (Exodus 1:13-20)

Because the midwives "feared God," He `gave them a name and a place in Israel, and they were greatly respected there.' (McGee) Now, we come to the place where "all" the Egyptians were ordered to kill the boy babies in Israel.

When my parents, Amram and Jochebed gave birth to me they "saw that I was a goodly child," and was healthy and had promise. They hid me for three months until they could no longer keep me at home without detection because, you see, I was a crying baby, which God would shortly turn to my good. My mother made an `ark of bulrushes, and daubed it with slime and with pitch, and put me in it and laid me in the reeds by the river's edge.' (Exodus 2:3)

My sister Miriam, was sent to watch me from afar, to see what would happen to me. One day "the daughter of Pharaoh came down to wash herself at the river; and her maidens walked along by the river's side; and when she saw the ark among the flags (reeds), she sent her maid to fetch it. When she opened the basket she saw me, the child: and behold, I, the baby wept. She then had compassion on me, and said, `This is one of the Hebrews' children." I told you God would use my baby ways to benefit my family and me. (Exodus 2:5-6)

Now, my sister Miriam made herself known and said to Pharaoh's daughter, "Shall I go and call to thee a nurse of the Hebrew women, that she may nurse the child for thee? Pharaoh's daughter said to her, `Go,' Miriam then went and called my mother. When she came, Pharaoh's daughter said unto her, "Take this child away, and nurse it for me, and I will give thee your wages. So my mother took me, her son, and nursed me" (as she had been doing all along). God had miraculously provided for our family through me.

"When I had grown to the appropriate age, my mother took me to Pharaoh's daughter, and I became her son. She called me by the name of Moses: Because she drew me out of the water." (Moses means, `drawer out.') Exodus 2:7-10)

Now, I had had training in the ways of the Hebrews, and I knew I was a Hebrew. When I lived in the courts of Pharaoh. I was trained and educated as an Egyptian, and I looked like an Egyptian. The Egyptians taught me all of their wisdom, and I was "mighty in words and in deeds." (Acts 7:22)

When I was forty years old, I decided to visit my "brethren the children of Israel. While I was there, I saw one of the men suffer wrong, so I defended him, and avenged him that was oppressed, and killed the Egyptian" that was doing him wrong. I looked both ways to see if anyone had seen me do this deed, but no one had, so I hid the body in the sand. (Exodus 2:12)

I was sure that my brethren would understand that I, Moses, "by the hand of God would deliver them:" but they understood not, because the next day I went among them again. This time I saw two of my brethren fighting, so I intervened and asked them why they were fighting each other? The man in the wrong told me to mind my own business. He asked, `who made you a ruler and judge over us? Are you going to kill me as you killed the Egyptian yesterday? (Acts 7:23-28)

I was afraid because this "deed" was known; I thought no one knew I had killed an Egyptian. Soon Pharaoh heard of this and, `he sought to kill me.' Before anyone could find me I fled the country and went to the land of Midian. When I got there I "sat down by a well." (Exodus 2:15)

THIS WAS THE FIRST FORTY YEARS OF MY LIFE. NOW BEGINS THE SECOND FORTY.

While I was sitting by the well, "seven sisters came to draw water to fill the troughs to water their father's flock. But before they could get the water, shepherds came and drove them away, but I stood up to help them, and got their flock watered for them." (Exodus 2:16-17)

When the girls arrived at home their father, Reuel who was the Priest of Midian, asked them, "How is it that you are home so soon?" They told him that I, `an Egyptian, had delivered them out of the hand of the shepherds, and that I had drawn water for them to water the flock,` (Exodus 2:18-19)

Their father asked them where I was, and why had they left me at the well? He told them to call me, so I could eat bread with them. They did fetch me, and I ended up staying with them for forty years, plus Reuel gave me his daughter Zipporah to be my wife. (Exodus 2:20-21)

Zipporah gave me two sons; I was content to live and work in Midian as a shepherd. These people were the offspring of Abraham and

Keturah, who had a son named Midian, so I felt right at home here. (McGee)

My brethren were still in bondage in Egypt, but I had no thought of them anymore. My life as a shepherd for my father-in-law was slow and quiet, but God had plans for me. The King of Egypt died and the Israelites were relieved, so they cried to God to deliver them from bondage. God heard their cries and remembered His covenant with Abraham, Isaac, and Jacob. (Exodus 2:23-25)

One day I was with the sheep at the backside of the desert when I came to Horeb, the mountain of God. There was a bush on fire before me, but it was not being consumed as it burned. No smoke, no black leaves, just a bright fire before me. I thought this was a great sight and went closer to see why it was not being burned up.

God called to me from the bush, and said, "MOSES MOSES," I said, 'Here am I' He said, "COME NOT NIGH HITHER: PUT OFF THY SHOES FROM OFF THY FEET, FOR THE PLACE WHEREON THOU STANDEST IS HOLY GROUND." He said, 'I AM THE GOD OF THY FATHER, THE GOD OF ABRAHAM, THE GOD OF ISAAC AND THE GOD OF JACOB.' I hid my face for I was very afraid to look upon God. (Exodus 3:3-6)

God went on to tell me that He had seen the affliction of His people in Egypt because of their taskmasters. He said, "I AM COME DOWN TO DELIVER THEM OUT OF THE HAND OF THE EGYPTIANS... AND TO BRING THEM INTO A LAND FLOWING WITH MILK AND HONEY; UNTO A PLACE OF THE CANAANITES, AND THE HITTITES, AND THE AMORITES, AND THE PERIZZITES, AND HIVITES, AND JEBUSITES." (Exodus 3:7-8) Next, He said to me, 'I WILL SEND THEE TO PHARAOH, THAT THOU MAY BRING FORTH MY PEOPLE, THE CHILDREN OF ISRAEL, OUT OF EGYPT. (Exodus 3:9-10)

I immediately protested and said, "Who am I, that I should go unto Pharaoh, and that I should bring forth the children of Israel out of Egypt?" (Exodus 3:11) Forty years before, I was ready to take on the Egyptians single handedly, but now I was content to be a shepherd and had no confidence in my ability, but this, my friend, is just where God wanted me. He wanted me to know I needed to lean on Him, and Him alone, so He could use me to deliver "His people,' from their bondage in Egypt. (McGee)

God said to me, "CERTAINLY I WILL BE WITH THEE, AND THIS SHALL BE A TOKEN UNTO THEE, THAT I HAVE SENT THEE: WHEN THOU HAST BROUGHT FORTH THE PEOPLE OUT OF EGYPT, YE SHALL SERVE GOD UPON THIS MOUNTAIN."

I, Moses, immediately asked why the people would accept me as their deliverer now, remembering forty years before, when they would have no part of me. I said to God, "Behold, when I come unto the children of Israel, and shall say unto them, The God of your fathers have sent me unto you; and they shall say to me, what is his name: what shall I say unto them?" (Exodus 3:12-13)

God said to me, "I AM THAT I AM:" THUS SHALL THOU SAY UNTO THE CHILDREN OF ISRAEL, "I AM" HATH SENT ME UNTO YOU. THUS, SHALT THOU SAY UNTO THE CHILDREN OF ISRAEL, THE LORD GOD OF YOUR FATHERS, THE GOD OF ABRAHAM, THE GOD OF ISAAC, THE GOD OF JACOB, HATH SENT ME UNTO YOU: THIS IS MY NAME FOR EVER, AND THIS IS MY MEMORIAL UNTO ALL GENERATIONS" (Exodus 3:14-15)

Next, God gave me the "procedure that I was to use." (McGee) God said, 'GO, AND GATHER THE ELDERS OF ISRAEL TOGETHER, AND SAY UNTO THEM, THE LORD GOD OF YOUR FATHERS, THE GOD OF ABRAHAM, OF ISAAC, AND OF JACOB, APPEARED UNTO ME, SAYING, I HAVE SURELY VISITED YOU, AND SEEN THAT WHICH IS DONE TO YOU IN EGYPT.'

"AND I HAVE SAID, I WILL BRING YOU UP OUT OF THE AFFLICTION OF EGYPT UNTO THE LAND OF THE CANAANITES, AND THE HITITTES, AND THE AMORITES, AND THE PERIZZITES, AND THE HIVITES, AND THE JEBUSITES, UNTO A LAND FLOWING WITH MILK AND HONEY.

"AND THEY SHALL HEARKEN TO THY VOICE AND THOU SHALT COME, THOU AND THE ELDERS OF ISRAEL, UNTO THE KING OF EGYPT, AND YE SHALL SAY UNTO HIM, THE LORD GOD OF THE HEBREWS HATH MET WITH US: AND NOW LET US GO, WE BESEECH THEE, THREE DAYS' JOURNEY INTO THE WILDERNESS, THAT WE MAY SACRIFICE TO THE LORD OUR GOD. "AND I AM SURE THAT THE KING OF EGYPT WILL NOT LET YOU GO, NO, NOT BY A MIGHTY HAND, AND I WILL STRECTH OUT MY HAND, AND SMITE EGYPT WITH ALL MY WONDERS WHICH I WILL DO IN THE MIDST THEREOF; AND AFTER THAT HE WILL LET YOU GO." (Exodus 3:16-20)

God went on to say this, "I WILL GIVE THIS PEOPLE FAVOUR IN THE SIGHT OF THE EGYPTIANS: AND IT SHALL COME TO PASS, THAT, WHEN YE GO, YE SHALL NOT GO EMPTY: BUT EVERY WOMAN SHALL BORROW OF HER NEIGHBOUR, AND OF HER THAT SOJOURNETH IN HER HOUSE, JEWELS OF SILVER, AND JEWELS OF GOLD, AND RAIMENT: AND YE SHALL PUT THEM UPON YOUR SONS, AND UPON YOUR DAUGHTERS; AND YE SHALL SPOIL THE EGYPTIANS." (Exodus 3:21-22)

"God meant that the people would collect their back wages from the Egyptians for all the hundreds of years of hard labor they have done as slaves." (McGee)

I was still not convinced; I still had many questions. I said to God, "But, behold, they will not believe me, nor hearken unto my voice: for they will say. The Lord hath not appeared unto thee."

The Lord said to me, "WHAT IS THAT IN THINE HAND?" I said, "A rod."

God said, "CAST IT ON THE GROUND."

I did as God had said and it became a serpent. I was afraid, so I fled away from it.

God said to me, "PUT FORTH THINE HAND, AND TAKE IT BY THE TAIL." I did as he told me to do, ` and I caught it, and it became a rod in my hand, again.' (Exodus 4:1-4)

Now God told me to put my hand into my bosom, and when I did and took it out again, my hand was as leprous as snow. Then God said, put your hand into your bosom again, and then take it out, and when I withdrew it, it was "turned again as my other hand." Exodus 4:6-7) `God was saying to me that he wants my hand and my heart, as I go forth. He is saying the same to you today. God does not want your money and your abilities, because when He gets all of you, He has all the rest.' (McGee)

I was not done complaining to the Lord. Next, I told Him that "I was not eloquent, but slow of speech and slow of tongue." God said, WHO HATH MADE A MAN'S MOUTH?" OR WHO MAKETH THE DUMB, OR DEAF, OR THE SEEING, OR THE BLIND? HAVE NOT I THE LORD? NOW THEREFORE GO, AND I WILL BE WITH THY MOUTH, AND TEACH THEE WHAT THOU SHALT SAY." (Exodus 4:11-12)

I persisted in my inability to do this, and asked that someone else would be better. God was angry with me now, and He said, "IS NOT AARON THE LEVITE THY BROTHER? I KNOW THAT HE CAN SPEAK WELL. HE WILL COME FORTH TO MEET THEE AND HE WILL BE GLAD IN HIS HEART. AND I WILL BE WITH THY MOUTH, AND WITH HIS MOUTH, AND I WILL TEACH YOU WHAT YE SHALL DO. HE WILL BE THY SPOKESMAN UNTO THE PEOPLE AND HE SHALL BE, EVEN HE SHALL BE TO THEE INSTEAD OF A MOUTH, AND THOU SHALT BE TO HIM INSTEAD OF GOD. (Exodus 4:14-16)

"God allowed me to use Aaron as a spokesman, but He did not like a divided command. Later this caused problems. God wanted me and me alone to deliver Israel out of Egypt, but I could not trust Him all the way. Please, friend, do not make this mistake, when God calls you to do a job. He is more than able to accomplish it through you." (McGee)

I went to my father-in-law, Jethro, and asked his permission to "return to my brethren in Egypt, and see if they were yet alive." Jethro told me to `Go in peace." God then told me it was safe to return to Egypt, "For ALL that sought my life were dead." I took my wife and sons, and `returned to the land of Egypt with the rod of God in my hand.' (Exodus 4:17-20)

God also told me that when I go to Egypt and did the "wonders" that God had showed me, God `would harden the heart of Pharaoh, and he would not let the people go.' Of course, Pharaoh hardened his own heart before God. God told me to say to Pharaoh, "THUS SAITH THE LORD, ISRAEL IS MY SON, EVEN MY FIRSTBORN, AND I SAY UNTO THEE, LET MY SON GO, THAT HE MAY SERVE ME: AND IF THOU REFUSE TO LET HIM GO, BEHOLD, I WILL SLAY THY SON, EVEN THY FIRSTBORN." (EXODUS 4:21-23)

The next thing that God did was, "seek to kill me." We had started for Egypt when I came near death. I had not been obedient to God while I was in Midian, because I had not circumcised my sons. `If I was to proclaim God's will to others, I had to be obedient to God's will, so God forcibly reminded me of my disobedience.' (McGee)

My wife, Zipporah took a sharp stone, and cut off the foreskin of her son, and cast it at my feet, and said, "Surely a bloody husband art thou to me, a bloody husband thou art, because of the circumcision." (Exodus 4:24-26) `Circumcision was the badge and seal of God's covenant with Abraham that was designed to teach the Israelites to have no confidence in the flesh. The flesh was to be cut away, and each Israelite was to place his trust in God. Abraham believed God, and it was counted unto him as righteousness. Isaac and Jacob followed the example of Abraham. They were Israelites by birth, but circumcision was the badge of it. It was an act of faith for them to perform that rite. Circumcision was the evidence that a man was the son of Abraham. It was evidence of their faith. In the 21st century the Christian must circumcise his heart before God, and let God have his dreams, his hopes, and his ideas, and let God be Lord of his life.' (McGee)

My wife Zipporah, did not like the act of circumcision so I had not resisted her will, but God would not let me get by with this. I was restored to health when the ritual was done, and we proceeded on.

As we went, my brother, Aaron met us and kissed me. I told him all that God had showed me, and we went together to the elders of Israel. Aaron spoke the words of God that I told him, "And did the sign in the sight of the people, and the people, and the people believed us and bowed their heads and worshipped." Exodus 4:27-31)

Aaron and I went to the Pharaoh of Egypt and told him this: "Thus saith the Lord God of Israel, let my people go, that they may hold a feast unto Me in the wilderness."

Pharaoh said, "Who is the Lord, that I should obey his voice to let Israel go? I know not the Lord, neither will I let Israel go." (Exodus 5:1-2)

Aaron and I then said, "The God of the Hebrews hath met with us: let us go, we pray thee, three days' journey into the desert, and sacrifice unto the Lord our God; lest he fall upon us with pestilence, or with the sword." (Exodus 5:3)

The king of Egypt would not let the Hebrews out of the work of brick making and decided if they wanted time off, they must not be working hard enough, so he commanded the taskmasters of the people to withhold the straw from them, but still they were required to make the same number of bricks per day and gather their own straw.

The people were very upset with Aaron and me because of his decree. And blamed us for interfering with their lives instead of helping them. (Exodus 5:15-21)

I went to the Lord and asked Him why He allowed this to happen to the people, and why had He sent me, because the people had not been helped and they were not delivered form the bondage of Pharaoh. (Exodus 5:22-23)

Then the Lord said to me, "NOW SHALL YOU SEE WHAT I WILL DO TO PHARAOH: FOR WITH A STRONG HAND SHALL HE LET THEM GO, AND WITH A STRONG HAND SHALL HE DRIVE THEM OUT OF HIS LAND." (Exodus 6:1)

He went on to tell me "I AM THE LORD: AND I APPEARED UNTO ABRAHAM, UNTO ISAAC, AND UNTO JACOB, BY THE NAME OF GOD ALMIGHTY, BUT BY MY NAME JEHOVAH WAS I NOT KNOWN TO THEM. I HAVE ESTABLISHED MY COVENANT WITH THEM, TO GIVE THEM THE LAND OF CANAAN, THE LAND OF THEIR PILGRIMAGE, WHEREIN THEY WERE STRANGERS. AND I HAVE ALSO HEARD THE GROANING OF THE CHILDREN OF ISRAEL, WHOM THE EGYPTIANS KEEP IN BONDAGE; AND I HAVE REMEMBERED MY COVENANT." (Exodus 6:1-5)

Next God went on to promise the people of Israel the seven "I wills" of redemption, which are: (Exodus 6:6-8)

1. "I will bring you out from under the burdens of the Egyptians.

2. "I will rid you out of their bondage.

3. "I will redeem you with an outstretched arm.

4. "I will take you to me for a people.

5. "I will be to you a God.

6. "I will bring you into the land.

7. "I will give it to you for a heritage." (McGee)

Still, the people of Israel did not accept me, and the Pharaoh and the people of Egypt did not accept me either. So, I asked the Lord, again, why Pharaoh would not listen to me? God told me that before this was over; "THE EGYPTIANS SHALL KNOW THAT I AM THE LORD, WHEN I STRETCH FORTH MINE HAND UPON EGYPT, AND BRING OUT THE CHILDREN OF ISRAEL FROM AMONG THEM." (Exodus 7:4-5)

Aaron and I did as the Lord commanded us, I was 80 years old and Aaron was 83. God told Aaron to "take thy rod, and cast it before Pharaoh, and it shall become a serpent." He did and it did, but Pharaoh was not to be outdone, so he called in his wise men and his sorcerers, and they did the same as we had done. Their rods became serpents, but Aaron's rod swallowed up their rods. Did this impress Pharaoh? 'No!' (Exodus 7:10-13)

God told me that Pharaoh's heart was hardened, and he refused to let the people go. So, now the first of ten plagues began that God would send to Egypt that would reveal the hardened heart of Pharaoh. I was to go to the Nile River and say, The Lord God of the Hebrews hath sent me unto thee, saying, "LET MY PEOPLE GO, THAT THEY MAY SERVE ME IN THE WILDERNESS: AND, BEHOLD, HITHERTO THOU WOULDEST NOT HEAR. IN THIS THOU SHALT KNOW THAT I AM THE LORD: BEHOLD, I WILL SMITE WITH THE ROD THAT IS IN MY HAND UPON THE WATERS WHICH ARE IN THE RIVER, AND THEY SHALL BE TURNED TO BLOOD." (Exodus 7:14-18)

All the fish would die in the river, and the river would stink, and no one would want to drink the water. Aaron was to take the rod, and stretch out his hand upon all the water of Egypt, and they would become blood along with all the water in the vessels. (Exodus 7:19)

"Each plague was leveled at a different god of Egypt. There were thousands of temples, millions of idols, and about three thousand gods in Egypt. There was power in the religion of Egypt; this power was satanic and Satan grants power to those who worship him. God directed His plagues against the idolatry in Egypt, against Pharaoh, and against Satan. It was a battle of the gods." (McGee)

A brief outline of each plague will help to show you how God "exposed the gods of Egypt as false, and He revealed to Israel His ability to deliver them and His superiority over them."

1. "With the water turned to blood, the Nile River was worthless as fertilizer and water. It brought death instead of life, but the wise men of Egypt imitated this plague with their sorcery."
2. The plague of frogs (Exodus 8:1-15): "One of the most beautiful temples in Memphis was the temple to Heka, the ugly frog-headed goddess. It was an offense to kill the sacred frog, but when they were in your house, bed, food, and everywhere, I'm sure the Egyptians wanted to kill them. The wise men also duplicated this plague."

3. The plague of lice (Exodus 8:16-20): "The Egyptians worshiped the earth-God Geb. But `the dust of the land became lice throughout all the land of Egypt.' Pharaoh did not ask that this plague be taken away, and the Egyptian sorcerers could not reproduce this pestilence. They seemed to acknowledge that the One who brought this plague was supreme over the gods of Egypt. Up to this point the magicians were able to duplicate every miracle wrought by the hand of God. They were powerless to reproduce this plague."

4. The plague of flies (Exodus 8:20-32): "It is thought by some that the swarms of flies were actually masses of the sacred beetle. And Khepara was the beetle-god. The beetle, or scarab, is found in the Egyptian tombs and speaks of eternal life. These beetles were sacred to Ra the sun god.

   1. "Up until this time the plagues had touched both the lands of Egypt and Goshen where the children of Israel lived. Everything becomes crystal clear at this juncture, however, when God declared that from now on there was to be distinction and none of the following plagues would touch the land of Goshen, the home of Israel. From now on, judgment would fall only upon the land of Egypt."

5. The plague of murrain (Exodus 9:1-7): "Murrain was a disease that affected cattle. The second largest temple of Egypt ever built was located in Memphis and was for the worship of the black bull Apis. Now the Egyptians were worshiping a sick cow."

6. The plague of boils (Exodus 9:8-17): "The priest of all the religions of Egypt had to be spotless with no mark or blemish on their bodies - in order to serve in the temples. During this plague the priests could not serve anywhere. It was actually a judgment on the entire religion of Egypt."

7. The plague of hail (Exodus 9:18-35): "God demonstrates His power with the plague of hail over the sky-goddess who is powerless in her own domain."

8. The plague of locusts (Exodus 10:1-20): "The judgment of the locusts was against the insect gods. The plague of locusts meant; the crops

were cursed. This was evidence of the judgment of God as found in the books of Joel and Revelation also."

9. The plagues of darkness (Exodus 10:21-29): "God moved in with darkness against the chief god that was worshiped – the sun-god Ra. The sun disc is the most familiar symbol found in Egyptian ruins. The plague of darkness shows the utter helplessness of Ra."

10. The Death of the firstborn (Exodus 11-12:36): "According to the religion of Egypt, the firstborn belonged to the gods of Egypt. In other words, God took what was set-aside for the gods of Egypt. God was teaching the Egyptians who He was. He was convincing Pharaoh that he was God. Also, He was bringing His own people to the place where they were willing to acknowledge him as their God. This was the final act of judgment that would free Israel from Egyptian bondage." (McGee 1-10)

"It is important to understand that there was purpose in the plagues of Egypt. God challenged the gods of Egypt to a contest and defeated them. You can imagine the idolatry that was in the land of Egypt. Yet God through Isaiah predicted that the time would come when every idol would disappear from Egypt. Today Egypt is a Moslem country that does not permit idols at all. Every idol had disappeared, as God said they would." (McGee)

I will tell you about the last plague and show you what God told Aaron and me to do. God said, "THIS MONTH SHALL BE UNTO YOU THE BEGINNING OF MONTHS: IT SHALL BE THE FIRST MONTH OF THE YEAR TO YOU, SPEAK UNTO THE CONGREGATION OF ISRAEL, SAYING, IN THE TENTH DAY OF THIS MONTH THEY SHALL TAKE TO THEM EVERY MAN A LAMB. ACCORDING TO THE HOUSE OF THEIR FATHERS, A LAMB FOR AN HOUSE." (Exodus 12:1-3)

"It was important for each house to have their own lamb, or a portion of a lamb according to what they were able to eat. Each individual member of the family is to receive a part of the lamb. The lamb speaks the Lord Jesus Christ that would come into the World to be the ultimate sacrifice for mankind. Each one in the family will have to participate and partake of this lamb in order to come in under the protection and the redemption of the blood that will be put on each doorpost." `One is not saved because they are a part of the family; they must each one-take part.' (McGee)

The lamb had to be without blemish, a male of the first year: taken from the sheep, or the goats. It had to be kept to the fourteenth day of the same month: and the whole assembly of the congregation of Israel had to kill the lamb in the evening. (Exodus 12:5-6)

The lamb was to be eaten, that night after it was roasted with fire, with the head and legs left on, with unleavened bread and bitter herbs. The meat was not to be soaked with water. (Exodus 12:8) "Each instruction connected with this feast had a specific meaning and message. The family entered into the celebration of the Passover together. The fire speaks of judgment. There must be judgment of sin. Leaven speaks of sin, so unleavened bread speaks of Christ as the One we are to feed upon. They were to partake of this meal with bitter herbs, which may mean that our experience will not always be sweet after we have received Jesus Christ as Savior. The bitter herbs go with redemption." (McGee)

Each person was to eat with his loins girded, his shoes on his feet, and his staff on his hand, in haste, because each one was to be ready to go on command. (Exodus 12:11) The meaning of this instruction is to the "believer of Christ who should have his loins girded to be ready to get out of the world, and no longer be involved in it. You can no longer be converted and continue living a sinful life. This does not mean that you will never sin again, but it does mean that you will not make a habit of living in a pattern of sin." (McGee)

God said, "I WILL PASS THROUGH THE LAND OF EGYPT THIS NIGHT, AND WILL SMITE ALL THE FIRSTBORN IN THE LAND OF EGYPT, BOTH MAN AND BEAST; AND AGAINST ALL THE GODS OF EGYPT I WILL EXECUTE JUDGMENT: I AM THE LORD, THE BLOOD SHALL BE TO YOU FOR A TOKEN UPON THE HOUSES WHERE YE ARE: AND WHEN I SEE THE BLOOD, I WILL PASS OVER YOU AND THE PLAGUE SHALL NOT BE UPON YOU TO DESTROY YOU, WHEN I SMITE THE LAND OF EGYPT." (Exodus 12:12-13)

The blood from the lamb was to be put in a basin, and then put on the lintel and the two side posts of the door with a bunch of hyssops, that was dipped in the blood. No one was to leave the house until the morning came. "The hyssop plant is fluffy and grows around rocks. This plant represents faith. That is the way the blood of Christ is applied to your heart and life. You trust, in faith, what Christ has done when He died for you." (McGee)

"The Lord passed through the land to smite the Egyptians," but when He saw the blood on the doorposts, He passed over that house, so no one in that house would die. (Exodus 12:22-23)

"At midnight the Lord smote all the firstborn in the land of Egypt, from the firstborn of Pharaoh that sat on the throne unto the firstborn of the captive that was in the dungeon; and all the firstborn cattle. Pharaoh rose up in the night, and all the servants, and all the Egyptians; and there was a great cry in Egypt; for there was not a house where there was not one dead." (Exodus 12:29-30)

Pharaoh was finally ready to let us go to serve the Lord, and to take our flocks and herds with us. The Egyptian people wanted us to go quickly before they would all become "dead men." I told the people (women) to `ask the Egyptians for jewels of silver, and jewels of gold, and raiment.' (Exodus 12:33-35) "This was God's way of simply collecting back wages for the years of slave labor in Egypt." (McGee)

When we left Egypt, we had about six hundred thousand men on foot, beside the children and all our flocks, herds, and cattle. With us was a mixed multitude, being those that were not true Israelites but "half - breeds." These were those, from Egypt, who had married Israelites, and made a decision to go with us. These would cause us trouble forever. We had been in Egypt for four hundred and thirty years and Egypt had gotten into our lives more than we understood at this time. (Exodus 12:37-38) (McGee)

We left the land of Egypt and moved toward the Red Sea. God told me to sanctify unto Him all the firstborn, both of man and beast." (Exodus 13:1-3)

"The firstborn of Egypt had died, and now God claims the firstborn of Israel as His own. In this passage and in the 21st century God wants each one to give himself to Him and all that one holds valuable." (McGee)

God told me to tell the people, "Remember this day, in which ye came out from Egypt, out of the house of bondage; for by strength of hand the Lord brought you out from this place: there shall no leavened bread be eaten." (Exodus 13:1-3)

God led us by way of the wilderness of the red sea because we were not able to defend ourselves in any way. God was our defense. (Exodus 13:18) When we left Egypt, I took the bones of Joseph with me. "Joseph wanted to be buried in the Promised Land, because he knew he would be raised from the dead someday and taken to heaven. because he believed in the resurrection of his people in that land for the Millennium – and then for eternity." (McGee)

As we journeyed the "Lord went before us by day in a pillar of a cloud, to lead the way; and by night in a pillar of fire, to give us light; to go by day and night." (Exodus 13:20-21) 'Our nation had something that no other nation has ever had: the Glory, the visible presence of God.' (McGee)

However we had not heard the last of Pharaoh. "He had spies watching us, but two and one half million people were not difficult to conceal." (McGee) When Pharaoh thinks we are trapped, he asks, 'Why have we done this, that we have let Israel go from serving us,' so he made ready his chariot, and took six hundred chosen chariots, and all the chariots of Egypt, and captains over every one of them, with him." (Exodus 14:5-7)

"When Pharaoh drew near to us, the children of Israel lifted up their eyes, and, were sore afraid; and they cried out unto the Lord. They turned to me and complained that I had taken them away to die in the wilderness." (Exodus 14:10-11)

I told the people to "fear ye not, stand still, and see the salvation of the Lord, which He will show to you today: for the Egyptians whom ye have seen today, ye shall see them no more forever. The Lord shall fight for you and ye shall hold your peace." (Exodus 14:13-14)

Next was a great miracle of God that was the beginning of many to come. The "Lord said to me, "Lift thou up thy rod, and stretch out thine hand over the sea, and divide it: and the children of Israel shall go on dry ground through the midst of the sea."

"I stretched out my hand over the sea; and the Lord caused the sea to go back by a strong east wind all that night, and made the sea dry land, and the waters were divided. All the people crossed over on dry ground, with the water as a wall on both sides of us. The Egyptians pursuing us went into the sea after us, and then the Lord took their chariot wheels off their chariots, so they were unable to move forward. They realized that God had caused this to happen, and they started to flee." (Exodus 14:14-25)

Again, the Lord told me to "stretch out my hand over the sea, that the waters may come again upon the Egyptians, their chariots, and their horseman." I did as instructed, and the sea returned to normal, so that all the chariots, and the horseman, and Pharaoh, were covered with water. (Exodus 14:26-28)

"The Lord saved Israel that day, and Israel saw the Egyptians dead upon the sea shore. Israel saw that great work which the Lord did upon the Egyptians: and the people feared the Lord, and believed the Lord, and me his servant Moses." There was a great celebration, to God, for His deliverance. (Exodus 14:30-31)

We then started on our way and traveled three days into the wilderness, we found only bitter water to drink at Marah. Again, the people murmured against me and I cried out to the Lord.

"The Lord showed me a tree, which when I cast it into the waters, the waters were made sweet. God then said, 'IF THOU WILL DILLIGENTLY HARKEN TO THE VOICE OF THE LORD THY GOD, AND WILL DO THAT WHICH IS RIGHT IN HIS SIGHT, AND WILL GIVE EAR TO HIS COMMANDMENTS, AND KEEP ALL HIS STATUES, I WILL PUT NONE OF THESE DISEASES UPON THEE, WHICH I HAVE BROUGHT UPON THE EGYPTIANS: FOR I AM THE LORD THAT HEALETH THEE." (Exodus 15:23-26)

You may know that the tree that God had me cast into the waters was a picture of Christ whom died on a tree for you and me. "It is the cross that makes the experiences of life sweet. He tasted death for every man, and took the sting out of death." O death, where is thy sting? O grave, where is thy victory? (1 Corinthians 15:55) "It is the cross of Christ that makes sweet the Marah experiences of life." (McGee)

Now we went on to "Elim, where there were twelve wells of water, and three score and ten palm trees: and we camped there by the waters." (Exodus 15:27) Now God blesses us greatly, but soon the people were murmuring against Aaron and me, because they were hungry and there was no food. All the murmuring of the people was aimed at Aaron and me, but it really was against God.

God then does a miracle that lasts for forty years. He rained bread from heaven for us. The people saw the bread and called it "manna" for they did not know what it was. I told them it was the `bread the Lord has given them to eat.' The people were to gather enough manna for one day, according to how many people were in the family. They were not to leave it until morning or it would spoil. On the sixth day of the week, they were to gather twice as much bread so they would not have to gather on the Sabbath Day. This double portion would not spoil. It came on the dew in the morning and melted when the sun became hot. (Exodus 13-21)

Again the "manna was a representation of the Lord Jesus Christ as the Bread of Life." Jesus said, `I am the living bread which came down from heaven: if any man eat of this bread, he shall live forever: and the bread that I will give is my flesh, which I will give for the life of the world.' (John 6:31) This bread was a "wonderful food that contained all the nourishment Israel needed. There was no sickness among the people for forty years, on this food. Manna could be fixed in many ways. They could grind it, beat it, bake it in pans, or make a casserole. But soon the people grew tired of God's heavenly food. They longed for the fleshpots of Egypt." (McGee)

God commanded us to journey to Rephidim, but again there was no water, so the people murmured against me and demanded, "Give us water that we drink. Why have you brought us up out of Egypt, to kill us and our children and our cattle with thirst?" So again, I cried to the Lord and He told me to take my rod and "smite the rock in Horeb, and water would come out of it, that the people may drink." (Exodus 17:1-7) The water did flow, and again this was a picture of Jesus. `And they remembered that God was their rock, and the high God their redeemer.' (Psalm 78:35) (McGee)

Next, we had to face a foe, Amalek, and fight with him. I told Joshua to choose his men to fight, because the next day the battle would begin. I stood on the hill with the rod of God in my hand while the battle raged below me. As long as my hand was up, Israel prevailed, but when I let down my hand down, Amalek prevailed. Aaron and Hur, one on one side and one on the other side, came to hold up my hands until victory was secure. (Exodus 17:11-14)

"I built an altar, and called the name of it Jehovah -nissi: For I said, 'because the Lord hath sworn that the Lord will have war with Amalek from generation to generation." (Exodus 17:15-16) 'Amalek represents the old nature of man and the Lord will never compromise with it, He got rid of it at the cross. As long as man lives in the world, the flesh and the spirit will always war against each other. Only the Holy Spirit of God can give you victory. Please recognize this fact.' (McGee)

My father-in-law, Jethro, heard all that God had done for me, and for Israel his people, and that the Lord had brought Israel out of Egypt. He brought Zipporah, my wife, and our two sons, back to me for I had sent them back to her home when we left for Egypt. (Exodus 18:1-12)

Jethro watched me as I "sat to judge the people from morning to evening." Then he made this suggestion to lighten my load. He believed I needed to appoint judges to help take care of the problems of the people. This would provide an orderly system and conserve time. Of course, God did not instruct me to do this, but it seemed wise, so I adhered to it.

"Really, God did not want a third party brought in, as He was dealing directly with me. There are many people that would rather go through a man, a church, a ceremony, a book, or even a musical concert, rather than go directly to God. God did not want others Involved. Actually, God gave me the power to do these tasks and arduous duties. Today, you may believe that the right method is what the church needs for success. This organization created the Sanhedrin, which about 1500 years later would meet together and plot the death of Jesus, the Son of God. Please friend, always listen and consult God before you go ahead with your plans, or the plans of your well- meaning friends and loved ones." (McGee)

We now arrive at Mount Sinai where God gives us His Law. God tells me this: "IF YE WILL OBEY MY VOICE INDEED, AND KEEP MY COVENANT, THEN YE SHALL BE A PECULIAR TREASURE UNTO ME ABOVE ALL PEOPLE: FOR ALL THE EARTH IS MINE. YE SHALL BE UNTO ME A KINGDOM OF PRIESTS, AND AN HOLY NATION." (Exodus 19:5-6)

God prepared the people to hear from Him. They were to wash their clothes and be ready on the third day when "God would come down in the sight of all the people upon mount Sinai." The people were not to go up into the mount, or 'touch the border of it: anyone touching the mount would be surely put to death.' (Exodus 19:12)

So, "on the third day in the morning, there were thunders and lightning's, and a thick cloud upon the mount, and the voice of the trumpet exceeding loud; so that all the people that were in the camp trembled;" `and when the voice of the trumpet sounded long, and waxed louder and louder, I spoke, and God answered me by a voice. And the Lord came down upon Mount Sinai, on the top of the mount: and the Lord called me, "MOSES", up to the top of the mount, and I went up.'

GOD THEN GAVE ME WHAT IS KNOWN AS THE TEN COMMANDMENTS, WHICH ARE A MORAL CODE

1. "Thou shalt have no other gods before me."

2. "Thou shalt not make unto thee any graven image, or any likeness of anything that is in heaven above, or that is in the earth beneath, or that is in the water under the earth: Thou shalt not bow down thyself to them, nor serve them: for I the Lord thy God am a jealous God, visiting the iniquity of the fathers upon the children unto the third and fourth generation of them that hate me."

3. "Thou shalt not take the name of the Lord thy God in vain; for the Lord will not hold him guiltless that taketh his name in vain."

4. "Remember the Sabbath day, to keep it holy. Six days shalt thou labor, and do all thy work: But the seventh day is the Sabbath of the Lord thy God: in it thou shalt not do any work, thou, nor thy son, nor thy daughter, thy manservant, nor thy maidservant, nor thy cattle, nor thy stranger that is within thy gates: For in six days the Lord made heaven and earth, the sea, and all that in them is, and rested the seventh day: wherefore the Lord blessed the Sabbath day and hallowed it."

5. "Honor thy father and thy mother: that thy days may be long upon the land which the Lord thy God giveth thee."

6. "Thou shalt not kill."

7. "Thou shalt not commit adultery."

8. Thou shalt not steal."

9. "Thou shalt not bear false witness against thy neighbor."

10. "Thou shalt not covet thy neighbor's house, thou shalt not covet thy neighbor's wife, nor his manservant, nor his maidservant, nor his ox, nor his mule, nor any thing that is thy neighbor's." (Exodus 20:3-17)

"What is the Law? Someone has defined it as the transcript of the mind of God. The Law is the expression of the mind of God relative to what man ought to be. There is no grace or mercy in the Law at all. The Law is an expression of the holy will of God. The Law requires perfection on your part. I have never met anyone who has measured up to God's standard. The Law is not some vague notion, and it does not have anything to do with good intentions. It requires perfect obedience, for the Law of the Lord is perfect. The Law of the Lord is right. There is no love in the law. There is no grace in the law. The Law sets forth what man ought to be. Grace sets forth what God is. The Law never made a man a sinner, it reveals the fact that man is a sinner." (McGee)

After the Ten Commandments were given God gave Israel instructions concerning the Altar. "The Altar is used for sacrifice. It speaks of the cross of Christ and the blood that He shed. We built this altar before the tabernacle was made." (McGee)

"God wanted a plain altar made of earth or plain stone, where a sacrifice of burnt offerings, peace offerings, sheep, and oxen would be made." There were to be no steps up to the altar that would reveal the nakedness of man. (Exodus 24-26)

The Lord went on to give us laws concerning all areas of our life. "He gave us laws concerning the master and servant relationship, laws concerning personal injuries, the law concerning property rights, the law concerning the land and the Sabbath, the law concerning national feasts, and the order of worship before the existence of the tabernacle." (McGee) (Exodus 21-25)

"God gave us the blueprint for the tabernacle and the pattern for the garments of the high priest. When we constructed the tabernacle, this structure was the center of Israel's life, because it was where we could approach God and His glory filled the place." (McGee) (Exodus 25-31)

While I was on Mount Sinai the people began to think I had died there, so they appealed to Aaron to make them idols (gods), so they would have something to lead them on their wilderness march. Aaron obliged by telling them to bring their golden earrings to him, and when he received them, he "fashioned" a golden calf. When the people saw it they 'offered burnt offerings and they brought peace offerings and they sat down to eat and to drink, and they rose up to play.' (Exodus 32:1-6)

Well, I had not died on the mount, but was still talking with the Lord, but God said to me, "GO, GET THEE DOWN; FOR THY PEOPLE, WHICH THOU BROUGHTEST OUT OF THE LAND OF EGYPT, HAVE CORRUPTED THEMSELVES. THEY HAVE TURNED ASIDE QUICKLY OUT OF THE WAY WHICH I COMMANDED THEM: THEY HAVE MADE THEM A MOLTEN CALF, AND THEY HAVE WORSHIPPED IT, AND HAVE SACRIFICED THEREUNTO, AND SAID, "These be thy gods, O Israel, which have brought thee up out of the land of Egypt." (Exodus 32:7-8)

God went on to tell me that these people were a "stiff-necked people" and that His 'wrath was waxed hot against them.' I prayed to God by saying, "Lord, you made a mistake, I did not bring the people out of Egypt and they are not my people but Yours. With Your mighty hand You have brought them out. I reminded Him that He made a promise to Abraham, Isaac, and Israel, that He would multiply their seed and give them a land." (Exodus 32:11-13) (McGee)

The Lord heard my prayer and "the Lord repented of the evil which He thought to do unto His people." (Exodus 32:14) I then went down from the mount carrying the two tables the Lord had written with His own hand. They were written on both sides. When I entered the camp, I saw the calf, and the dancing, and I was so angry I cast the tables down and they broke on the rocks. I took the calf and ground it to powder and mixed it with water and made the people drink it.

I then turned to Aaron and asked him how he had been involved in such a great sin as this. He said he threw the gold earrings in the fire and the calf came out, all on its own. I then ordered the "sons of Levi" to kill those involved, and about three thousand men died that day. (Exodus 32:24-28) 'Sin is a very serious thing, so please do not compromise with it; weed it out when you see it invading your churches today.' (McGee)

I then returned to the Lord, and asked God to "forgive their sin or else blot me out with them." The Lord said to me, 'WHOSOEVER HATH SINNED AGAINST ME, HIM WILL I BLOT OUT OF MY BOOK. GO NOW, LEAD THE PEOPLE UNTO THE PLACE OF WHICH I HAVE SPOKEN UNTO THEE: MINE ANGEL SHALL GO BEFORE THEE.' "The Lord plagued the people, because they made the calf, which Aaron made." (Exodus 32:31-35) 'The Lord graciously heard my prayer and His heart was moved.' (McGee)

God gave us instructions to construct the tabernacle; it was set up outside the camp. I then entered the tabernacle, and the cloudy pillar descended and stood at the door of the tabernacle, and the Lord talked with me here. The Lord spoke to me "face to face," but I really did not see God, literally face to face. In John 1:18 we learn 'that no man has seen God at any time." (Exodus 33:11-13)

I asked God that I might "know Him and find grace in His sight," and He assured me that 'His presence would go with me, and He would give me rest and He was with the people of Israel too'. I asked God to show me His glory, but God said to me, "THOU CANST NOT SEE MY FACE: FOR THERE SHALL NO MAN SEE ME, AND LIVE." (Exodus 33:20)

Since I broke the tablets of stone on the rocks, God told me to "hew two tables of stone like the first. He told me to be ready in the morning, and come up to Mount Sinai and present myself there. No man was to come with me. I went up to the mount and the Lord descended in the cloud, and stood with me there." God said, 'I, THE LORD GOD AM MERCIFUL AND GRACIOUS, FORGIVING INIQUITY AND TRANSGRESSION AND SIN, AND WILL BY NO MEANS CLEAR THE GUILTY, VISITING THE INIQUITY OF THE FATHERS UPON THE CHILDREN, AND UPON THE CHILDRENS'S CHILDREN, UNTO THE THIRD AND TO THE FOURTH GENERATION. BEHOLD, I MADE A COVENANT: BEFORE ALL, THY PEOPLE I WILL DO MARVELS, SUCH AS HAVE NOT BEEN DONE IN ALL THE EARTH, NOR IN ANY NATION: AND ALL THE PEOPLE AMONG WHICH THOU ART SHALL SEE THE WORK OF THE LORD. BEHOLD, I DRIVE OUT BEFORE THEE THE AMORITE, AND THE CANAANITE, AND THE HITTITE, AND THE PERIZZITE, AND THE HIVITE, AND THE JEBUSITE.' (Exodus 34:6-11)

When I came down from Mount Sinai with the two tables, my face shone with the glory of God. The people wanted me to put a veil over my face because they were afraid to come close to me. When I went before the Lord I removed the veil, but when I spoke to the people, I covered my face. (Exodus: 34:29-35)

The Lord God reemphasized the importance of the Sabbath day and said the "Sabbath was a peculiar sign between Himself and the children of Israel." God said that anyone doing work on the Sabbath should be put to death. The Lord commanded the children of Israel to 'take an offering and with a willing heart give gold, silver, and brass, and blue, purple, and scarlet, and fine linen, and goats' hair; rams' skins dyed red, and badgers' skins, and shittim wood; oil for light, and spices for anointing oil, and for the sweet incense, and onyx stones, and stones to be set for the ephod, and for the breastplate for the tabernacle.' (Exodus 35:2-9)

"The Lord gave us detailed instruction - on how to build the tabernacle, because - the tabernacle is God's portrait of Christ - revealed." (McGee)

There came a time when Miriam and Aaron, my sister and brother, spoke against me because of the Ethiopian woman that I had married. They questioned whether God had spoken to me only, or had He not spoken to Miriam and Aaron too? God made it plain that He had spoken to me only, and because they had spoken against me Miriam was stricken with leprosy and became "white as snow". She was put out of the camp for seven days. I prayed for her and God healed her of the leprosy. We did not move for the seven days while she was outside the camp. (Numbers 12:1-16)

When we reached the border of the Promised Land God spoke to me and told me to send one man from each tribe of Israel, twelve in all. These men were to "spy out the land of Canaan" by seeing what the land was like, good or bad, and the kind of people that dwelled there, whether they be strong or weak, and the kinds of dwelling they had, tents or strong structure. Also, they were to report whether the land was fat or lean, whether there was wood or not. They were to be of good courage, and bring a sample of the fruit of the land back with them. (Numbers 13:1-20)

The men went into the land to search it out. They came to a brook and cut down a branch with one cluster of grapes that took two men to carry it between them. They also brought back pomegranates, and figs, and were gone for a total of forty days. (Numbers 13:17-20)

When they returned, they gave a report to Aaron and me and to all the congregation of the children of Israel. They said, "The land flowed with milk and honey" and they showed us the fruit they had gathered. They went on to say that the people were strong that dwelled in the land,

and the cities were walled and very great. They believed we could not' go against these people for they were stronger than us. They said that the people were giants and we looked like grasshoppers next to them.

There were two men who disagreed with the ten. They were Caleb and Joshua; they believed that "we should go at once and possess the land because we were well able to overcome it." (Numbers 13:26-30)

The majority of the people believed the ten, and refused to go into the Promised Land. They "cried and wept all night," and murmured against Aaron and me. They said, 'We should have died in Egypt or in the wilderness instead of God bringing us to this land, to fall by the sword, that our wives and our children should be a prey; would it not be better for us to return to Egypt? (Numbers 14:1-3)

God did not intend the people to make this decision; they were only to go in and report what they saw; God was to be our protector and defender and go before us to defeat the people in the Land. The people did not have faith in God; their faith was in themselves, so we did not go in at this time. It would be forty years before the people of Israel would finally enter the Promised Land.

Aaron and I fell on our faces before the people, but they wanted to stone us. God then appeared to us and said, "YOUR CARCASES SHALL FALL IN THIS WILDERNESS; ACCORDING TO YOUR WHOLE NUMBER, FROM TWENTY YEARS OLD, AND UPWARD, WHICH HAVE MURMURED AGAINST ME, DOUBTLESS YE SHALL NOT COME INTO THE LAND, WHICH I SWEAR TO MAKE YOU DWELL THEREIN, SAVE CALEB, AND JOSHUA, BUT YOUR LITTLE ONES WHICH YE SAID SHOULD BE A PREY, THEM WILL I BRING IN, AND THEY SHALL KNOW THE LAND WHICH YE HAVE DESPISED. YOUR CHILDREN SHALL WANDER IN THE WILDERNESS FORTY YEARS, UNTIL YOUR CARCASES BE WASTED IN THE WILDERNESS." (Numbers 14:29-33)

So began our forty-year wandering in the wilderness. During these many years God sent manna, daily, for us to eat, and our clothes did not wear out. After thirty-seven years, my sister Miriam died, and was buried. Again, we ran out of water, and again the people complained to Aaron and me, as was their custom. We fell upon our faces before God at the door of the tabernacle, and He spoke to me and said, "TAKE THE ROD, AND GATHER THOU THE ASSEMBLY TOGETHER, THOU, AND AARON THY BROTHER, AND SPEAK YE UNTO THE ROCK BEFORE THEIR EYES:

AND IT SHALL GIVE FORTH HIS WATER AND THOU SHALL BRING FORTH TO THEM WATER OUT OF THE ROCK: SO, THOU SHALT GIVE THE CONGREGATION AND THEIR BEAST DRINK." (Numbers 20:7-8)

So I look my rod, and Aaron and I gathered the congregation together before the rock, and I said, "Hear now, ye rebels; must we fetch you water out of this rock?" `I lifted up my hand and with my rod I smote the rock twice: and the water came out abundantly, and the congregation drank, and their beasts also.' (Numbers 20:7-11)

I just had made the biggest mistake of my life by not obeying what God told me to do. I struck the rock, "twice," out of my anger, when I was to `speak' to it only. The Rock represented Christ; He suffered once for our sins, and He died once for our sins, so "The Rock" had already been smitten when Christ died on the cross. (McGee) Immediately, the Lord spoke to me and Aaron and said, `BECAUSE YE BELIEVED ME NOT, TO SANCTIFY ME IN THE EYES OF THE CHILDREN OF ISRAEL, THEREFORE YE SHALL NOT BRING THIS CONGREGATION INTO THE LAND WHICH I HAVE GIVEN THEM.' (Numbers 20:12)

Next, my brother Aaron died at mount Hor. He, being the high priest had to pass his garments on to his son, Eleazar, before his death. This took place on mount Hor, so when Eleazar came down from the mount, he was the new high priest. "Today you have the Great High Priest of Jesus Christ who never changes. He died once for all, so He will never die again. He is always there for you and you can depend on Him. He knows each one individually and knowing Him will occupy us for all eternity." (McGee) We mourned for Aaron for thirty days. (Numbers 20:23-29)

Again, the people murmured against God and me. They continued to complain that they were brought out of Egypt to die in the wilderness. They said that there was no bread, or water, and they loathed the light bread, they called "manna". Because the people murmured God sent fiery serpents that bit the people, and many died.

They realized that they had sinned for speaking against the Lord and me. They asked me to pray to the Lord that He would take the serpents away. I prayed and the "Lord told me to make a fiery serpent, and set it upon a pole: and it would come to pass that every one that is bitten when he looks upon it, shall live." (Numbers 21:6-9)

"I made a serpent of brass and put it upon a pole, and it came to pass, that if a serpent had bitten any man, when he beheld the serpent of brass, he lived." There is a lesson for you today in the 21st century. When the Lord Jesus was talking to Nicodemus, He said, `And as Moses lifted up the serpent in the wilderness, even so must the Son of man be lifted up: That whosoever believeth in him should not perish, but have eternal life. FOR GOD SO LOVED THE WORLD, THAT HE GAVE HIS ONLY BEGOTTEN SON, THAT WHOSOEVER BELIEVETH IN HIM SHOULD NOT PERISH, BUT HAVE EVERLASTING LIFE.' (John 3:14-16) (McGee)

"How was the son of man lifted up, you ask; on a cross? Our Lord was made sin for us, and took our place in death. God wants us to look to Christ for our salvation, and live. The serpent of brass, that I made, was representative of Jesus on the Cross, and any that look to Him, live." Many in my day did not want to look at the serpent of brass. They believed that it was silly or they were too proud to look. `People would rather look to themselves and to their own good works hoping that this will save them. It is a problem for people to admit they are sinners and need a savior, and to look to Christ and trust Him alone for salvation.' "If one did not look at the serpent then, or you do not look to Christ now, you will die as an unforgiven sinner." (McGee)

The next story that came to my attention was about the "daughters of Zelophehad, the son of Hepher, the son of Gilead, the son of Machir, the son of Manasseh, of the families of Manasseh the son of Joseph: and these are the names of his daughters, Mahlah, Noah, and Hoglah, and Milcah, and Tirzah." (Numbers 27:1)

They stood before Moses, and before Eleazar the priest, and before the prince and all the congregation, by the door of the tabernacle of the congregation, saying, "Our father died in the wilderness, and he was not in the company of them that gathered themselves together against the Lord in the company of Korah; but died in his own sin, and had no sons."

"Why should the name of our father be done away from among his family, because he hath no son? Give unto us therefore a possession among the brethren of our father. And I, Moses, brought their cause before the Lord."

And the Lord, spoke to me, saying, "THE DAUGHTERS OF ZELEPHEHAD SPEAK RIGHT: THOU SHALT SURELY GIVE THEM A POSSESSION OF AN INHERITANCE AMONG THEIR FATHER'S

BRETHREN; AND THOU SHALT CAUSE THE INHERITANCE OF THEIR FATHER TO PASS UNTO THEM. SPEAK UNTO THE CHILDREN OF ISRAEL, SAYING, "IF A MAN DIE, AND HAVE NO SON, THEN YE SHALL CAUSE HIS INHERITANCE TO PASS UNTO HIS DAUGHTER." (Numbers 27:2-9)

You can see the Lord is on the side of women's rights. This is one of the most remarkable laws that can be imagined. You live in the 21st century when a ruling such as this is commonplace. If any of you women think that Jesus was against women, or God only spoke and worked with men, you are wrong. It is in the Bible; God's Word that first gave women their rights. This law was made about 1500 years before Christ came into the world." (McGee)

"These five girls wanted to possess their father's inheritance. It was not the custom of the day nor a written law that they could have it. Therefore, they asked by faith, and by faith God gave the inheritance to them. This is a marvelous lesson for you today. God hears and answers us, not only in the spiritual blessings but also in the material things. Many are paupers because they do not come to God as His children and ask Him for things. God wants to be good to us." (McGee)

Now it is of God's timing that I "was to pass from the earthly scene." God told me "To go up mount Abarim, and see the land, which He had given to the children of Israel." (Numbers 27:12-14) He told me that I would not go into this land, as was my heart's desire. "God told me I could not go in because of my rebellion in the desert of Zin, when I smote the rock twice, when God had told me to speak to the rock, only." (McGee)

You can see friend that "disobedience is a terrible sin which will keep you from entering into your spiritual possessions that God has for you." (McGee) However, it was not my disobedience that kept me out of the Promised Land; it was what I said when I hit the rock twice, "Must we fetch thee water from the rock?" I put myself in the place of God and in my wrath spoke and acted as if I was God. God will not let any person supercede His place as God over all.

The Lord then told me to "take Joshua the son of Nun, a man in whom is the Spirit, and lay thine hand upon him. I was to set him before Eleazar the priest, and before the whole congregation; and charge him with the responsibility of leading the people." I did as I was commanded and I laid my hands upon him, and he became God's new leader of the people of Israel. (Numbers 27:15-23)

I reviewed, for the people, our journeys from Egypt and restated and interpreted the Law God had given us, as this would prepare the new generation to enter the Promised Land. I reminded them of who God is: "The Lord our God made a covenant with us in Horeb. The Lord made not this covenant with our fathers, but with us, even us, who are all of us here alive this day." (Deuteronomy 5:2-3)

I reminded them of the Ten Commandments God gave us and what God told us, "Hear, O Israel; The Lord our God is one Lord. And thou shall love the Lord thy God with all your heart, and with all thy soul, and with all thy might. And these words, which I command thee this day, shall be in your heart. And thou shall teach them diligently unto thy children, and shall talk of them when thou sit in your house, and when thou walk by the way, and when thou lie down, and when thou rise up, and thou shall bind them for a sign upon your hand, and they shall be as frontlets between your eyes. And thou shall write them upon the posts of thy house, and on thy gates." (Deut.6:9)

"All the commandments which I command thee this day shall ye observe to do, that ye may live, and multiply, and go in and possess the land which the Lord swear unto your fathers. And thou shall remember all the ways which the Lord thy God led thee these forty years in the wilderness, to humble thee, and to prove thee, to know what was in your heart, whether thou would keep his commandments, or no." (Deut. 8:1-2)

Of course, none can keep the law in their own strength. In Philippians 1:6 we learn: "Being confident of this very thing, that he which hath begun a good work in you will perform it until the day of Jesus Christ." 'God tested us in the wilderness to humble us, and to prove what was really in our hearts.' (McGee)

I continued to tell the people how God fed us manna and we did not get sick a day on it, and how our clothes did not wear out in forty years. I also reminded them of past failures, God called Israel a stiff-necked people, the making of the golden calf, the breaking of the tablets of stone on the rocks, and the many times Israel murmured against God while in the wilderness, and because of their lack of faith in God, they would not go into the Promised Land.

My emphasis was on "two words: love and obedience - not law and obedience. You and I express our love for God in our obedience." In John 14:15, Jesus said, 'IF YOU LOVE ME, KEEP MY COMMANDMENTS.' (McGee)

In 1 John 4:19 we realize that we can only love the Lord, because He first loved us, and Jesus cited the greatest commandment of all as: "And thou shalt love the Lord thy God with all thine heart, and with all thy soul, and with all thy might." (Deut. 6:5) (McGee)

So God promised to bless His people who respond to His love by obedience: "Wherefore it shall come to pass, if ye hearken to these judgments, and keep, and do them, that the Lord thy God shall keep unto thee the covenant and the mercy which he swear unto thy fathers: And he will love thee, and bless thee, and multiply thee, he will also bless the fruit of thy womb, and the fruit of thy land, thy corn, and thy wine, and thine oil, the increase of the kine, and the flocks of thy sheep, in the land which he swear unto thy fathers to give thee.

"Thou shall not be afraid of them: but shall well remember what the Lord thy God did unto Pharaoh, and unto all Egypt. Thou shall not be affrighted at them: for the Lord thy God is among you, a mighty God and terrible, and the Lord thy God will put out those nations before thee by little and little: thou mayest not consume them at once, lest the beasts of the field increase upon thee.

"But the Lord thy God shall deliver them unto thee, and shall destroy them with a mighty destruction, until they be destroyed." (Deuteronomy 7:10-23)

I then gathered the people around me and I gave a blessing to each tribe. I then said, "Happy art thou, O Israel: who is like thee, O people saved by the Lord, the shield of thy help, and who is the sword of thy Excellency! And thine enemies shall be found liars unto thee; and thou shalt tread upon their high places." (Deuteronomy 33:29)

"I then went up from the plains of Moab unto the mountain of Nebo, to the top of Pisgah, that is over against Jericho." The Lord showed me the land promised to Abraham, Isaac, and Jacob, but God said I could only see the land; I could not cross over into the land.

"I then died there in the land of Moab, according to the word of the Lord, and God buried me in a valley in the land of Moab," with the location of my sepulcher known only to God Himself. God did not want the people making any kind of monument to me that would keep them from moving forward to the Promised Land. God wanted them to leave the past behind and look to, Him, only for their future.

I was one hundred and twenty years old when I died. My eyes were good and I had plenty of energy, which should encourage you that you do not have to consider yourself old, and take on the sicknesses of the world. My strength was from God and so can be yours.

The people of Israel were allowed to weep and mourn for me for thirty days only, and then they had to move on to the Promised Land without me. (Deut. 34:1-8) I am the one that wrote the first five books of the Bible given to me by inspiration of God. (Genesis, Exodus, Leviticus, Numbers and Deuteronomy)

God designed my life from birth to its completion 120 years later. Let God direct your life too, you will never be sorry. His design is the one that will make you most satisfied and happy at the end. May the Love of God go with you always?

I DID IT MY WAY

THE HARD SOIL

That "shepherd, that old man," Moses, came to me to request that I let his people go out of Egypt to worship their God. Who is he that I should let the Israelis go to worship a God that I know nothing of. I have my own gods that I worship, and they are good enough for Israel too. I am Pharaoh; no man can tell me what to do and no god will tell me what I must do with Israel.

I have no knowledge of Moses once being the son of the Princess of Egypt. He is no Egyptian now; he is nothing now. He has nothing but a rod and a word from his God, named "I am." What is that to me? As if a rod could scare me in to submission to him and his God.

My magicians have rods too, and they performed all the same, "so-called - signs," that Moses did. I did. Of course, Moses' rod did swallow up all the snakes of my magicians, but that means nothing.

No, there is nothing, or no one, or any God, that will tell me what I must do, because, "I AM PHARAOH, KING OF EGYPT." The Israelites belong to me now, and they are MY servants. No person and no 'God' can take them away from me.

Those plagues are little troublesome, but we are a tough people, we can get through them one-by-one. I repeat, "NO ONE, OR NO GOD, WILL TELL, ME, THE "PHARAOH" OF EGYPT, WHAT I 'MUST' DO~ I WILL PREVAIL NO MATTER WHAT."

Exodus 12:30-31 "And Pharaoh rose up in the night, he, and all his servants, and all Egyptians; and there was a great cry in Egypt, for there was not a house where there was not one dead. And he called for Moses and Aaron by night, and said, 'rise up, and get you forth from among my people, both you and the children of Israel: and go, serve the Lord, as ye have said."

Exodus 15:9-11 "The enemy (Pharaoh) said, I will pursue, I will overtake, I will divide the spoil; my lust shall be satisfied upon them; I will draw my sword, my hand shall destroy them. Thou dist blow with thy wind, the sea covered them: they sank as lead in the mighty sea. Who is like thee, O Lord, among the Gods?"

Goliath

Jonathan

Abigail

Bathsheba

David

WHO'S TO BLAME?

"I don't see how God can blame David for everything. That foolish woman shouldn't have been taking a bath on the roof."

"I don't think she was necessarily on the roof, David looking around. It was evening, and he might have been able to see into her house. Maybe she had candles or something that lit up her bathroom." The verse says: `And it came to pass in an evening tide, that David arose from off his bed, and walked upon the roof of the king's house: and from the roof he saw a woman washing herself; and the woman was very beautiful to look upon.' (2 Samuel 11:2)

"Well, even so, it seems like she should get some of the blame instead of it all going onto David."

"She did not go unpunished. She lost her husband Uriah, and she lost the first baby she and David had together, because of David's sin. God holds his people responsible to Him for their actions, and David had the power and the position to influence Bathsheba."

They lost their baby because of the adultery?"

Yes, God sent Nathan to David to expose his sin. Nathan said this to David, `because of your sin the child that is born unto thee shall surely die." (2 Samuel 12:14)

"There it is again, God blaming David."

"Yes, but their next baby, Solomon, was the next King of Israel, and the wisest man that ever lived until Jesus. So, we know God forgave David, however, people are not so forgiving, so we might conclude that Bathsheba endured the scorn of people until her death, and we know that David's sin is still talked about today, and movies shown around the world, have been made about it."

A MAN AFTER MY OWN HEART – DAVID

Sometimes the most innocent of moments can lead to a lifetime of remorse, I, David, was standing on my roof enjoying the evening alone. My men were off fighting a war, but I decided to stay at home to get a much-needed vacation, and my men encouraged me to do this. I neglected to ask God if this was a good idea, and now I am paying the price.

God has lead me all of my life, and He brought me to this place of being King over all Israel by His Devine direction; I was a very young shepherd boy, the youngest of eight boys born to my father, Jesse. After Saul turned away from God "to do what was right in his own eyes," God told Samuel, His prophet, to go to the house of Jesse to anoint a new king of Israel. When Samuel arrived at our home, I was out in the field tending my father's sheep. My seven older brothers were ready to be presented to Samuel, and everyone was sure one would be anointed as the next king of Israel.

Samuel started with the oldest, Eliab; he was sure he had the right one to lead Israel, because he was well-built and he was handsome to look at. "But the Lord said unto Samuel, `Look not on his countenance, or on the height of his statue; because I have refused him: for the Lord sees not as man sees; for man looks on the outward appearance, but the Lord looks on the heart." (1 Samuel 16:7)

Again, my father, Jesse had all seven of my brothers pass before Samuel, but Samuel said to Jesse, "The Lord has not chosen these. Are all your children here?" My father then told him that I, David, the youngest was keeping the sheep. Samuel asked for me to be brought in from the field. He could not eat until he anointed the next king.

I was brought in before Samuel, and God said to him, "Arise, anoint him: for this is he." Samuel took the horn of oil and anointed me in the midst of my brethren: and the spirit of the Lord came upon me from that day forward." (1 Samuel 16:10-13)

My life did not change, as Saul was still the king of Israel. However, Saul was troubled in his spirit because of his disobedience to God. He asked one of his servants to find a man that could play a harp for him, and to "refresh" him. I was that man, so I went to the palace to play for Saul. He loved me at first because when I played my music, the "evil spirit departed from him." (1 Samuel 17:17-23)

"Now the Philistines gathered together their armies to do battle with Israel. The Philistines stood on a mountain on the one side, and Israel stood on a mountain on the other side: and there was a valley between them. A champion of the Philistines, named Goliath, of Gath, was about nine feet, nine inches tall. He had great armor and spear like a weaver's beam. He stood and cried to the armies of Israel, 'Choose you a man from among you, and let him come down and fight me." (1 Samuel 17:1-8)

My father, Jesse, sent me to take bread and cheese to my brothers and their captain, at the battlefield. When I arrived there, I heard the champion Goliath challenging the army of Israel to send a man to fight him. I saw the men were so afraid of him, and they wondered who could go against this giant and live. The men told me that Saul would give his daughter and great riches to the one that defeated Goliath, and also his family would not have to pay taxes in Israel.

I spoke to the men of the army saying, "Who is this uncircumcised Philistine, that he should defy the armies of the living God?" My oldest brother, Eliab, took offense to me and he said, 'Why did you leave the sheep and come down here; you have pride in your heart because you wanted to see the battle.'

I turned away from him and again spoke freely against Goliath. Saul sent for me to come before him. I told him, "Let no man's heart fail because of Goliath; thy servant will go and fight with this Philistine." Saul said that I was not able to fight because I was a youth and Goliath a man. I told Saul that I kept my father's sheep, and I had killed a lion, and a bear, when they tried to kill the sheep. I went on to say, 'The Lord that delivered me out of the paw of the bear, he will deliver me out of the hand of this Philistine.' Saul told me to "Go, the Lord be with thee."

Saul put his armor on me and it was so heavy that I could not take a step, so I took it off. I then went to the brook and took five smooth stones and put them in my shepherd's bag, and then I took my sling and drew near to Goliath. When the Philistine saw me, he mocked me, and said,

"Am I a dog, that thou comest to me with a sling?" He then cursed me by his gods, and said he would feed me to the fowls of the air.

Some may believe that I chose five stones so in case I missed, I could try again. I had no intention of missing the mark, and besides I would only have one chance to kill Goliath. The reason I choose five smooth stones, was because Goliath had four brothers, I was sure that they would come forth when I killed Goliath.

I spoke unto him, saying, "Thou comest to me with a sword, and with a spear, and with a shield: but I come to thee in the name of the Lord of hosts, and God of the armies of Israel, whom thou hast defied. This day will the Lord deliver thee into my hand; and I will smite thee, and take thine head from thee; and I will give the carcasses of the host of the Philistines this day unto the fowls of the air, and to the wild beasts of the earth; that all the earth may know that there is a God in Israel. All this assembly shall know that the Lord saveth not with sword and spear: for the battle is the Lord's, and He will give you into our hands." (1 Samuel 17:9-47)

"Next, I ran toward the Philistine, put my hand in my bag, took a stone and slung it and smote him in his forehead; the stone sunk deep into his head, and he fell upon his face to the earth. I ran to where Goliath lay, took his sword, drew it out of the sheath, and slew him, and cut off his head. When the Philistines saw their champion was dead, they fled."

"The men of Israel and of Judah arose, and shouted, and pursued the Philistines and killed them; then they returned from chasing them and destroyed their tents. King Saul sent for me, and I went before him with the head of Goliath in my hand. Saul inquired as to whose son I was; I told him I was the son of Jesse. Saul would not let me go home again; he gave me his robe, and his sword, and his bow, and his other garments, and Saul made me head over the men of war." (1 Samuel 17: 48-58)

While Saul was speaking to me, his son Jonathan stood listening. As he listened, our two souls were knit together, and Jonathan loved me as his own soul. We made a covenant among ourselves that we would stick together for life, and our friendship has been equal to none other in history. (1 Samuel 18:1-5) (McGee)

Soon my reputation was known throughout the land. Women sang songs saying, "Saul has slain his thousands, and David his ten thousands."

Saul was very wroth when he heard this, and he was filled with hate for me. While I played for him, he threw his javelin at me twice, but I managed to get out of its path and left his presence quickly. (1 Samuel 18:6-16)

Soon Saul made it plain to his son, Jonathan, and to all his servants, that they should kill me. Because Jonathan loved me like his brother, he told me of this plot by his father, to kill me. He told me to go out and hide myself until morning: at that time, he would speak with his father, Saul, about me, to see if he could change his mind. He reminded Saul that I had slain Goliath, and saved Israel; he said that I had done good toward Saul, and that if he killed me, he would shed innocent blood. (1 Samuel 19:1-7)

Saul let Jonathan bring me back to the palace and into Saul's presence, as in times past. There was war again, and I went out to fight the Philistines and defeated them again. But this truce between Saul and me did not last long. Again, Saul sent his messengers to my house to kill me in the morning. My wife Michal, Saul's daughter, helped me to escape. (1 Samuel 19:8-18)

I did not understand why Saul was so angry with me, and wanted to kill me. I asked Jonathan to find out what intent Saul had concerning me. We had a plan for me to find out if it was safe for me to return to the palace. Since Saul's servants watched Jonathan, we decided that I would hide in a field nearby; in three days Jonathan would say he was going to practice his archery and when he shot his arrow, he would direct it toward where I was hiding. If the arrow landed behind me, I would know Saul wanted to kill me, if it landed in front of my hiding place, I would know it was safe to return.

Before we departed from our secret place, we made a pact that when I became king, we would not forget our friendship and our families would be honored between us. On the third day, Jonathan went out to shoot his arrows. His first arrow went flying through the air and landed way on the other side of me. I knew then the news was not favorable, and that Saul wanted to slay me. Jonathan sent his armor-bearer to pick up the arrows, that he had shot, and then had them take the artillery into the city. (McGee)

When they had left, we met and talked. Jonathan said to me, "Go in peace for as much as we have sworn both of us in the name of the Lord, saying. The lord be between me and thee, and between my seed and thy seed forever." Then Jonathan departed and went into the city. I knew that from this day on I was in danger because of Saul. (1 Samuel 20:1-42)

"I departed and escaped to the cave of Adullam; men that were in distress, in debt, or discontented, gather themselves to me, and I became captain over them; they numbered about four hundred men." (1 Samuel 22:1-2)

As time goes on, Saul becomes more and more unreasonable. He was so bitter and hateful toward me, that he slays all the priests of Nob, because they had helped me, "killing eighty five persons that wore a linen ephod. He also killed both men and women, children and babies, and oxen, and donkeys, and sheep, with the edge of the sword." (1 Samuel 22:19)

The people of Keliah were being robbed of their grain supply, so I inquired of the Lord, asking if I should go and smite these Philistines? The Lord said unto me, "GO, AND SMITE THE PHILISTINES, AND SAVE KEILAH." So I, and my men, who numbered about six hundred now, went and slaughtered the Philistines and saved Keilah. (1 Samuel 23:1-5)

"Saul heard of this and sought me every day in the wilderness, but God delivered me out of his hand. Jonathan came to me in the wood, and strengthened me. He said to me, "Fear not: for the hand of Saul my father shall not find thee; and thou shall be king over Israel, and I shall be next unto thee." We again made a covenant before the Lord, before we departed back to his house. (1 Samuel 23:17-18)

I had two chances to kill Saul, but would not because he was the "Lord's anointed, so I could not stretch forth my hand against him. "(1 Samuel 24:6)

Next, I encountered a man, named Nabal, in Maon; he was very great, and he had three thousand sheep, and a thousand goats; and he was shearing his sheep in Camel. "He was a churlish and evil man. but his wife, Abigail, was a woman of good understanding, and of a beautiful countenance." (1 Samuel 25:2-3)

I had been protecting Nabul's property and keeping his sheep from marauders, so "I sent out ten young men and told them to go to Nabal, in my name, and ask him for food for my men. Nabel answered my servants this way, "Who is David? And who is the son of Jesse? There be many servants now a days that break away every man from his master. (Nabal was implying that I had betrayed Saul and was disloyal to him) Shall I then take my bread, and my water, and my flesh that I have killed for my Shearers', and give it unto men whom I know not who they are."

My young men returned to me with this report, I said to my men in wrath, "Gird ye on every man his sword." And they girded on their swords and so did I. I was planning on taking four hundred of my men with me, and leaving two hundred to watch our stuff. (1 Samuel 25:4-13)

Unbeknown to me, one of my men told Abigail, Nabal's wife, what Nabal had said, and what I was planning to do. Abigail quickly gathered together "two hundred loaves, and two bottles of wine, and five sheep ready dressed, and five measures of corn, and an hundred clusters of raisins, and two hundred cakes of figs, and laid them on donkeys." And she said to her servants, "Go on before me, behold, I come after you." But she told not her husband Nabal.' (1 Samuel 25:14-19)

My intention was to kill every man that belonged to Nabal because "he had requited me evil for good." As we advanced toward Nabal, we met Abigail. She quickly lighted off her donkey, and fell before me on her face, and bowed herself to the ground, and fell at my feet, and said, "Upon me let this iniquity be; and let thine handmaid, I pray thee, speak to you, and please hear the words of thine handmaid."

She went on to say that her husband was a "fool and a brute," and if I did what I intended, I would shed blood with my own hand, and up until this time I had honored the Lord and lived for Him. She admired me for this, and did not want me to act in haste, and become an offense before God. She reminded me that I was to become the ruler over Israel (and when I did became King over Israel, to please remember her), and it was unworthy of me to disgrace myself by shedding blood without a cause.

I instantly realized my mistake, and was very thankful to Abigail for coming to me in humility, and reminding me of my position before God. I said to her, "Blessed be the Lord God of Israel, which sent thee this day to meet me: And blessed be thy advice, and blessed be thou, which hast kept me this day from coming to shed blood, and from avenging myself with mine own hand."

"I accepted all the food she had brought, I accepted her advice, and I accepted her kindness, I told her "Go in peace to your house." (I Samuel 25:20-35)

When Abigail arrived home, Nabal was holding a feast in the house and he was very drunk. Abigail waited until morning when he was sober, and told him all she had done concerning me. Nabal became "as a stone, and after ten days, the Lord smote him."

When I heard that Nabal was dead, I said, "Blessed be the Lord, that hath pleaded the cause of my reproach from the hand of Nabal, and has kept his servant from evil: for the Lord has returned the wickedness of Nabal upon his own head. And I sent for Abigail, as she requested of me, and because of my love for her I took her to be my wife." (1 Samuel 25:36-39)

I also took Ahinoam for my wife, as Saul had taken my wife Michal and given her to another man, named Phalti. Did God approve of me taking more than one wife because I was "the man after His own heart?" "No," I held no favors from God when I went against his will. Taking more than one wife would lead me into sin later on in my leadership over Israel.

"While I and my men were away from home (our home being in the city of Ziklag), an enemy from the south, the Amalekites, invaded the Philistine country and destroyed Ziklag. When we returned expecting to be reunited with our families, we found the city burned with fire and deserted. We had lost our wives and children and we did not know if they were slaves or they had all been killed." (McGee)

"My men were ready to stone me because it was my idea to go and help the Philistines (whom had become my friends) and leave our families unprotected. I had made a great blunder and `I was greatly distressed; for my people spoke of stoning me, because the soul of all the people were grieved, every man for his sons and for his daughters (they believed their wives were dead); but I encouraged myself in the Lord my God." (1 Samuel 30:6) (McGee)

"I was so distraught and discouraged, but I could not give up, so I threw myself on the mercy of God." I inquired of the Lord, saying, `shall I pursue after this troop? Shall I overtake them?' And God answered me, "FOR THOU SHALL SURELY OVERTAKE THEM, AND WITHOUT FAIL RECOVER ALL." (1 Samuel 30:8)

So, I went with my six hundred men with me, and came to the brook Besor, where two hundred men were too faint (from marching double time) to go on. Next we came upon an Egyptian who had been left behind by the Amalekites because he was sick. We gave him food and water to revive him; he agreed to lead us to Amalekites if I agreed not to return him to his master. I agreed.

When we came upon the Amalekite camp, "they were eating and drinking, and dancing, because of all the great spoil that they had taken from us." My men and I `smote them from the twilight even unto the evening of the next day: and there escaped not a man of them, except the four hundred young men which rode away on camels, and fled.' (1 Samuel 30:16-17) (McGee)

"We recovered our wives, our children, and all our flocks and herds that had been captured, as God had told me. Then an argument broke out among my men; they thought that the men that had participated in the battle should not be entitled to any of the spoil. In fairness, I laid down a principle that required all six hundred men to share equally in the booty." (McGee)

Now comes a very sorrowful time in my life. "While my men and I were hunting down the Amalekites, Israel is fleeing before the Philistines. They are being defeated in this battle because they are out of the will of God." (McGee)

"Now the Philistines fought against Israel: and the men of Israel fled from before the Philistines. And the Philistines followed hard upon Saul and upon his sons; and the Philistines slew Jonathan, and Abinadab, and Melchi-shua, Saul's sons. And the battle went against Saul, and the archers hit him; and he was wounded of the archers." (1 Samuel 31:1-3)

"When Saul saw that he was mortally wounded, he felt that the enemy would come and abuse him and taunt him, so he asked his armor-bearer to thrust him through with a sword. His armor-bearer could not lay a hand on the king, so Saul fell upon his own sword and killed himself." (McGee)

I heard of the defeat of Saul and his death on the third day after the battle, when a messenger, an Amalekite, came and reported all to me: the war, the defeat, and the deaths of Saul and Jonathan, and Saul's three sons.

"I then rent my clothes, and all the men with me did likewise. We mourned, and wept, and fasted, for Saul, and for Jonathan, and for the people of the Lord, and for the house of Israel; because they were fallen by the sword. I lamented over Saul and Jonathan. Saul and Jonathan were lovely and pleasant in their lives, and in their death, they were not divided: they were swifter than eagles; they were stronger than lions. I am distressed for thee, my brother Jonathan; very pleasant hast thou been unto me: thy love to me was wonderful, passing the love of women." (2 Samuel 1:1-27)

"Now I asked God if I should go up to Hebron, a city of Judah. God told me to "GO" While there, the men of Judah came, and there they anointed me king over the house of Judah. I thanked Saul's men for burying Saul, and I asked for their support and devotion to me as king, even as they had given it to Saul." (2 Samuel 2:1-7) (McGee)

The beginning of my leadership over Judah started with a civil war. "There were those loyal to Saul, and Saul's captain took Ish-bosheth, was the son of Saul, and made him king over all Israel. Ish-bosheth was forty years old when he began to reign over Israel, and he reigned two years. But still the house of Judah followed me." (2 Samuel 2:8-9)

"Now there was a long war between the house of Saul and my house: but I waxed stronger and stronger, and the house of Saul waxed weaker and weaker." (2 Samuel 3:1) Now my wives numbered six, and each had a son by me; my son Absolom, born to my wife Maacah, the daughter of Talmai king of Geshur. When I invaded the Geshurites I killed the king of Geshur, and took his daughter captive. God did not approve of my actions, and later I would pay the price, when my son Absolom leads a rebellion against me. Always remember, God never lets a person get by with sin. There is a price to pay. (McGee)

After seven years of a bloody civil war, Ish-bosheth is defeated, and I am made king over all the tribes of Israel. "I was thirty years old when I began to reign, and I reigned for forty years over Israel." (2 Samuel 5:4) 'My first move to consolidate the kingdom was to move the capital of Israel from Hebron to Jerusalem. I was considered a great military leader, a great political leader, and a great king, but most and best of all I was a man of God.' (McGee)

"I built my palace on Mount Zion above Jerusalem. This was my strong hold and it came to be known as the city of David. Later, the temple was built below Mount Zion." (McGee) "I took more concubines and wives out of Jerusalem, and there were more sons and daughters born to me." (2 Samuel 5:13) "Two of my sons born in Jerusalem were Nathan, and Solomon." `From the line of Nathan came Mary the mother of Jesus, and from Solomon came Joseph, Mary's husband. Jesus Christ received the blood line and the legal title to the throne of David through Nathan and Solomon.' (McGee)

"I smote the Philistines, and subdued them. I extended the borders of Israel to the south and to the east; Syria, Moab, Ammon, the Philistines, and the Amalekites; all became subject to me and became my servants. And the Lord preserved me wherever I went. I reigned over all Israel; and executed judgement and justice unto all my people." (2 Samuel 8:1-5) (McGee)

I remembered my good friend, Jonathan, and our promise that we would always be friends and we would live side by side when I became king. I inquired of my servants if there were any left that belonged to the house of Saul? A servant of Saul, named Ziba, was brought before me; I inquired of him if there were any left in the house of Saul that I may show God's kindness to?

Ziba told me that Jonathan had a son named Mephibosheth, who was alive, but was lame in both his feet. He revealed to me his location, so I sent for him to be brought before me. When he came into my presence, he fell on his face, expecting the worst, I, as king had the right to kill him, but instead I said to him, "Fear not: for I surely show thee kindness for Jonathan thy father's sake, and I will restore to thee all the land that belonged to Saul; and you shall eat bread at my table continually."

Mephibosheth bowed himself before me and said, "What is thy servant, that thou should look upon such a dead dog as I am? I then called for Ziba, Saul's servant, and I said unto him, `I have given all that pertained to Saul and to all his house, to Mephibosheth. Thou therefore, and thy sons, and thy servants, shall till the land for him, and you shall bring in the fruits, that thy master's son may have food to eat: but Mephibosheth shall always eat at my table.' ("Now Ziba had fifteen sons and twenty servants.") Ziba told me that all would be done according to what I had told him. (2 Samuel 9:1-13)

Now, we come to my great sin against God. I, of course, knew that all sin is against God, and that we pay a very high price for it. As I mentioned at the beginning of this account of my life, that I stayed at the palace when my men went out to fight for the kingdom. "I arose from off my bed, (yes, I was taking a nap in the middle of the afternoon) and walked upon the roof of my house: and from the roof I saw a woman washing herself; and she was beautiful to look upon." (2 Samuel 11:2)

I immediately inquired to find out who she was. I was told her name was Bathsheba, the daughter of Eliam, the wife of Uriah the Hittite. But none of this stopped me from sending messengers to bring her to me. I lay with her and then sent her back to her house. Soon I received a message from her saying, "I am with child." I had an idea; I would send for her husband who was in battle: I would bring him home so he could sleep with his wife, and thus cover my sin.

He was brought to me, and "I demanded of him how Joab did, and how the people did, and how the war prospered." I then sent him to his house to be with his wife. Uriah departed, but he did not go to his home. Instead, he slept at the door of my house. The next day I asked him why he did not go to his home. He told me that he 'could not go to his house to eat and drink, and to lie with his wife, because the army and his commander were out in the field, in danger.' (2 Samuel 11:3-11)

I then told him to stay in Jerusalem for two days more, giving him food and drink to make him drunk. Still, he would not go to his home to sleep with his wife. "" I then wrote a letter to Joab, and sent the letter with Uriah; I gave orders to Joab to set Uriah at the frontline of the hottest battle, and then to leave him alone to be smitten, so he would be killed." (2 Samuel 11:12-15)

Soon word came from Joab, by messenger, that Uriah the Hittite was dead. Uriah's wife mourned for him when she learned of his death in battle. When her mourning was done, I sent for her to become my wife, and she gave birth to my son. Can you believe that I would commit such a sin as this before the living God? Yes, I did, but the Lord was very displeased with me, and would not let get away with adultery and murderer. (2 Samuel 11:25-27)

Time passed; I went on as if nothing had happened until one day God sent Nathan, His messenger, to tell me a story of two men living in one city. One was very rich; he had many flocks and herds; the other was very poor and only owned one ewe lamb that was a favored pet of the man and his family.

One day a traveler came to the rich man's home and instead of preparing a meal for the man from his own herds, he took the poor man's lamb, and dressed it for the man that came to him. (2 Samuel 1:1-4)

"My anger was greatly kindled against the man; and I said to Nathan, 'As the Lord lives, the man that has done this thing shall surely die.' I thought Nathan had brought this case to me for me to rule upon it. I sprang to my feet and demanded, "Where is this man? We will arrest him and have him executed! He shall restore the lamb four-fold, because he did this thing, and because he had no pity." (2 Samuel 12:5-6)

Then Nathan said to me, "Thou art the man." Thus says the Lord God of Israel, 'I ANOINTED THEE KING OVER ISRAEL, AND I DELIVERED THEE OUT OF THE HAND OF SAUL; AND I GAVE THEE THY MASTER'S HOUSE, AND THY MASTER'S WIVES INTO THY BOSOM. AND GAVE YOU THE HOUSE OF ISRAEL, AND OF JUDAH; AND IF THAT HAD BEEN TOO LITTLE, I WOULD MOREOVER HAVE GIVEN UNTO THEE SUCH AND SUCH THINGS;

YOU HAVE DESPISED THE COMMANDMENT OF THE LORD, TO DO EVIL IN HIS SIGHT? YOU HAVE KILLED URIAH THE HITTITE WITH THE SWORD, AND HAVE TAKEN HIS WIFE TO BE YOUR WIFE, AND HAVE SLAIN HIM WITH THE SWORD OF THE CHILDREN OF AMMON. NOW, THEREFORE THE SWORD SHALL NEVER DEPART FROM YOUR HOUSE; BECAUSE YOU HAVE DESPISED ME, AND HAVE TAKEN THE WIFE OF URIAH THE HITTITE TO BE YOUR WIFE. Thus says the Lord, 'BEHOLD, I WILL RAISE UP EVIL AGAINST YOU OUT OF YOUR OWN HOUSE, BEHOLD, AND I WILL TAKE YOUR WIVES BEFORE YOUR EYES, AND GIVE THEM TO YOUR NEIGHBOR, AND HE SHALL LIE WITH YOUR WIVES IN THE SIGHT OF THE SUN. BEHOLD, FOR YOU DID THIS SECRETLY: BUT I WILL DO THIS THING BEFORE ALL ISRAEL, AND BEFORE THE SUN." (2 Samuel 12:7-12)

I said to Nathan, 'I have sinned against the Lord." Nathan said to me, 'The Lord has put away your sin; you shall not die.' But because I gave the enemy reason to blaspheme God, "the Lord struck the child that Uriah's wife bare unto me, with sickness unto death." (2 Samuel 12:13-14)

Friends, you can see that I did not get by with this great sin. In the 21st Century my sin is still talked about, and made into movies, and it has brought great shame to me, and all those connected to God. No, you will not get by with your sin either; no one can. It seems so innocent at the time, like God is not watching you while you break His heart. His love for me and for you cannot overrule His truth. "Your sin will find you out."

Actually, I was greatly relieved to have this sin of mine out in the open. When the little one was very sick, I fasted and lay upon the earth all night; I pleaded with God to spare this child's life, because it was my sin, not his. But the child died. My servants were afraid to tell me of his death, because of my fasting and praying. I perceived that the child was dead and asked the servants if it was so? They said, "He is dead."

"I then arose from the earth, and washed and anointed myself, and changed my clothes, and come to the house of the Lord and worshipped: I then went to my own home and did eat bread that was set before me." My servants could not understand my behavior because they thought I would be in great grief after the baby's death. I told them this, 'While the child was yet alive, I fasted and wept: for I said, "Who can tell whether God will be gracious to me, that the child may live?" But now that he is dead, why should I fast? Can I bring him back again? I shall go to him, but he shall not return to me.' (2 Samuel 12:15-23)

"I comforted my wife Bathsheba and went into her and lay with her: and she bore a son to me, and we called his name Solomon: and the Lord loved him." The name Jedidiah was given by God through Nathan to Solomon. This name means 'beloved of the Lord.'

I then gathered all the people together, and went to Rabbah, and fought against it, and took it." The Lord continued to extend and expand my kingdom. (2 Samuel 12:24-29)

A great trouble came upon my family because of my son, Amnon. He was in love with my son Absalom's sister, Tamar, who was very fair. He could not eat because of his love for her and Jonadab, my brother's son, asked why he could not eat? Amnon told him of his great love for Tamar, but he had a fear of Absolom, so could not make known his love.

Jonadab told Amnon to pretend to be sick, and when I, David, came to see what the matter was, Amnon would tell me to send Tamar to come and give him a meal made in his sight by her hand. I called for Tamar to go and help her brother and make this meal for him.

I did not know that Amnon would take hold of her and insist she lie with him, as she was a virgin. She told him not to force her into this union to bring her shame and to make him a fool in Israel, but to ask me for her hand in marriage. He would not listen to her, and did as he intended, but then he hated her as much as he had loved her. Amnon put her out of his room and bolted the door. Tamar went to her brother's home for refuge. (2 Samuel 13:1-22)

When I heard what had been done to Tamar, I was very angry, but I did nothing about it. Absalom spoke to his brother Amnon about the deed, but to no avail. Absalom now hated Amnon and waited for a chance to kill him. Two years went by and Absalom gave a party for all my sons. I did not believe Absalom was going to take out any revenge on Amnon, so I let him go to the party. Absalom made sure Amnon "was merry with wine," and then he had him killed.

Absalom fled, and went to Talmai, the son of Ammihud, king of Geshur where his mother was from. (11 Samuel 13:37) I knew of Amnon's death, but I mourned for Absalom, because he was my favorite son and he had to flee the country. I still did nothing about all of this. Absalom wished for me to confront him on this issue: I was in distress but did not act.

After two years, I still did not permit Absalom to return to me, until one day a woman came to me and told me of a story of her two imaginary sons. She said that one killed the other, but now she wanted to receive a full pardon for the murderer because she was a widow and needed her son to support her, and give an heir to the family. The widow applied this to Absalom, because she wanted him to return to Jerusalem.

I half-heartedly let him return, but I could not forgive him completely for what he had done. God had forgiven me totally, but I was not willing to do the same for my son, Absalom, even though he was my favorite.

Absalom decided to lead a rebellion against me because he was angry with me. He started to win the hearts of the people to himself, by going to the busiest gate of the city. When men had complaints requiring justice, he listened to them with a great show of sympathy. In this way he "stole the hearts of the men of Israel." (2 Samuel 15:1-6) (McGee)

Absalom continued to conspire against me with lies and by building his own army. Soon there came a messenger to me saying, "The hearts of the men of Israel are after Absalom." So I said to my servants that were with me in Jerusalem, 'Arise, and let us flee; for we shall not else escape from Absalom: make speed to depart lest he overtake us suddenly, and bring evil upon us, and smite the city with the edge of the sword.' (2 Samuel 15:13-14)

In exile I found that I had many allies in the people around about; they knew of my past victories, so they brought supplies to us as I readied my troops for combat against Absalom and his army. When the civil war did come, "there was a great battle in the wood of Ephraim; where the people of Israel were slain before my servants, and there was a great slaughter of twenty thousand men." I had much experience and three loyal captains that Absalom's men could not match. (2 Samuel 18:6-7) (McGee)

Before we went into battle with Absalom, I commanded my captain saying, "Deal gently, for my sake, with the young man, Absalom. All the people heard my plea concerning Absalom." During the battle, Absalom's men started to flee before my army into the forest; they were 'bottled' in, and lost their life there instead of in battle.

Absalom decided to flee the battle as his men had, but during his fight he became entangled in a great oak tree by being caught in the boughs by his thick hair. The donkey he was riding left him hanging there helpless. When Joab heard of the predicament of Absalom, he quickly goes to where Absalom is hanging and kills him with three darts in his heart.

The death of Absalom ended the battle; I did not want to know how the battle was going or how my men were faring. I only wanted to know if Absalom was safe. A runner came to me with the news of his death, and my heart was stabbed through with grief for his rebellious son of mine that I loved more than my own life. I mourned loudly by weeping for Absalom and I cried out, "O my son Absalom, my son, my son Absalom! Would God I had died for thee, O Absalom, my son, my son~" (2 Samuel 18:4-33)

I knew this trouble had come to Israel and me because of my sin. God had told me that strife would never depart from my house because of it. I continued in my grief for Absalom until Joab spoke sharply to me saying, "Thou hast shamed this day the faces of all thy servants, which this day have saved thy life, and the lives of thy sons and daughters, and the lives of thy wives, and the lives of thy concubines; In that thou lovest thine enemies, and hatest thy friends? For thou hast declared this day, that thou regardest neither princes nor servants: for this day I perceive, that if Absalom had lived, and all we had died this day, then it had pleased thee well." (2 Samuel 19:5-6)

My people were in despair because I was grieving. I realized this was not a good situation, so I went to the gate to let my men know that I deeply appreciated their loyalty to me, and in their loyalty, they restored me to the throne.

After many years of ruling over Israel, I was "old and stricken in years." My successor was to be named, but my fourth son, Adonijah decides to set himself up as the next king. He did this behind my back. However, Nathan let it be known that Bathsheba's son, Solomon was to be the next king.

Bathsheba comes to me in my chamber and bows low before me, saying, "My lord, thou swarest by the Lord thy God unto thine handmaid, saying, 'Assuredly Solomon thy son shall reign after me, and he shall sit upon my throne. And now, behold, Adonijah reigneth; but, O king, the eyes of all Israel are upon thee, that thou shouldest tell them who shall sit on the throne of my lord the king after him." (1 Kings 1:1-20)

I then called Bath-sheba, Nathan the prophet, Zadok the priest, and Benaiah the son of Jehoiada to come before me. I said unto them, "Take with you the servants of your lord, and cause Solomon my son to ride upon my own mule, and bring him down to Gihon, Zadok the priest took a horn of oil out of the tabernacle, and anointed Solomon. They blew the trumpet; and all the people said, `God save the king." (1 Kings 31-39)

Adonijah feared Solomon, so he came before him and bowed himself to the King." Solomon dismissed him in peace.

Now, the days of my life are short, so I charge Solomon saying, "I go the way of all the earth: be thou strong therefore, and show thyself a man. Keep the charge of the Lord thy God, to walk in His ways, to keep His statutes, and His commandments, and His judgments, and His testimonies, as it is written in the law of Moses, that you may prosper in all that you do, and wherever you go; That the Lord may continue His word which He spoke concerning me, saying, 'IF MY CHILDREN TAKE HEED TO THEIR WAY, TO WALK BEFORE ME IN TRUTH WITH ALL THEIR HEART AND WITH ALL THEIR SOUL, THERE SHALL NOT FAIL (TO BE) A MAN ON THE THRONE OF ISRAEL." (1 Kings 2:3-4)

With this I come to the end of my days on the earth. The Lord never "left me or forsook me" He led me in my victories, and in my failures. I was called 'a man after God's own heart,' but I am not the one to be admired. God is the great "I Am;" He is the one for you to keep your eyes upon; He is the 'FAITHFUL ONE, THE LOVELY ONE, THE ONLY GOD.'

Please read of my life and learn of the ONE AND ONLY GOD, the "GOD OF ABRAHAM, OF ISAAC, and OF JACOB."

HEAVY HAIR – ABSALOM

11 SAMUEL 13-19

I was "praised in all Israel," both by men and by women I had beautiful hair that I had to cut once a year, because it was too 'heavy on me' to bear it any longer than that. The amount that was cut off weighed 200 shekels, or about five pounds. I was a very handsome man; "No blemish was found in me from the crown of my head to the sole of my foot,' but none of this satisfied me. (Genesis 14:25-26)

I was the third son of my father David; he loved me but "I" took offense to him on many occasions. When I was growing me up my father was absent most of the time; off fighting battles and being King over all Israel. My father had many wives and many children, so I was just one of the "many." He favored me, but he didn't discipline me, and I resented it.

I knew that if he really loved me, he would take the time to teach me how to be a man of self-control, and give me direction for my life. I was left to get my own justice on many occasions, and my father did not intervene or help me, or give me guidance, or stop me from doing wrong.

Tamar was my beautiful sister. We had the same mother, Maacah, the daughter of Talmai, king of Geshur, in Aram. (11 Samuel 3:3) Our half-brother Amnon decided that he was in love with Tamar, and he wanted her for his own. He could have asked our father, David, for her hand in marriage, but instead he chose to deceive her. He pretended to be sick, and then he asked our father to send Tamar in to him to make him some "cakes" of food, so he would feel better.

Tamar came to Amnon's chamber in good faith; Amnon watched her as she "took flour, and kneaded it, and then baked cakes for him." When she brought the cakes to him to eat, 'he took hold of her,' and said,

"Come lie with me, my sister." She said, 'Do not force me, for this is wrong in Israel and you will cause me great shame, and you will be listed as one of the fools in Israel.'

Amnon played the fool and would not listen to her; "he being stronger than her, forced her, and lay with her." Then Amnon 'hated her exceedingly, greater now than his love for her.'

Tamar came to me, Absalom, crying profusely, and I protected her in my home. When our father heard of this, he was angry, but took no action against Amnon. This made me very angry and I hated Amnon. Two years later, I figured out a way to kill him and I did. I then fled for my life back to my mother's relatives in Geshur, and there I stayed for three years. I thought David, my father, would confront me and take the necessary action, but nothing happened.

I then returned to Jerusalem and stayed there for two more years before I was allowed to see David, my father. He kissed me after I bowed myself low before him, but it was a half-hearted gesture on his part to forgive me, or make amends between us. I was still offended by him, and my rebellion could not be stopped now.

I realized that I was not to succeed David on the throne, but I had heard that the next king of Israel would be Solomon. I decided this to be unfair as I was the eldest, so "I set myself to win the hearts of the people away from the king." I did succeed in winning the mass of the people to me, but the priests and the Levites stayed with my father.

I underestimated my father's abilities and mine. My advisors were not competent. My father fled Jerusalem, and "I" in my conceit, and on the advice of Ahithophel, one of my father's chief counselors that had defected to me, 'spread a tent on top of the palace, and I went in unto the ten concubines,' that were my fathers' that he had left behind to keep the palace in his absence. I did this in the sight of all Israel, so they would see that I had no regard for my father and that I was in control now. (11 Samuel 16:21-22)

I then went to war with my father. My rebels were untrained and no match for my fathers' skilled veterans, so we were immediately out numbered. "I retreated on my mule, and in my haste became entangled by my long flowing hair in the spreading branches of an oak tree." My mule left me and I hung there dangling.

David had given specific orders for my life to be spared, but Joab, one of my father's commanders, "thrust three darts through my heart, and Joab's followers finished me off." (Davis Dict.) My vanity ended up being the reason for my death.

My father, David, mourned for me saying, "O my son Absalom, my son, my son Absalom! Would God I had died for thee, O Absalom, my son, my son!" David knew my rebellion against him and he knew God would separate us from being united in eternity."

I did what I had to do as I saw it.

THE WISEST "MAN" – SOLOMON
11 SAMUEL 13-19

I am Solomon, considered to be the wisest man to have ever lived on the earth, except for Christ Himself. But even the wisest man can become very "foolish" if he uses his wisdom to satisfy himself, and forgets that God is his only source of wisdom. I wrote Proverbs, Ecclesiastes, and Song of Solomon: all books in the Bible. Since all writings of the Bible are God inspired, mine are too. (All scripture is given by inspiration of God..." 11 Timothy 3:16)

You may ask how I got to be so wise, I am the son of David by his wife Bathsheba. My mother was married to Uriah when my father fell in love with her. Because she was expecting my father's child, while still married, my father devised a scheme to have Uriah killed in battle.

David had sinned before God because of this murder, so the child my mother bore, before me, died shortly after birth. (Nathan said unto David, "Because by this deed thou have given great occasion to the enemies of the Lord to blaspheme, the child also that is born unto thee shall surely die." (11 Samuel 12:14) But because God is the God who forgives, my mother conceived me next. (`And David comforted Bathsheba his wife, and went in unto her, and lay with her: and she bare a son, and he called his name Solomon: and the Lord loved him.' (11 Samuel 12:24)

This still does not explain how I became wise. When I was made king of Israel, after my father David's death, the Lord appeared to me in a dream by night: and said, "ASK WHAT I SHALL GIVE THEE." I said to the Lord: `and now, O Lord my God, thou hast made thy servant king instead of David my father: and I am but a little child: I know not how to go out or come in, and thy servant is in the midst of thy people, which thou hast chosen, a great people, which cannot be numbered nor counted for multitude. Give therefore thy servant an understanding heart to judge thy people, that I may discern between good and bad: for who is able to judge this thy so great a people?' (1 Kings 3:5-9)

And God said unto me, "BECAUSE THOU HAST ASKED THIS THING, AND HAST NOT ASKED FOR THYSELF LONG LIFE; NEITHER HAST ASKED RICHES FOR THYSELF; NOR HAST ASKED THE LIFE OF THINE ENEMIES; BUT HAST ASKED FOR THYSELF UNDERSTANDING TO DISCERN JUDGMENT; BEHOLD, I HAVE DONE ACCORDING TO THY WORDS; LO, I HAVE GIVEN THEE A WISE AND AN UNDERSTANDING HEART; SO THAT THERE WAS NONE LIKE THEE BEFORE THEE, NEITHER AFTER THEE SHALL ANY ARISE LIKE UNTO THEE. AND I HAVE ALSO GIVEN THEE THAT WHICH THOU HAST NOT ASKED, BOTH RICHES, AND HONOR: SO THAT THERE SHALL NOT BE ANY AMONG THE KINGS LIKE UNTO THEE ALL THY DAYS. AND IF THOU WILL WALK IN MY WAYS, TO KEEP MY STATUTES AND MY COMMANDMENTS, AS THY FATHER DAVID DID WALK, THEN I WILL LENGTHEN THY DAYS."

I awoke and realized it was a dream. I was in Gibeon at this time, so I went on to Jerusalem and "stood before the ark of the covenant of the Lord, and offered up burnt offerings, and offered peace offerings, and made a feast to all my servants." (1 Kings 3:11-15)

While at this feast "there came two women, that were harlots, unto me, and stood before me." And the one woman said, 'O my lord, this woman and I dwell in one house; and I was delivered of a child with her in the house. And it came to pass the third day after that I was delivered, that this woman was delivered also; and we were together; there was no stranger with us in the house, (only) we two in the house.'

"And this woman's child died in the night; because she laid on it. And she arose at midnight, and took my son from beside me, while I slept, and laid it in her bosom, and laid her dead child in my bosom. And when I rose in the morning to give my child suck, behold, it was dead: but when I had considered it in the morning, behold, it was not my son, which I did bear. And the other woman said, Nay, but the living is my son, and the dead is thy son."

And each woman said the living son belonged to her, and the dead son belonged to the other. So, I said, "One woman says the living son is mine, and the dead son is hers: And the other woman says, 'No,' the dead son is hers and the living son is mine."

So, I, as the king, said, "Divide the living child in two, and give half to the one, and half to the other." Then spoke the woman unto me, who's the living child was, for she yearned for her son, and she said, `O my lord, give her the living child, and in no wise slay it.' But the other said, "Let it be neither mine or hers, but divide it."

I then answered and said (to the first woman), "Give her the living child, and in no wise slay it: she is the mother thereof." (1 Kings 3:16-27)

"God gave me wisdom and understanding exceedingly, and largeness of heart, even as the sand that is on the sea shore. And my wisdom excelled the wisdom of all the children of the east country, and all the wisdom of Egypt. I was considered wiser than all men... I spoke three thousand proverbs; and my songs were a thousand and five. I spoke of trees, from the cedar tree that is in Lebanon even unto the hyssop that springs out of the wall: I spoke of beasts, and of fowl, and of creeping things, and of fishes."

People and kings came from all over the earth to hear the wisdom God had given me (and to gain advice), because the stories of me had spread everywhere. (1 Kings 4:29-34)

In the spring of the fourth year of my reign, actual construction of the Temple was started. My father David had wanted to build the Temple for God, but God prevented him from doing so because he was considered a "man of war, and had shed blood." (1 Chronicles 28:3)

God gave my father David credit for his desire to "build God a house." Instead of David building God a house, God said, `I WILL BUILD YOU A HOUSE (David), AND WHEN THY DAYS BE FULFILLED, AND THOU SHALL SLEEP WITH THY FATHERS, I WILL SET UP THY SEED AFTER THEE, WHICH SHALL PROCEED OUT OF THY BOWELS, AND I WILL ESTABLISH HIS KINGDOM.' (2 Samuel 7:12)

God was not speaking to David about me (Solomon) here, but he was referring to Jesus Christ. You can read in Romans 1:3, "The Lord Jesus Christ was made of the seed of David." The kingdom speaks of the throne of David that the Lord Jesus Christ will one day sit upon, here on the earth. In Luke 1:32 you read of Gabriel's message to Mary (the mother of Jesus): `He shall be great, and shall be called the son of the Highest: and the Lord God shall give unto him the throne of his father David.' (McGee)

God went on to tell David: "I WILL BE HIS FATHER, AND HE SHALL BE MY SON, IF HE COMMIT INIQUITY, I WILL CHASTEN HIM WITH THE ROD OF MEN, AND WITH THE STRIPES OF THE CHILDREN OF MEN." (2 Samuel 7:14)

God is still speaking of Jesus here: "I WILL BE HIS FATHER," At His resurrection the Lord Jesus Christ said to Mary Magdalene, `TOUCH ME NOT; FOR I AM NOT YET ASCENDED TO MY FATHER; BUT GO TO MY BRETHREN, AND SAY UNTO THEM, I ASCEND UNTO MY FATHER, AND YOUR FATHER; AND TO MY GOD, AND YOUR GOD,' (John 20:17)

"God is the father of Jesus Christ because of His position in the Trinity, God is the Father of believers by regeneration -- `But as many as received him, to them gave he power to become the sons of God, even to them that believe on his name." (John 1:12) (McGee)

The next part of this verse: "I will chasten him with the rod of men, and with the stripes of the children of men." These words have been translated this way: 'When guilt is laid upon Him (Jesus Christ), and when iniquity is laid upon Him—when my sin and your sin were laid upon Him - it is with His stripes that we are healed.' Jesus died on a cross for you and me: "Who his own self bare our sins in his own body on the tree, that we, being dead to sins, should live unto righteousness: by whose stripes ye were healed." (1 Peter 2:24) Isaiah said of Jesus, 'Yet it pleased the Lord to bruise him; he hath put him to grief..' (Isaiah 53:10) "The one coming in David's line would bear the sins of the world." (McGee)

Isaiah continues to speak of Jesus: "Surely, he hath borne our griefs, and carried our sorrows: yet we did esteem him stricken, smitten of God, and afflicted. But he was wounded for our transgressions, he has bruised for our iniquities: the chastisement of our peace was upon him; and with his stripes we are healed. All we like sheep have gone astray; we have turned everyone to his own way; and the Lord hath laid on him the iniquity of us all." (Isaiah 53:4-6)

"With his stripes we are healed," "Healed of what? We are healed of sin, the bondage of serving sin', sickness, anger, unforgiveness, all sin that is the awful disease that afflicts mankind,' That is why God said, "I WILL CHASTEN HIM WITH THE ROD OF MEN, AND WITH THE STRIPES OF THE CHILDREN OF MEN." (McGee)

So, what does all this have to do with my building the Temple in my fourth year as king? The Temple I built represents Jesus Christ. Jesus said, referring to His body, "Destroy this temple, and in three days I will raise it up." (John 2:19) The believer in Jesus Christ also becomes the Temple of Christ.

God did mention me, Solomon, as the builder of the Temple of Jerusalem. "He shall build a house for my name, and I will establish the throne of his kingdom forever." (2 Samuel 7:13) "The kingdom, however, goes beyond me and looks to the future.' (McGee)

The construction of the Temple took seven years to complete. The work was started when God provided peace "on every side," and no wars were being fought anywhere. The Temple was not built as a house in which God would dwell, it is an approach for man to God, and an access to God through sacrifices.' David, my father, said that the Temple was 'a house of rest for the ark of the covenant of the Lord, and for the footstool of our God." (Chronicles 28:2) (McGee)

My father, David, was given the blueprint of the temple, by God, and he gave it to me. David said to me, "Solomon my son, know thou the God of thy father and serve him with a perfect heart and with a willing mind: for the Lord searches all hearts, and understands all the imaginations of the thoughts: if thou seek Him, he will be found of thee: but if thou forsake Him, He will cast thee off for ever." (1 Chronicles 28:9)

"Then David gave to me his son the pattern of the porch, and of the houses thereof, and of treasuries thereof, and of the upper chambers thereof, and of the inner parlors thereof, and of the place of the mercy seat, and the pattern of all that he had by the spirit, of the courts of the house of the Lord, and of all the chambers round about, of the treasuries of the house of God, and of the treasuries of the dedicated things." (1 Chronicles 28:10-12)

My father, David, also gathered the material: "Now I have prepared with all my might for the house of my God the gold for things to be made of gold, and the silver for things of silver, and the brass for things of brass, the iron for things of iron, and wood for things of wood; onyx stones, and stones to be set, glistering stones, and stones of many colors, and all manner of precious stones, and marble stones in abundance." (1 Chronicles 29:2)

"With all the accumulation of material at hand, I contracted with Hiram, king of Tyre, for cedar and fir timber for the actual construction of the edifice. The temple was twice as large as the tabernacle (which was the tent house of God used by the Israelites after they left Egypt and wandered in the wilderness for 40 years). The temple was surrounded on three sides by a three-story building. This was the place where the priests lived during their course of service. In the front there was a portico that was 10 x 20 x 120 cubits – half as long as a football field. The brazen altar was 20 x 30 x 10 cubits, while the altar of the tabernacle was 5 x 5 x 3 cubits. There were ten lamp stands to replace the one of the tabernacles. There were ten tables of showbread rather than one. There was a multiplication of some of the articles of furniture.

"There were 30,000 Israelites used in the construction; they were drafted for the work. There were 150,000 extra workers and 3,300 overseers used in the construction of the building. The temple was made of stone, and the sound of a hammer was not heard during the building." (And the house, when it was in building, was built of stone made ready before it was brought forth: so that there was neither hammer nor axe nor any tool of iron heard in the house, while it was in building.' 1 Kings 6:7) The cost of the building is estimated around five million dollars (21st century figures)." (McGee)

"The temple was like a jewel box. There were two pillars in it that were very impressive. ('And he (Hiram) set up the pillars in the porch of the temple: and he set up the right pillar, and called the name thereof Jachin: and he set up the left pillar, and called the name Boaz.' 1 Kings 7:21) Jachin means, "God shall establish," Boaz means 'in it is strength,' Spiritually, these two pillars Jachin and Boaz speaks of that which worship really is – a redeemed soul who comes into the presence of a Holy God. (McGee)

Some believe that the temple was inferior to the tabernacle. "The temple was complicated; the simplicity of the tabernacle was lost. There may be a comparison to you living in the 21st century. You are living in a day when the emphasis is put on methods rather than on the Word of God, the church is filled with new programs and new methods. (McGee)

"I (Solomon) put narrow windows in the temple, but there had been no windows in the tabernacle. The windows only let in a little light, but some believe that this represents that the people no longer depended upon divine light as they had in the tabernacle. Also, I made the cherubim out of olive wood that were ten cubits high (15 feet) – I then overlaid them with solid gold. This Temple was a very ornate and gaudy, whereas the tabernacle was very simple in style. We did have more ceremony and ritual connected with it". (McGee) I thought this 'permanent' temple should be lovely to behold.

When the temple was finished "I offered a sacrifice of peace offerings unto the Lord, two and twenty thousand oxen, and an hundred and twenty thousand sheep. Because the altars in the temple could not accommodate all the animal sacrifices, temporary altars were erected to handle the large number of animals that were sacrificed at this time. After the animals were offered, they were taken off the altars and divided among the people. This was a time of great celebration of all 'that the Lord had done for David his servant, and for Israel his people." (1 Kings 8:63-66) (McGee)

Unfortunately, Nebuchadnezzar destroyed the temple I built in David's name, when he invaded Jerusalem; he took Daniel and his friend's captive at this time. Later Zerubbabel put up a temple, but this was ultimately destroyed too. While the Jews were captive in Rome, Herod built a temple for them. This temple took forty-six years to build, and it was the temple Jesus used while he lived on the earth. (McGee)

After the temple was built, I spent thirteen years building houses for myself. I built a house in the forest of Lebanon, which was like a vacation house. It was "a hundred cubits long," which is half the length of a football field. The "width was 50 cubits," which is seventy-five feet. The "height of it was thirty cubits;" that is forty-five feet. It was built 'upon four rows of cedar pillars, with cedar beams upon the pillars.' This house was very ornate and elaborate, like the temple. I liked to be surrounded with beautiful things in the buildings I lived in, and in everything I owned.

Next, I "built a house for Pharaoh's daughter, whom I had taken for a wife." This marriage formed an alliance with Egypt. This too was a palace of beauty to behold. I favored this wife, but I did not use wisdom when I married her, as God did not want me to marry foreign women, or have more than one wife. Before I died, I had 700 wives and 300 concubines, so in all I had 1000 wives. They were the undoing of my life and my walk with God, and ultimately lead to my foolishness. (1 Kings 7:1-8) (McGee)

God appears to me a second time to encourage me, "God tells me that He will meet with me at the temple. This is the place for me to come to, for the people to come to, and for the world to come to, as the meeting place with God." (1 Kings 9:1-3)

God says to me at this time, "IF THOU WILL WALK BEFORE ME, AS DAVID THY FATHER WALKED IN INTEGRITY OF HEART, AND IN UPRIGHTNESS, TO DO ACCORDING TO ALL THAT I HAVE COMMANDED THEE, AND WILL KEEP MY STATUTES AND MY JUDGMENTS, THEN I WILL ESTABLISH THE THRONE OF THY KINGDOM UPON ISRAEL FOR EVER, AS I PROMISED TO DAVID THY FATHER," saying 'THERE SHALL NOT FAIL THEE A MAN UPON THE THRONE OF ISRAEL'

BUT IF YE SHALL AT ALL TURN FROM - FOLLOWING ME, YE OR YOUR CHILDREN, AND WILL NOT KEEP MY COMMANDMENTS AND MY STATUES WHICH I HAVE SET BEFORE YOU, BUT GO AND SERVE OTHER GODS, AND WORSHIP THEM: THEN WILL I CUT OFF ISRAEL OUT OF THE LAND WHICH I HAVE GIVEN THEM; AND THIS HOUSE, WHICH I HAVE HALLOWED FOR MY NAME WILL I CAST OUT OF MY SIGHT; AND ISRAEL SHALL BE A PROVERB AND A BY WORD AMONG ALL PEOPLE.

"AND AT THIS HOUSE, WHICH IS HIGH, EVERY ONE THAT PASSETH BY IT SHALL BE ASTONISHED, AND SHALL HISS; AND THEY SHALL SAY, WHY HATH THE LORD DONE THUS UNTO THIS LAND, AND TO THIS HOUSE? AND THEY SHALL ANSWER, BECAUSE THEY FORSOOK THE LORD THEIR GOD, WHO BROUGHT FORTH THEIR FATHERS OUT OF EGYPT, AND HAVE TAKEN HOLD UPON OTHER GODS, AND HAVE WORSHIPPED THEM, AND SERVED THEM: THEREFORE, HATH THE LORD BROUGHT UPON THEM ALL THIS EVIL. (1 Kings 9:4-9)

"My fame had spread, and multitudes were coming to Jerusalem to worship the living and true God. The queen of Sheba came to me because of what she had heard of a temple where man could approach God. She had heard of my wisdom, and she came to me to test me with difficult questions. She did not believe half of what she had been told, and she came to find that the half had "NOT" been told her." (1 Kings 10:1-9) (McGee)

The Queen believed God and she said, "Happy are thy men, happy are these thy servants, which stand continually before thee, and that hear thy wisdom. Blessed be the Lord thy God, which delighted in thee, to set thee on the throne of Israel: because the Lord loved Israel forever, therefore made he thee king, to do judgment and justice." (1 Kings 10:8-9)

"She brought a great amount of wealth with her: `And she gave (to me) the king a hundred and twenty talents of gold, and of spices, a very great store, and precious stones: there came no more such abundance of spices as these which the queen of Sheba gave to me, Solomon." (1 Kings 10:10)

Because of my father David and all he had done in his lifetime, I was able to enjoy the peace, the plenty, and the prosperity. "In one year, I received about $20,000,000 in gold, besides sales taxes and profits from trade with the kings of Arabia and the other surrounding territories. I had some of the gold beaten into two hundred pieces of armor (gold worth $6,000 went into each piece) and three hundred shields ($1,800 worth of gold in each.) And I kept all these in my palace in the Hall of the forest of Lebanon." (1 Kings 10:14-17)

"I made a huge ivory throne and overlaid it with pure gold. It had six steps and a rounded back, with armrests; and a lion standing on each side. And there were two lions on each step – twelve in all. This was the most splendid throne in the entire world. All my cups were of solid gold, and in the Hall of the Forest of Lebanon my entire dining service was made of solid gold. (Silver wasn't used because it wasn't considered to be of much value)." (1 Kings 10:18-21)

"My merchant fleet was in partnership with King Hiram's, and once every three years a great load of gold, silver, ivory, apes, and peacocks arrived at the Israeli ports. So I, Solomon, was richer and wiser than all the kings of the earth. Great men from many lands came to interview me and listen to my God-given wisdom. They brought me annual tributes of silver and gold dishes, beautiful cloth, myrrh, spices, horses, and mules." (1 Kings 10 22-25)

"I had a great stable of horses with a vast number of chariots and cavalry 1,400 chariots and 12,000 cavalrymen who lived in the chariot cities and with me at Jerusalem. Silver was as common as stones in Jerusalem in my day, and cedar was of no greater value than the common sycamore! My horses were brought to me from Egypt and

southern Turkey, where my agents purchased them at wholesale prices."
(1 Kings: 26-29)

God had forbidden me to expand in the department of horses and chariots, but I did it anyway, and it was my undoing. Even the vast riches I accumulated were later a subject of spoil by other nations when the Kingdom was divided and weakened, but at this time, I had cornered the market on gold, silver, and precious stones. (McGee)

As I mentioned before, I married many "strange women," women from foreign nations who brought with them their `gods' and soon they turned my heart away from the Lord. You might say I collected women, until I had a harem of one thousand wives. Because I turned from the Lord, God stirred up enemies against me and allowed Jeroboam to rise to prominence and finally split the kingdom. (McGee)

The Lord was angry with me, because He had come to me twice and told me: "not to go after other gods," but I kept not that which the Lord commanded to me. God said to me, `FOR AS MUCH AS THIS IS DONE OF THEE, AND THOU HAS NOT KEPT MY COVENANT AND MY STATUTES, WHICH I HAVE COMMANDED THEE, I WILL SURELY REND THE KINGDOM FROM THEE, AND I WILL GIVE IT TO THY SERVANT. HOWEVER, FOR THE SAKE OF YOUR FATHER DAVID, I WILL NOT DO THIS WHILE YOU ARE STILL ALIVE, I WILL TAKE THE KINGDOM AWAY FROM YOUR SON. AND EVEN SO I WILL LET HIM BE KING OF ONE TRIBE, FOR DAVID'S SAKE AND FOR THE SAKE OF JERUSALEM, MY CHOSEN CITY.' (1 Kings 11:9-13)

The tribe of Benjamin went with my son, and because I am of the tribe of Judah, they stood with me. So these two tribes went with the family of David. The other ten tribes in the north would follow Jeroboam, my servant. (McGee)

"I had the greatest opportunity of any man who ever lived, but I became the most colossal failure in the pages of Scripture...' `To whomsoever much is given, of him shall be much required...' (Luke 12:28) I had the greatest opportunity of any man, who ever lived, to speak for God, but I failed to remove false religion, and it became a plague of leprosy. My one thousand pagan wives turned my heart away from the Lord. (McGee)

Before I tell you of my downfall, let me point you to my writings. In the Book of Proverbs God has a message for every person. "It is particularly slanted to young men - and it applies to young women too. It has a special message for youth and will help them find answers for their everyday life." (McGee)

"The key verse is found in the first chapter, "The fear of the Lord is the beginning of knowledge: but fools despise wisdom and instruction." (Proverbs 1:7) You can see I forgot my own proverb. (McGee)

"But let me tell you, Proverbs bears no unscientific statement or inaccurate observation. For example, `Keep thy heart with all diligence for out it are the issues of life.' (Proverbs 4:23) This is a remarkable statement; because it was about 2,700 years later that Harvey found that the blood circulates and that the heart is the pump. In contrast, in an apocryphal book called the Epistle of Barnabas, mention is made of the mythical phoenix, a bird that consumes itself by fire and rises in resurrection. Such a fable does not appear in the Book of Proverbs or anywhere in the Bible. You may find it strange that Proverbs is an ancient book, compared to the 21st century, but not one of the proverbs, I wrote, is unscientific today. This should alert you that this book is God inspired." (McGee)

"The Book of Proverbs is written on a high moral plane, unlike other writings: for instance, Justin Martyr said that Socrates was a Christian before Christ - which, of course, would be an impossibility. Socrates also gave instructions to harlots on how to conduct themselves! The best that can be said of him is that he was amoral." (McGee)

"None of the Proverbs recorded in the Bible, contradict themselves, while man's proverbs are often in opposition to each other. For example: `Look before you leap' contrasted with "He who hesitates is lost." A man gets no more than he pays for,' contrasted with "The best things in life are free." `Leave well enough alone' has over against it, "Progress never stands still." `A rolling stone gathers no moss.' Versus "A setting hen does not get fat." The proverbs of man contradict each other, because men's ideas differ." (McGee)

"You may believe that these Proverbs are a collection of sayings without any particular regard for orderly arrangement, but they tell a story of a young man starting out in life and they give a thumbnail sketch of every character in the Bible, and there is a proverb that will fit every one of you that read them." (McGee)

"The literary form of these Proverbs is mostly in the form of couplets. The two clauses of the couplet are generally related to each other by what has been termed parallelism, according to Hebrew poetry. Parallelism is a parallelism of ideas and three kinds of parallelism is pointed out here." (McGee)

1. "Synonymous Parallelism:" Here the second clause restates what is given in the first clause. (It expresses the same thought in a different way)

    'Judgments are prepared for scorners, and stripes for the back of fools.' (Proverbs 19:29)

2. Antithetic (Contrast) Parallelism:" Here a truth, stated in the first clause, is made stronger in the second clause by contrast with an Opposite truth

    "The light of the righteous rejoiceth. But the lamp of the wicked shall be put out." (Proverbs 13:9)

3. "Synthetic Parallelism:" The second clause develops the thought of the first.

    "The terror of a king is as the roaring of a lion; He that provokes him to anger sins against his own life." (Proverbs 20:2) (McGee)

These Proverbs were stated by me (Solomon) to "teach the people knowledge that they may heed these words and master them; fear God, and keep his commandments, for this is the whole duty of man, for God shall bring every work into judgment, including every hidden thing, good or bad." (Ecclesiastes 12:9-14)

"Fear God is the theme of Proverbs, it means to: reverence, worship, and obey Him, and keep His commandments: would mean to meet God's conditions for salvation – grounded on faith in God. For you living in the world today, it means to "… Believe on the Lord Jesus Christ, and thou shall be saved…" (Acts 16:31) Christ bore the judgment of man; He died a judgment death. Your sins must be on Christ by faith in Him, or you must answer for your own sins at the Great White Throne judgment as mentioned in Revelation 20:11." (McGee)

"In Ecclesiastes I write an autobiography of my life, apart from God. Here is where I go into 'foolishness' trying to be happy without God, and using my God-given wisdom to try every field of endeavor and pleasure that is known to man. I prove in these writings that mankind cannot be satisfied without Christ, even if we possess the whole world and all of its content ("What profits man, if he gains the whole world and loses his own soul?") I reach conclusions by my own intelligence and my own experiments. I reached the conclusion that `all is vanity under the sun." (Ecclesiastes 1:2) (McGee)

"The man under the sun is a great deal different from the child of God who has been blessed `... With all spiritual blessings in heavenly places in Christ." (Ephesians 1:3) (McGee)

These are some of the things I tried to make myself happy: "laughter, wine, I built houses, planted vineyards, I made gardens and orchards, planted trees, and made pools of water; I had servants and maidens, I had great possessions, cattle, silver, and gold, I had singers and musical instruments, I withheld nothing from my eyes, I labored, I ate and drank all that pleased me, but I hated my life because all was vexation of my spirit." (Ecclesiastes 2:2-26)

"I concluded that God (Jesus Christ) is the only solution for the problems of life, and to satisfy the deep longings of man's heart. The Lord Jesus has given His promise to people of any and all ages: '...him that cometh to me I will in no wise cast out." (John 6:37) (McGee)

"The Song of Solomon' is not a story at all, but a song: "The Song of Songs is written by me." (Song of Solomon 1:1) I wrote three thousand proverbs and one thousand and five songs. The Bible has recorded only a portion of what I wrote, but these are the best of all that I wrote." (McGee)

"In this song, `Beloved is the name for Him (the bridegroom); and "love" is the name for her (the bride)." "I am my beloved's and my beloved is mine; He pastures his flock among the lilies." (Song 6:3) `Many waters cannot quench love, neither can the floods drown it: if a man tried to buy it (love) with everything he owned, he could not do it." (Song 8:7) (McGee)

"This song has been misunderstood above all other books of the Bible. Peter wrote this concerning Paul's epistles… Paul has talked about these same things in many of his letters. Some of his comments are not easy to understand, and there are people who are deliberately (unlearned and unstable), and always demand some unusual interpretation – they have twisted his letters around to mean something quite different from what he meant, just as they do the other parts of the Scripture – and the result is disaster for them. (2 Peter: 15-16) I think this is also true of my `Song of Solomon." (McGee)

"This song should show you that wedded love is a wonderful thing, a glorious experience 'between one man and one woman.' It is as a glorious experience as an elaborate, vivid, striking, and bold picture of our relationship with the Lord Jesus Christ. You may wonder how I could write such a book after Ecclesiastes, and knowing that I had 1000 wives, but this book is truly inspired by God; it is holy ground, like a fragile flower that requires delicate handling, and you will see why." (McGee)

"There are four different and important meanings found in this book:"

1. The first, sets forth the `glory of wedded-love.' Here, it is declared the sacredness of the marital relationship, and that marriage is a God-given institution. This song will show you what real love is. The Jews taught it to reveal the heart of a satisfied husband, and that of a devoted wife."

   "Today, in the 21st century, you have seen a great movement toward `sexual freedom,' which many people think is good. One young man, who had lived and believed in "free love" said that such a life is "living like an animal.' People living such a life know what an animal knows about sex, but know little about real love. There is a stark contrast between the ideas of your generation and the glory of wedded love, as it is portrayed in Song of Solomon." (McGee)

2. "The second idea sets forth the `love of Jehovah for Israel.' The prophets also spoke of Israel as the wife of Jehovah. Hosea has this same theme in his writings. According to

   Hosea, idolatry in Israel is likened to a breach in wedded love, and is the greatest sin in all the world." (McGee)

3. "The scribes and rabbis of Israel have given these two interpretations to this book, but the church has given two more interpretations; one being a picture of 'Christ and the Church: The Church is the bride of Christ.' This is a familiar figure in the New Testament as read about in Ephesians 5, and Revelation 21. However, in my "Song of Solomon," God uses a picture of human affection to convey to all people His most great love. He uses the very best of human love to rouse us to realize the wonderful love that He has for us. This song may lead you into marvelous relationship with the Lord Jesus Christ that you would have never known before. All people need a knowledge of the Word of God, and a personal relationship with God through Jesus Christ, to come into this intimacy; my 'Song of Solomon' can lead you into this relationship." (McGee)

4. "The fourth interpretation, of this book, depicts 'the communion of Christ with the individual believer.' It portrays the love of Christ for the individual, and the soul's communion with Christ. Many saints have experienced this down through the years, Paul said in Galatians 2:20 that, "… the Son of God, who loved me, and gave Himself for me." This is not a kind of experience; it is a personal relationship with Jesus Christ

   - seeing how wonderful He is, and how glorious He is. This book should be like the breaking of Mary's alabaster box of ointment; the fragrance of it will fill your life and spread out to others." (McGee) "There have been many interpretations of my book over the centuries, some being that of liberalism, which is simply unbelief☐ One states that the Shulamite girl was kidnapped by me, Solomon; at first she did not want to go with me, but finally she did." (McGee)

"I will give you an interpretation of my book as I see it, and others, like Dr. Harry Ironside, have interpreted it by God's direction. These are some of the observations that I write for you living in the 21st century The setting: a drama in the palace in Jerusalem; some of the scenes are flashbacks to a previous time. The daughters of Jerusalem carry along the tempo of the story. These dialogues are to be sung. Several lovely scenes are introduced at Jerusalem, which have a counterpart in the church." (McGee)

"The Shulamite girl says, 'Look not upon me, because I am black, because the sun hath looked upon me: my mother's children were angry with me; they made me the keeper of the vineyards; but mine own vineyard I have not kept.' (Song 1:6) The elder daughter of a poor Shulamite family is a sort of Cinderella; she has been forced to keep the vineyard because her family are tenant farmers in the hill country of Ephraim. This comes from Song 8:11, where I state that I have a vineyard at Baal-hamon, that I let out to keepers that paid me one thousand pieces of silver, for the use of it." (McGee)

"The Shulamate girl is tanned from exposure to the sun, and she feels disgraced because she is dark and hasn't been able to take care of her looks, or enhance her beauty in any way. Also, she takes care of the sheep, as you read in Song 1:8. 'If thou know not, O thou fairest among women, go thy way forth by the footsteps of the flock, and feed thy kids beside the shepherds' tent." (McGee)

"The girl worked along a caravan route in the very rugged territory of the hill country. As she worked, she would see the caravans that passed by going between Jerusalem and Damascus. Her reaction to this is: 'who is this that cometh out of the wilderness like pillars of smoke, perfumed with myrrh and frankincense, with all powders of the merchant?' (Song 3:6) She observed the beautiful ladies of court with their white skin; they had canopies over them as they traveled on camels or elephants. She saw their beautiful jewels and satins, but could only dream about herself in their position." (McGee)

"The Shuamite girl would smell the frankincense and myrrh as the caravans passed by. These fragrances also portray a wonderful picture of Jesus Christ both, at His birth and His death. The wise men brought Him frankincense and myrrh as a gift when He was born; when He was dead, Joseph and Nicodemus brought myrrh to put on His body." (McGee)

"In Song 1:13 my 'love' (my bride) makes this statement: 'A bundle of myrrh is my well-beloved unto me; he shall lie all night betwixt my breasts.' The myrrh speaks of Jesus entire life from birth to death. Christ should be heavy on your heart at night when you awake, and are worried and anxious about the next day. When you "get to the end of your rope," think on these things as written in Philippians 4:8

'Whatsoever things are true (that is Christ), whatsoever things are honest (that is Christ, also), whatsoever things are just (that is the Lord Jesus), whatsoever things are pure (He is pure), whatsoever things are lovely, of good report; if there be any virtue, and if there be any praise, "think" on these things.' In other words, meditate upon the Lord Jesus Christ, night and day; my book, the 'Song of Solomon' will help you to do this." (McGee)

"One day while my 'love' (my bride) was tending her sheep, I, a handsome shepherd appeared, and fell in love with her. This is what I said to her, "As the lily among thorns, so is my love among the daughters." (Song 2:2) Again I said, 'Behold, thou art fair, my love beholds, thou art fair; thou hast doves' eyes within thy locks: thy hair is as flock of goats that appear from mount Gilead.' (Song 4:1) I used beautiful poetic language to woo her, but this is a picture of the love of Christ for the church. "Christ loved the church and gave Himself for it." (McGee)

"Finally, my 'love' (my bride, gave her heart to me: "As the apple tree among the trees of the wood, so is my beloved among the sons. I sat down under his shadow with great delight, and his fruit was sweet to my taste." (Song 2:3) This refers to the Lord Jesus Christ's invitation to you: 'come unto me, all ye that labor and are heavy laden, and I will give you rest (rest you).' Do you, readers, know what it is to rest in Jesus Christ? Is He a reality to you? Do you rest in Him? I am talking, here, about a personal relationship with Jesus Christ." (McGee)

"After she (my love)) gave her heart to me, we were madly in love. There is nothing like marital love as we experienced it. 'My beloved is mine, and I am his: he feedeth among the lilies.' (Song 2:16) It was wonderful to have this personal intimate relationship." (McGee)

"At first 'my Love' only knew me as a shepherd. "He brought me to the banqueting house, and his banner over me was love." (Song 2:4) But she thought that I was a peculiar shepherd, because she couldn't see any sheep. She asked me, 'Tell me, O thou whom my soul loveth, where thou feedest, where thou makest thy flock to rest at noon…?'" (Song 1:7) (McGee)

"Then one day I, (as beloved) announced that I was going away, but I would return. This parallels the words of the Lord Jesus: 'Let not your heart be troubled: ye believe in God, believe also in me. In my father's house are many mansions: if it were not so, I would have told you. I go to prepare a place for you. And if I go to prepare a place for you, I will come again, and receive you unto myself; that where I am, there ye may be also." (John 14: 1-3) (McGee)

"The days passed, 'my love' waited. Her family and friends began to ridicule her. They said, "You are just a simple country girl taken in by him." Peter predicted this would happen in your time also: 'Knowing this first, that there shall come in the last days scoffers, walking after their own lusts, and saying, where is the promise of his coming: for since the fathers fell asleep, all things continue as they were from the beginning of the creation.'" (2 Peter 3: 3-4) (McGee)

"But my 'love' trusted me; she loved me; she dreamed of me. By night on my bed, I sought him whom my soul loveth: I sought him, but I found him not." (Song 3:1) Do you ask yourself: 'Do I miss Christ? Do I long for Him? Then one night my "love" lay restlessly upon her couch when she noticed a fragrance in the room. In my day it was the custom for a lover to put some myrrh or frankincense in the opening to the door handle. She smelled the perfume and went to the door. 'I rose up to open to my beloved; and my hands dripped with myrrh, and my fingers with sweet smelling myrrh, upon the handles of the lock.' (Song 5:5) She knew now that I had been there; that I had not forgotten her." (McGee)

"Again, you can associate this fragrance with the perfume of Christ in your life today. Never be satisfied with religious gimmicks. What does Christ mean to you right now? Is the fragrance of Christ in your life today?" (McGee)

"Now, she knew that I, her 'beloved' was nearby. The Lord Jesus said, "... Lo, I am with you always, even unto the end of the world." (Matthew 28:20) Paul said while in prison that the Lord stood by him. Jesus promised, '...I will never leave thee, not forsake thee.' (Hebrews 13:5) (McGee)

"One day she, (my love) was working with the vines in the vine-yard. She raised the grapes that were down on the ground and put a rock under them, so that the little foxes could not get to them. "Take us the foxes, the little foxes, that spoil the vines: for our vines have tender grapes." (Song 2:15) (McGee)

"While 'my love' is working with the vines, she sees a pillar of smoke down the road. 'Who is this that cometh out of the wilderness like pillars of smoke, perfumed with myrrh and frankincense, with all powders of the merchant?' (Song 3:6) The cry is passed along. "Behold, King Solomon is coming!" Then someone comes to her excitedly and says her, 'Oh, King Solomon is coming!' But she is busy, and she doesn't know King Solomon. Then someone comes to her and says, "King Solomon is asking for you!" She says, 'Asking for me? I don't know King Solomon; I've never met him, why would he ask for me? (McGee)

"The voice of my beloved! 'Behold, he cometh leaping upon the mountains, skipping upon the hills. My beloved is like a roe or a young hart: behold, he standeth behind our wall, he looketh forth at the windows, showing himself through the lattice." My beloved spoke, and said unto me, "Rise up, my 'love, my fair one.' And come away." (Song 2:8 - 10) So my love is brought into my presence. I asked if she knew me. She recognized me as her shepherd, and now she knew I had come for 'her!'" (McGee)

"My promise to return for 'my love,' parallels the promise of the Lord Jesus: My sheep hear my voice and I know them, and they follow Me: And I give unto them eternal life; and they shall never perish, neither shall any man pluck them out My hand." (John 10:27 - 28) Also this written by Paul (the Apostle), For the Lord himself shall descend from heaven with a shout, with the voice of the archangel, and with the trump of God; and the dead in Christ shall rise first: Then we which are alive and remain shall be caught up together with them in the clouds, to meet the Lord in the air: and so shall we ever be with the Lord.' (1 Thessalonians 4:1 - 17) The Lord Jesus has promised the He is coming again for His own." (McGee)

"'For, lo, the winter is past, the rain is over and gone; The flowers appear on the earth; the time of the singing birds is come, and the voice of the turtle is heard in our land; The fig tree putteth forth her green figs, and the vines with the tender grape give a good smell. Arise, "my love, my fair one," and come away.' (Song 2:11 - 13) Today, Jesus is calling 'you' out this world." (McGee)

"Please ask yourself right now: 'how much am I involved in the world? Would it break my heart if Jesus were to come right now and take me out of the world?' Many, as I, Solomon became, are satisfied in the world, they are doing very well in an affluent society; so if Jesus should come to them today, they would be crying all the way to heaven, because they have so much here on the earth to leave behind." Remember Lot's wife whom looked back (at her world) and turned into a pillar of salt." (McGee)

"Arise, "my love, my fair one," and come away, O my dove that art in the clefts of the rock. In the secret places of the stairs, let me see thy countenance, let me hear thy voice; for sweet is thy voice, and thy countenance is comely.' (Song 2:13 - 14) Jesus puts us in the "cleft of the rock' until the storm passes. How glorious to hear the voice of Jesus and to be in His constant care." (McGee)

"He brought me to the banqueting house, and his banner over me was love." (Song 2:4) 'Salvation is a love affair - we love Jesus because He first loved us. This is my story (Solomon) as told in this little book. "Song of Solomon." (McGee)

"Now, I must finish the story of my life on the earth. I am not proud of the way it ended, with God angry with me. My friend, it is not how you start a race, but how you finish; even if you give your heart to God in the last minutes of your life, as the thief on the cross did: He said to Jesus as they both hung on the cross: 'Lord, remember me when thou comest into thy kingdom.' Jesus answered him saying: "Verily I say unto thee, today shalt thou be with me in paradise." Seek God every day of your life and when you reach the end of it, you will hear the voice of Jesus say, 'Well done good and faithful servant."

"I had enjoyed peace in my reign as King of Israel, but now God stirs up trouble for me; this is the first time since I had come to the throne that we had warfare. 'And the Lord stirred up an adversary unto (me), Solomon; Hadad, the Edomite: he was of the king's seed in Edom." (1 Kings 11:14) (McGee)

"I had elevated Jeroboam (a son of a servant) to a high position, as overseer of my public works, because he had considerable ability and talent. Ahijah was a prophet in the land, and one day he found Jeroboam wearing a new garment. He took this new garment off Jeroboam and rent it into twelve pieces. He gave ten of the pieces to Jeroboam and said to him, 'God is going to give you ten tribes. The kingdom is going to be divided.'" (1 Kings 29 - 32) (McGee)

God said to me: "BECAUSE THAT THEY HAVE FORSAKEN ME, AND HAVE WORSHIPPED ASHTORETH THE GODDESS OF THE ZEDONIANS, CHEMOSH THE GOD OF THE MOABITES, AND MILCOM THE GOD OF

THE CHILDREN OF AMMON, AND HAVE NOT WALKED IN MY WAYS, TO DO THAT WHICH IS RIGHT IN MINE EYES, AND TO KEEP MY STATUTES AND MY JUDGMENTS, AS DID DAVID HIS FATHER." (1 Kings 11:33)

God told Ahijah that my kingdom would not be taken from me, because of my father David, but God would take it from my son, Rehoboam. I sought to kill Jeroboam, so he fled into Egypt and there he stayed until my death. Let me explain briefly what happened when my kingdom was divided.

"Jeroboam returned from Egypt; he leads ten tribes in demanding a reduction in taxes. Rehoboam, my son, being on the throne in my place, turns down the request of the ten northern tribes to lower taxes (but he actually raises taxes), so Jeroboam leads the ten tribes in revolt. Jeroboam succeeds in separating the ten tribes, and sets himself on the throne as their king; this constitutes the northern kingdom. He puts a golden calf in Beth- el and one in Dan, so that the people would not have to go to Jerusalem to worship in the temple." (McGee)

"This is the beginning of the kingdom divided. Eventually the northern kingdom will go into - captivity in Assyria, and the southern kingdom will go into captivity in Babylon. The kingdom of Judah lasted longer than the kingdom of Israel, before going into captivity; most all of the prophets, except the post - captivity prophets, prophesied during this period. The southern kingdom of Judah followed the line of David right into the New Testament, to the birth of the Lord Jesus Christ. This was a very sad period in the life of the nation Israel, and unfortunately, I was the beginning of it. Remember, that your life has eternal significance and it will influence someone, maybe millions, so don't be "foolish" as I became, please 'LIVE for the Glory of God (McGee)

"The northern kingdom never had a good king, and the southern kingdom only had eight good kings during this 200 - year period. Here is a chronological table of the kings and the prophets during the divided kingdom:"

JUDAH

KING	REIGN	CHARACTER	PROPHET
1. Rehoboam	931-913 B.C. (17 years)	Bad	Shemaiah
2. Abijah	913-911 B.C. (3 years)	Bad	
3. Asa	911-870 B.C. (41 years)	Good	
4. Jehoshapat	870-848 B.C. (25 years)	Good	
5. Jehoram	848-841 B.C. (8 years)	Bad	
6. Ahaziah	841 (1 year)	Bad	
7. Athaliah	841-835 (6 years)	Bad	
8. Joash	835-796 (40 years)	Good	Joel
9. Amaziah	796-767 (29 years)	Good	
10. Azariah or Uzziah			Isaiah
11. Jotham	740-732 (16 years)	Good	Micah
12. Ahaz	732-716 (16 years)	Bad	
13. Hezekiah	716-687 (29 years)	Good	
14. Manasseh	687-642 (55 years)	Bad	Nahum
15. Amon	642-642 (2 years)	Bad	Habakkuk
16. Josiah	640-608 (31 years)	Good	Zephaniah
17. Jehoahaz	608 (3 mo.)	Bad	Jeremiah
18. Jehoiakim	608-597 (11 years)	Bad	
19. Jehoiachin	597 (3 mo.)	Bad	
20. Zedekiah	597-586 (11 years)	Bad	

ISRAEL

1. Jeroboam	931-909 B.C. (22 years)	Bad	Ahijah
2. Nadab	910-909 (2 years)	Bad	
3. Baasha	909-886 (24 years)	Bad	
4. Elah	886-885 (2 years)	Bad	
5. Zimri	885 (7 years)	Bad	
6. Omri	885-874 (12 years)	Bad	Elijah
7. Ahab	874-853 (22 years)	Bad	Micaiah
8. Ahaziah	853-852 (2 years)	Bad	
9. Joram	852-841 (12 years)	Bad	Elisha
10. Jehu	841-814 (28 years)	Bad	
11. Jehoahaz	814-798 (17 years)	Bad	
12. Jehoash	798-782 (16 years)	Bad	Jonah
13. Jeroboam II	782-753 (41 years)	Bad	Amos
14. Zechariah	753-752 (6 mo.)	Bad	Hosea
15. Shallum	752 (1 mo.)	Bad	
16. Menahem	752-742 (10 years)	Bad	
17. Pekahiah	742-740 (2 years)	Bad	
18. Pekah	740-732 (20 years)	Bad	
19. Hoshea	732-721 (9 years)	Bad	

"I, Solomon, ruled over all Israel for forty years, and then I died and was buried in the city of David, my father, and Rehoboam reigned in my stead." (1 Kings 11:40-43)

"Friend, let me tell you what happened to me as a ruler over Israel. God gave me a special dispensation of wisdom to administer the kingdom. Yet that wisdom did not enter into my own personal, private, or spiritual life. You, today, talk of separation of church and state; and I say that if you do try to make such a separation you will lose your own soul. I never really broke with false religion; I closed my eyes to it; I never took a stand against it. I became obsessed with prosperity, materialism, and 'WOMEN." (McGee)

"Immorality and false religion always go together. Don't kid yourself, you cannot serve God, and have fellowship with Him if you live in sin; John made it clear in 1 John 1:6, 'If we say that we have fellowship with Him, and walk in darkness, we LIE, and do not (tell) the truth.' May I say to you that the wealth and achievements of this world are a passing glory? This brings me to the end of my life as recorded in the Bible." (McGee)

Samson

STRONG HAIR – SAMSON

JUDGES 13-16

My life ended with me blind, and forced to grind grain like a common donkey, in the land of the Philistines where they mocked me night and day. God chose me for His prophet before my birth. My parents tried to tell me that my life belonged to God and not to me, but I was self-willed and did my "own thinking."

I laughed in the face of those silly Philistines, who believed they could tie me up, and bind me with ropes to confine me. I was the strongest man in the world. No one could compare to me. I killed a lion with my bare hands. I tied the tails of 300 foxes together with torches of fire between their tails, and set them loose in the Philistines grain fields, because my father-in-law gave my wife to another man. Another thing I did, was to kill a thousand men with a new jawbone of a donkey.

"An angel appeared to my parents before I was born, and said that God Himself, would set me aside from the womb to the day of my death, as a Nazarite, to 'begin' to deliver Israel out of the hand of the Philistines. (Judges 13:5,7) No razor was ever to touch my head.

My parents called me Samson, and as I grew the Lord blessed me. (Judges 13:24) When I was grown, "I saw a woman among the Philistines, and I told my mother and father to get her for me. My parents asked me to take a wife from among our own people, but I again told my father to get her for me, for she pleased me well. My mother and father did not know that this was of the Lord, because He sought an occasion for me to go against the Philistines; Israel was under the dominion of the Philistines at this time, and that is why God had raised me up." (Judges 14:1 - 4) However, my love for Philistine 'women' would be my downfall, because I loved them more than they "deserved." and finally I loved 'one' more than God.

I did judge Israel for twenty years, "rightly," and God was with me. 'One day I went to Gaza and took a harlot unto myself; the Gazites heard of this, and laid in wait for me so they could kill me in the morning. But I arose at midnight, and took the doors of the gate of the city, and two posts, and went away with them, bar and all.' (Judges 16:3) But then, I saw 'Delilah.' I could not get her off my mind; I thought of her beauty night and day. She betrayed me over, and over, trying to discover the source of my strength, so she could turn me over to her people to bind me forever. You see my strength was in 'God,' and not in my muscles, or any visible appearance.

I knew what Delilah was doing, but I could not resist her conniving ways. Finally, I told her if my hair was cut, I would be as weak as any man. I should have realized that God had departed from me, when I started to make a game of the gifts, and secrets, that He had given to me alone.

So, I ended up, "blind," grinding grain, 'alone,' because the Philistines had gouged my eyes out, after they cut my hair; I was mocked and cursed by them year after year. The Philistines did not notice that my hair had grown back, and they could not know that I had prayed to God for forgiveness; I asked Him to remember me once again, to strengthen me one last time to do His will at my death.

One day, about 3000 Philistines gathered together for a great party, and they brought me out of the prison to mock me once more. They, "foolishly," bound me between the two center pillars that held up the house; I asked God to 'let me die with the Philistines, and then I bowed myself with all my might, and the house fell upon the lords, and all the people that were therein. So the dead that I slew at my death were more than I slew in my lifetime.' (Judges 16:30) "Then my brethren and all the house of my father came and took my body to be buried in the place of Manoah, my father. I had judged Israel for twenty years." (Judges 16:31) Please read of 'my life,' and then ask yourself, whom you will serve all the days of "your life?"

AMEN

JOB

"How do you know God loves you?"

"Because Jesus died on the cross for my sins, so now I am forgiven, and I can go to heaven when I die.

"What if your livestock were condemned to die, because of disease, your income was gone, and your savings were wiped out, and your children were killed by a hurricane; all in one day. Would you still believe in God loved you?"

"No!"

"Why not?"

"How could I believe God would let such terrible things happen and still be loving."

"This all happened to Job in the Bible, yet we are assured that God loved him beyond compare."

"I don't understand."

"Satan said to God, "Of course, Job loves You, you have put a hedge of protection around him and You have blessed his work and have increased his goods."

"Satan talks to God?"

"Apparently."

"So go on, what happened next?"

"Job refused to hate God and still believed and honored Him, but Satan would not give up, so he asked God to let him plague Job with poor health, and then he believed Job would hate God."

"Did he."

"No, but Job had boils on his skin from the top of his head to the souls of his feet."

"That is something to think about."

"Yes, Job's wife told him to curse God and die."

"His wife was still alive?"

"Yes, Satan didn't care if she was there or not because she seemed to be on Satan's side, and she didn't comfort Job at all, in fact she sent him outside to the ash pile to scrape his boils."

"?????"

BLESSED BE THE NAME OF THE LORD
JOB 1-42

Oh, a darker day could not be lived by man or beast, but this day in my life.

First, a messenger came with news that all my oxen were stolen by thieves, and all the servants were slain, but one; then another messenger came, even while the first was speaking, and told me all the sheep had been burned up by fire from heaven, and all the servants were consumed too, but one; then another messenger came and told me thieves had taken all the camels away and killed all the servants who cared for them, but one; and then while he was yet speaking, one came to tell me the most crushing news of all, that my "sons and daughters" were together at my eldest sons' house, and a great wind pushed the walls in upon them, and that they were all dead.

I fell to my knees and worshiped God and said, "Naked I came out of my mothers' womb, and naked shall I return thither: the Lord gave, and the Lord hath taken away; blessed be the name of the Lord." (Job 1: 21) I realize now that God was not the one that took away all my possessions and my family; God can give only 'good and perfect gifts' to His people who love Him. I had expressed many times to myself, and to others, the things that made me afraid. When these things happened to me, I spoke these words: 'for the thing which I 'greatly feared' is come upon me, and that which I was afraid of is come unto me.' (Job 3:25) Because of these fears I had let Satan into my life, and he took advantage of it by going to God and getting permission to cause all of these wicked circumstances to take place. God only allowed all these troubles to come upon me because I "GREATLY FEARED" bad things "WOULD," come upon me. In my unbelief I didn't trust in God's protection.

Even though my heart was broken, I knew my God would not forsake me or leave me alone, but still my problems continued. Satan was not content to take away from me all that I held dear, but because I did not forsake God, he went back to God, and God said, "Have you considered My servant Job, that there is none like him in the earth, a perfect and an upright man, one that feareth God, and avoids evil? And still he holds fast his integrity…" Satan said, 'Skin for skin, yea, all that a man has will he give for his life, but put forth thine hand now, and touch his bone and his flesh, and he will curse You to Your face.' (Job 2:3 - 5) Satan believed if I were sick, I would then curse God. God said to Satan, "Behold, he is in thine hand, but save his life." (Job 2:6) I soon broke out in boils, from the soles of my feet to the crown of my head, and my whole body was in unbearable pain, but my heart was grieved even more.

It was then that my wife came to me, her heart broken as was mine, and she said "Do you still retain integrity? Curse God and die." (Job 2:9)

I said to her that she was speaking as one of the "foolish" women speaks. I said, 'Shall we receive good at the hand of God, and shall we not receive evil? (Job 2:10) In her pain, she believed life was no longer worth living, and that we should kill ourselves and be done with it.

I told her that God had given us all our beloved children, all of our animals, and all of our servants, and all of our possessions, and the breath of life within us, and that He alone decides what our life will be like. He wants us to trust Him in everything and with everything that we have, and He is worth honoring in all circumstances. He would never let us down, even though he seemed to be far away from us at that time.

This, however, was just the beginning of the test of my faith in God. For many years I did question God over and over again. Three of my friends came at once, and stayed with me for seven days and seven nights without speaking a word to me. They knew my heart was broken and my body ached day and night, and that there were no words to comfort me. Their presence did help me a little, to know someone cared enough to stay with me in my time of terrible trouble.

When we did start talking, my first friend insisted, over and over again, endlessly, that if I would just "admit my sin," God would restore me to health. He was sure I had done great sins and that I needed to repent of them.

My second friend told me if I would just be more religious, God would be pleased to heal me and my life would be restored again. He wanted me to "pray more, and study the Word more, and to give more."

My third friend explained to me if I would have more "faith," I would be healed and well.

All of this talk and criticism was very disturbing to me, and I came to the point that I wished I had never been born; "let the day perish wherein I was born, and the night it was said. "There is a man child conceived." (Job 3:1 - 2) But I never let go of the thought that God would help me get through this. The wait, however, and all the endless chatter did defeat my resolve, and questioned God as to why this was happening to me.

I wanted to speak to God and ask Him what he wanted of me. "If only someone could plead my case before God; a middleman that could talk for me and help me. You know this person to be Jesus Christ, but I did not know Him then." (McGee)

I was sure God wasn't listening to me, because He seemed to be so far away. I pleaded with God to answer my call. I felt so sick and so alone, even with my friends nearby, and all I asked was to be healed. That was forever on my mind. If only God would heal me. If I could have my health, I could be happy once again.

I tried different approaches to get God's attention. "I first agreed with Him that whatever He decided was right for me. Then, I tried telling God why He should heal me. I was a good person and had done only good in my life. I was 'walking on thin ice' with this approach, as there is only ONE that is good, and that is God in Jesus Christ." (McGee)

After years of pleading, talking – reasoning, asking, discussing, thinking, and speaking, God spoke to me. He asked me where I was when He created the World, and the Universe, and all that is in it. He asked me 135 questions about Himself. I was finally, "speechless," and 'I abhorred myself, and repented in dust and ashes.'

When God was done with His questions, I surrendered my life and my will, and all that I am to Him. He told me to make sacrifices for my friends, because they were wrong in their reasoning. God said to my friends, "Therefore take unto you now seven bullocks and seven rams, and go to my servant Job, and offer up for yourselves a burnt offering: and My servant Job shall pray for you: for him will I accept: lest I deal with you after your folly, in that ye have not spoken of Me the thing which is right, like My servant Job." (Job 42:8) When I prayed for my friends, all my resentment was gone, and 'the Lord reversed my captivity, and He restored twice as much as I had before.' (Job 42:10) I realized that in the "good" times of my life, I was not really trusting God. I was hoping I was acceptable to Him, and that my sacrifices were acceptable. I questioned God's love for me, even though He had 'blessed' me so much.

In my years of stress and sickness, God was with me. He would "never leave me nor forsake me." He taught me to trust Him and Him only, in 'all' circumstances. "In everything give thanks, for this is the will of God, in Christ Jesus, concerning you," (1 Thessalonians 5:18) This is a verse that will comfort you in ways that I could not be comforted because I did not know of Jesus Christ as you know Him, as your Lord and Savior.

He taught me to wait for His timing and His will to be accomplished: He set me on my feet and restored to me all my possessions "double," and he gave me ten more lovely children, seven boys and three girls. The girls were the most 'beautiful' in all the land.

I no longer relied on "my ability" to please God, because I learned, during this trial, of God's great love and concern for me. His love was not dependant on anything that I did. God loved me before 'He set the foundations of the World in place.' (Ephesians 1:4) His nature was to bless me forever, and He is delighted when I accepted His blessing without question. Even when everything was black, God was engineering circumstances for my good. (Romans 8:28)

God wants to change the heart of man to conform to His. He will put us in circumstances that make us lean on Him, and Him only. When we meditate on God we realize "Heaven" is our eternal home, and He uses our life on earth to prepare for this. Our suffering is but for 'a moment,' compared to FOREVER and EVER, WITH HIM!

I no longer struggled with the rest of my life, because I knew my life was with God, I think back to the long dark years, and all the anguish I felt in my soul for so long. I am thankful that God did not let me give up on "Him." They were the years that brought me to know God as I could never have known Him otherwise. God is faithful and can be trusted in all things, and my eternity is so delightful because of all that God let me endure. May you know Him as I know Him now? I must tell you I lost everything that I valued. My wife and friends were still with me. Did I value them then? No, but I understand now that God gave me a new beginning to enjoy Him, and all those who shared in my life, even if they did not believe as I did.

My book of Job ends with these words: "After this Job lived a hundred and forty years, and saw his sons, and his sons' sons, even four generations. So Job died, being old and full of days." (Job 42:16 - 17)

MAY YOUR LIFE END WITH THESE GREAT WORDS OF BLESSING TOO!

PSALM 151

O my Lord, my heart is panicked within me.

It races and beats wildly at will,

I cry out for someone to help me, but none can.

Fear fills my every organ, my every moment.

I cry out for deliverance, but no one comes to stop the pain.

Some are sympathetic, but none can calm me.

I gulp vitamins by the handfuls; I lunge at my food of only raw vegetables, apples, chicken, and lean meat. I dutifully walk each day for thirty minutes, even on days when I am so sick, I can hardly get out of bed; I pretend to laugh to increase endorphins in my brain; surely my deliverance is near.

Still the storm rages, no one can see it, no one knows what is happening to me, no one

They tell me, "I look good," oh what do they know?

I feel I must be delivered from this anguish, or I will surely die.

I must work at being peaceful,

I must work to gain joy in my spirit,

I must work at being calm,

I must work to gain quietness in my soul.

Two years pass, three years, four… "Where are you, Lord? Can't You see, don't You know, can't You feel my torment within?"

I question and wonder what has happened to me,

I call unto you, Lord, you answer me; "YES, I AM HERE, I SEE, I KNOW, I FEEL, I HEAR YOUR EVERY CALL", and I say, 'HERE I AM, I WILL NEVER LEAVE YOU OR FORSAKE YOU.'

You are the only One that watches me with Your eye and listens to me with Your ear.

You are the only One that gives me all of Your care, all of Your joy, all of Your Peace, and all of Your love endlessly; this is beyond my understanding!

Now the years are still passing, and my body still feels it is out of control at times, and my soul still has questions, and my thoughts still may lead me to fear, but Your Spirit "has never left me or forsaken me," not even for a minute.

I do not need to rush You, God. I have been 'bought with a price, by Your precious blood,' I am a new creation in Christ, the old man is dead, the feelings of rejection are a lie from Satan; my life belongs to You, and to alone, dear Lord.

You have assured me that You will never reject me, You are weaving my heart and mind together, to look like You.

I can trust Your love, and Your direction no matter how I feel, or how things look.

"Selah!"

PSALM 152

"This is the day You, Lord, have made, that we can be glad together and rejoice in it." (Psalm 9:2)

A day I can be with You, and You will let Your light shine in my heart, and lead me with Your Holy Spirit.

You "have blessed me with all spiritual blessings in heavenly places; because You have chosen me before the foundation of the world, that I should be holy and without blame before You, Lord, in love." (Ephesians 1:3 - 4)

A day to search Your lovely creation, together outside in the fresh air and sunshine, and to realize You are in everything, and in all the obscure places, too. And I thank you for keeping all the rattlesnakes away from me, while we walk.

A day You will dust, and vacuum, and wash clothes with me, and we can sing songs of delight, as we go together to get the work done.

A day to bake cookies: oatmeal raisin, or pecan crescents, or peanut butter, chocolate chip with peanuts, and we can enjoy the taste of sugar and chocolate together.

A day, mostly a day, to have confidence in Your nearness, and in Your unconditional love for me, and to be overwhelmed by You, because You have "delivered me from all of my fears," and replace them with Your perfect love and peace.

A day to know that You are always, always with me, and I will never need to be afraid, as you hold me in the "Palm of Your hand."

Jesus, You are so willing to bless me with all "Your riches in glory," according to the sacrifice You made for me at the cross. You give me 'favor' and security all the days of my life.

AMEN

PROVERBS

"The Christian life is like riding a bicycle: You go forward or you go off."

"What you pursue is what you will get, so make sure it is what you want."

"Every choice produces a result."

"One must choose to be excellent."

"Without God, we cannot, without us, God will not."

"You cannot curse what God has blessed."

"Sin brings a curse."

"Your thinking determines your life. If you fail in your thinking, you will fail in your life."

"Everything you are looking for can be found in Jesus."

"Your outside life cannot be raised until the inside life is raised."

"The instruction you follow will determine the outcome of you life."

"The question is not, 'what can I do?' The question is, "What can God do?"

"God's only pain is to be doubted; God's only pleasure is to be believed."

"A day of favor is worth a lifetime of labor."

"The day will come when all you have, is what you have given to God."

All you can take with you into the next life, is your attitude. "The devil does not need us helping him."

Could the World, the Flesh, and the Devil translate into, "Me, Myself, and I?"

"You can't go beyond your own thinking."

"With God it is all about the next time."

"Teaching our children how to control their anger is the best thing a parent can do for them."

"No one knows what they know, until they are tested."

"You're only a coward if you won't stand and face the fear."

"Submission is choosing to be under the authority of an equal."

"It is not the job of people to make me happy."

"God does not wait for me to be perfect before He speaks a word to me."

"I am not moved by what I see, but I am moved by what I believe."

"Make decisions according to the Word of God."

"Doubt is a way of blaming God."

"Addictions are man's way of handling the pain in his life, and filling up the place in him that only God can fill."

"We believe in our experience more than we believe in God."

"Do not try to do what God asks of you, but get on your knees and ask God to do it in you."

"Believing God is a choice, not a time decision."

"The way you love God, shows, in how you treat people."

"All children need is structure and routine."

"When you concentrate on your sins, you are still trying to do it yourself."

"There is an appointed time for me to be taken off the earth, and no devil in hell can take me before this time."

"Delayed obedience is disobedience."

"Jesus could not die, but He chose to die, for you and for me."

"There is no truth apart from God's Word."

"Think before you speak."

"A legalist is not thankful."

"What is my sin, do I mean to give it up?"

"To be set free from ourselves is the greatest freedom we can have."

"Go humming along all day long."

"It is never too late to be the person you wished you could be."

"Do things the way you think God would do them."

"Take care of other people's property, as if it is your own."

"God judges in love and justice."

"Living in the power of the Holy Ghost, is to have a problem, but not to be upset by it."

"We want the blessing and benefits of God, but we don't want the servant hood."

"When you are in darkness, do not light your own fire."

"Nobody comes to God in steps."

"Refuse to fear."

"I have everything in God, but I must take it by faith."

"How long will you be in the wilderness before you obey God."

"You can control your life if you let God control your time."

"Do all things without grumbling or complaining."

"Anything you can tolerate will not change."

"Live with your eyes fixed on the Lord."

"Remember that you can be here today, and gone tomorrow."

"Falling down is not the end, but staying down is a sin."

"Truth comes before love."

"The reason you are angry is because you are hurting: to live in happiness, learn to forgive."

"God created us for His pleasure."

"You can only renew your mind by speaking the Words of God."

"Make yourself, by choice, do the sayings of God.'

"Do you want God or the devil?"

"God has already worked it out, but you must walk it out."

"You can't, or you won't?

"What you make happen for other people, God will make happen for you."

"Every time you hear a Christian message, you must be ready to take on more responsibility."

"If we forget where we came from, and where we are going, then we are going nowhere."

"God's will, my choice."

"God has a plan to BLESS you; Satan has a plan to 'kill' you."

"It doesn't matter where you start, but where you finish."

WORDS, WHAT DO THEY MEAN?

A CHRISTIAN IS: "One beggar telling another beggar, where to get food."

CHARACTER IS: "How you act when you believe no one is watching you, and you have no one to impress."

HUMILITY IS: "Knowing how much I am loved by God, and realizing how much He has forgiven me."

GRACE IS: "God giving to us what we don't deserve."

MERCY IS: "God withholding from us what we do deserve."

COURAGE IS: "To put myself at risk for the safety of another."

CHANGE IS: "Not change, until I change."

GLORY IS: "All the excellence that God has, living on the inside of me."

CURSE IS: "Whatever can go wrong "will" go wrong."

SUCCESS IS: "Fulfilling the Divine plan God has for you."

FAITH IS: "Hoping for the manifestation of the things God has promised to you."

GRATITUDE IS: "Thanking God for answered prayer, before it happens"

VICTORIOUS CHRISTIAN IS: "One that believes God's Word, no matter what."

FREEDOM IS: "The state of being exempt from the control of another."

WORRY IS: "Meditating on your problem night and day."

WORDS ARE: "Containers for power."

STRESS IS: "Little faith in God.

GUILT IS: 'Believing you are wrong."

SHAME IS: "Believing you deserve the wrongs done to you."

FORGIVENESS IS: "My letting go of my right to get even."

HOPELESSNESS IS: "Believing God is not faithful."

SIN IS: "Knowingly or unknowingly acting in disobedience toward God, and refusing to go to Him for forgiveness."

FEAR IS: "False evidence appearing to be real."

IDOLATRY IS: "Putting your love, time, and attention, for anything or anybody in first place (including yourself), ahead of God."

THE WRATH OF GOD IS: "God giving up on a person to let him do what he desires."

SEARCH YOUR HEART MEANS: "To be honest with yourself."

TOLERANCE SAYS: "You can do anything or believe anything as long as you don't infringe on someone else's belief."

PATIENCE IS: "Not the ability to wait, but how you act while you are waiting."

TRUTH IS: "Having your sin exposed, and taking responsibility for it."

EDUCATION IS: "Not just getting knowledge, but it is acting on the knowledge you have learned."

MEEKNESS IS: "Power under control: i.e. a man acts in gentleness when it is in his power to act in severity."

RELIGION IS: "God has your will, but not your heart (trust)."

LOVE IS: "Forgiving those, and doing right to those who have done you wrong."

HATE IS: "Not being able to forgive others, and ignoring their needs."

WALKING IN THE SPIRIT IS: "Agreeing with God in your thoughts, words, and actions,"

WALKING IN THE FLESH IS: Living your life in your own understanding.

BLESS MEANS: "To speak well of people."

WORSHIP IS: "Living your life in the presence of God, always knowing that He is there with you."

REPENTANCE MEANS: "To turn around and go in God's direction."

SELF-RELIANT HEART IS: "Doing God's will in you own steam." (i.e. – Saul)

COMPASSION IS: "Just being there."

GIVING IS: "Doing what you can, with what you have, as long as you can."

A FOOL IS: "One who puts his confidence in his own ability to get the job done."

RIGHTEOUS ANGER: "Being ready to help when injustice is done to another."

UNRIGHTEOUS ANGER: "Being ready to kill when injustice is done to you."

PRAYER: "God pouring Himself into you."

PEACE: "Is not the absence of trouble, but the presence of God."

DANIEL, "THE PROPHET" AND 'A MAN GREATLY BELOVED BY GOD'

DANIEL 1-2

You may know me as Daniel who went to the lion's den and lived to tell the story. You may know me as the man who insisted on eating vegetables and water, with my three friends, as a way to set us apart for the living and "only" God. You may know my three friends, Shadrach, Meshach, and Abed-nego, as the men who would not bow down before the statue of Nebuchadnezzar, and were thrown into the fiery furnace, but lived to talk about it. Please let me tell you some things about myself that you may now know.

The Babylonians carried me into captivity in the third year of the reign of Jehoiakim, king of Judah, in about 606 B.C., when Nebuchadnezzar, king of Babylon, came into Jerusalem and besieged it; I was in captivity until the first year of King Cyrus's reign, about 536 B.C. It started when I was in my teens and lasted for seventy years.

Along with the "cream of the crop" taken from the captives, Nebuchadnezzar took the 'vessels of the house of God; into the "treasure house of his god" My three friends and I were made eunuchs (in fulfillment of prophecy) and were trained as advisors to the king of Babylon. In Isaiah 39:7 we read, "And of thy sons that shall issue from thee, which thou shall beget, shall they take away; and they shall be eunuchs in the palace of the king of Babylon." (McGee)

Did being a eunuch ruin my life; actually, God brought good from this to me, and glory to Himself. "I was able to study with the great minds of my day, in science, in math, and in the advanced knowledge that was in Babylon," (McGee) so I determined in my heart, that I would honor God in all that I did. The test of this honor was soon upon me, and my three friends. (Daniel 1:1 - 4)

"The king appointed to us a daily provision of the king's meat, and of the wine he drank. This, also, was to be our nourishment for three years, and then we were to be brought before the king for judgment. Because "we were Jews and under the Mosaic Law, we were not able to eat certain meats, certain fowls, and certain fish," (McGee) so I, "purposed in my heart that I would not defile myself with the portion of the king's meat, nor with the wine which he drank: therefore, I requested of the prince of the eunuchs that I might not defile myself." My friends stood with me in this. (Daniel 1:5 - 8)

The prince of the eunuchs said to me, "I fear my lord the king," for he has decided that you should eat meat and drink: I fear you will become weak and gaunt, and the king will surely have my 'head' for this.

Then I said to Melzar, whom the prince of the eunuchs had set over me and my friends, "prove thy servants, I beseech thee, (for) ten days; that during this time we will eat vegetables, and grain, and have only water as our drink, then look upon our countenance and see how we compare to the others, and then deal with us."

"So, he consented" to let us do this for the ten days, and then he would take us before the king. At the end of this time, we 'appeared to be fairer and fatter' than those who did eat the king's meat. "Thus, Melzar took away the meat and wine, and gave us the food we requested. Because we were faithful to God, He gave us knowledge and skill in all our learning, and He gave us wisdom; and I Daniel, had understanding in all visions and dreams." (Daniel 1:9 - 17)

When Nebuchadnezzar saw that we were healthier than the others, he tested us and "found us to be ten times better than all the magicians and astrologers that were in his realm." I continued as the king's advisor until my death. (Daniel 1:18 - 21)

"In the second year of the reign of Nebuchadnezzar, he dreamed a dream, and was very troubled in his sleep wondering what the dream meant, and what the future held for his empire. The king called his magicians, and his astrologers, and his sorcerers, and the Chaldreans," and he told them he had dreamed a dream, and that he was very troubled by it. (Daniel 2:1 - 2)

Nebuchadnezzar explained that he had an unusual dream, which he believed had some far-reaching significance as God had told him this. (McGee) The Chaldeans spoke to the king, saying, "Tell thy servants the dream and we will show you the interpretation."

The king answered the Chaldeans, "The thing is gone from me: if you will not make the dream known to me with the interpretation of it, you shall be cut in pieces, and your houses shall be made dunghill. But if you show me the dream, and the interpretation thereof, you shall receive from me gifts, and rewards, and great honor: so show me the dream and the interpretation of it." (Daniel 12:5-6)

Again, the wise men asked the king to tell them the dream and then they would show him the interpretation. The king replied, "I see plainly that you are trying to gain time: because you see capital punishment awaits you." (McGee) But he insisted they tell him the dream first, because he realized they had told him 'lying and corrupt words,' in the past. This was the test of their competence, to tell him the dream and then tell him the interpretation. He had not forgotten the dream, but he wanted an accurate interpretation, and knew he could only get this if they could tell him his dream first.

The Chaldeans answered before the king, and said, "There is not a man upon the earth that can show the king's matter: therefore, there is no king, lord, nor ruler, that asked such things from any magician, or astrologer, or Chaldean. It is a rare thing that the king requires, and there is none that can show it before the king, except the gods, whose dwelling is not the flesh." (Daniel 2:7 - 11) (They were right on this point, no man on earth could give the dream, only God could)

The king was furious and very angry, and commanded all the wise men of Babylon to be destroyed. The decree went forth that the wise men should be slain; and they sought my friends and me to be slain also. I was puzzled at the hasty and unjust decree of the king, so I approached, Arioch, the captain of the king's guard and asked him why the king made this decree? (McGee)

When he had told me all, I "went in, and desired of the king that he would give me time, and that I would show the king the interpretation." I then went to my home and made this thing known to my three companions, Shadrach, Meshach, and Aben-nego. We went to the 'God of heaven' to ask for His mercy on us and the rest of the wise men, that

He might show me the interpretation of the kings' dream (Daniel 2:12 - 18)

God did reveal the king's dream to me that very night, as I had the same dream as he had had. I answered God for giving me this wonderful answer to our prayers. I praised Him mightily; "Blessed is the name of God for ever and ever: for wisdom and might are His. He changes the times and the seasons: He removes kings, and sets up kings: He gives wisdom unto the wise, and knowledge to them that know understanding: He reveals the deep secret things: He knows what is in the darkness, and the light dwells in Him.

"I thank Thee, and praise Thee, O thou God my fathers, who has given me wisdom and might and has made known unto me now what we desired of Thee: for thou has now made known unto us the king's matter." (Daniel 2:19 - 23)

I then went to Arioch, who by the king's orders was to destroy the wise men of Babylon, Arioch took me to the king in haste, and told him he had found a man of the captives of Judah, that would make known unto the king the interpretation.

When I went before the king, he asked me, "Are you able to make known unto me the dream which I have seen, and the interpretation thereof?" I answered that no man could tell him what he desired to know, but I told him that 'there is a God in heaven that reveals secrets, and makes known to king Nebuchadnezzar what shall be in the latter days.'

I went on to explain to the king that I could take no credit, but only the God in heaven could reveal this dream to him, and I then told him what God had told me about the dream. (Daniel22:24 - 30)

"O king, you saw a great image. This great image, whose brightness was excellent, stood before you; and the form was terrible. This image's head was of fine gold, his breast and his arms of silver, his belly and his thighs of brass, his legs of iron, his feet part iron and part of clay. Thou saw a stone was cut out without hands, which smote the image upon his feet that were of iron and of clay, and broke the statue to pieces." (Daniel 2:31 - 35)

This was the dream I saw, and then I told the king the interpretation of it: "Thou, O king, art a king of kings: for the God of heaven has given thee a kingdom, power, and strength, and glory. And wheresoever the children of men dwell, the beasts of the field and the fowls of the heaven,

God has given into thy hand, and has made thee ruler over them all. Thou art this head of gold."

"After thee shall arise another kingdom inferior to thee, and another third kingdom of brass, which shall bear rule over all the earth. And the fourth kingdom shall be strong as iron: for as much as iron breaks in pieces and subdues all things: and as iron breaks all these, shall it break in pieces and bruise. And where as thou saw the feet and toes, part of potters' clay, and part of iron, the kingdom shall be divided; the kingdom shall be partly strong and partly broken. As iron cannot be mixed with clay, these kingdoms shall mingle themselves with the seed of men, but they shall not cleave one to another." (Daniel 2:36 - 43)

"And in the days of these kings shall the God of heaven set up a kingdom, which shall never be destroyed: and the kingdom shall not be left to other people, but it shall break in pieces and consume all these kingdoms, and it shall stand forever. As thou saw that the stone was cut out of the mountain without hands, and that it broke in pieces the iron, the brass, the clay, the silver, and the gold; the great God has made known to the king what shall come to pass hereafter: and the dream is certain, and the interpretation is sure." (Daniel 2:44 - 45)

"Then king Nebuchadnezzar fell upon his face and worshipped me, Daniel, and commanded that they should offer an oblation and sweet odors unto me." The king then said to me, 'Of a truth it is, that your God is a God of gods, and a Lord of kings, and revealer of secrets, seeing thou could reveal this secret.'

"Then the king made me a great man, and gave me many great gifts, and made me ruler over the whole province of Babylon, and chief of the governors over all the wise men of Babylon. I then requested of the king, that he set Shadrach, Meshach, and Abed-nego, over the affairs of the province of Babylon: but I sat in the gate of the king." (Daniel 2:46 - 49)

You in the 21st Century know that this dream has come to pass except for the stone, cut without hands, to break the statue into many pieces, and the final kingdom of God being set up. But you also know that you live in the time of the iron and clay of the feet and toes: so, the kingdom of God must be close at hand for you.

Let me tell you what empires each metal represents. The head of gold was Nebuchadnezzar's kingdom; In Jeremiah 27:5 - 11, we learn that God said: "I have made the earth, the man and the beast that are upon the ground, by my great power and by my out-stretched arm, and have given it unto whom it seemed meet (right) unto me. And now have I given all these lands into the hand of Nebuchadnezzar the king of Babylon, my servant; and the beasts of the field have I given him also to serve him. And all nations shall serve him and his son, and his son's son, until the very time of his land come..." 'God made Nebuchadnezzar the great world ruler, and there has been none like him since then.' (McGee)

"The kingdom which will come after Nebuchadnezzar will be inferior to his. The third one will be inferior to the second, and the fourth will be inferior to the third. That means the fourth one is the worst form of all. That is where you are today in the 21st century." (McGee)

The arms of silver represent Media and Persia. Babylon would be divided and given to the Medes and Persians. "The third kingdom would be a kingdom of brass and would 'bear rule over all the earth.' This is the Graeco- Macedonian Empire of Alexander the Great." (McGee) (Daniel 2:39)

The fourth kingdom is the kingdom of the latter days. I told Nebuchadnezzar that was the reason for the image; what the world would be like in the latter days. "The legs of iron, is the fourth kingdom, which is Rome. The feet of clay and iron mixed, is the last form of the Roman Empire. There is a definite deterioration from one kingdom to another." (McGee)

"The deterioration of these kingdoms is contrary to modern philosophy and opinion. Man believes that we are all getting better and better every day. We feel we have the best form of government and that we are a superior people, which is not true" according to this image that God told Nebuchadnezzar and me about, 'The definite division of sovereignty denotes weakness.' (McGee)

"The Roman Empire fell apart from within, no enemy destroyed it. Rome is living in the great nations of Europe today: Italy, France, Great Britain, Germany, and Spain are all part of the old Roman Empire: the law of Rome lives on, and her language also. No one speaks Latin today but it is basic to understanding French, Spanish and other languages. Her warlike spirit lives on also: Europe has been at war ever since the empire broke up in these kingdoms." (McGee)

There have been a lot of men who tried to put the Roman Empire together again, but they have not succeeded. The Roman Catholic

Church wanted to do it at the beginning of it's inception, Charlemagne attempted it, Napoleon tried to do it, and Hitler and Mussolini tried it too." (McGee)

"You ask, what the final end of this last kingdom of iron mixed with clay will be? The clay, I believe, represents the masses, the different nations of the ten toes. The iron speaks of the fact that Rome lives on in the final form of the old empire." (McGee)

I give you the answer in Daniel 2:44 - 45; "And in the days of these kings shall the God of heaven set up a kingdom, which shall never be destroyed: and the kingdom shall not be left to other people, but it shall break in pieces and consume all these kingdoms, and it shall stand for ever. Forasmuch, I saw that the stone was cut out of the mountain without hands, and that it broke in pieces the iron, the brass, the clay, the silver, and the gold; the great God hath made known to the kings what shall come to pass hereafter: and the dream is certain, and the interpretation thereof sure."

"The stone represents none other than the Lord Jesus Christ. This is not a man; this is God's Anointed. In Matthew 21:44, Jesus said, 'and whosoever shall fall on this stone shall be broken: but on whomsoever it shall fall, it will grind him to powder.' "For other foundation can no man lay than that is laid, which is Jesus Christ." (I Cor. 3:11) (McGee)

"If you fall on that Stone, that is rest in Him by faith. Come just as you are, without one plea, but that His blood was shed for me, you are broken, you come as a sinner, with nothing to offer, then He (Jesus) becomes the wonderful Stone to rest upon." This time Jesus is coming to the earth as a Judge to put down earth's rebellion against God. The reference here is to the second coming of Christ to the earth, which is depicted for you in detail in Revelation 19:11 - 21. His coming is going to be climactic, catastrophic, and cataclysmic.' (McGee)

"My friend, you need to trust Christ as Savior, especially in the 21st century, because you are living in the toes, so close to His return. Please bow to Him and acknowledge Him today as 'The Stone,' or the Stone will be coming to you. It is better to come to the Stone while there is still time, you will never regret it or lose anything." (McGee)

Nebuchadnezzar set up a golden image before the people, and they were to fall down and worship it whenever they heard the sound of the "cornet, flute, harp, sackbut, psaltery, and all kinds of music." My three friends called, "Shadrach, Meshach, and Abed-nego (their Babylonian names)," had not been bowing at the sound of the music, because they recognized their God only, so the Chaldeans accused them before the king.

This infuriated Nebuchadnezzar a great deal, so he had the three of them brought before him, to give them a chance to change their minds. He asked them, "Is it true, O Shadrach, Meshach, and Abed-nego, you do not serve my gods, nor worship the golden image which I have set up? Now, if you be ready at what time you hear the sound of the music, you fall down and worship the image which I have made; well: but if you worship not, you shall be cast the same hour into the midst of a burning fiery furnace; and who is that God that shall deliver you out of my hands? (Daniel 3:9 - 15)

My three friends answered and said to the king, "O Nebuchadnezzar we have carefully weighed the consequences of refusing to obey the king. If it be so, our God whom we serve is able to deliver us from the burning fiery furnace, and He will deliver us out of your hand, O king. But if not, be it known unto you, O King, that we will not serve thy gods, nor worship the golden image which you have set up." (Daniel 3:17 - 18) (McGee)

Then Nebuchadnezzar was full of fury, and "he vented his anger against these three men whom he had previously favored." He commanded that the furnace be heated to seven times hotter than usual. He bound them fully clothed and had them thrown into the "fiery furnace," 'Those chosen to cast the captives into the furnace, that Nebuchadnezzar could look into, were slain from the heat. He expected the three men to expire at once, but he was amazed to see them alive and walking about in the fire.'

"Another amazing fact was to see a fourth Man whom Nebuchadnezzar described as being in the form 'like the Son of God.'" Of course, the king did not know our God, but he recognized Him as a god. We believe that "fourth Man was the Son of God, the preincarnate Christ." (McGee)

"Nebuchadnezzar came near to the mouth of the burning fiery furnace, and said, Shadrach, Meshach, and Abed-nego, you servants of the most high God, come forth, and come to me. My friends came forth of the midst of the fire, and the princes, governors, and captains, and the king's counselors, being gathered together, saw these men upon whose bodies the fire had no power, nor the smell of fire had passed on them." 'This was a clear-cut miracle.' (Daniel 3:19 - 27) (McGee)

Then Nebuchadnezzar spoke, and said, "Blessed be the God if Shadrach, Meshach, and Abed-nego, who has sent His angel, and delivered his servants that trusted in Him, and have changed the king's word, and yielded their bodies, that they might not serve nor worship any god, except their own God. Therefore, I make a decree, "That every people, nation, and language, which speak anything amiss against the God of Shadrach, Meshach, and Abed-nego, shall be cut in pieces, and their houses shall be cut in pieces, and their houses shall be made a dunghill: because there is no other God that can deliver after this sort. Then the king promoted my friends in the providence of Babylon." (Daniel 3:28 - 30)

Nebuchadnezzar, after the incident of the "fiery furnace," acknowledged God's rule and God's kingdom, is above all, and above his, and he sends a message of peace to 'all peoples, nations, and languages' of his kingdom. "Nebuchadnezzar the king, unto all people, nations, and languages, that dwell in all the earth; Peace be multiplied unto you." (Daniel 4:1)

Then Nebuchadnezzar had a dream that disturbed him very much. "Again, he called in the wise men to give interpretation, and again they could not. I was called as a Spirit-filled man that interpretations were given to by God, to tell the dream to Nebuchadnezzar." (McGee)

"The dream was of a tree that grew tall to heaven, wide enough to fill the whole earth. It was a fruit tree that provided fruit for all. Beasts stood in its shadow, and the birds rested in its branches." There was a 'watcher and an holy one (that) came down from heaven; he cried aloud and said thus,' "Hew down the tree, and cut off his branches, shake off his leaves, 'and scatter his fruit: let the beasts get away from under it and the fowls from his branches: Nevertheless leave the stump of his roots in the earth, even with a band of iron and brass, in the tender grass of the field; and let it be wet with the dew of heaven, and let his portion be with the beasts of the field, till seven times pass over him."

I Daniel, gave this interpretation: "The tree is Nebuchadnezzar and he will be cut down, but not totally rejected. For seven years, Nebuchadnezzar was to live with and like the beasts of the field. He himself and no one else will recognize him during this time. The reason for this trouble was that Nebuchadnezzar was lifted up with pride. He asked himself, "Is not this great Babylon, that I have built for the house of the kingdom by the might of my power, and for honor of my majesty?" (Daniel 4:30) (McGee)

While Nebuchadnezzar was still-speaking a voice came from heaven: "O KING NEBUCHADNEZZAR, TO THEE IT IS SPOKEN; THE KINGDOM IS DEPARTED FROM THEE. THEY SHALL DRIVE THEE FROM MEN, AND THY DWELLING SHALL BE WITH THE BEASTS OF THE FIELD: THEY SHALL MAKE THEE TO EAT GRASS AS OXEN, AND SEVEN TIMES SHALL PASS OVER THEE, UNTIL THOU KNOW THAT THE MOST HIGH RULETH IN THE KINGDOM OF MAN, AND GIVETH IT TO WHOMSOEVER HE WILL." (Daniel 4:31 - 33)

"At the end of the seven years Nebuchadnezzar lifted up his eyes unto heaven, and his understanding returned to him, he blessed the most High, and praised and honored Him that lives forever, whose dominion is an everlasting dominion, and whose kingdom is from generation to generation." (Daniel 4:34)

"Nebuchadnezzar's reason returned to him. His position as king of Babylon was restored to him, and his officials once again surrounded him. The kingdom was not jeopardized during his long period of absence, and added majesty came to him because he had now come to the knowledge of the living and true God." (McGee)

Many years later, Nabonidus's son, Belshazzar, was acting as king of Babylon in his father's absence while he (Belshazzar's father) was at war, away from Babylon. "Belshazzar made a great feast to a thousand of his lords, and drank wine before the thousand. While this feast was going on, the armies of Gobryas, Median general, were in full view of the city. Belshazzar believed that Babylon was constructed of brick: it was three hundred feet high, and wide enough for four chariots to travel abreast around the city walls. There were enough supplies within the walls of the city to eat and drink for years, and the Euphrates River was channeled right through the middle of the city." (Daniel 5:1) (McGee)

"Belshazzar's feast may have been in defiance of the enemy on the outside, or perhaps he wanted to build up the morale of those within. This feast started with a big cocktail party. Liquor has been a prop for weak men and women all though the centuries. In the 21st century alcohol is still the leading drug problem in the countries of the world. Liquor is a big home wrecker, and many nations have gone down because of liquor." (McGee)

"Belshazzar in his drunken state, decided to bring the golden and silver vessels which Nebuchadnezzar had taken out of the temple which was in Jerusalem; so that the king, and his princes, his wives, and his concubines, might drink from them." (Daniel 5:2 - 3)

"By using these vessels, Belshazzar is defying God, because these are Holy vessels, set aside by God, for the use of God in Israel." Now Belshazzar and his friends are toasting the gods of Babylon with these Holy vessels. 'Their sin is cloaked as worship and veiled in blasphemy in the name of religion.' (McGee)

"In the same hour came forth fingers of a man's hand, and wrote over against the candlestick upon the plaster of the wall of the king's palace: and the king saw the part of the hand that wrote. Then the king's countenance was changed, and his thoughts troubled him, so that the joints of his loins were loosed, and his knees smote one against another. The king cried aloud to bring in the astrologers. Whosoever shall read this writing, and show me the interpretation shall be clothed with scarlet, and have a chain of gold about his neck, and shall be the third ruler of the kingdom." (Daniel 5:5 - 7)

The king's wise men came, but could not interpret the writing. The queen (the wife of Nebuchadnezzar) came to the banquet hall and told her grandson that there was a man in the kingdom, named Daniel, who could decipher this writing. (McGee)

So, I was brought before the king. I spurned the gifts he offered me, but I preached a very pointed and powerful sermon to Belshazzar on how God had given the kingdom to Nebuchadnezzar, and how he had been an absolute sovereign whom no man could question or hinder, and whose wishes and whims were the law of the land. However, when Nebuchadnezzar became filled with pride, God humbled him to a tragic episode. Then I reminded Belshazzar of Nebuchadezzar's humiliating experience. This is a reminder to all of us that God only destroys those who have known the truth and have refused it." (McGee)

Now I conclude my sermon by stating that the handwriting, on the wall, was from God whom Belshazzar had spurned and ridiculed and blasphemed. He now had an opportunity to receive the truth of God and who He is , but he turned it down. I read the words on the wall: "MENE, MENE, TEKEL, UPHARSIN." This is the interpretation of the thing: 'MENE; God has numbered thy kingdom, and finished it. TEKEL; Thou art weighed in the balances, and art found wanting. PERES; Thy kingdom is divided, and given to the Medes and Persians.' (Daniel 5:20 - 28)

Belshazzar commands they put the robe of scarlet on me and the chain of gold around my neck, and proclaim me the third ruler of the kingdom. But it was too late for Belshazzar to save himself. "That very night Belshazzar was slain by the Chaldeans and Darius the Median took the kingdom." At the very time that this banquet was being held, the Medes were marching underneath the walls of Babylon where the waters of the canal had flowed. These waters, unbeknown to Belshazzar, had been cut off and channeled back into the main stream of the Euphrates River. The army marched into the inner city where the palace was located and thus killed Belshazzar.' (Daniel 5:29 - 31) (McGee)

"Now that the Media-Persian Empire is ruling, we have moved into the 'arms of silver' in the dream of Nebuchadnezzar. Darius Cyaxares 11 is the ruler if the kingdom; he has "an hundred and twenty princes" who shared the responsibility and leadership with him. Over this group Darius placed 'three presidents' who served as liaison officers between the princes and the king. These presidents were to prevent the princes from stealing from or undermining the king in any way. I was one of these three presidents. Because God had placed "His excellent spirit in me," I became to be placed next to the king in position and power." (Daniel 6:1 - 3)

Because I was in this coveted position, there were those who were jealous of me. They watched me to see if they could discover a weak spot in my character so that could use it against me. Since the Lord had greatly blessed me, they could only fault my belief in the one and only God. They went to Darius and flattered him that he should make a decree, "that whosoever shall ask a petition of any God or man for thirty days, except the king, shall be cast into the den of lions."

"They knew that I kneeled to pray toward Jerusalem three times a day, 'to give thanks before God.' Because of the decree, they watched me to see what I would do? I knelt to pray, before my window, as usual, and made supplication before my God." (Daniel 6:6 - 11) (McGee)

My accusers ran to the king with the news that I had broken the royal statute by making my petition to God, three times a day. Because Darius could not change his own law, I was to be put in the den of lions. Darius regretted his decision now, but it was too late. I was brought to Darius and "cast into the lion's den." The king said to me, 'Thy God whom thou servest continually, he will deliver thee.' This was more of a question than true belief in my God. (Daniel 6:12 - 16)

"A stone was put over the month of the lion's den: and the king sealed it with his own signet, and with the signet of his lords; that the purpose might not be changed concerning me." 'Now, the king was very distressed over my situation and he spent the night fasting: no music was played before him, and he didn't sleep at all, all night. (Daniel 6:17 - 18)

The king arose very early in the morning, and went in haste to the den of lions. He cried to me in a loud voice, 'O Daniel, servant of the living God, is thy God, whom thou servest continually, able to deliver thee from the lions?' "I called back to the king, 'O king live forever. My God has sent His angel, and has shut the lion's mouths, that they have not hurt me: for as much as before Him innocence was found in me; and also, before thee, O king, have I done no hurt.' (Daniel 6:19 - 22)

"The king was exceeding glad that I was alive, and commanded they take me up out of the lion's den; and no hurt was found on me." 'The dastardly plot of those who were my enemies was now uncovered. The king had them, and their families, thrown into the lion's den. The lion's pounced upon them and in all viciousness broke their bones and ate them alive. (Daniel 6:23 - 24)

Darius sent out a worldwide decree: "Peace be multiplied unto you." 'Darius commands men to fear the God of Daniel, and testifies that He is the living God, and that He is sovereign.' "I now prospered in the reign of Darius, and in the reign of Cyrus the Persian." (Daniel 6:25 - 28) (McGee)

I Daniel, had dreams and visions while in captivity in Babylon, coming at different times: in the first reign of King Belshazzar, I had the vision of the four beasts; in the third year of King Belshazzar, I had more prophetic understanding of this first vision. In the first year of Darius, I had the "prophecy of the Seventy Weeks." In the third year of Cyrus, I had a vision of the final "willful ruler."

The four great beasts came up from the sea, diverse one from another. The first was like a lion, and had eagle's wings: I beheld till the wings thereof were plucked, and it was lifted up from the earth, and made stand upon the feet as a man, and a man's heart was given to it. And behold another beast, a second, like to a bear, and it raised up itself on one side, and it had three ribs in the mouth of it, between the teeth of it: and they said thus unto it, 'Arise, devour much flesh.'

"After this I beheld, and lo another, like a leopard, which had upon the back of it four wings of a fowl; the beast had also four heads; and dominion was given to it. After this I saw in the night visions, and behold a fourth beast, dreadful and terrible, and strong exceedingly; and it had great iron teeth: it devoured and broke in pieces and stamped the residue with the feet of it: and it was diverse from all the beasts that were before it; and it had ten horns." (Daniel 7:3 - 7)

In my vision of the four beasts I see, "the lion, the bear, the panther (or leopard), and a composite beast which is called the nondescript beast." "These beasts correspond to the four metals in the image of Nebuchadnezzar's vision. The head of Gold, and the two-winged Lion, is the nation of Babylon; the Arms of Silver, and the Bear with three ribs in its mouth, the nation Media-Persia; the Sides of brass, and the Panther (leopard) with four wings on its back, is the nation of Greco-Macedonia; the Legs of Iron, and the Composite beast which is strong exceedingly; has great iron teeth: and it has ten horns, which represents the Roman Empire; the Feet of Iron and Clay represents the Roman Empire after it fell apart. The ten horns represent the ten toes of the image and the ten most powerful nations that rule in the end times; where you are living now, my friend, in the 21st century." (Daniel 7:1 - 16) (McGee)

As a connection to the 21st Century may I offer another explanation of these beasts? (1) The lion represents England and the eagle wings represent the United States. England's wings were clipped when the U.S. broke away and became an independent nation. The eagle now represents the United States. (2) The bear represents the family; the bear is the man or the head of the family. The family had devoured itself in divorce, violence, cohabitation without marriage, and the demand of same sex marriage. (3) The Panther has four wings and four heads. These four represent the four parts of a democratic government: the President, the Congress, the Judicial Branch, and the People. It has dominion in the earth. (4) The Composite beast is strong exceedingly, and has ten horns, which represents the end times or modern day culture: this represents the businessmen, or business that is conducted in the world. Business represents money and the making of money. The world is consumed with making money, and spending money, and getting money, and wanting money. Illicit sex is also a part of the "love of money." Sex has taken the world by storm with pornography, movies videos, and the computer. (McGee)

"These great beasts, which are four, are four kings, which shall arise out of the earth. But the saints of the most High shall take the kingdom, and possess the kingdom forever, even for ever and ever." (Daniel 7:17 - 18) The four kings are Nebuchadnezzar and Alexander the Great, to name two of them. The saints represent those righteous ones who believe in God. (McGee)

"I wrote of the fourth beast; 'Then I would know the truth of the fourth beast, which was diverse from all the others, exceeding dreadful, whose teeth were of iron, and his nails of brass; which devoured, broke in pieces, and stamped the residue with his feet; And of the ten horns that were in his head, and of the other which came up, and before whom three fell; even of that horn that had eyes, and a mouth that spoke very great things, whose look was more stout than his fellows." (Daniel 7:19 - 20)

"Everything here speaks of power and fierceness; the ferocity of the beast, with its iron teeth and brass nails. Rome was hated by her captive nations. Rome rejected the Son of God, the Savior, through her puppet Pilate, who asked the cynical contemptuous question of Jesus, 'What is truth?' Rome crucified Jesus and persecuted the church." (McGee)

"I beheld, and the same horn made war with the saints, and prevailed against them. Until the Ancient of days (Jesus) came, and judgment was given to the saints of the most High; and the time came that the saints possessed the kingdom. (Daniel 7:21 - 22)

"It should be noted that Rome will again be a world power under Antichrist, and in Revelation 13:7 we are told, 'And it was given unto him to make war with the saints and to overcome them: and power was given him over all kindreds, and tongues, and nations.' "The Ancient of days" is Christ; He is the only One Who is going to be able to put down Antichrist (McGee)

"And he shall speak great words against the most High, and shall wear out the saints of the most High, and think to change times and laws: and they shall be given into his hand until a time and times and the dividing of time. But Judgment shall sit, and they shall take away his dominion, to consume and to destroy it unto the end."

"The characteristics of Antichrist are that he is against God and against Christ. That is one of the meanings of 'antichrist'; the other meaning is to "imitate Christ." I believe that the two beasts of Revelation 13 represent these two aspects of Antichrist: (1) that he is against Christ and a blasphemer; and (2) that he is a false prophet, and attempts to imitate Christ; although he acts like a lamb, he really is a wolf in sheep's clothing." (McGee)

"And thinks to change times and laws,' means the little horn will change customs and laws. The period of the little horn's reign is of short duration. The Lamb who is the executor of the judgment determines "The judgment shall sit," and it is the agreement of all God's created, and redeemed intelligences of heaven, that the beast must be put down. His dominion must be ended, and he himself judged. 'The judgment shall sit,' means it cannot be changed." (McGee)

I Daniel, "was much troubled by these visions and my countenance changed in me: but I kept the matter in my heart." (Daniel 7:28)

Next, I had the vision "of the ram and he goat." 'I saw in my vision, that I was at Susa, the capital of Media-Persia in the palace or "near the fortress', which is in the Province of Elam, and I was by the river of Ulai, which is the Kerkhah River which flowed by Susa. This vision concerns the second and third world empires. You know now, that this vision was fulfilled within two hundred years. Some try to say I wrote this after it's happening, but God is into the miraculous, and thus the real author of this vision. (Daniel 8:2) (McGee)

"Then I lifted up my eyes, and saw, and behold, there stood before the river a ram which had two horns: and the two horns were high; but one was higher than the other, and the higher came up last. I saw the ram pushing westward, and northward, and southwards; so that no beasts could stand before him, neither was there any that could deliver out of his hand; but he did according to his will, and became great.

"And as I was considering, behold, an he goat came from the west on the face of the whole earth, and touched not the ground: and the goat had a notable horn between his eyes. He came to the ram that had two horns, which I had seen standing before the river and ran unto him in the fury of his power. And I saw him come close unto the ram, and he was moved with (anger) against him, and smote the ram, and broke his two horns: and there was no power in the ram to stand before him, but he cast him down to the ground, and stamped upon him: and there was none that could deliver the ram out his hand.

"Therefore, the he goat waxed very great: and when he was strong, the great horn was broken; and for it came up four notable ones toward the four winds of heaven. And out of one of them came forth a little horn, which waxed exceeding great, toward the south, and toward the east, and toward the pleasant land (this is Israel).

"Yea, he magnified himself even to the prince of the host, and by him the daily sacrifice was taken away, and the place of his sanctuary was cast down. And a host was given him against the daily sacrifice by reason of transgression, and it cast down the truth to the ground; and it practiced, and prospered. Then I heard one saint speaking, and another saint said unto that certain saint, who spoke, 'How long shall be the vision concerning the daily sacrifice, and the transgression of desolation, to give both the sanctuary and the host to be trodden under foot? And he said unto me, "Unto two thousand and three hundred days; then shall the sanctuary be cleansed.'" (Daniel 8:3 - 14)

I, Daniel wanted to know the meaning of this vision. The angel Gabriel came to explain the vision, but I was very afraid, and "fell upon my face. While he was speaking with me, I was in a deep sleep on my face, toward the ground: but he touched me, and set me upright. He told me that this vision was for the time of the end." 'This vision was for the fulfillment in Antiochus' and for the "end of the Times of Gentiles." (McGee)

"The ram represents the kings of Media and Persia. The 'rough goat' is the king of Greece, and the "great horn" is the first king. Alexander the Great. The 'little horn' is Antiochus Epiphanes that took Syria. He is a picture of the coming Antichrist. Antiochus slaughtered "The Holy People," or Israel. He was as bad as Hitler, but is a picture of Antichrist who is coming. (McGee)

"Antiochus did four things, on a small scale, that the Antichrist will do throughout the whole world:" (1) 'He shall cause craft to prosper in his hand. 'We are told in Revelation 13:17 that no man will be able to buy or sell save the one who has the mark of the beast. He will control the economy with vengeance. (2) "He shall magnify himself in his heart," Revelation 13:5 says that 'he is given a mouth speaking great things and blasphemies.' Humility is not a characteristic of the Antichrist! He is like Satan who was filled with pride. (3) "By peace shall destroy many." He comes in as a lamb, but he goes out as a lion. He brings war and a false peace. (4) 'He stood up against the prince of princes.' He will oppose and fight against Christ. Revelation 13 tells us he is against Christ." (Daniel 8:23 - 25) (McGee)

"I was told that the vision would be for the distant future: 'for it shall be for many days.' I fainted and was sick for several days after this vision for I was astonished at the vision, but no one understood it." (Daniel 8:26 - 27) (McGee)

I, Daniel knew that prayer was my connection to God, and a great privilege that I took very seriously; it was because I prayed openly three times a day to my Lord, that I was put into the lion's den. And because of answered prayer, I was spared from the lion's den.

In the first year of Darius the Mede or Cyaxares 11, I began to wonder about the future of my people, the Israelites. I turned to the prophet Jeremiah who said that Israel would be in captivity for seventy years. I was an old man of over eighty, when I pondered the will of God for us now. In Jeremiah 29:10 I read, "And this whole land shall be a desolation and an astonishment; and these nations shall serve the king of Babylon seventy years for thus saith the Lord, 'That after seventy years be accomplished at Babylon I will visit you, in causing you to return to this place."

Because I read these words, "I set my face unto the Lord God, with fasting, and sackcloth, and ashes. I said, 'O Lord, the great and dreadful (worthy of reverence) God, keeping the covenant and mercy to them that love Him, and to them that keep his commandments. We have sinned, and have committed iniquity, and have done wickedly, and have rebelled, even by departing from Thy precepts and from Thy judgments: Neither have we harkened unto Thy servants the prophets, which spoke in Thy name to our kings, our princes, and our fathers, and to all the people of the land.

"O Lord, righteousness belongs unto Thee, but unto us (our shame), as at this day; to the men of Judah, and to the inhabitants of Jerusalem, and unto all Israel, that are near, and that are far off (scattered), through all the countries…because of their trespass… against Thee.

"Yes, all Israel have transgressed Thy law…they (did) not obey Thy voice; therefore, the curse is poured upon us, and the oath that is written in the Law of Moses…because we have sinned against Him. As it is written in the Law of Moses, all this evil is come upon us: yet made we not our prayer before the Lord our God, that we might turn from our iniquities, and understand Thy truth. Therefore (has) the Lord watched upon the evil, and brought it upon us: for the Lord our God is righteous in all His works which He (does): for we obeyed not His voice."

"O Lord our God; You have brought thy people forth out of the land of Egypt with a mighty hand. Now therefore, O our God, hear the prayer of thy servant, and his supplications, and cause Thy face to shine upon Thy sanctuary that is desolate, for the Lord's sake. O Lord, hear; O Lord, forgive; O Lord, hearken and do; defer not, for thine own sake, O my God : for Thy city and Thy people are called by Thy name." (Daniel 9:1 - 19)

"And while I was speaking, and praying, and confessing my sin and the sin of my people Israel, and presenting my supplication before the Lord my God for the holy mountain of my God (Jerusalem and the kingdom of God). Yes, while I was speaking in prayer, the man Gabriel…touched me about the time of the evening oblation (sacrifice) at Jerusalem, or three o'clock in the afternoon).' God sent Gabriel immediately to answer me.

"He informed me, and talked with me, and said, 'O Daniel, I am now come forth to give thee skill and understanding. At the beginning of thy supplications the commandment came forth, and I am come to show thee; for thou are greatly beloved: therefore, understand the matter, and consider the vision.'" (Daniel 9:22 - 23)

"Seventy weeks ate determined upon thy people and upon thy holy city, to finish the transgression, and to make reconciliation for iniquity, and to bring in everlasting righteousness, and to seal up the vision and prophecy, and to anoint the most Holy." (Daniel 9:24)

"Seventy weeks" does not mean weeks of seven days. The Hebrew word for "seven" is shabua, meaning "a unit of measure." So here, Seventy Weeks means seventy sevens. It could be seventy sevens of anything. In this context, I Daniel, had been reading in Jeremiah about years, seventy years. Jeremiah had been preaching and writing that the captivity would be for seventy years. The seventy years of captivity were the specific penalty for violating seventy Sabbatic years. That would be seventy sevens, a total of 490 years. In those 490 years, Israel had violated exactly seventy Sabbatic years; so, they would be in captivity for seventy years. "To fulfill the word of the Lord by the mouth of Jeremiah, until the land had enjoyed her Sabbaths: for as long as she lay desolate, she kept Sabbath, to fulfill threescore and ten years." (2 Chron. 36:21) (McGee)

1 week = 7 years

70 weeks = 490 years

70 weeks divided into 3 periods:

7 weeks–62 weeks–1 week

"I Daniel was puzzled as to how the end of the seventy years of captivity would fit into the long period of Gentile world dominion which I saw in the previous visions. However, the Seventy Weeks, or the seventy sevens, answer two questions. Israel's kingdom will not come immediately. The seventy sevens must run their course. These seventy sevens fit into the Times of the Gentiles and run concurrently with them.

"They are broken up to fit into Gentile times. The word for 'determined' literally means "cutting off." These seventy sevens for Israel and the Times of the Gentiles will both come to an end at the same time, that is, at the second coming of Christ. This is important to know in the correct understanding of the prophecy.

"The Seventy weeks concern 'thy people,' meaning my people. That would be Israel; however, Israel means "strives with God" or 'one man with God.' And they concern "thy holy city," which can be none other than Jerusalem. Six things are to be accomplished:

(1) 'To finish the transgression:' This refers to the transgression of Israel. The cross provided the redemption for sin—for the sin of the nation, but all must accept it. In the 21st century the word has gone out to the ends of the earth that there is redemption for mankind. But in that last "week" God says, "And I will pour upon the house of David, and upon the inhabitants of Jerusalem, the spirit of grace and

supplications…" (Zechariah 12:10) Zechariah 13:1: 'In that day there shall be a fountain opened to the house of David and to the inhabitants of Jerusalem for sin and for uncleanness' You know, that has not been opened yet. As you look at the land of Israel, you will know this has not been fulfilled.

(2) "To make an end of sins." "The national sins of Israel will come to an end at the second coming of Christ. They and all nations are sinners as individuals and as a nation. Israel and all nations have made mistakes as a nation, but God will make an end to that.

(3) "To make reconciliation for iniquity." "During this period of Seventy Weeks, God has provided redemption through the death and resurrection of Christ. This is for Jew and Gentile alike.

(4) "And to bring in everlasting righteousness" refers to the return of Christ at the end of the 490 years to establish the kingdom.

(5) "To seal up the vision and prophecy," 'means that all will be fulfilled, which will vindicate this prophecy as well as all other prophecies in Scripture.'

(6) "To anoint the most Holy, has reference to the anointment of the holy of holies in the millennial temple about which Ezekiel spoke." (Ezekiel 41-46) (McGee)

You my friend, have access to all of history and the complete Scripture. This makes the vision of prophecy that I had, more understandable for you. But I had more prophecy given to me.

"Know therefore and understand, that from the going forth of the commandment to restore and to build Jerusalem unto Messiah the Prince shall be seven weeks, and threescore and two weeks: the street shall be built again, and the wall, even in troublous times."

"And after threescore and two weeks shall Messiah be cut off, but not for himself: and the people of the prince that shall come shall destroy the city and the sanctuary; and the end thereof shall be with a flood, and unto the end of the war desolations are determined."

"And he shall confirm the covenant with many for one week: and in the midst of the week, he shall cause the sacrifice and the oblation to cease, and for the overspreading of abominations he shall make it desolate, even until the consummation, and that determined shall be poured upon the desolate." (Daniel 9:25 - 27)

"The starting point for this period of 490 years is essential to the correct understanding of the prophecy. Since this period is projected into the Times of the Gentile, it must fit into secular history and originate from some date connected with the Times of the Gentiles. I believe that the decree of Artaxerxes in the twentieth year of his reign (Nehemiah 2:1-8) meets the requirement of the commandment to rebuild the city of Jerusalem was issued in the month Nisan 445 B.C. So, this is my starting point." (You realize I am giving you understanding I did not have when I got this prophecy: I am telling you what you know in the 21st century.)

"The first seven weeks of forty-nine years bring us to 397 B.C. and to Malachi and the end of the Old Testament. These were 'troublous times,' as witnessed to by both Nehemiah and Malachi. Sixty-two weeks, or 434 years, bring us to the Messiah. Sir Robert Anderson in his book, The Coming Prince, has worked out the time schedule, from the first of the month Nisan to the tenth of Nisan (April 6) A.D. 32, are 173,880 days. Dividing them according to the Jewish year of 360 days, he arrives at 483 years (69) sevens. On this day Jesus rode into Jerusalem, offering Himself for the first time, publicly and officially as the Messiah."

"After the 69 weeks, or 483 years, there is a time break. Between the sixty - ninth and Seventieth Week two events of utmost importance are to take place:

(1) Messiah will be cut off. This was the crucifixion of Christ, the great mystery and truth of the gospel: 'From that time forth began Jesus to show unto his disciples, how that He must go to Jerusalem, and be killed, and be raised again the third day' (Matthew 16:21). "That whosoever believeth in him should not perish, but have eternal life" (John 3:15).

(2) "Destruction of Jerusalem, which took place in A.D. 70, when Titus the Roman was the instrument. The final 'week' (the seventieth), a period of seven years, is projected into the future and does not follow chronologically the other sixty-nine. The time gap between the sixty-nine and seventieth weeks is the age of grace—unknown to me or to the prophets (Ephesians 3:1 - 12; 1 Peter 1:10 - 12). The Seventieth Week

is eschatological; it is the final period and is yet unfulfilled as you are reading this.

"The prince" is a Roman; he is the little horn' that I referred to; he is "the beast" of Revelation 13. He will make a covenant with Israel and Israel will accept him, but in the midst of the "week" he will break his covenant by placing an image in the temple (Revelation 13). This is the abomination of desolation, or the Great Tribulation period (Matthew 24:15 - 26) Only the coming of Christ can end this frightful period." (Matthew 24:27 - 31) (McGee wrote the previous six paragraphs)

"In the third year of Cyrus king of Persia, a thing was revealed unto me Daniel, whose name was called Belteshazzar; and the thing was true, but the time appointed was long: and (I) understood the thing, and had understanding of the vision (because it was made crystal clear to me)." (Daniel 10:1)

"I Daniel was mourning for three full weeks, I ate no pleasant bread, neither came flesh nor wine in my mouth, neither did I anoint myself at all, till three whole weeks were fulfilled. I was by the side of the great river, which is Hiddekel." (Daniel 10:3 - 4)

"Then I lifted up mine eyes, and I looked, and behold a certain man clothed in linen, whose loins were girded with fine gold of Uhaz: His body also was like the beryl, and his face as the appearance of lightning, and his eyes as lamps of fire, and his arms and his feet like in color to polished brass and the voice of his words like the voice of a multitude." (Daniel 10:5 - 6)

"And I Daniel alone saw the vision: for the men that were with me saw not the vision: but a great quaking fell upon them, so that they fled to hide themselves. Therefore, I was left alone, and saw this great vision and there remained no strength in me: for my comeliness was turned in me into corruption, and I retained no strength. Yet I heard the voice of His words: and when I heard the voice of His words, then was I in a deep sleep on my face, and my face toward the ground." (Daniel 10:7 - 9)

"I believe this 'certain man' was the Lord Jesus in His post incarnate state. Christ, in His office as priestly Intercessor and Judge and the great Shepherd of the sheep. My experience here is like unto the experience that the apostle Paul had on the road to Damascus when he alone saw the glorified Christ, as reported in Scripture in Acts 9:7 - 8." (McGee)

"And behold, a hand touched me, which set me upon my knees and upon the palms of my hands. And he said to me, 'O Daniel, a man greatly beloved, understand the words that I speak unto thee, and stand upright: for unto thee am I now sent.' And when he had spoken this word unto me, I stood trembling. Then he said to me, "Fear not, Daniel: for from the first day that thou did set thine heart to understand, and to chasten thyself before thy God, thy words were heard, and I am come for thy words, but the prince if the kingdom of Persia withstood me one and twenty days: but, lo, Michael, one of the chief princes, came to help me; and I remained there with the kings of Persia." (Daniel 10:10 - 13)

"This vision made me realize that my words were heard by God on the first day that I prayed unto Him, but there is heavenly warfare going on. Yours and my mind is a place of this warfare, and it is very significant to each person and should be taken seriously. It is the unseen conflict between good and evil, light and darkness, God and Satan. Many times, our prayers are short-circuited by the evil one. We desire the blessings of God in our life, but we must 'take the Word by force,' it is not enough to want the blessings. ("O Lord, I wish you would send healing to my body; I wish you would send the money I need to pay all my bills; I wish you would make my country strong; I wish people would stop harassing me"): desires are not the same as taking the blessings of God by faith and perseverance. (McGee)

"Often public prayer and prayer meetings are dead because those praying do not realize that there is a battle going on. There is a war that must be fought and won. In 2 Corinthians 10:3 - 5 Paul writes this to you: 'For though we walk in the flesh, we do not war after the flesh: (For the weapons of our warfare are not carnal, but mighty through God to the pulling down of strong holds:) Casting down imaginations, and every high thing that exalteth itself against the knowledge of God, and bringing into captivity every thought to the obedience of Christ.'" (McGee)

Take your life in Christ seriously: recognize your need for the power of the Holy Spirit in your life, and practice the presence of Christ within you. Life and death is a privilege, a gift from the Almighty Father that must not be cast aside out of anger, denial, or a whim.

My heavenly messenger said to me, "Now I am come to make thee understand what shall befall thy people in the latter days: for yet the vision is for many days." (Daniel 10:14) I learned that this vision is for 'my people,' it is for "the latter days." And 'it will not be accomplished for a long period of time.'

I was greatly drained of "all my strength and breath," but the 'angel came and touched me and he strengthened me'. He told me he must get back to the battle that was going on: "Now I will return to fight with the prince of Persia, but I will show thee that which is noted in the scripture of truth." 'He turned me to the Word of God.' I would not hear or see anything that is contradictory to the Word of God.' You, my friend, have the Word of God as the only weapon available for effective use in spiritual warfare. It is called the "sword of the Spirit," and please let me tell you these truths I have recorded for you, and then use this sword as God's words in you. (Daniel 10:15 - 21) (McGee)

"What I record next has caused my critics to insist that I wrote this after it had become history, because of it's detailed accuracy. I did not live to see it fulfilled. God gave this to me to record, to comfort and encourage those beloved ones that would have to live through the difficult days I describe." (McGee)

"The angel told me that there would be four notable kings of Persia to follow Cyrus. You can identify them in the 21st century as: (1) Cambyses, 529 B.C.; (2) Pseudo - Smerdis, 522 B.C.; (3) Daius Hystapsis, 521 B.C: and (4) Xerxes who invaded Greece in 480 B.C. He was defeated and never again did Media - Persia make a bid for world dominion. You may believe that Xerxes is the Ahasuerus of the Book Ester. He was very rich as this prophecy said he would be." (Daniel 11:2) (McGee)

"And the king of the south shall be strong, and one of his princes; and he shall be strong above him, and have dominion…And in the end of years they shall join themselves together; for the king's daughter of the south shall come to the king of the north to make an agreement: but she shall not retain the power of the arm; neither shall he stand, nor his arm: but she shall be given up, and they that bought her, and he that begat her, and he that strengthened her in these times." (Daniel 11:5 - 6)

"The king of the south; South of what? Directions in the Bible are reckoned from Israel as the center of the earth. The king of the South is not from south of Los Angeles, or Chicago, or New York. It is the king from the south of Israel, so this would be the king from Egypt. This king of the south would be one of the Ptolemies. 'The king of the north' refers to the line of the Seleucidae. This verse brings us to about 250 B.C.

Historians have recorded some of the manipulations that went on in the courts of that day, which fulfill this prophecy very accurately. To form an alliance between these two warring families, Ptomely Philadelphus of Egypt gave his daughter Berenice in marriage to Antiochus Tkheos of Syria. Antiochus was already married to Laodice, whom he divorced. After two years Ptomely Philadelphus died; so, Antiochus Theos put away Berenice with her son and took back his first wife, Laodice. She in turn, poisoned Antiochus Theos and ordered the death of Berenice and her son. Then Laodice put her own son, Deleucus Callinicus, on the throne. That was some juggling act, and God covered it all in the prophecy given to me, Daniel." (McGee)

"But out of a branch of her roots shall one standup in his estate, which shall come with an army, and shall enter into the fortress of the king of the north, and shall seal against them, shall prevail. And shall also carry captives into Egypt their gods, with their Princes, and with their precious vessels of silver and of gold; and he shall continue more years than the king of the north. So the king of the south shall come into his kingdom, and shall return into his own land." (Daniel 11:7 - 9)

"Out of a branch of her roots,' to Ptolemy Euregetes, brother of Berenice, who came with an army and captured Syria, and he seized the fort, which was the port of Antioch in that day. It is reported that Ptomely Eurgetes took into Egypt as booty four thousand talents of gold, forty thousand talents silver, and twenty-five hundred idols. So, this Scripture was literally fulfilled." (McGee)

"Next there was continual warfare between Egypt and Syria. During this period Israel seemed repeatedly to make wrong choices, and found herself being made captive first by one, then by the other. Many in the nation Israel were slain at this time. They incurred untold sufferings from both the king of the north and the king of the south." (Daniel 11:10 - 14) (McGee)

"So, the king of the north shall come, and cast up a mount, and take the most fenced cities: and the arms of the south shall not withstand, neither his chosen people, neither shall there be any strength to withstand. But he cometh against him shall do according to his own will, and none shall stand before him: and he shall stand in the glorious land, which by his hand shall be consumed." (Daniel 11:15 - 16)

"He shall stand in the 'glorious land.' I now know why this has been given to me to record because it concerns the "glorious land." Which is Israel, the land that God vouchsafe to Abraham and to those coming after him. These two verses predict what history now records as the victory of Antiochus the Great over Egypt. It was a decisive victory, and it caused Israel to suffer immeasurably. All of my prophecy was fulfilled in a remarkable way, although I will not go into all the secular history now. There was a period of 125 years that was fulfilled in detail. Go to your history books to read all the details." (McGee)

"He shall also set his face to enter with the strength of his whole kingdom, and upright ones with him; thus, shall he do: and he shall give him the daughter of women, corrupting her: but she shall not stand on his side, neither be for him." (Daniel 11:17)

"This brings us to about 198 or 195 B.C. when Antiochus the Great made a treaty with Egypt and gave his daughter Cleopatra to Ptomely Epiphanes in marriage." (McGee)

"After this shall he turn his face unto isles, and shall take many: but a prince for his own behalf shall cause the reproach offered by him to cease; without his own reproach he shall cause it to turn upon him. Then he shall turn his face toward the fort of his own land: but he shall stumble and fall, and not be found. Then shall stand up in his estate a raiser of taxes in the glory of the kingdom: but within few days he shall be destroyed, neither in anger, nor in battle." (Daniel 11:18 - 20)

"He shall turn his face unto the isles' refers to Greece and all the Greek Islands. This where Antiochus the Great was beginning to move at this time – not only against Ptomely in the south, but against Lysimachus in the west. "A prince for his own behalf" would refer to another line, that is, Rome which was beginning to arise in the west and move toward the east; Rome, exacted taxes from the Syrians. As Rome began to rise, she was building a tremendous empire by taxing the people she was capturing." (McGee)

"Next to come to power will be an evil man not directly in line for royal succession. But during a crisis he will take over the kingdom by flattery and intrigue." (LBT) (Daniel 11:21)

"Now I introduce a most vile person, Antiochus Epiphanes, who was king in Syria and is easily identified in history. Most fundamental interpreters of Scripture, who have studied this since I wrote it, consider this section to be a direct reference to this man. He is considered to be the "little horn" that I mentioned earlier, and he is also the same type as the Antichrist, the Man of sin, who is yet to come. The Antichrist that will be revealed in your day; Christ said there would be "many antichrists" so this is what they will be like. Antiochus Epiphanes came to the throne in 175 B.C. He is called vile because of his blasphemies. He came to the throne with a program of peace, with deceit and flattery." (McGee)

"Then all opposition will be swept away before him, including a leader of the priests. His promises will be worthless. From the first his method will be deceit; with a mere handful of followers, he will become strong. He will enter the richest areas of the land without warning and do something never done before: he will take the property and wealth of the rich and scatter it out among the people. With great success he will besige and capture powerfull strongholds throughout his dominions, but this will last for only a short while." (LBT (Daniel 11:21 - 24)

"Then he will stir up his courage and raise a great army against Egypt; and Egypt, too will raise a mighty army, but to no avail, for plots against him will succeed. Those of his own household will bring his downfall; his army will desert, and many will be killed. Both these kings will be plotting against, each other at the conferences table, attempting to deceive each other. But it will make no difference, for neither can succeed until God's appointed time has come." (LBT) (Daniel 11:25 - 27)

"Then shall he return into his land with great riches; and his heart shall be against the holy covenant: and he shall do exploits, and return to his own land. At the time appointed he shall return, and come toward the south, but it shall be as the former, or as the latter. For the ships of Chittim shall come against him: therefore he shall be grieved, and return, and have indignation against the holy covenant: so shall he do; he shall even return, and have intelligence with them that forsake the holy covenant."

"These verses describe the campaign of Antiochus and his victory over the king of Egypt which brought him much riches and prestige. 'Both these kings were plotting against each other…attempting to deceive each other." This refers to the fact that both were lying to each other. Today you have conference tables that are much the same, where nations meet and make treaties, which become meaningless scraps of paper. Antiochus made a second campaign against Egypt but was not successful due to the navy of Rome, "the ships of Chittim." He broke his covenant with Israel, but notice that some of the Jews betrayed their own people, "he shall even return, and have intelligence with them that forsake the holy covenant."" (McGee)

"For Roman warships will scare him off, and he will withdraw and return home. Angered by having to retreat, the Syrian king will again pillage Jerusalem and pollute the sanctuary, putting a stop to the daily sacrifices, and worshipping idols inside the Temple ('abomination that maketh desolate'). He will leave godless Jews in power when he leaves— men who have abandoned their father's faith. He will flatter those who hate the things of God and win them over to his side. But the people who know their God shall be strong and do great things. Yet they shall fall by the sword, and by flame, by captivity, and by spoil, many days." (LBT) (Daniel 11:30 - 34)

One hundred thousand Jews were slain! He took away the daily sacrifice from the temple, offered the blood and broth of a swine upon the altar, and set up an image of Jupiter to be worshiped in the holy place of the temple of God. This 'abomination that maketh desolate' is still to come in the latter days that Jesus referred to. This is Antichrist who is portrayed in these verses also. You can see that those who know God will suffer many things, by the sword, by fire, by captivity, and all that they own will be taken from them." (McGee)

"And some of them of understanding shall fail, to try then, and to purge, and to make them white, even to the time of the end: because it is yet for a time appointed." (Daniel 11:35) These ones with understanding will be refined, and cleansed to make them pure, until the end of their trials. "The time of the end" leaps forward in prophecy from Antiochus Epiphanes to the Antichrist. We move now from the history of that time into that which be yet in the future. All of this prophecy was in the future for me, Daniel, but to you, some is now history and some is yet future." (McGee)

"The king will do exactly as he pleases, claiming to be greater than every god there is, even blaspheming the God of gods, and prospering— until his time is up. For God's plans are unshakable. He will have no regard for the gods of his fathers, nor for the god beloved of women, nor any other god, for he will boast that he is greater than them all. Instead of these he will worship the Fortress god—a god his fathers never knew— and lavish on him costly gifts! Claiming his help, he will have great success against the strongest fortresses. He will honor those who submit to him, appointing them to positions of authority and dividing the land to them as their reward." (LBT) (Daniel 11:36 - 39)

My prophecy corresponds with the prophecy in Revelation that John wrote. For instance, "Therefore rejoice, ye heavens, and ye that dwell in them. Woe to the inhabiters of the earth and of the sea! For the devil is come down to you, having great wrath, because he knows that he has but a short time. (Revelation 12:12)

"This is Satan's hour. He will make the most of it, as he knows his time is short. Antichrist will do completely the will of Satan in that day. He will rule over many people and dispose of property as he pleases. He is the willfull king and the final world dictator." (McGee)

"And at the time of the end shall the king of the south push at him: and the king of the north shall come against him like a whirlwind, with chariots, and with horseman, and with many ships; and he shall enter the countries, and shall overflow and pass over." (Daniel 11:40)

"It is the time of the end,' not the end of time. It is the last days of my nation Israel that he Lord Jesus labeled the Great Tribulation. "The king of the south" is evidently a ruler of Egypt and the 'king of the north' I believe is Russia." (McGee)

"He shall enter also into the glorious land, and many countries shall be overthrown: but these shall escape out his hand, even Edom, and Moab, and the chief of the children of Ammon. He shall stretch forth his hand also upon the countries: and the land of Egypt shall not escape. But he shall have power over the treasures of gold and of silver, and over all the precious things of Egypt: and the Libyans and the Ethiopians shall be at his steps." (Daniel 11:41 - 43)

"When antichrist enters Israel, that is, 'the glorious land,' he will find that he is going to have trouble with Edom, Moab, and Ammon. That is the territory where the sons of Ishmael, the Arabs, are in the 21st century or your day. He will have trouble for a while. Egypt and the king of the south will yield to the Antichrist, and he will have control of the wealth of the world. He will control the entire money markets of the world at that time, and he will have control of Africa, too." (McGee)

"But tidings out of the east, and out of the north, shall trouble him: therefore, he shall go forth with great fury to destroy, and utterly to take away many. And he shall plant the tabernacles of his palace between the seas in the glorious holy mountain, yet he shall come to his end and none shall help him." (Daniel 11:44 - 45)

"Tidings out of the east'—that means the Orient with its millions. A great army will come from there to the Battle of Armageddon and the world ruler will be very troubled. At this time there will be no hope in the world, and no hope for God's people, except for God Himself. "The seas" refers to the Mediterranean Sea, and 'the glorious holy mountain' is Jerusalem. Antichrist will establish his headquarters for world conquest between the Mediterranean Sea and Jerusalem. However, instead of ruling from there, he will be destroyed by the personal return of the Lord Jesus Christ as written in (Revelation 19:17 - 20). Evil will have taken over, and only in the personal coming of Christ to establish His kingdom will any on this earth be delivered and saved." (McGee)

"And at that time shall Michael stand up, the great prince which standeth for the children of Thy people: and there shall be a time of trouble, such as never was since there was a nation even to that same time: and at that time Thy people shall be delivered, every one that shall be found written in the book." (Daniel 12:1)

"This is called the 'Great Tribulation Period' as Jesus spoke of also in Matthew 24:15 - 26, when He said that this would be a brief period, a time of trouble, and that there would never be a time like it before or afterward. This is now the end of the vision given to me, Daniel, as it ends with the "Great Tribulation Period." (McGee)

"And many of them that sleep in the dust of the earth shall awake, some to everlasting life, and some to shame and everlasting contempt. And they that are wise shall shine as the brightness of the firmaments; and they that turn many to righteousness, as the stars forever and ever. But thou, O Daniel, shut up the words, and seal the book, even to the time of the end: many shall run to and fro, and knowledge shall be increased. (Daniel 12:2 - 4)

"God's servants in the dark days of the Great Tribulation will shine as lights. The remnant in that day will be God's witness in the world, and they are going to "turn many to righteousness." That righteousness is Christ, the only righteousness that is acceptable to God. Our righteousness is as filthy rags (Isaiah 64:6) in His sight. God is not accepting our works; He is accepting the righteousness of Christ, and that is provided only by faith. These prophecies given by me, Daniel, were to be sealed until "the time of the end". This does not mean the end of time, but refers to that the period of time I have written about as the Seventieth Week." (McGee)

"Many shall run to and fro, and knowledge shall be increased,' are referring to, as you understand now, as in the end times when scholars will be running up and down the Bible in the study of prophecy, and the knowledge and study of prophecy will increase." (McGee)

I had no understanding of these words when I wrote them. "And I heard, but I understood not:" then said, 'O my Lord, what shall be the end of these things?' And He said, "Go thy way, Daniel: for the words are closed up and sealed till the time of the end. Many shall be purified, and made white, and tried; but the wicked shall do wickedly: and none of the wicked shall understand; but the wise shall understand." (Daniel 12:8 - 10)

"And from the time that the daily sacrifice shall be taken away, and the abomination that maketh desolate set up, there shall be a thousand two hundred and ninety days. Blessed is he that waiteth, and cometh to the thousand three hundred and five and thirty days. But go thou thy way till the end be: for thou shall rest, and stand in thy lot in the end of the days." (Daniel 12:11 - 13)

"In thy lot,' means that I Daniel will be raised with the Old Testament Saints to enter into Christ's kingdom. Jesus is coming to this earth to establish His kingdom. This is the hope each one of us has to keep before us as we live our lives, in my life and in yours." (McGee)

May this book of my life and of God's prophecy to you, be of great comfort and encouragement to all who read, and seek understanding of it.

"MAD AS "SPIT," AT GOD?

JONAH 1 - 4

God's Word came to me, Jonah the son of Amittai, saying, "ARISE, GO TO NINEVEH, THAT GREAT CITY, AND CRY AGAINST IT; FOR THEIR WICKEDNESS IS COME UP BEFORE ME." (Jonah 1:1 - 2)

I had a different idea. I could not, "I WOULD NOT," witness to those 'heathen,' those "wicked people," those 'terrorists.' I lived in Gath-hepher in the northern kingdom of Israel. To go to Nineveth, I would have to go east, but I decided to go "down" to Joppa, and flee unto Tarshish, which was west, away from the presence of the Lord. I found a ship going my way, (away form Nineveh and I thought God) so I paid the fare, and went 'down' into the bottom of the ship and fell asleep. I thought it was such good fortune that there was a ship waiting there, and that I could get aboard. (Jonah 1:3)

"The Lord sent out a great wind into the sea." It was so bad that the ship I was on was about to break into pieces, but I knew nothing of it because I was asleep. The sailors were very afraid, and each one cried to his own god; they threw the cargo overboard to try to lighten the load in an attempt to keep the ship from breaking into pieces. (Jonah 1:4 - 5)

The captain came to me and screamed at me; "WHAT MEANEST THOU, O SLEEPER? ARISE, CALL UPON THY GOD, THAT HE MIGHT HAVE MERCY ON US ALL, AND SAVE US." The shipmen decided to cast lots to decide which one of us had caused this evil storm to come upon us. The lot fell to me, Jonah. They questioned me: "WHY IS THE EVIL ON US, WHAT IS YOUR OCCUPATION, WHAT COUNTRY DO YOU COME FROM, AND WHO ARE YOUR PEOPLE?" (Jonah 1:6)

I told them that I was a "Hebrew and that I feared the Lord, the God of heaven, which had made the sea and the dry land." This was very hypocritical of me given the circumstances, but I added that my God made the sea and the dry land, as 'dry land' looked very well to us all at this point. The men became "exceedingly afraid" because I had told them that I fled the presence of the Lord. They said to me, 'What shall we do to thee, that the sea may be calm unto us?' I said that they "must cast me into the sea, that it would become calm." (Jonah 1:7 - 12)

The sailors did not want to throw me overboard, so they did their best to get the ship out of the storm by rowing as hard as they could to bring the ship to dry land, but nothing helped. Finally, they decided they had no alternative but to throw me overboard, so they cried to the Lord, and said, "We beseech thee, O Lord, we beseech thee, let us not perish for this man's life, and lay not upon us innocent blood: for thou, O Lord, has done as it pleased thee." (Jonah 1:13 - 14)

"They took me up and cast me into the sea: and the sea immediately ceased from her raging. Then the sailors feared the Lord exceedingly, and offered a sacrifice unto Him, and made vows to Him." (Jonah 1:15 - 16)

You may realize that I did not pray to my God, but the pagan sailors did. I was determined that I was not going to Nineveh even if it meant my life. "Now the Lord had prepared a great fish to swallow me up. I went 'down" into the belly of the fish and was there for three days and three nights; I prayed unto the Lord from within the fish's belly.' (Jonah 2:1)

I finally realized there was something worse than going to Nineveh, so "I cried out of my affliction to the Lord. I knew He had cast me into the deep, in the middle of the seas; and the floods compassed all around me: the waves passed over me. The water was everywhere even in the depths of my soul. The weeds were wrapped around my head and I went 'down' to the bottom of the mountains. My soul fainted within me, and I remembered the Lord." (Jonah 2:2 - 6)

"I was imprisoned in the land of death, but the Lord my God snatched me from the jaws of death, when I had lost all hope. I was no longer playing the game of 'lying vanities' with the Lord. I appealed to God's mercy and I found He was merciful to me. I told God that I would pay that I had vowed now to go to Nineveth. I prayed to Him "Salvation is of the Lord." I knew that God was the only one that could save me because 'Salvation is God's work for man, it is never man's work for God.' (Jonah 2:6 - 7) (McGee)

"The Lord heard me when I cried out of the belly of hell; the Lord heard my voice. I sacrificed unto God with the voice of thanksgiving. The Lord spoke to the fish, and it vomited me upon the dry land." (Jonah 2:2,9,10)

"The word of the Lord came to me the second time, saying, 'ARISE GO UNTO NINEVEH, THAT GREAT CITY, AND PREACH UNTO IT THE PREACHING THAT I BID THEE.' I immediately arose, and went unto Nineveh, according to the word of the Lord. Nineveh was an exceeding great city that took me three days' journey to get through it." (Jonah 3:2 - 3)

"When I entered the city, I cried, and said, 'Yet forty days, and Nineveh shall be overthrown.'" You may wonder how I got the people to listen to me? There was a man in the twentieth century that was swallowed by a fish, and spent two days inside of it. He lived to tell the story, so you today living in the 21st century have a close-up look at what happened to his appearance. The man did not have a hair on his body, and his skin was yellowish-brown color, due to the gastric juices of the fish working on his skin, trying to digest him." (Jonah 3:4) (McGee)

When I told the people of Nineveh that I had been swallowed by a great fish, and was inside of it for three days and three nights, and was now returned from the dead because of the mercy of God, they listened to me. They could see something had happened to me. Also, stories travel fast when they are remarkable, so we can presume that the shipmen were talking of their experience with me, and it was being heard.

After I crossed the whole city with the message of judgment from God, "YET FORTY DAYS, AND NINEVEH SHALL BE OVERTHROWN," 'the people of Nineveh believed God, and proclaimed a fast, and put on sackcloth, from the greatest of them even to the least of them. For word came unto the king of Nineveh, and he arose from his throne, and he lay his robe from him, and covered himself with sackcloth, and sat in ashes. And he caused it to be proclaimed and published through Nineveh by the decree of the king and his nobles, saying, "Let neither man nor beast, herd nor flock, taste anything: let them not feed, nor drink water."' (Jonah 3:5 - 7)

The king continued, "But let man and beast be covered with sackcloth, and cry mightily unto God: yea, let them turn everyone from his evil way, and from the violence that is in their hands. Who can tell if God will turn and repent, an turn away from His fierce anger that we perish not. (Jonah 3:8-9)

"God saw their works, that they turned from their evil way; and God 'repented' of the evil, that He had said that He would do unto them; and He did it not." Since God does not need to repent, and to repent means to have "a change of mind," we must look at what happened here. The people of Nineveh did the repenting, and the changing, by believing God would do what He said. God had stated to Nineveh what He would do if they did not repent, implying that there could be forgiveness if they did repent. So, they called to Him for forgiveness, and He did forgive them, as is His nature." (Jonah 3:10) (McGee)

"This was revival like I had not seen in Israel, and revival like you have probably not seen in your lifetime. From the highest position in the kingdom, to the lowest position in the kingdom, the people repented, and the animals were changed too, because the people dealt with them differently. There is a story of a mining town that had a revival, and the miner's hearts were turned toward God. When they returned to their work in the mines, their ponies would not cooperate with them because they were used cursing, and kicking, as a way to bringing them into obedience. Now the miners were kind to their animals, and the animals did not understand this compassionate treatment." (McGee)

So the change was most impressive to all who had been forgiven, but not to me. "I was displeased exceedingly, and I was very angry." I prayed unto the Lord, and said, 'I pray thee, O Lord, was not this my saying, when I was yet in my country? Therefore, I fled before You unto Tarnish: for I knew that thou art a gracious God, and merciful, slow to anger, and of great kindness, and repentest thee of the evil.'" (Jonah 4:1 - 2)

I went on in my discouragement saying, "Therefore now, O Lord, take, I beseech thee, my life from me; for it is better for me to die than to live." 'I was overwrought, over stimulated, exhausted and absolutely drained from my experiences of the past few days. I just gave up, I quit, I didn't want to go any further and I wished to be dead.' (Jonah) (McGee)

God spoke to me in my despair, "DOEST THOU WELL TO BE ANGRY?" or in other words, 'Is this displeasing to you that I have saved these Ninevites? God went on to remind me that He is in the SAVING

BUSINESS and he wants all men to come to repentance. (Jonah 4:4) (McGee)

So, I went out of the city, and sat on the east side of the city and there made a booth. I sat under it in the shadow, till I might see what would become of the city." 'I did not trust the Ninevites; I expected them to go back to their old ways, and I was hoping they would, so God would have to destroy them. You may believe that you must love people before you can go as a missionary to them, but I hated the Ninevites, so my story proves that is not true.' (Jonah 4:5) (McGee)

"The Lord God prepared a gourd, and He made it to come up over me, that it might be a shadow over my head to deliver me from my grief. I was exceeding glad of the gourd." 'This was the first time I had been happy about anything since this ordeal started. I got very attached to the gourd and took very good care of it.' (Jonah 4:6) (McGee)

"But God prepared a worm when the morning rose the next day, and it smote the gourd so that it withered. And it came to pass when the sun did arise, that God prepared a vehement east wind; and the sun beat upon my head, so that I fainted, and wished to die." I said, 'It is better for me to die than to live.' I wished to die again. (Jonah 4:7 - 8)

"And God said to me, 'Doest thou (do) well to be angry for the gourd?' I said, "I do well to be angry, even unto death." Then the Lord said, 'You have not labored, neither did you make it grow; it came up in the night, and it perished in the night. Should I not spare Nineveh, that great city, wherein are more than (120,000) persons that cannot discern between their right hand, and their left hand; and also, much cattle:' God was telling me that a gourd is nothing compared to a person who has a soul that is going to spend eternity in heaven, with God, or separated from Him in hell." (Jonah 4:9 - 10) (McGee)

You may wonder if I was a real person, I was, I am. No one else in the Bible is named Jonah so you cannot confuse me with anyone else in the pages. You may ask what is the significance of this book? "My book sets forth the resurrection of Jesus Christ." In Luke 11:30 we read, 'For as Jonas was a sign unto the Ninevites, so shall also the Son of man be to this generation; Then in (Matthew 12:39-41) we read: "But He answered and said unto them, an evil and adulterous generation seeketh after a sign; and there shall no sign be given to it, but the sign of the prophet Jonas: For as Jonas was three days and three nights in the whale's belly, so shall the Son of man be three days, and three nights in the heart of the earth. The men of Nineveh shall rise in judgment with this generation, and shall condemn it: because they repented at the preaching of Jonas; and, behold, a greater than Jonas is here."" (McGee)

"My book of Jonah also teaches that salvation is not by works, but by faith, which leads to repentance. The way to God is not by works of righteousness, which we have done, but by the blood of a substitutionary sacrifice provided by the Lord Jesus." (McGee)

"The third great purpose of my book is to show that God's purpose of grace cannot be frustrated. I refused to go to Nineveh, but God was still going to get the message to Nineveh. I was determined not to go to Nineveh, but God was determined that I was: God's will, will always prevail." (McGee)

"The fourth great truth in my book is that God will not cast a person aside for faithlessness. He may not use you, but He will not cast you aside. He may put you on the bench, but anytime you want to get back in the game of life, and do His will, He will permit you to do it," (McGee)

"The fifth truth is that God is good and gracious. Did I not say unto God, 'Thou art a gracious God, and merciful, slow to anger, and of great kindness, (and forgives evil).' You may believe that God is portrayed as a "God of wrath." in the Old Testament, and a 'God of love,' in the New Testament: but God is no vengeful Deity in my Book of Jonah. (McGee)

"The sixth and last great teaching is that God is the God of the Gentiles. In Romans 3:29 Paul writes, "Is He the God of the Jews only? Is he not also God of the Gentiles? Yes, of the Gentiles also.' I reveal, in my book of Jonah, that even in the Old Testament, God did not forget the Gentiles. He was willing to save a woman like Rahab the harlot, and the brutal inhabitants of Nineveh, because God is in the business of saving sinners." (McGee)

However, I did not approve of this city repenting, and being forgiven, and saved by God. You may ask how I got to this place in my life. I said this to God in my anger, "I" pray thee, O Lord, was not this 'my' saying, when "I" was yet in 'my' country? Therefore "I" fled unto Tarshish: for 'I' knew that thou art a gracious God...Therefore now, O Lord, take, "I" beseech thee, 'my' life from "me," for it is better for 'me' to die than to live. (Jonah 4:3) live."

I used the personal pronoun ten times, because "my" life was all about 'me,' "my" preferences, 'my' perspectives, "my" desires, and 'my' wants, because I was headed way down the wrong path. "Followers of Jesus Christ understand this; that life is not about 'me' and "my" preferences, and 'my' perspectives: life is about Jesus, and about "His" perspectives, and 'His' dreams, and "His" desires. I had a heart problem, because 'my' life was all about "me" and not about God. I didn't get my way, so I pouted about it. I pouted long enough so that I got angry with God." (Joseph Stowell)

"The church in the United States, in the 21st century, has a heart problem; the church believes that church is all about 'me.' You must realize that church is about Jesus, and His preeminence. You may judge the service like this: "I didn't like the sermon today, I don't like the choir," and you may get very angry when church doesn't go your way. The sermon may not have been for you, and the music may touch the heart of a struggling Christian, or a new member, in ways you cannot understand." (Joseph Stowell)

"Please remember my story and ask yourself, and ultimately God, if there is any part of your life that is unpleasing to Him? God will always do what is best for you and by you. If you will trust Him, you will see great rewards in your life on earth and in heaven. Please realize that it is not worth it to stay mad at God, and let your life be all about "you." The lost in this world are always on the heart of God, and they should weigh heavy on the heart of every believer." (Joseph Stowell)

ONLY FORTY MORE DAYS

GOD TOLD JONAH TO REPORT TO THE NINIVITES THAT THEY HAD "FORTY DAYS TO REPENT"

WHAT IF GOD TOLD YOU PERSONALLY THAT YOU HAD FORTY MORE DAYS, FROM TODAY, TO LIVE ON THIS EARTH,

WHAT WOULD YOU SAY?

"I don't believe in God, so I'm okay."

"Well, I will eat, drink, and be merry, for tomorrow I die; that's life."

"I'm feeling pretty good, so I'm sure it won't happen."

"I've got a dentist appointment in eight weeks, and everyone knows nothing ever happens to cancel a dentist appointment."

"A few of my friends have died lately, but I don't think it will be my turn for a long time yet."

"I'm sure someone will come up with a shot, by then, to keep me alive longer."

"I'm going to pump-up on vitamins, so I'm sure I will live a long time yet,"

"Life is short, I know, but not that short."

"RIGHT! God has killed most of my friends, so it only stands to reason He wants to kill me, too."

"I've got BIG plans for my future, so I'm sure God won't stop me now."
"I eat right, and EXERCISE, so I'm sure I'm okay."

Jesus said, "Verily, verily, I say unto you, He that hears my word, and believes on Him that sent Me, has everlasting life, and shall not come into condemnation; but is passed from death unto life." (John 5:24

"I will 'repent' and ask God to forgive me, and maybe He will give me more time."

"He which testifies of these things says, Surely, I come quickly. Amen. Even so, come Lord Jesus. The grace of our Lord Jesus Christ be (is) with you all. Amen." (Revelation 22: 20 - 21)

THE NEW TESTAMENT

John the Baptist

MY NAME IS JOHN

LUKE 1 - 2

My name is John, given to me by God. Was my name important? God thought so because He told my father to call me John. In Hebrew John means: "God is gracious."

What about your name: Is your name important, and how did you get it? Did your parents give you a Biblical name, or did they make up a name for you, or are you named after someone? Do you think you have the wrong name; God knows you, and He knew what your name would be long before the earth was made; "He chose you, in Christ, before the foundation of the world, that you should be holy and without blame, before Him in love." (Ephesians 1:4)

Some popular names being used in your day are: Girls name - Madison (meaning: former surname), Olivia (meaning: symbol of peace), Emma (meaning: artistic), Isabella (meaning: she who is consecrated to God), and Chloe (meaning: profusion of blooms); some popular Boys names being used are - Ethan (meaning: firm), Jacob (meaning: conqueror), Jordan (meaning: flow down), Matthew (meaning: a gift of the Lord) and Gabriel (meaning: man of God).

Let me tell you how I was destined to be called, John, by God, but my parents had agreed to it. When I was eight days old our relatives and neighbors came to a ceremony to circumcise me. Because of the covenant God made with Abraham, all boy babies were, and are circumcised on the eight days after their birth.

Genesis 17:6 - 13 "And I will make thee exceeding fruitful and I will make nations of thee, and kings shall come out of thee. And I will establish thy covenant between me and thee and thy seed after thee in their generations for an everlasting covenant to be a God unto thee, and to thy seed after thee."

"THIS IS MY COVENANT WHICH YE SHALL KEEP, BETWEEN ME AND YOU AND THY SEED AFTER THEE; EVERY CHILD AMONG YOU SHALL BE CIRCUMCISED AND HE THAT IS EIGHT DAYS OLD SHALL BE CIRCUMCISED AMONG YOU, EVERY MAN CHILD IN YOUR GENERATIONS...AND MY COVENANT SHALL BE IN YOUR FLESH FOR AN EVERLASTING COVENANT."

So, you can see why the people gathered for my circumcision. My name was given to me on this day and those present called me "Zacharias after my father." My mother answered and said, 'Not so, he shall be called John.' And they said to her, "There is none of your kindred that is called by this name."

So they went to my father and "made signs unto him to ask him what he would have me called?" He asked for a writing table, and wrote, saying, 'His name is John.' And they all marveled that I should be called "John."

I must go back to why my father Zacharias was writing on a tablet instead of speaking. My father belongs to the tribe of Levi, and as a priest he "was serving in the temple executing the priest's office before God in the order of his course." He was serving at the golden altar, the place of prayer. It was the time of the evening sacrifice, and in this particular part of the service he placed incense upon the altar. (McGee)

Suddenly an angel appeared and said to my father, "Fear not, Zacharias: for thy prayer is heard; and thy wife Elisabeth shall bear thee a son, and thou shall call his name John. And thou shall have joy and gladness; and many shall rejoice at his birth. For he shall be great in the sight of the Lord, and shall drink neither wine nor strong drink; and he shall be filled with the Holy Ghost, even from his mother's womb. Many of the children of Israel shall he turn to the Lord their God. And he shall go before Him in the spirit and power of Elijah, to turn the hearts of the fathers to the children, and the disobedient to the wisdom of the just; to make ready a people prepared for the Lord." (Luke 1:13 - 17)

Such wonderful things the angel said about me. The Lord has a wonderful plan for your life too, so please ask Him what you should do day by day and He will "direct your paths," and you will love the life He gives to you through His Son Jesus Christ.

Now here is where my father got into trouble. He said to the angel "How shall I know this? For I am an old man, and my wife well stricken in years." Another reason he was in unbelief is that his prayer for a son was no longer being offered, because he thought he and his wife were too old to conceive. He was already forgetting that Sarah and Abraham had a baby when they were 90 and 100 years old. However, the Lord hears all prayers prayed in His Will, and He will answer in His due time. (Jimmy Swaggart)

The angel answered him and said, "I am Gabriel, that stands in the presence of God, and am sent to speak unto thee, and to show thee these glad tidings. You shall be unable to speak, until the day that these things shall be performed, because thou believed not my words, which shall be fulfilled in their season."

Now my father had to be stopped from speaking any more doubt and unbelief or I could not have been born. Our words are so very important and we must speak according to what the Lord tells us to speak.

The people were waiting for my father to come out of the temple. They marveled that he tarried so long. When he did come out, he could not speak to them: they perceived that he had a vision in the temple: for he beckoned to them, and remained speechless. (Luke 1:21 - 22)

When his time of administration was accomplished, he departed to his home. My mother then conceived me and was thankful to God that He had looked upon her, and took away her reproach among men." She hid herself in our home for five months rejoicing constantly that I, a son, would soon be born. (Luke 1: 24 - 25)

Six months after the angel Gabriel appeared to my father, he was sent by God to a city of Galilee, named Nazareth, to a virgin, named Mary, who was engaged to a man whose name was Joseph, who was of the house of David. (Luke 1:26 - 27)

The angel said to her, "Hail, you are highly favored by the Lord, as He is with you to bless you among women." (Luke 1:29)

When Mary saw him, she was troubled in her mind, wondering what kind of salutation was this. The angel said to her, "Fear not, Mary; for thou have found favor with God. Behold, thou shall conceive in thy womb, and bring forth a son, and you shall call his name JESUS. He shall be great, and shall be called the Son of the Highest: and the Lord God shall give Him the throne of his father David. He shall reign over the house of Jacob forever; and His kingdom will never end." (Luke 1:29 - 33)

Mary said, "Be it unto me according to thy word." Then the angel told her that her cousin Elizabeth had conceived a son in her old age, and that she was in her sixth month. So, Mary arose and went to the hill country with haste, into the city of Judah, and entered the house of Zacharias and saluted Elizabeth. (Luke 1:38 - 41)

When my mother heard the salutation of Mary, I, the baby, leap in her womb. My mother was filled with the Holy Ghost and spoke with a loud voice saying, "Blessed art thou among women, and blessed is the fruit of thy womb and how is it that the mother of my Lord should come to me?" (Luke 1:42 - 43)

As soon as my mother spoke, I leapt in her womb for joy. My mother continued to speak to Mary in the Holy Ghost saying, "Blessed is she that believed: for there shall be a performance of those things which were told her from the Lord. Mary stayed with us for about three months and then returned to her own home. (Luke 1:43-45,46)

Now it was time for me to be born and all our relatives and neighbors rejoiced with my mother and father. This brings me up to my circumcision.

When my father, Zacharias, wrote my name as John, his mouth was immediately opened, and his tongue loosed, and he spoke in the Holy Ghost praising God, saying, "Blessed is the Lord God of Israel; for he has visited and redeemed his people, and has raised up a Horn of Salvation for us in the house of his servant David." (Luke 1:68 - 69)

The miracle of my birth was told throughout all the hill country of Judea, and all those who heard of it said in their hearts, "What manner of child shall this be! The hand of the Lord is with him." (Luke 1:65 - 67)

We go forward to the fifteenth year of the reign of Tiberius Caesar, Pontius Pilate being governor of Judea, and Herod being tetrarch of Galilee, and his brother Philip tetrarch of Itunea and of the region of Trachonitis, and Lysanias the tetrarch of Abilene. (Luke 3:1)

When I, John, was a grown man God spoke to me in the wilderness. It has been stated that "Tiberius Caesar is emperor, Annas and Caiaphas are high priests, Tiberius Caeser is a brilliant and brutal man. He is clever and cunning, very inhuman and profane. He wants to master the world." (McGee)

You know that my birth was miraculous, but my ministry was even more miraculous. I was a priest, a prophet, and a preacher called by God. My message was very strong as "I preached the baptism of repentance for the remission of sins." I was preparing the way for Israel and for you, my friend, making the way straight so you ALL will know the Word, Jesus Christ, when you are called to Him. (Luke 3:3) (McGee)

I was not a man that would fit into most of your churches in the United States of America in the 21st century. "I was unshaven, and shaggy, wearing camel's hair clothes, with a leather girdle about my loins; eating locusts and wild honey; but called to speak the truth of man's sin, declaring he must turn away from idols (himself), repent and "turn to the salvation of God and serve only the living and true God." (One cannot turn to God without turning from something; that something is personal sin) I declared to those who came to be baptized, "You are a generation of vipers and I am warning you to flee from the wrath of God that surely comes to "All" that reject the Messiah (Jesus Christ)." (Matthew 3:3) (Luke 3:4 - 7) (McGee)

"I am one voice calling in the wilderness, called to prepare you the way of the Lord." (Matthew 3:3) What does wilderness mean, why the wilderness? "The wild place, or the desert where no life can be sustained, a place of thorns, nothing grows, a place of thirst, all the wells are dry, there is no bread there because you can't grow wheat, just thorns, nothing grows, there is no water there, a place of thirst and a place of terrible loneliness because it can't support a community. It can't support life." (Tim Keller)

"So why did God send me out to the wilderness, why did everyone have to go out to the wilderness to be baptized? As you read the Bible you will see, in general, that man meet's God in the wilderness. In the history of Israel, they met God in the wilderness: where did Moses meet God? At the burning bush, in the wilderness: where did Jacob wrestle with God, "face to face," in the wilderness: where did Israel meet God, in Egypt, no, at Mt. Sinai, that's where they were made the people of God in principle, but after forty years of wandering in the wilderness the place where we meet God? The wilderness is the place where we can't stay alive without the intervention of God; all the wells go dry, so we have to have the water of God; all the bread goes moldy, so we need the bread (manna) of God. In the wilderness we all learn that God is not an add-on, apart from the saving intervention of God we have no hope of surviving." (Tim Keller)

"Your man of the 20th century, C.S. Lewis, explains what the wilderness experience is; the place where we meet God: 'Most people if they really learn how to look into their own hearts. would know what they do want, and want acutely something that cannot be had in this world.' There are all sorts of things in this world that offer to give you satisfaction, but they never keep their promise. A longing that puts a rise in you when you first fall in love, or first think of a foreign country you want to visit, or first take up some subject that excites you; a longing that no marriage, no amount of travel, no amount of education, can satisfy. I'm not referring to unsuccessful marriages, or bad trips, or terrible circumstances, or loss of money, or a loss of a good job; I am speaking of acquiring, with success, what you grasped at in your first moment of longing: you soon discover that the hope of happiness always fades away in the reality. You discover that something is evading you." (Tim Keller)

"This is what it means to meet the King (Jesus Christ); something happens in you that makes you look at the foundations of your life, and realize that I am going to die without God. It's not my career, it's not my family, it's not my husband, it's not my wife, it's not great kids, it's not my looks, it's not my friends, it's not the money, it's none of these things, that will ever, ever, ever, make me "HAPPY." I finally realized that every well "will" run dry, except the water of God; all the bread 'will' go moldy, except the bread of God. I finally realized that without a direct intervention of God into my life, "I am dead!"" (Tim Keller)

"When you admit that you are in the wilderness with no hope of making your life meaningful. THEN, you are ready to meet the "KING" (Jesus). I, John, am making this perfectly clear to you so you will understand that you must die to all other idols that you are using to try to give your life meaning, and make your life happy: then you can embrace the only One Who will set you free from your own sin; that is Jesus Christ." (Tim Keller)

"So, all of this may help you to understand why I was called to baptize; before me there was 'washings, and ablutions, and infusions, and immersions.' The Jews knew they needed to wash their hands before going into the temple to worship God as an expression that they needed to be cleansed of sin They knew they had a certain uncleanness in their life; it was a certain ritual for the purification of sin. If a Gentile wanted to go into the temple and worship God, they had to cleanse their whole body with water, and infusion of water because they were unclean. This type of cleansing had been done for centuries but, you always did it yourself. Now, I am saying, "NO," I have to baptize you, and that includes, all of you, everybody: Jews, Gentiles, Prostitutes, and Bible Scholars; it doesn't matter your background. You must receive your fitness for this kingdom by the hand of another.

Later, Jesus will have to baptize you with His Holy Spirit, but now I baptize you with water; the fact of the matter is you cannot save yourself, "YOU CANNOT EVER SAVE YOURSELF." (TIM KELLER)

"One must accept the finished work of Jesus Christ: this means He does something to you and for you. I was called to speak the message of impending judgment by baptism; I was not called to bring the message of the redeeming love of God." (McGee)

"The axe is laid to the root of the tree: every tree therefore which brings not forth good fruit, is hewn down, and cast into the fire." (Luke 3:9) "The message from God for Israel then, and for you today is: if a nation is not productive, as God expected, judgment is to be their portion." (McGee) However, God wants to lead you back to your 'first Love,' and make you productive again.

The people who came to me to be baptized asked: "What shall we do then?" I answered them and said, 'If a man has two coats, let him give to one who has none, and he that has food, let him do likewise.' I was telling them that they were living for "self" and not attempting to share what they had with others. The publicans and the soldiers then asked me what they should do? I said that whatever your occupation, reveal that you are a believer in Jesus Christ by the way you live within that occupation.

The people then wondered in their hearts if I was the Christ. I made it clear that I was not the final one, but I was preparing the way for the One to come (Jesus). I was baptizing with water, but Jesus, when He came, baptized with the Holy Spirit, and this is what I was leading them to.

I knew I was not worthy to unloose the laces of "His" shoes (the one coming after me). At this time, I did not know who the Christ was, but the day came when Jesus came to me to be baptized. I said of Him, 'Behold the Lamb of God, which takes away the sin of the world: This is the one who comes and is preferred before me, for He was before me: I did not know Him until I saw the Spirit descending from heaven like a dove, and it abode upon Him.' God had told me that I would know the Savior by seeing the Spirit descending, and remaining on Him.

You may ask, was Jesus not your cousin? Yes, I was acquainted with Him and had spent some of my boyhood with him, but until God revealed Him as Savior, I did not know Him as Lord.

When I baptized Jesus, I bore witness of Him. I spoke of Jesus as the One who has the bride and therefore is the bridegroom. I am only the friend of the bridegroom, which stands and hears Him and rejoices greatly because of His voice, therefore I am fulfilled. "He must increase and I must decrease." (John 3:27 - 30)

When Jesus came to me to be baptized, "I forbad Him," saying, I have need to be baptized of Thee, and You come to me? Jesus answered me and said, "Let it be so now; for I must do all that is right." I then did baptize Him.

When Jesus was baptized, He came out of the water: and, lo, the heavens were opened up, and I saw the Spirit of God descending like a dove, and lightning upon Him. And lo a voice from heaven said, "THIS IS MY BELOVED SON, IN WHOM I AM WELL PLEASED." (Matthew 3: 16 - 17) This is a manifestation of the Trinity, Jesus coming out of the water, the Spirit of God descends upon Him like a dove, and the Father speaks from heaven.' (McGee)

"So, why was Jesus baptized? Jesus' primary reason was to identify Himself completely with sinful mankind. Isaiah had prophesied that He would be numbered with the transgressors (Isaiah 53:12). Jesus, the King, identifies Himself with His subjects. Baptism means identification, and Jesus identified with you and me. Also, water baptism is symbolic of death. His (Jesus) death was a baptism. He entered into death for you and for me." (McGee)

"Another reason Jesus was baptized was because He was set-aside for His office of priest." Everything Jesus did was done by the power of the Holy Spirit. 'For He has made Him to be sin for us, who knew no sin; that we might be made the righteousness of God in Him' (2 Corinthians 5:21) "There was sin on Him, but there was no sin in Him. My sin was put on Him. not in Him. This is an important distinction, because being identified with Him saves you and me. This is why I was called to baptize Jesus." (McGee)

"He that comes from above is above all: he that is of the earth is earthly, and speaks of the earth: He that comes from Heaven is above all. For He whom God has sent speaks the words of God and has the Spirit of God. He that believes on the Son has everlasting life, he that believes not the Son shall not see life; but the wrath of God abides on him." (John 3:31 - 36)

How wonderful it is for me to be a testimony for the Lord Jesus Christ.

Soon after Jesus started His ministry, I was "cast into prison" by Herod the tetrarch, because I had reproved him publicly for marrying, Herodias, who was his brothers Philip's wife, and for all the evils which he had done. Herodias was furious over my proclamations and insisted Herod put me in jail. (Luke 3:19 - 20)

As time passed in prison, my disciples were keeping me up to date as to what Jesus was doing. I decided to send two of them to Jesus to ask Him if He was the one to come? Or should we look for another?

Many wondered why I was questioning Jesus in this way: was I depressed, discourage, or dejected because I had been in prison so long, and began to doubt Jesus as the Messiah. This was not the case, because I could not be shaken from my belief in Jesus as the Lord. I was expecting Christ to establish the kingdom in all of its glory and power. Since this had not happened, I sent those to find out why. (McGee)

My disciples asked this question of Jesus, but He continued to perform many miracles while they watched. He "cured many of their infirmities and plagues, and cast out evil spirits; and unto many that were blind he gave sight." (Luke 7:21)

Then Jesus answered and said unto them. "Go your way and tell John what things you have seen and heard; how that the blind see, the lame walk, the lepers are cleansed, the deaf hear, the dead are raised, to the poor, the gospel is preached. He said, "Blessed is he, whosoever shall not be offended in me." (Luke 7:22 - 23)

"Jesus realized that He was not moving as fast as I wanted Him to, and He was asking me to trust Him. He is asking the same thing of you, my friend, when you cannot understand your circumstances. 'For the preaching of the cross is to them that perish foolishness; but unto us which are saved it is the power of God.' (1 Corinthians 1:18)

I believe the Word of God, and I hope you do too." (McGee)

"After my disciples departed, Jesus began to speak unto the people concerning me, John. He asked what the people went out into the wilderness to see: A reed shaken with the wind? A man clothed in soft raiment: A prophet, 'yes,' and much more than a prophet. This is the one of whom it is written; a messenger which shall prepare thy way before thee." (Luke 7: 24 - 27) (Malachi 3:)

Jesus then gave me tremendous tribute when He said, "Among those that are born of women there is not a greater than he." (Luke 7:28 - 29)

"All the prophets before me said that Jesus was coming; I said, 'Behold, He is here.' I introduced Christ, which made me greater: but since the Cross, the Covenant affords you, (the believer in Christ in the 21st century) far greater privileges than those had under the Old Covenant, of which I am a part." (Jimmy Swaggart)

I was satisfied to know that Jesus was to be trusted above all others. But the day came when Herod's wife, Herodias, was able to get her revenge on me. It was Herod's birthday and Herodias' daughter had danced for him, and pleased him much. "Herod promised, with an oath, to give her whatsoever she would ask. The girl went to her mother to be instructed by her, as to what she should ask Herod? Herodias saw her chance to have me killed. She told her daughter to ask for the head of John the Baptist delivered in a charger, or you may call it delivered on a platter." (Luke 14:5 - 9)

"Herod was sorry that he had made this oath, but he was afraid of what his guests might think of him for having made a promise and not making good on it, so he ordered me to be beheaded in prison. My head was brought in a charger, and given to the damsel: and she brought it to her mother." (Matthew 14:10 - 13)

Thus, my life on earth ended, but now I am in eternity with Jesus awaiting you, my friend. There is more to my story; "my disciples came to the prison and took my body and buried it, then they went to Jesus and told Him of my death." (Matthew 14:12

"When Jesus heard of my death, He was greatly grieved and departed immediately by ship across the Sea of Galilee to have a time to be alone,' but the people followed Him on foot, and walked around the shore of Galilee and met Him on the other side. Jesus saw the multitude, and was moved with compassion toward them, and he healed their sick (Matthew 14:13 – 15)

Jesus' way of dealing with my death was to stop the Devil's evil deed of destruction by healing the sick that had been following Him all day. The needs of the people continued after my death, and Jesus went on to show us, His people, that God wants us to go on with living, and doing good, after we spend a time of mourning for our loved one. (McGee)

Why didn't Jesus save my life? I came as the fore runner to Jesus, to proclaim him as Savior to the World: I did the Will of God by the Holy Spirit: I finished the work God gave me, so I left the earth. You can do God's Will for your life, by His Holy Spirit. It is the only life I wanted, and it will be the only one you will want to live. "And I (God) will put My Spirit within you, and cause you to walk in my statues, and you shall keep my judgments, and do them." (Ezekiel 36-27)

AMEN

Rich Young Man

HOW DO I GET TO HEAVEN FROM HERE?

MATTHEW 19:16 - 22

"Good Master, what good thing shall I do that I may have eternal life?" (Matt. 19:16)

"If thou will enter into life, keep the commandments." I asked the Master which ones I should keep?

The master said to me, "Thou shall do no murder, thou shall not commit adultery, thou shall not steal, thou shall not bear false witness. Honor thou father and mother, and thou shall love thy neighbor as thyself."

"I have since my youth honored my father and mother; I've never killed anyone. I haven't committed adultery. I have never stolen from anyone, I have never brought false witness against my neighbor, and I love my neighbor as myself, all as you have said that I should. Do I lack anything?" (Matt. 19:18 - 19)

"If you will be perfect, go and sell what you have, and give it to the poor, and then you shall have treasure in heaven: and come and follow Me." (Matt. 19:21)

Oh! I can't imagine this man thinks I should sell all my beautiful possessions, and then give it to the poor? Some of my possessions have been in the family for generations, and I must pass them on to my children, (that is when I marry and have children) or what would they ever have as an inheritance? I can't imagine living without money and possessions, and following someone around that doesn't sleep regularly, or eat regularly, and be with all those poor people that don't wash regularly, or talk right, and are not educated.

"Well, Master, this makes me very sorrowful, so I must go and think all of this over for a very, very, long, time."

As I was leaving, I heard Jesus say, "It's easier for a camel to go through the eye of a needle, than for a rich man to enter heaven with God."(Matt. 19:24) What could he mean by that? Of course, it is impossible for a camel to go through the eye of a needle!

Also, when I addressed him, he asked me why I called him "good?"

What does he mean by that, 'isn't He good?' He said that there was only one that is good, and that is God. He mentioned I should come and follow him. I don't see how I could when he makes no sense to me.

Jesus looked so sad when I left, but I just can't follow him now, not on "His terms!"

HOW RICH WAS HE?

LUKE 16:19 - 31

I can't believe that Lazarus is in Paradise, "in the bosom of Abraham" while I'm here in this 'ENDLESS TORMENT!"

Oh, how good I had it on earth, and did I know it? When I think of all the money I left behind; of course, my brothers have it all now. I wonder how my investments are doing?

I can't believe my money isn't any good here. What a shame I had to leave everything behind! That purple silk cloth, embroidered with gold thread, the rarest on the earth, and my hand-made linen robes, and the sheets on my bed were so soft and lovely.

All that imported wine; it took me years to stock that wine cellar. I had to study all about wine and how each one was different, and which ones to use with which food, which ones were best served alone, and which bottles made the best gifts, and how to get the best bargain when I bought it by the case; now it all belongs to someone else.

I keep thinking of all the diamonds and rubies I left behind. I loved that special snake ring I had, which had the diamond eyes, and all the perfectly matched rubies inlaid all around. Then there was my rare coin collection. Some were so rare I wouldn't even let my brothers see them. Now they got 'um!

And I can't even think about my art collection, with all those priceless paintings that I traveled the earth to find. I ate daily from bone china plates rimmed in gold, with matching gold goblets. All I had to do was lift my hand my cup was filled, now I ask Father Abraham to send Lazarus over here with one drop of water to cool my tongue; to relieve the torment of this flame and He says it's impossible, because of the "great gulf fixed between us. (Luke 16:26)

I would think I could at least have that. I'm not asking much. One little finger dipped in the water to touch my tongue; besides I can't see any great gulf or chasm between us. I can see and hear them just fine.

After all, Lazarus had nothing on earth, of course he would be happy now; I did him a favor when we were on earth, by letting him be laid at my gate every day so he could be fed from the crumbs that came from my table; and mighty good crumbs they were too.

He was quite the eyesore for my friends and me to see every day, but I allowed it. I even allowed those pesky dogs to stay around him that licked his wounds all the time.

Oh! When I think of all the luscious food, I ate every day, and the most wonderful French cook money could buy. That chocolate velvet pie was a melt in your mouth delicacy, but meat, potatoes, an gravy can't be topped. Oh, what a loss for me!

I only asked Father Abraham for a little favor, to send Lazarus back to warn my five brothers not to come here to this place of torment. But Abraham said they had Moses and the prophets, and they had not heard them, so they would not even believe if someone rose from the dead. (Luke 16:27 - 31)

What is Father Abraham talking about, "Moses and the prophets?" My brothers and I know all about them. I studied Hebrew with the best of them. We memorized scripture before we were twelve, and we could recite endless passages and psalms. We could recite the Ten Commandments on cue. We were circumcised on the eighth day, and we celebrated all the Holy Days. I gave tithes at the temple and I even gave coins to the poor that begged in the streets. That was way more than was required of me.

I prayed loudly and well on street corners and in the temple, and in any public place regularly, because there were all those who needed to be prayed for. If I had seen someone come back from the dead, surely it would have left an impression on me.

Again, I think of all I had, and all I "had" to leave behind, and now this endless torment with no servants to help me. I think of the waxed hardwood floors throughout my lavish home, and the marble baths and ornate carved furniture, especially that special bed I had made just for me. I had servants to bath me, servants to dress me, servants to buy the best fruits and vegetables at the market, and fish and meat. I had servants to take me anywhere I wanted to go, servants to keep the house spotless and clean. Servants to help me at bedtime and to bring me food and drink anytime I desired it, even in the middle of the night if I couldn't sleep.

My life was so "sumptuous" and so SHORT, and now all I have is this 'endless torment' for all eternity. God isn't fair at all. I can't believe He let that poor, no-account Lazarus into Heaven before me. I think of my funeral that I planned from start to finish, in advance, so it would be appropriate to the life I lived, so all my friends and neighbors would remember all the "good" I did.

My estate was a work of art to behold. People came from miles around to gaze upon its loveliness. So many beautiful and colorful flower gardens each with its own walkway, so each flower could be smelled individually. I loved to sit at the fountains and watch the water flow in interesting designs, and the rainbows that were captured when the sun hit a shower of water as it sprayed forth in delightful ways.

I can't believe Lazarus is over there dancing, and laughing, and talking with Jesus like he knows Him personally. He acts as if he can't even "see, or hear me." He has no concern for my torment. This is all SO UNFAIR!

HOW POOR WAS HE?

LUKE 16:19 - 31

"Lord, my Lord and my God," this is a dream come true to be here in Paradise with YOU at last. What a glorious place this is. My suffering and pain was but for 'a little season' as YOU promised. (1 Peter 1:6) Now I see You "face to face" every moment of every day forever and ever. I am so full of Joy all the time because YOU are with me constantly.

Your endless love for me, even me, by dying on the cross in my place, has brought me here. You told me to "run with patience the race that was set before me (Hebrews 12:1), to always pray and not faint, to believe," to hold onto Your faith that You put in me, and it would lead me here. But this is beyond all my hopes, and all my dreams, and all my wildest imagination. You, my Lord and my God are beyond compare.

I remember what You did for me, and I can barely walk because I want to fall down in worship of You continually. You took my place, on earth, on the cross, in death, so all my iniquities were laid on You, and in exchange I got Your life, Your righteousness, Your position in eternity with You. My life, for Yours!

Oh, thank you Lord, that I cannot stop Your joy, your peace, your love, and Your goodness that wells up in my soul continually. Only You are the worthy One: the "Lamb slain for me." Your light shines out of every part of me; it bathes me, and clothes me in Your righteousness constantly. I am never out of Your LIGHT. You have given me my 'desire so that I can behold Your beauty, inquire of You daily, and dwell in Your house all the days of my life, which is forever.' (Psalm 27:4)

To You goes all the glory, the entire honor, and all the praise forever and ever. Amen! Your Blood has cleansed me, and now sits on the Mercy Seat for me!

Any agony that I suffered on earth could not be compared to what You, Jesus, endured for me. As I gaze upon Your face daily my suffering is as nothing...NOTHING! All the money on earth, all the jewels, all the beautiful homes, all the lavish food, had they been mine, would have been of no comparison to this endless satisfaction given to me for the asking, because You Lord, are the same "yesterday, and today, and forever." (Hebrews 13:8)

"The fear of the Lord is the beginning of wisdom: a good understanding have all they that do His commandments.' (My praise for Him') endureth forever." (Psalm 111:10)

AMEN!

THAT SON OF YOURS

"I think the older brother had good reason to be angry with his younger brother."

"Why?"

"That 'coyote' ran off with all the money and spent it on wine, women, and song."

"So."

"So, he had no right to come back home as if nothing had happened."

"You believe this story is about the younger son taking his 'fathers' money and squandering it?"

"Well, isn't it?"

"Jesus seemed to think the older brother had the problem. He was not only mad at his younger brother, but he was mad at his father too."

"Oh?"

"Do you believe the father had the right to forgive the younger son?

"I suppose he had the right."

"Should he forgive him?"

"That is the question."

"What about the older son, should the father forgive him?"

"I didn't realize he needed to be forgiven."

"His Father said, 'all that He had belonged to His son.' That should have been enough, but he was unable to forgive, so he lacked love.

Should God forgive us?"

"?????"

LIVIN AT HOME

LUKE 15: 11-32

"Dad, I know we've talked about this before and I appreciate all you've done for me, but I'm so 'fenced-in' here! I need to have "excitement" in my life. The cows just don't do anything for me anymore; The routine, up at 6:00 a.m., feedin' cows, movin' cows, roundin' up cows, brandin', fixin' fence, an' RIDIN', RIDIN', RIDIN'; It all seems so ordinary now. I just want to get away to a place where I can REALLY LIVE!"

"The food is always good, but I'd like to try somethin' besides MEAT, POTATOES, AN' GRAVY, and the family chocolate cake, an' peppermint ice cream. Even banana cream pie is getting to be 'old hat' to me now.

"Bob an' I used to be close, but now he's married and he's got his family. All he thinks about is the business. And Mary Ann, next-door; talks about horses and ridin' an' the next rodeo all the time. Besides she rides and ropes better than I do.

"Dad, if you'd give me my share of the inheritance, I'll be on my way. I won't bother you anymore about being so bored."

"Okay son, I don't want you to go, but I'll give you your inheritance; I'll divide it up according to your age, Bob gets two thirds and you will get one third of all that I have. Remember, if you ever change your mind, I'll be here waiting and watching for you to come home again."

"Don't worry Dad, I won't, but thanks for the money and for letting me go. I know you'll never regret it.

"Good bye Buster. You be a good dog now and take care of Dad."

RIOTOUS LIVING

This is some riot livin' here in this pigpen. I never realized how smelly pigs are and how selfish. Boy, talk about FRIENDS, the minute the money's gone, so are they. I can't believe I went through all my money so fast. Where'd it all go?

SHANTEL! I never thought she'd go with the others. I was so in love with her, and what was all that, that she said to me? ALL a LIE!

I've lost thirty pounds in six weeks. I've got to get some food somehow.

Dad! Yeah, DAD! What was it he said; I could come back home if I wanted to. Oh, I don't know. Bob was sure mad when I left with my money. He said, "Good Riddance!" I don't know if I can face him and Dad again, and what about Mary Ann? She was so hurt because I was leaving. The whole town thought Dad was a fool letting me go off with the inheritance.

I've got to chance it. I've got to, or I'll be a dead man. I'll tell Dad that "I have sinned against heaven, and before him, and I am no longer worthy to be called his son, and I'll tell him I'll be the hired man now." (Luke 15: 18-19) I'll milk the cow and clean the horse barn and fix fence. I'll sleep in the bunkhouse. Boy, that trailer will look like a palace to me now.

An' BUSTER! Yeah, he'll be so glad to see me; he'll probably knock me down lickin' my face all over. I sure hated leavin' him, but now we'll be together again.

REALLY LIVING

Well here goes; all or nothin'!

Boy there's the house...I think I see someone running. What the...Is that Dad? Running in cowboy boots toward me yelling my name as if he's glad to see me. How'd he see me from the house? Does he still have that spotting scope pointed out the window, or what? Is that Buster running beside him?

"My son, my son!"

Did Dad just kiss me on the neck? WOW!... "Father, I have sinned against heaven, and against You, and am no more worthy to be called your son." (Luke 15: 21) I have spent all 'your' hard-earned money in a foreign land."

"What are you talkin' about, you're home at last! Let me look at you...we've gotta get some flesh on you, BOY! When we get to the house, we'll get you a bath, and I'll give you the new jacket and the new cowboy boots I've been savin' for ya. I'll get your name back on the checkbook and you can get you some real clothes. You can get yourself another pair of boots, ten pairs if you want 'um, some cowboy hats and a goose down jacket, and all the new clothes you need. You can buy yourself some long johns; a wool cap and a pair of elk hide gloves too, and some gloves with liners, because winter will be here before you know it.

"I'm going to get Millie to call all the neighbors so we can have us a barbeque in your honor; roast beef like you've never tasted it before. 'For you, my son, were dead, but now you are alive again, you were lost, but now you are found. Let's sing and dance and be merry.' (Luke 15: 24) Let's celebrate your homecoming in style!"

"Dad, I can't thank you enough for taking me back after what I did. Being home with you and Buster is like heaven on earth. Having beef at every meal and eating banana cream pie again, is more than I could ever have imagined. "The Lord has restored my soul: He has prepared a table before me in the presence of my enemies; surely goodness and mercy will follow me all the days of my life: and I will dwell in the house of the Lord forever!" (Psalm 23: 4-6)

BOB, WHAT ABOUT BOB?

What's all that racket comin' from the house? I hear music and it looks like all the neighbors are here. It sounds like a party, but it's too early for that! I'm all sweaty and tired from workin' hard all day and Dad is havin' a party? I can't believe it! What could have happened to make Dad have a party without telling me about it first? Hey Willy, what's going on at the house?"

"Haven't you heard? Your brother is home again and your father is ecstatic with joy and is having a beef barbeque in his honor. Everybody's here and there's a lot of celebratin' goin' on in there. You better hurry in, your father is looking for you."

"WHAT? I can't believe it! Tell Dad I'm out here and I want to talk to him, NOW!"

"SON, I wanted to tell you that your brother is home again, so we are making merry over his safe return."

"Dad, I can't believe you are doing this for 'THAT SON of YOURS!' I have been here all the time 'working my tail off', and I have "never" failed you once, but did you ever give me a beef to have a party with my friends? But the minute that COYOTE shows up, you fall all over him like he hasn't squandered all 'my' money on loose women and whisky and heaven knows what else. The main thing is the money's all gone, and all we've got is him: AND YOU GIVE "HIM" A PARTY?"

"Bob, you are my eldest and most beloved son. All that I have is yours. Remember, 'your brother was dead, but now he is alive, he was lost, but is found,' (Luke 15:32) He turned his back on us and God, but now his rebirth is a time to celebrate."

WISE, OR FOOLISH?

MATTHEW 25: 1-30

J. Vernon McGee said he never met a "foolish virgin." How foolish were we, and why are we considered so foolish? Here is our story:

There were ten of us that had gone forth to wait for the bridegroom to come for us. We all had our lamps, and we were all sleeping because the "Bridegroom tarried." Then at midnight the cry came: 'Behold, the Bridegroom cometh; go ye out to meet Him.' We all arose and trimmed our lamps, but five of us, foolishly, had brought no extra oil along and could not light our lamps.

The five wise virgins had, however, brought along extra oil and thus they lit their lamps. We five, with no extra oil, begged them to give us some of their oil; they said that they could not because they would not have enough for themselves. They told us to hurry and go and buy some for ourselves. We agreed we must hurry and buy more oil, so we rushed off. We knew where to go; we went to the church as we had all come from the church to begin with.

We raced in breathless and told them of our plight. They sold us the oil and we ran back to where the bridegroom was, but now the other "five virgins, that were ready, went in to the marriage with the bridegroom, and the door was shut."

We pounded on the door screaming and demanding of the Lord "Open to us," for now we had our lamps lit again. But the Bridegroom called to us through the closed door and said "I SAY TO YOU, I KNOW YOU NOT."

We continued to demand to be let in; after all, "He" should know US. We are the ones who keep the church afloat. We are the ones who teach Sunday school, we put on Christmas programs, we knock ourselves out over vacation Bible school every summer, we have meetings with the children every Wednesday after school, we are the Elders and the Deacons and the Trustees, and the hard workers of the church. We give our money and we keep track of everybody else's to make sure it is used 'right.' When the Pastor insisted on draining our bank account by using too much gas, running all over visiting the sick in distant hospitals, we were outraged, and all the extra trips he took, demanding to be paid, was not acceptable to us. He spent our money like it was his, and his alone, to use as he pleased.

When the Sunday school spent thousands of dollars, over the years, on art supplies and special Bible food for children's activities, we didn't agree, but we said nothing because the kids needed this kind of stuff to win them to the Lord.

When an addition was added to our church we rallied around and raised the necessary funds, and volunteered our valuable time to get the project done as soon as possible. Of course, some of our "brothers in Christ" had to be put in their place when they tried to tell 'us' how the project should be done. We had the blueprint, we had the plan, we were putting in the most effort (and money), and no one could change our "work for the Lord." If we had to get a little ugly, so be it.

Sure, we murmured and complained to each other about the others, the "wise virgins," so to speak, but who do they think 'they' are, trying to tell us how to do things. And their Bible studies; they speak as if "they" are the only ones who have authority from God. Who do 'they' think "they" are, trying to speak like God? We know the Word too; we go to church; we are the Sunday school teachers; we are the direct descendants of those that started the church, way back 100 years ago. Most of 'them' are outsiders who came to our church though marriage or the Pastor brought them in: all kinds of "riffraff:" You wouldn't believe some of their backgrounds!

Well, we know our "rights"; we are the 'chosen ones,' the "right ones;" remember, we are the Sunday school teachers. Some may call 'us' foolish, but that is a matter of opinion. We brought in our own people; we told them how they belonged to the "right" church now. Of course, they had their problems, and most had sicknesses, and they were all broke, but we assured them that prayer and more prayer solves all things. Besides, we all look good enough, and we all have our problems, and sickness is a part of life, and no one ever has enough money, and as Christians we aren't supposed to be rich anyway, because 'money is the root of all evil.' We couldn't dwell on anybody's problems for long, because God's work had to be done regardless of our own suffering or ailments.

So now, "What is this?" The Bridegroom telling 'us' that, "I KNOW YOU NOT." He never knew 'US!' We can't believe our ears. It cannot be, just because we had to leave and get more oil. This is most unfair; we are going to fight this. We "all agree" that there is some kind of mistake and we will make a 'stink' like no one has ever seen the likes of. We'll take this to a "court of law" that understands what is going on here, and will 'agree with us.' We will never go into "outer darkness" as long as we can buy more oil to keep our lamps burning. We can keep this fight going for a very, very, long time yet!

SET FREE

LUKE 8: 1-2, JOHN 20: 1-20

I, Mary Magdalene had an encounter with Jesus Christ when He cast seven devils out of me and changed my life forever.

I was full of anger from all the things that had happened to me in my lifetime. I hated everybody, especially MEN. I was jealous of anybody that had a nice life, with a family that loved and cared for them. I was guilty and ashamed that maybe I was at fault for all of these bad things that had happened to me.

I had unforgiveness in my heart for what had been done to me; fear filled me when I realized that I could not depend on any one. People did not want to be around me, but my pride kept me from revealing what was really in my heart. I would not take any help from anyone, especially God! All my sins made me sick and kept me in constant pain, in my body and in my soul.

Then, I came face to face with the loveliest man I had ever met. Jesus touched me with his hand, and lifted me up and spoke to me in the most melodious voice I had ever heard in my life. He looked directly at me with such kindness and love in His eyes, that I was in shock that anyone could show love to me.

He spoke to me as if He knew me, and still He loved me as I was. He changed my stony heart in a twinkling of an eye, and gave me a heart of flesh that could cry and laugh, and face evil and not be afraid, so I could now receive love and give love in return.

I floated on air everywhere I went, and I had such joy in my heart. I could hardly believe this could happen to me. I followed Jesus everywhere He went and became one of His most devoted disciples. I spoke of Him to everyone I met and told them what He had done for me.

But now Jesus has been crucified before my very eyes, and before the whole world, in a most shameful way. My heart is so broken because of the pain He suffered, and because He was an "innocent Lamb," and because He has been taken from me and from those that loved Him deeply.

Today, I "came early to the grave when it was yet dark."(John 20:1) When I got there I found the stone was rolled away from the entrance of the grave. I immediately ran to the home of Simon Peter and John and told them that "Jesus had been taken away and I did not know where they had laid Him."

The three of us ran to the gravesite and Peter and John saw for themselves that what I said was true. They went into the grave and saw the linen clothes were there, but Jesus was not. They then went away to their own homes," but I stayed weeping outside the tomb. I stooped down to look again into the cave and saw 'two angels in white sitting, one at the head and one at the feet, of where Jesus' body had been.'

They said to me, "Woman, why weepest thou?" I said, 'Because they have taken away my Lord, and I know not where they have laid Him.' Then I turned around and saw Jesus standing there, but I did not know it was He. Jesus said to me, "Woman, why weepest thou? Whom seekest thou? I believed Him to be the gardener, so I said to Him, 'Sir, If thou have borne Him, hence, tell me where thou hast laid Him, and I will take Him (John 20:15)

Jesus then said to me, "Mary." I immediately turned and said unto Him, 'Master!' I grabbed onto His feet with all my might, for fear that He may disappear from my sight. He said to me, "Touch me not; for I am not yet ascended to my Father: but go to my brethren, and say unto them, I ascend unto my Father; and your Father, and to my God, and your God."

I was convinced that He would not disappear from my life again, so I ran as fast as I could to tell the Disciples that I had seen our Lord and that He had spoken to me. I told them all that he had said to me. They had me tell them over and over again what He had said. We were all in hiding because of what had happened to Jesus and we were afraid of what might happen to us if we went out on the streets.

In the evening of the same day, the first day of the week, Jesus appeared to all of us assembled there and said to us, "Peace be with you." Then He showed us His nail-pierced hands and His pierced side. The Disciples were so glad to see Jesus alive again and they knew it was Him.

Then He said to them again, "Peace be unto you: as my Father hath sent me, even so I send you." Then He breathed on them, and said, 'Receive you the Holy Ghost; Whosesoever sins you remit, they are remitted unto them, and whosesoever sins you retain, they are retained.' (John 20:19 - 21)

This was the most marvelous encounter I had with Jesus. My heart was so full of joy; death had no fear for me ever again. "Jesus Is Risen. Hallelujah!

LORD, LET'S KEEP OUR PRIORITIES STRAIGHT

"Jesus...Jesus, could I talk to You for a minute? I know you're on Your way to the bath house so I will not keep You."

"Yes, Martha, what is it, you seem so upset?'

"I need help in the kitchen, because I am preparing a special meal for You and the others, and the work is so slow without Mary to help me. Would You please send Mary in here to help me, now?"

"Martha, Mary has been in the sitting room listening to Me. I will quickly wash and then I will help you; we can talk and laugh together, and the work will go quickly,"

"Oh no, no, no, heavens 'NO'; I couldn't let YOU help me; You, Jesus, with an apron on; You, Jesus, peeling potatoes? It wouldn't be right because You are the guest of honor, and this meal is for You. I must serve "You, you cannot serve me! Please, just get Mary!"

"Martha, my dear Martha, you are so worried about this meal and all the ones to come, but don't you see, that Mary has chosen the good part that cannot be taken away from her?" She has chosen the part of Me that is always with her: MY WORD."

JESUS, WHERE ARE YOU?
MARTHA, MARY, AND LAZARUS

JOHN 11: 1-46

My brother Lazarus was very sick; Mary and I were afraid he would die so we sent for Jesus to come and heal him. We know that Jesus loved Lazarus, and Mary and Me very much, so we believed He would come at once and save his life. We were wrong, because He did not come to us immediately but in fact; He waited two days before He and His Disciples even started for our home in Bethany.

'We learned later that Jesus told His Disciples that "this sickness is not unto death, but for the Glory of God, that the Son of God might be glorified thereby." After two days, He said to His Disciples, 'Let us go into Judea again.' Jesus' Disciples did not think He should go to us, because the Jews wanted to stone Him. Jesus was not concerned that His life would be taken from Him in this way.

Jesus said to His Disciples, "Our friend Lazarus sleeps, but I go that I may awake him out of sleep." The Disciples did not understand that Lazarus was dead, so they said, 'Lord, if he sleeps, he is doing well.' Then, Jesus told them plainly that Lazarus was dead, but He said that He was glad for the Disciples sake, that He was not there. Nevertheless Jesus said, "Let us go to him."

Thomas thought Jesus was going to His death, but said that the Disciples should go with Him anyway, and die with Him. When they all arrived in Bethany, which was about two miles from Jerusalem, they found that Lazarus had been in the grave four days already.

When I found out that Jesus was coming, I went out to meet Him, but my sister Mary stayed in the house with the guests. Upon meeting Jesus I told Him that if He had been here my brother would not have died. I went on to say, "I know, even now, whatever You will ask of God, God will give it to You." I still doubted Jesus even though it sounded like I trusted

Him.

I didn't really understand who Jesus was, because I said, "If You will ask God," who did I think Jesus was? 'He is God, manifest in the flesh. 'Yet still, I believe God was out there someplace, and later you will see I believed that God would do something someday. Jesus was correct about me, when He said that I needed to spend much time at His feet listening to Him.

Jesus goes on to answer me saying, "Thy brother shall rise again." I replied, 'I know that he (my brother, Lazarus) shall rise again in the resurrection at the last day.'

Again Jesus said to me, "I am the resurrection, and the life: he that believes in Me, though he were dead, yet shall he live: And whosoever lives and believes in Me shall never die. Do you believe this?"

I said, "Yes, Lord: I believe You are the Christ, the Son of God, which should come into the world.' (John 11:23-27) As you can see, I believed in the resurrection, but I believed it was coming for a future day; because it was easier for me to believe that the Lord is still coming someday when the dead will be raised, than for me to look into Jesus' eyes and realize I can live for Him today. I knew from the Old Testament that there would be a resurrection from the dead; I didn't believe that Jesus could help me now, and I still thought that cooking and cleaning were very important tasks that I needed to do before spending much time with Jesus. (McGee)

Later I said this. I went to our home secretly, and called Mary, my sister, and said, "The master comes, and calls for you." As soon as she heard this she arose quickly and went to Jesus. The Jews went with her because they thought she was going to the grave to weep there. (John 11:28-31)

When Mary saw Jesus, she fell down at His feet saying unto Him "Lord, if thou had been here, my brother, Lazarus, would not have died." Mary said the same thing that I had said to Jesus earlier, but there was one difference; I had spoken to Jesus' face, but Mary fell at His feet and spoke to Him. This tells me that she trusted Him as her Lord, and whatever He did was right.

When Jesus saw Mary weeping, and the Jews with her, He groaned in the Spirit, and was troubled, and He said, "Where have you laid Lazarus?" Those with Mary said, 'Come and see.' Then "JESUS WEPT."

(This is the shortest verse in the Bible) (John 11:33-35)

We did not really grasp what was going on with Jesus. "He was showing His great compassion for us, and for you, beloved one in the 21st century, that death is a frightful thing, and Jesus enters into sympathy with you and me whenever our loved one dies. He showed us that death is not pretty: He groans within Himself and He shows us how to feel the loss of our loved one. (McGee)

Some Christians try to tell us to be brave and not to cry at a funeral because after all, your loved one is already in heaven." (McGee)

The Jews said, "Behold how He loved him!" Some said, 'Could not this Man, which opened the eyes of the blind, have caused that even this man should not have died?' We realize now that Jesus was not weeping for the dead, but for the living. (John 11:36-37)

As Jesus again groaned within Himself, He came upon the grave. It was a cave with a stone rolled in front of the opening. Jesus said, "Take away the stone." I immediately said to Jesus, 'Lord, by this time he stinks: for he has been dead for four days.' Jesus said to me, "Did I not say that if you would believe you should see the glory of God?" (John 11:38-40)

'Then those took away the stone from the place where the dead was laid." And Jesus lifted up His eyes, and said, 'Father, I thank Thee that Thou hast heard Me. And I know that Thou always hears Me: but because of the people which stand by I said it, that they may believe that thou has sent Me.' (John 11:41-42)

And when Jesus had thus spoken He cried with a loud voice, "LAZARUS, COME FORTH!" And he, my brother, came forth bound hand and foot with grave clothes, and his face was bound with a napkin. Jesus said unto them, 'Loose him, and let him go.' (John 11:44)

"WOW!" I could hardly contain myself. Mary and I ran to our brother, and flung our arms around him, with such thankfulness to Jesus. What a wonderful day for us and for you, beloved one, to know whom Jesus is, and how much He loves you, and how much He loves all of us. Of course, His greatest sacrifice for us was still to come; in a few short days He went to the Cross-to die for my sins and your sins, and for sins of the whole World.

There is such meaning in the raising of my brother, Lazarus, from the dead. "He came out of the grave in his old body, and he had to be set free from the grave clothes that bound him. Even though Jesus saves us from death, we are held back in this earth by grave clothes. When Jesus was crucified, and put in the tomb, He arose from the dead never to die again. He came out of His grave clothes with His glorified body. The stone was rolled away from His tomb to show us that the tomb was empty, not to free Him from death, because He had conquered death once and for all. Jesus' grave clothes were left in the exact same position as if He was still in them. After His Resurrection, nothing on this earth could hold him back; He now could enter a room with all the doors locked." (McGee)

It is hard for me to realize that many of the Jews that witnessed the raising from the dead, of my brother, Lazarus, did not believe in Jesus. They ran to tell the Pharisees "what things Jesus had done."

"They wanted to plot ways to have Jesus put to death because they hated Jesus, and did not want to lose their position with the Romans if there was a mass turning to Jesus.' (McGee)

You would think that this crowning miracle would have turned the skeptics to Jesus, but it did not. Our Lord said to the rich man, "…If they hear not Moses and the prophets, neither will they be persuaded, though one rose from the dead." (Luke 16:31) People are not saved by miracles: the problem is not in the lack of evidence. The problem is the unbelief of man. (McGee)

"God so loved the world, that He gave His only begotten Son, that whosoever believeth in Him should not perish, but have everlasting life." (John 3:16)

I, Martha will end my story here. You and I know that soon after Jesus raised my brother from the dead, He went to the cross to be crucified. We were so sad then, but soon our "mourning was turned to joy" when Jesus was raised from the dead by the Holy Spirit on the third day after His death. Friend, I finally understood that 'He is God,' and the only One worth listening to. I was privileged to live on the earth at the time of His life and death. He wanted to be with my family and me, where we lived, and He wants to be with you too, even though you cannot see Him physically. He will make Himself more real to you today than when I saw Him "face to face," if you will turn your whole life over to Him and BELIEVE!

Paul

THE THORN IN MY FLESH

11 CORINTHIANS 12:2-10

I Paul, write to you from my Heavenly Home here with my Lord and Savior, Jesus Christ.

I am astounded at the discussion down through the centuries about my "thorn in the flesh." Believers seem to be consumed with what the thorn was exactly. They believe that God gave me this thorn to keep me humble.

Nothing could be further from the truth. Please turn with me to 11 Corinthians 12, and starting with verse seven, let us read together; "And lest I should be exalted above measure through the abundance of the revelations, there was given to me a thorn in the flesh, the messenger of Satan to buffet me, lest I should be exalted above measure."

Now you can see for yourself that Satan was the one to "buffet me" not God. God did not suddenly attack me to keep me weak and humble. Just the opposite. God gave me all of His strength to resist Satan, and thus to take His authority over this thorn of weakness. My weakness was listening to the words of Satan that would then discourage me; instead of using the Word of God to defeat Satan and his wiles against me, and thus receive the victory over any thorns that came against me.

When I asked God, "three times to take the thorn away, God told me His grace was sufficient for me, for His strength was made perfect in my weakness." (2 Corinthians 12:9)

In other words God was telling me that I had all of His power (from His Word), and all of His strength (for what He did for me at the cross), and I had His authority to not let any feelings of sickness, or rejection, to effect me in any way. I had to go forward in the power of His Word, to halt any evil forces that might overtake me that would stop the message of Jesus Christ from going forth.

I said, "Most gladly therefore will I rather glory in my infirmities, that the power of Christ may rest upon me." (2 Corinthians 12:9) I meant that whenever I felt weak in myself, either in sickness or distress of any kind, I could use God's own powerful words to stop the onslaught of the evil one on me. God never gave me any power of my own, but only His power in me through His Holy Spirit and His word to use in my life for all occasions.

I wanted Him to step in and do something for me, to bail me out of all my troubles, but God said that I had all the authority of Jesus Christ to calm the sea, feed the hungry, heal the sick, raise the dead, and overcome those who would come against me to stop the Gospel from going forth.

Did I have just one thorn in my flesh? No, I had many thorns, as do you. The thorn is not the issue; it is how to over come the trouble, the sickness, the rejection, and the problems of all kinds that come into our lives. God does not want us to be overcome by the enemy, and thus to become weak in our Spirit, so that our focus will go back to fleshly thinking again; trying to take care of oneself, instead of relying on Jesus and His finished work at the cross.

These are some of the trials I endured in my life. "From the Jews, five times I received forty stripes save one, three times was I beaten with rods, once was I stoned, three times I suffered shipwreck, I was in perils of waters, robbers, my own countrymen, the heathen, the wilderness, the sea, and false brethren. I was weary and in pain, I was in hunger and thirst, often cold and naked, but I said that I will glory in the things which concern my infirmities, through the God and Father of our Lord Jesus Christ." (11 Corinthians 11:23 - 33)

So you can see I had many thorns in my walk with Jesus Christ, that only the power of the Holy Spirit could endure for me and in me.

Today Christians speak of being stressed. Stress covers a multitude of sins; fear, anxiety, anger, unforgiveness, hate; stress can also be brought on by sickness and disease. People act as if stress is some kind of badge of honor, something they must endure, a part of life in the 21st century.

Not so, all sin, and thorns, and distress, is to be let go of, given over to Christ to take care of. He already endured all of your sin for you, so that you would not have to deal with it yourself, because you can not. You cannot do anything to make your sin go away, except trust Christ to wash it away with His blood. This was the same for me. Jesus gives us His Word to have His authority on this earth over Satan and his demons.

When you feel sick, or angry, or anxious, or fearful, you can be sure that Jesus Christ has already taken the consequences of sin of all kinds. Because that is true, you do not want to give your time and energy to trying to figure things out. The Devil wants you to focus on yourself. He wants to "steal (Jesus' way), and to kill (Jesus' truth), and to destroy you (Jesus' life in you)." you(Jesus' life in you)." (John 10:10)(John 14:6) If he can get your attention on something besides God, then he has succeeded; a sick body, a troubled spirit, or a dead person, cannot be a witness to Christ and all He is.

So as I return to my most glorious life here with Christ in Heaven, please go forth with courage, knowing that the Lord will never "leave you or forsake you" (Hebrews 13:5) And He gives you all of His life, and 'life abundantly' (John 10:10) to overcome any thorns you may encounter. Remember you will only come to health and happiness forever with God because you are in Him and He in you. You will never lose. Now you know why I said, "I desired to leave and to be with Christ," (Philippians 1:23-24) but I also wanted to stay and witness for Him. I want you too to be His ambassador on the earth.

"THE GRACE OF OUR LORD JESUS CHRIST IS WITH YOU ALL."

AMEN

BEFORE WE MARRY

"Before we marry, we've got to figure out the divorce. We've each got our own lawyer, so we can go over EVERYTHING together! Okay, Honey?" (I can't have anyone stealing me blind, not with my millions and all the hard work I have put into making money)

"Un Huh."

"I'll give you one million if you stick with me from one to three years. You get two million if we last five years. If we can tolerate each other ten years, you get a cool five million. What do you think so far, Hun?"

"Really!"

"For every year we stick it out over ten years, you get one million more each year. Are you getting this, Love?"

"Yes, I've got it alright!"

"Now for the houses; the one in Palm Beach is off limits to a settlement. That's mine and that's it, period! You can share it while we're married, also the one in New York, the one in Chicago, and the ranch in Montana. After the divorce, I mean if we divorce, you can have the house in Chicago, but the one in New York is mine and the ranch in Montana is much too perfect to go to you, Okay?"

"Un Huh."

"Now the cars: I love all my cars. You can drive the Explorer and maybe the BMW, but I and only I, drive the Audi, and the 62 Corvette, and the Mercedes. The 57 Thunderbird is only to look at; I start it up once in a while and take it to a show some times. I might let you see it through the glass after the wedding. The Rolls Royce and the Ferrari and the Lamberdini only leave the house if I am in the driver's seat!"

"The chauffer will take you, In the limo, anywhere you want to go, so you won't have any trouble getting around. Okay, Babe?"

"O... kay."

"Now, for the precious coin and rare stamps collections. I might consider letting you have one or two of the lesser ones when we separate, but mostly I don't let anyone see them. My art collections are my most cherished of all my possessions. I went the world over and had to do some fancy bidding and negotiating to obtain the most beautiful of all paintings and sculptures. I can't see letting any of them go because they fit so perfectly in the rooms, I had special made for them."

"The antiques and the Oriental rugs are part of the house and will never leave it. My wine collection is a work of art in itself and not negotiable."

"So, Sweetheart, my lawyer has already drawn up the necessary papers. Your lawyer can look them over and you can sign them tomorrow, so we can be married next Saturday as we planned; you'll soon be Mrs. Multimillionaire or Ms. Multimillionaire, whichever you prefer."

"My lawyer would like to speak."

"Is there a problem? You couldn't possibly have anything of value to quibble over...do you?"

"Miss Penniless would like you to know this: She would only marry you over her penniless dead body, but if you were to sell all that you have and give the money to the poor, she might consider marrying you."

"WHAAAT...GIVE AWAY MONEY? I don't know what she's talking about. Boy was I crazy to get mixed up with the POOR anyway! I need to find a RICH woman who will appreciate my money...I mean...ME!"

IT'S ANOTHER GIRL

It came to pass that there was a "Big war" in the world and all the people in the land were having their food, and their clothes, and their supplies rationed. And so it was that during this 'Big War,' with hard times everywhere, in a small town in New York State, that a mother and a father brought forth their third born daughter, who was wrapped in a receiving blanket, and laid in a hospital bassinette, to be close to her mother at the hospital.

And there were in the same country relatives and friends abiding, and doing the work of assembling war materials for the fighting men. The angels in heaven rejoiced with joy over this baby, as they do over every baby born. The relatives and friends came to see this new baby, and brought small gifts.

God looked upon this baby and knew the "plans he had for her, to prosper her, and to do her good, all the days of her life." God made her "fearfully and wonderfully, and her frame was not hidden from Him when she was in the secret place, when He wove her together in the depths of the earth." (Psalm 139)

"She is blessed in all spiritual blessing in heavenly places in Christ, and God chose her before the foundation if the world to be holy and without blame before Him in love. God predestined her as an adopted child in Jesus Christ to do according to the good pleasure of His will." (Ephesians 1:3)

"As she grows in favor and statue with God and man," God will choose her to accept His great gift of Jesus Christ; He will forgive her for her sins, so that she might live with God forever and forever, on earth, and in heaven.

GLORY HALLELUJAH!

ME, MYSELF, AND I MUST DECREASE

"I wrote this book myself, ya know."

"It could have been a serious accident, but my quick thinking saved us."

"Well, you'd be thinner too if you ate salad and exercised everyday, like me."

"Besides, I healed myself by eating right and taking lots of vitamins."

"My kids turned out right because I raised 'um right."

"I worked hard getting everything I have out of my husband."

"So don't think I'm going to just give you everything."

"I always know the Bible questions on Jeopardy."

"I'm pretty smart."

"I used to play the flute, ya know?"

"I'm the one that gave him the idea, ya know.?"

"I told you so!"

"I had perfect attendance at church for 25 years, and I had to drive 50 miles, one way, to do it, plus I had little kids to contend with."

"I prayed it would rain and it did, I believe my prayer did it."

"I look pretty good for my age and eating right is what does it too."

"I am one good cookie cook."

"Yep, just me."

"HE" MUST INCREASE

"That wasn't You Lord, was it, that told me to give "HER" a hug and a pie, when You know how she has said all those mean things about me over and over. If it was You, You certainly didn't mean APPLE PIE did You?

"That couldn't have been You that told me to OBEY my husband, all the time, was it?

"That wasn't You that told me to be tolerant of the slow driver in front of me, when You know that I am in a BIG HURRY…to be about Your business, after all.

"That wasn't You that told me to wait patiently and calmly with a smile on my face, while waiting in that LONG line at the airport, was it?

"Now, I know that I'm not supposed to worry, but You didn't mean EVER, did You?

"Now, I know You told Your children never to fear anything or anyone, but that is not the same as being afraid, is it?

"Everybody doubts things, that's not the same as doubting You, is it?

"Sometimes I lie without realizing it, so You understand that don't You,

Lord, You do automatically forgive me for that, "LITTLE WHITE LIE," don't You, even if I don't confess it to you?

"That wasn't You Lord, was it that told me to pray for the youth in our church, even when they come all dressed in black and wear clothes so tight one can see everything including the bare midriff and the bellybutton ring?

"Was that You Lord that told me I should pray for that disheveled woman I met at the grocery store; she stopped me and told me she was raising her grandchildren alone, and that she had had these children since they were babies?

"Did you really want me to pray for the single Moms in our church, and help them when I can with baby sitting and other needs they may have?

"I don't believe You meant for me NEVER to be jealous or angry with my loved ones and friends, did You?

"You certainly understand NEVER is impossible for me, and everyone else, after all."

"BUT 'NEVER' IS NOT IMPOSSIBLE FOR ME, (THE LIVING GOD) FOR I WILL GIVE YOU MY GRACE TO DO MY WILL IN YOUR LIFE AS YOU YIELD ALL OF YOUR HEART TO ME."

"An Jesus looking upon them said, "WITH MEN IT IS IMPOSSIBLE, BUT NOT WITH GOD: FOR WITH GOD ALL THINGS ARE POSSIBLE." (Mark 10:27)

ONE WAY TO PRAY

Dear Lord,

You've got to help me, Oh Lord, please help me, or I'm a goner. I'm so afraid, I'm nearly finished; I'm so nervous I can't think straight, and I'm so sick I'm seeing double, and I'm so jittery I can't sit still. My insides all hurt and I can't do my work, I can barely get through the day.

I have the bills to send out and I can't even talk on the phone. I'm so weak and done for. My cries seem to go unanswered.

I'm so wound-up; yet, I can barely move I'm so tired. I can't sleep and I have dishes to do and clothes to wash and meals to microwave, and I can't get off the sofa except to drag myself to the bathroom. I can hardly get dressed, because I'm so stressed out and anxious.

If you don't help me, Lord, I don't know what I will do. I'm so worried and I'm going down fast. Please, please, I have to crawl on the floor sometimes so my heart won't take off on me.

I'm really hurting here, so if you just heal me now, Lord, I would be so grateful.

In Jesus Name,

    Amen

"THE LORD SHALL PRESERVE THEE FROM ALL EVIL: HE SHALL PRESERVE THY SOUL. THE LORD SHALL PRESERVE THY GOING OUT AND THY COMING IN FROM THIS TIME FORTH, AND EVEN FOR EVERMORE. (PSALM 121:7-8

ANOTHER WAY TO PRAY

Dear Lord,

I come before You with Your word open in front of me. I know I am your beloved one and your righteous one. I am the one that You purified and sanctified by the blood shed by Your son Jesus Christ. I am worthy to be called a son, an adopted son now, because I asked YOU for redemption. I come before You, assured that You are a loving and kind God, who has already provided salvation and healing for me, who answers me and knows my every need before I even ask. The one who has planned my life before you set the foundations of the earth in place? You formed me in my mothers' womb to be exactly as You would have me to be.

You planned prosperity into each moment, each second of my long life. You planned each "jot and tiddle" of my life, all for me. Oh, how wonderful You are. I can barely believe how much you care and listen to my every word, and You read my every thought. I am never out of Your mind. All of my sicknesses were and are healed by the "stripes" You bore 2000 years ago. Any suffering or pain I have, is felt by You. You experience every tempting thought I have or will ever have, and have provided a way for me to escape.

You know the desires of my heart and will give them all to me. You lavish Your Mighty Love on me constantly. I have Your endless protection, and You call me by name. I will be Your delight for all eternity.

All my concerns have your immediate attention, with all of Your power and strength to bring them to bear. Any waiting I do is done in Your loving care, and in Your Holy Presence. Every word I have uttered, and every deed I have done, has been woven into a tapestry of eternal joy for me, by Your gracious hand and guided by Your all-seeing eye.

Oh Lord, could I ever thank you enough, or praise you enough, or love you enough, or adore you enough? The words I utter to You in praise are small indeed, but I know You relish each one, and You will forever keep them in your safekeeping.

My Lord and my God, to You goes all of the honor, and all of the praise, and all of my love, forever and ever.

Amen.

WHAT'S YOUR SECRET

"Hi, how are you doing? I've wanted to talk to you. Remember that Weight Loss Bible Study we had years ago? Ya know, we should try to get that going again! But it looks like you're keeping your weight off. How do you do it? I know you've been sick, is that how you've done it?"

"Well…"

"I bet you walk everyday, don't you? Well you've got the time. I find it almost impossible to exercise with my schedule."

"Well…"

"I suppose you're on a special diet. I can't eat all those raw vegetables, they don't agree with me. They give me indigestion; say nothing about the GAS! Plus, I don't have the time to chop, chop, chop all day. I've got a job you know."

"Well…"

"You're lucky you can stay home and be sick and that you don't have any kids at home either. I got three kids, ya know."

"Well…"

"Fast food, it's the only way I can survive in this world. Besides, I love cheeseburgers with everything on 'um. You're in the beef business so you can understand that, besides without McDonalds where would we be? Right?"

"Well…"

"I suppose you take vitamins? I heard you were seeing a nutritionist and some sort of 'Blood Doctor.' I don't understand all those vitamins and things; besides, it takes the bank of London to buy them. I've got my health insurance at work and I can get prescriptions at a discount too."

"Well…"

"I'm allergic to fruit. Well most of it. Watermelon makes me swell up like a balloon and peaches make me break out."

"Well…"

"Well, I gotta go. I've got to pick up a pizza for supper and get home. I drink diet pop, ya know, that keeps me from gaining too much."

"Well…"

"Wonderful to see you looking so good, and we'll think about getting together again if we could ever find the 'TIME!'"

OH LORD, WHERE ARE YOU?

Another day. I must drag myself out of bed.

MY BELOVED YOU'RE AWAKE; I COULD HARDLY WAIT FOR YOU TO WAKE UP, I HAVE SO MUCH TO TALK TO YOU ABOUT.

Let's see, I've got to go to the bathroom. I don't see why I have to go to the bathroom all the time. All that toilet paper!

DON'T YOU LIKE YOU'RE BATHROOMS, AND ESPECIALLY THE ONE WITH THE NEW BLUE TOWELS AND RUGS. INDOOR BATHROOMS WITH TOILET PAPER ARE STILL A LUXURY IN MOST PLACES OF THE WORLD.

Oh, that reminds me I've got to clean the bathroom, "Yuk," so I can put out the new towels and rugs. I'm not sure blue, dark blue, is my favorite color, but I had to comprise someplace.

RUNNING WATER, FLUSH TOILETS, CLEANING SUPPLIES, NEW ACCESSORIES, AND TOILET PAPER; ARE THINGS THAT I HAVE GIVEN TO YOU FOR YOUR ENJOYMENT.

I've got to get the breakfast on. Oatmeal, toast, and grape juice again, the same-old, same old…

OATMEAL IS SUCH A WONDERFUL NUTRITIOUS FOOD THAT I HAVE MADE FOR YOU; WHOLE WHEAT BREAD IS THE "STAFF OF LIFE," AND GRAPE JUICE MADE FROM SUCCULENT GRAPES IS JUST ABOUT THE BEST MEAL EVER, DON'T YOU THINK?

I'd better wash my hair today even though it takes a lot of time to wash long hair. It always gets a lot of snarls in it if I don't use "tons" of conditioner. I suppose I've got to put color on it even though it started to turn brown again when I started to use vitamins.

"OH, MY BELOVED ONE, I'VE GIVEN YOU YOUR HAIR AND YOUR WHOLE BEING. I LOVE THE WAY YOU LOOK, AND REMEMBER THERE IS NO ONE ELSE LIKE YOU. I LOVE TO LOOK AT YOU, AND TO ADMIRE WHAT I HAVE CREATED, AND REMEMBER, HAIR COLOR IS ALSO A LUXURY IN MOST OF THE WORLD."

Vitamins, vitamins, I take so many; they seem to be helping me, but I worry about all the money they cost. I wonder if it is worth it because it has been years since I started them, and it has been a very long regimen.

MY PRECIOUS ONE, YOU WERE SO DEPLETED IN YOUR HEALTH AND IN YOUR SPIRIT, THAT I CHOSE TO BUILD YOUR BODY UP WITH NUTRITIONAL CARE, AND PURE HERBS, AND VITAMINS; TO GIVE YOU A CHANCE TO GAIN STRENGTH SLOWLY. YOU NEEDED TO LEARN ABOUT ME EACH DAY AT A TIME. AS FAR AS MONEY GOES, I HAVE PLENTY, AND WILL GIVE TO YOU ALL YOU NEED WHENEVER YOU ASK.

Let's see, I'll get the dishes into the dishwasher, but of course I've got to unload it first. Then there's the dusting and the vacuuming and I've got to pay the bills; life is so humdrum.

MY CHILD, I AM RIGHT HERE WITH YOU AS YOU DO YOUR DAILY CHORES; AS YOU GO TO TOWN TO GET GROCERIES; AS YOU LAY DOWN TO SLEEP, AND WHEN YOU GET UP IN THE MORNING. I LONG TO TALK TO YOU, AND I WANT TO SHOW YOU THE WONDERS AND SECRETS IN MY WORD; YOU ARE MY MOST "PRICELESS CREATION!"

I suppose I've got to find time to walk this morning, before it gets too hot. Walking is good for my health, and heaven knows I need to get back on my feet again, somehow.

OH "MY PRECIOUS ONE, MY ADORED ONE, MY LOVELY ONE," SEE HOW STILL IT IS OUTSIDE TODAY; ALL OF MY CREATION WAS MADE JUST FOR YOU; THE AIR IS CLEAN, AND THE BIG SKY IS SO BLUE, AND YOU CAN TALK TO ME ALL THE TIME YOU ARE WALKING. I CAN TELL YOU OF MY GREAT CONCERN FOR YOU, AND SOME THINGS THAT I WANT TO BLESS YOU WITH TODAY. I WANT TO REMIND YOU THAT I WILL 'NEVER LEAVE YOU OR FORSAKE YOU,' AND EVERYTHING IN YOUR LIFE IS IN MY DIVINE CARE; IT IS WORKING OUT FOR A WONDERFUL, JOYOUS, ETERNAL LIFE, FOREVER, AND EVER, WITH "ME."

Lord, what am I thinking? You are always with me, making my path straight, and protecting me and working out my salvation to Your glory. Thank you seems to be not enough, but still, I give You all of my heart, all of my mind and soul. I know my end is most lovely as we spend eternity together, THANK YOU FOREVER! Amen.

TIRED, SO TIRED

"What are you doing?"

"I'm trying to get some SLEEEEP!"

"It's 9:30…in the morning!"

"I couldn't get to sleep last night until 12:30 a.m. and I was up every hour and a half going to the bathroom, then I woke up at 6:16 a.m. and couldn't go back to sleep."

"So?"

"SO, I have to go the dentist at 2:00 o'clock this afternoon, and I have to get groceries and shop a little, and I'm in no shape for any of that!"

"Who told you you were in no shape for that? You have all of My strength in you, so you can do all of those things and more, if necessary."

"Well it only stands to reason that if I don't sleep much , and in my condition, I wouldn't be able to keep up."

"Who told you that? And what condition is that, exactly?"

"You know what condition I am in. I've been sick for years, fighting mono, panic attacks, parasites, kidney infection, sinusitis, and…need I go on?"

"Hold on there, don't you think I know what goes on in your body? Don't you know I have every hair of your head numbered? Don't you know I knit you together in your mother's womb? Don't you know you are not your own, that I bought you with a price, and I would not let you be hurt in any way. You have all of My power working in you."

"I'm not being hurt? Lack of sleep doesn't hurt my body at all?"

"No, My beloved one. I spent many a night in prayer, when I was on the earth, and it was for you for this moment, so you are able to do all I did and much more. I also intercede for you from My heavenly home."

"Oh, my Lord and my God, how great you are to me. Help me to believe You always, and trust You."

AMEN

WHERE CAN YOU RUN?

WHERE ARE YOU RUNNING TO, MY LOVE?

ARE YOU RUNNING TOWARD MY LOVE? ARE YOU RUNNING TOWARD MY PEACE? ARE YOU RUNNING TOWARD MY HOPE? ARE YOU RUNNING TOWARD MY JOY? ARE YOU RUNNING TOWARD MY LIFE?

ARE YOU RUNNING FROM MY LIFE? ARE YOU RUNNING FROM YOUR SIN? ARE YOU RUNNING FROM YOUR CIRCUMSTANCES? ARE YOU RUNNING FROM YOUR PARENTS? ARE YOU RUNNING FROM YOUR SPOUSE? ARE YOU RUNNING FROM YOUR ENEMIES? ARE YOU RUNNING FROM YOUR HOME? ARE YOU RUNNING FROM YOUR JOB? ARE YOU RUNNING FROM YOUR SCHOOL? ARE YOU RUNNING FROM YOUR COUNTRY?

IF YOU MUST KEEP RUNNING, KNOW THAT YOU CAN ONLY RUN INTO "ME," EVERYWHERE YOU RUN, I AM THERE!

EVERYWHERE YOU RUN I WILL RUN WITH YOU. I WILL ALWAYS BE WITH YOU FOREVER. YOU WILL ONLY RUN INTO ME IN THIS LIFE AND IN YOUR PHYSICAL DEATH, AND IN YOUR LIFE TO COME.

EVERYWHERE YOU RUN, I AM "THERE," I HAVE ALWAYS BEEN "THERE," WAY BEFORE YOU EVER GET "THERE."

SO, YOU CAN ONLY RUN INTO ME; IF YOU GO AHEAD, OR IF YOU GO BEHIND, OR IF YOU GO EAST, OR IF YOU GO WEST, OR IF YOU GO UP, OR IF YOU GO DOWN, OR IF YOU GO AROUND, OR IF YOU GO BACK, OR IF YOU GO FORTH, OR IF YOU GO INTO SPACE, OR IF YOU GO INTO CYBERSPACE; YOU WILL ONLY RUN INTO ME, THE ONE WHO LOVES YOU SO DEARLY.

PLEASE STOP RUNNING; PLEASE CATCH YOUR BREATH AND KNOW THAT I AM ALL YOU NEED, OR EVER WILL NEED. I AM ALL YOU

WANT OR YEARN FOR, OR LONG FOR; YOUR "GOD" AND YOUR "LORD," THE ONE WHO WATCHES OVER YOU AND PROTECTS YOU, AND LEADS YOU IN THE RIGHT PATH, NOW AND FOREVERMORE!

    AMEN!

WHAT DO YOU WANT ME TO DO?

"Lord, what do you want me to doooo? I'll lay on the alter, I'll go to ends of the earth for You, I'll be in church every Sunday, I'll pray an hour every day, I'll double up on my giving, and I'll bake more cookies for church functions and the poor.

"I'm ready and waiting to do anything and all things for You. I could maybe go to Africa and maybe live without electricity, and maybe teach them to bake cookies. I could volunteer at the homeless shelter, or go to the rest home, or go to the sick and hungry and give out cookies.

"I could maybe teach Sunday school, or help out with the Youth Group, or volunteer to chaperone on a camping trip, if I can take my RV, and I could maybe teach them to bake cookies on an open fire, if it doesn't rain all the time.

"Lord, Lord, what do You want me to DOOO? Here I am, ready to do whatever you tell me to DOOO!"

"LOVE ME, LOVE YOUR HUSBAND, LOVE YOUR FAMILY, LOVE YOUR NEIGHBOR. KEEP ON BAKING COOKIES!"

"That's it, Lord? You, husband, family, neighbor, COOKIES! I believe I can do that!"

"YES, MY BELOVED, YOU CAN, AND YOU WILL DO IT AS I ANNOINT YOU WITH MY LIFE AND LOVE EACH DAY, AS WE GO FORTH TOGETHER."

MY LIFE

"So God, are You saying that my life has nothing to do with me, but everything to do with YOU? When I get up in the morning that's Your life that rises up, it is not my strength that lifts me out of bed? And when I lay down to sleep it is Your peace in me that rests, and Your protection that keeps me safe even when trouble is all around me? (Proverbs 3:24 "When thou liest down, thou shall not be afraid: yea, thou shall lie down, and thou sleep shall be sweet.")

"I'm thinking of Peter when he was in jail, with a death sentence hanging over his head in the morning, yet he slept soundly enough that the angel, You sent, had to shake him awake, help him on with his sandals, and lead him out of the jail, while the others knew nothing.

"But surely the food I eat, the exercise I do, and the water I drink, and the vitamins I take, sustain the life You give me; I certainly couldn't live without them, could I?"

"I HAVE PUT YOU IN MY CREATION AND IN TIME, AND THE FRUITS, AND VEGETABLES, AND WATER, AND MEAT, ARE ALL THERE FOR YOUR ENJOYMENT, BUT THEY DO NOT GIVE YOU LIFE. 'I' AND "I" ALONE 'AM' YOUR LIFE; MY LIFE MOST ABUNDANT. REMEMBER, I WENT FORTY DAYS IN THE WILDERNESS WITHOUT FOOD OR WATER. PAUL SUFFERED MANY THINGS IN THE FLESH, BUT NONE OF THEM COULD KILL HIM UNTILL MY PLAN FOR HIS LIFE AND HIS TIME ON EARTH WAS ENDED. THE WHIPPINGS I ENDURED AND THE CROSS- COULD NOT KILL ME; I HAD TO GIVE UP MY PHYSICAL BODY TO DEATH, BECAUSE MY SPIRIT WOULD HAVE KEPT IT ALIVE FOREVER. DO YOU UNDERSTAND THIS?"

"Yes"

"DO YOU KNOW HOW I CREATED THE EARTH, THE ANIMALS, THE BIRDS AND MAN AND ALL THE UNIVERSE?"

"By Your Word, all is created by Your Word, and everything is held up by Your Word."

"SO YOU SEE YOUR LIFE IS NOT YOUR OWN; 'YOU WERE BOUGHT WITH A PRICE, BY MY PRECIOUS BLOOD." THE WORLD BELONGS TO "ME" AND EVERYTHING IN IT. I WILL ONLY TAKE GOOD CARE OF YOU SO, YOU MUST NEVER BE AFRAID OF 'ME,' OR DOUBT MY CARE, AND GREAT LOVE FOR YOU."

GOD'S WILL, MY CHOICE

Do I love You Jesus, with all of my heart?

Am I waiting for a feeling?

Or is it by my choice.

Do I have the health you gave me, Jesus, by "Your stripes" so long ago?

Am I waiting for a feeling? Or is it by my choice.

Do I have Your joy of life, Lord?

Is it within me now?

Am I waiting for a feeling?

Or is it by my choice.

Do I have the peace you gave me, Lord,

That "passes all my understanding?"

Am I waiting for a feeling?

Or is it by my choice.

Do I try to change my husband?

Am I waiting to see results?

Will I bless him with Your Words Lord?

As I choose to by my choice.

Do I try to change my children?

By my power and my might, or can I trust Your Spirit Lord,

As I choose to walk by faith, not by sight.

These neighbors are a problem Lord,

No change can I see.

Is there hope for their salvation?

By choosing Your Words and Your Life: that is the key.

Is the Pastor "Right" with You, Lord?

Is he Your 'anointed' man?

I need to pray for him daily, as I choose to trust him to Your Hand?

Will I ever forgive myself, Lord?

Can Your Word be all I need?

You told me I am "righteous" now,

Because Jesus paid the price,

By His choice and by His deed!

You told me: You are "THE WAY, THE TRUTH AND THE LIFE, LORD" (John 14:6)

This is your plan for me,

And I embrace it and accept it,

By Your Grace, and in faith, by my CHOICE,

I Know You have set me free!

JUST GIVE UP

Lord, I come to You as I am. You have always known what I am like, but until now I have denied that I am bad enough to be called a "sinner". I hate all of my sins now, and I 'repent' and turn away from all the wrong thoughts I have had toward You in my lifetime. I give up my fear of not being able to please You, and trying to make myself acceptable to You and to others. I give up trying to get justice for myself for the wrongs that I feel others have done against me. (Hebrews 10:30 "For we know Him that hath said, "Vengeance belongs unto me, I will repay, saith the Lord,")

I believe and receive your forgiveness for all I have done against You. I accept Your precious gift of eternal life. I believe my old self was crucified with You on the cross, and in Baptism You washed me clean. Now I have only Your new life living in me for all eternity.

Thank you, Dear Lord, for dying in my place on the cross so that now I am acceptable before the Father as if I had never sinned at all; my past sins, my sins of today, and the sins I may commit in the future, are all forgiven. It is beyond my comprehension, but I don't have to understand it all to know of Your great love for me. Love without end.

All that I am, that You created me to be is under Your shed Blood, I am a new creation.

AMEN

"FEAR NOT, I WILL HELP YOU"

ISAIAH 41:10

"You have gotten fat since the last time I saw you."

"Well, I've gained some."

"SOME! I think you're kidding yourself."

"Wellll..."

"I bet you could lose forty pounds now! You've got to get back to TOPS."

"Well, I'm asking God to get the weight off this time."

"GOD! Look, praying helps I'm sure, but God expects you to eat right and EXERCISE. There is no other way, and that's 'His' only way, He invented it, ya know."

"Well, I understand diet and exercise, and I was the queen of calorie counting and walking every day, come rain or snow, or sunshine, or blow."

So, let's get with it child. There is no time like the present. You obviously are not walking and countin' those calories now.

Well, I walk a little.

"Okay, that settles it, I'm signing you up at TOPS. Be there Tuesday at ten sharp!"

"Well, in Matthew 6:31 God said, 'Therefore take no thought saying, "What shall I eat? Or, what shall I drink? Or, (how) shall I be clothed?" For your Heavenly Father knows that you have need of all these things, but seek you first the kingdom of God, and His righteousness; and all these things shall be added unto you. Take therefore no thought for the things of itself. Sufficient unto the day is the evil thereof,"

"That doesn't make any sense. God doesn't mean not to think about what you eat, or drink, or wear; no matter how much you misconstrue it."

"Well, in another place God said to, 'Go your way, eat the fat and drink the sweet, and send portions unto them for whom nothing is prepared." (Nehemiah 8:10)

"You better get your head on straight, 'honey-bunny.' This is America, the 21st century you're livin' in. The fat and the sweet have made you FAT, and everybody has access to McDonald's now; portions have already been prepared in "fast-food-land." So, let's be sensible about this!"

"Well, Jesus provided my healing by His stripes. 'With His stripes we are healed." (Isaiah 53:5) In Jeremiah 30:17 it is written: "For I will restore health unto thee, and I will heal thee of thy wounds, saith the Lord."

"That has nothing whatever to do with you being FAT: that only applies to spiritual healing or people with incurable cancer. Otherwise we have doctors to help us. They are telling you to eat your salad, fresh fruit, lean meat, and EXERCISE, EXERCISE, EXERCISE!"

"Well, God says in Timothy 4:8 that, 'Bodily exercise profiteth little; but godliness is profitable unto all things, having promise of the life that now is, and of that which is to come."

"Oh pleeeese, 'help me God' to convince you that none of this applies to the FAT person who obviously needs EXERCISE badly."

"Well, again God says that 'we have not because we ask not, and if we ask anything in the name of Jesus, He will do it, and when we seek God first, all will be added to the one in need." (John 14:14) (Matthew 7:33)

"What we need here is subtraction not addition. To get thin takes, hard work, good sense about food, eating less, and EXERCISE, EXERCISE, EXERCISE! Seeking God will tell you that you got yourself into this, and there is only ONE who can get 'herself out."

"Well, in another place in the Bible, God says 'there are those that will forbid you to marry, and commanding you to abstain from meats, which God hath created to be received with thanksgiving of them which believe and know the truth. For every creature of God is good, and nothing to be refused if it is received with Thanksgiving; for it is sanctified by the Word of God and prayer." (Timothy 4:3-5)

"I think you should thank God for the skinless chicken breast, and the sword fish (say nothing about the kale and Romaine lettuce) He gave you to eat while you're on your weight loss program, and then incorporating it into your lifetime eating plan."

"Well, what about in Colossians 2 (Living Bible) where God says, 'so don't let anyone criticize you for what you eat or drink, or for not celebrating Jewish holidays and feasts or new moon ceremonies or Sabbaths, For these where only temporary rules that ended when Christ came. They were only shadows of the real thing—of Christ himself. Since you died, as it were, with Christ, and this has set you free from following the world's ideas of how to be saved—by doing good and obeying various rules as "not eating, tasting, or even touching certain foods? Such rules are mere human teachings, for food was made to be eaten and used up. These rules may seem good, for rules of this kind requires strong devotion and are humiliating and hard on the body, but they have no effect when it comes to conquering a person's evil thoughts and desires. They only make him proud."

"I GIVE UP! I can't believed you found all this in the Bible, and you make it sound like God said it just to you. Can't you see that weight loss is a whole different problem than any other? We were born with certain metabolisms and they can't be changed by anyone or anything. In-put must equal out-put, or the body gets FAT, FAT, FAT! That is where you are at, right now. Please live in reality, not by ancient words spoken thousands of years ago that really have nothing to do with processed foods, candy and pop, that we live with in the 21st century."

"Well, I believe Jesus fulfilled the law for me at the Cross, and did what I am unable to do. So I must disagree."

"Of course you would, because you are the FAT one, even though you have spoken these words. I think you should see they are NOT helping you to lose weight."

"Well, please hang around and you will see that God is faithful. and He will get the weight off, as 'I can do nothing without Him.' "Without faith it is impossible to please God." I thank God that he has heard me, and that He always hears me. He will tell me if I am believing a lie." (John 1:41-12) (John 5:19)

WHAT IS IT LIKE TO BE YOKED TO JESUS?

"I am crucified with Christ; nevertheless, I live; yet not I, but Christ lives in me: and the life which I now live in the flesh I live by the faith of the Son of God who loves me, and gave Himself for me."

Matthew 11:29-30, Galatians 2"20, Matthew 6:9-13, 1 Peter 2:24, Jeremiah 30:17

I woke up: Jesus was waiting for me, and He was smiling.

I didn't feel very happy to be awake; my whole body was racked with pain since I fell and broke a rib, but He said, "WHAT A WONDERFUL DAY TO BE ALIVE; WE WILL BE GLAD AND REJOICE IN IT."

When I stood up my knees buckled, and I was beside Jesus by the bed. Jesus put His arm around me and He started praying to our heavenly Father.

"OUR HOLY HEAVENLY FATHER, TODAY YOUR WILL BE DONE IN US, AS IT IS IN HEAVEN, YOU GIVE US YOUR WONDEFUL FOOD TO EAT: WE ARE THANKFUL THAT WE HAVE SOMEONE TO SHARE OUR FOOD WITH, AND THAT WE HAVE SUCH A WONDERFUL SELECTION OF NOURISHING FOOD TO CHOOSE FROM. WE ARE THANKFUL FOR WHAT IS PUT BEFORE US, AND FOR THOSE WHO HAVE PREPARED IT.

"WE PRAY THAT EVERYONE WILL ENJOY THEIR FOOD TODAY AND WILL HAVE FOOD TO EAT. MAY WE PROVIDE, FROM THE ABUNDANCE YOU HAVE GIVEN US, FOOD FOR SOMEONE ELSE THAT HAS NONE.

"THANK YOU FOR YOUR FORGIVENESS TO SINNERS: WE FORGIVE ALL WE WILL MEET TODAY IF WE MIGHT BECOME OFFENSIVE TO THEM.

"WE BELIEVE, FATHER, THAT YOU WILL KEEP OUR EYES STAYED ON YOU TODAY, SO THAT WE WILL BE DELIVERED FROM ALL TEMPTATION. I, JESUS, WAS TEMPTED IN ALL WAYS AND DID NOT SIN, AND I CAN KEEP MY LOVED ONE HERE, ALSO FROM SIN, BECAUSE OUR WORD, FATHER, GIVES OUR BELOVED ONES A WAY TO ESCAPE ALL EVIL..

"TO YOU, OUR FATHER, BELONGS THE KINGDOM: THE KINGDOM OF OUR HEART, AND ALL THE POWER AND AUTHORITY WE HAVE TODAY BELONGS TO YOU: AND ALL OF YOUR GLORY SHINES IN US TODAY, TO REFLECT IN US WHO YOU ARE, AND THIS LIFE WE HAVE IS FROM YOU TO US, FOREVER AND FOREVER! AMEN!"

Now, Jesus pulled me to my feet and said, "LET'S GO! WHAT IS ON YOUR AGENDA TODAY?"

"Well," I said, 'Don't you make the agenda?"

He said, "WHATEVER WORK IS BEFORE YOU IS THE WORK OF OUR FATHER."

"It is? How can that be? You mean making oatmeal, and cleaning the house and washing the clothes, is the 'work of our Father?' How can I do anything with all this pain?"

"I WILL BE YOUR STRENGTH, AND AS WE GO ON TOGETHER, 'I SAY I WILL RESTORE YOU TO HEALTH, AND HEAL YOU OF ALL YOUR WOUNDS, AND YES, ALL THAT YOU AND I DO TOGETHER IS THE WORK OF OUR FATHER. WE WILL SEE WHAT WE CAN DO TO HELP PEOPLE AS WE DO OUR WORK, BECAUSE OUR FATHER IS CONCERNED HOW WE TREAT HIS PEOPLE, FOR THIS IS HIS GREATEST WORK, AND HOW HE IS GLORIFIED IN US."

What good news! The cloud that hung over me was completely gone now; pain was still with me, but now my heart was burning with great joy and love for Jesus. I watched Jesus as he looked at me with great loving concern. He said to me, "BY MY STIPES I HEALED YOU; IT'S ALREADY DONE." (1 Peter 2:24)

"WHAT HAVE I BEEN THINKING?" 'Life is so worth living with You Jesus looking me right in the eyes every day, you assure me that You will "never" leave me! In my aches and my pains, and my sorrows and my duties, and my joys; You feel everything as much as I do. You told me to rest knowing that You will stay with me through it all: which means there is an end to the pain! Yes, I love being yoked to, You Jesus, as my constant Companion, my loving Friend, my forgiving Savior, my knowing Guide, you are 'closer than a brother,' and my Comforter forever and forever: You will not let me forget that Your Glorious Presence is Living in me every day,'

Amen!

HOW DEFEATED IS HE?

"Satan is a real person you know?"

"Oh?"

"Yes, he goes around like a roaring lion seeking whom he may devour."

"Oh?"

"Lions don't leave anything but the bare bones, so I'm told."

"Oh?"

"Yep, they slick a person clean, clean as a whistle!"

"Oh?"

"That's like us, if Satan (that ol' devil) gets a hold on us, he eats us up for dinner and we have to fight like crazy to get away,"

"Oh?"

"Yeah, we have to cast him out everyday, and be on guard against him!"

"Oh?"

"Satan is mean and powerful, you know?"

"Oh?"

"He can tell you to be angry and you can fall for it before you think."

"Oh?"

"He can tell you to be jealous of your best friend, and before you know what hit you, you say things you wish you didn't."

"Oh?"

"Oh yes, the devil is a formidable force to recon with, I'll tell you. Job had to put up with him, you know, and look how he lost everything, including his health!"

"What about Jesus?"

"Jesus?"

WHO'S RESPONSIBLE?

"I just fell into sin."

"I didn't mean to do it."

"I wasn't thinking."

"I said I was sorry, afterward."

"I didn't know what was happening."

"He lied to me."

"They were supposed to do that, not ME!"

"I tried."

"I did my best."

"It seemed like a good idea, so I couldn't help myself."

"There was no way out."

"I'm not to blame."

"I'm innocent."

"I'm just not in love anymore,"

"I was never in love."

"We have nothing in common anymore."

"We just grew apart."

"The children will be happier if we live apart."

"I was only thinking of the children."

"I just couldn't help myself."

"We just couldn't stop ourselves."

"It just smelled so good.!"

"It just happened."

HOW DID I GET DOWN HERE IN HELL?

I know the Bible says that, "All have sinned, and come short of the glory of God. (Romans 3:23) But everyone tells me that I am a good person and I agree with them.

I know the Bible says to "Honor thy father and thy mother."(Exodus 20:12) I was nice enough to them, but they did me wrong when I was growing up. They always favored my older brother who never did an honest day's work in his life, so I had to do all the work and I never got any credit for it. Even though years have passed and both are dead now, I'll never forgive them.

I know the Bible tells me to "love my wife," but she spends all my money and she always criticizes me for everything, so I can't forgive her for that, unless she changes her ways.

I know the Bible says, "to teach the children in the ways of the Lord," but I did the best I could. They are all educated and successful in business, so surely that's all God asks of me, "Right?"

I know the Bible says to "pray for people in high places," but the past President got us into a war that had nothing to do with our nation's security, and our young men and women are getting killed everyday. "He was just no good." The present President has taken away most of my constitutional rights and is taxing my wages by all the spending bills, and the huge budget. How can I be expected to pray for people like that?

I know the Bible says to "love my neighbor as myself," but my neighbor is selfish and he doesn't keep his yard neat, he is opinionated about everything. I don't "hate" him, but I'll never love him unless he changes his ways.

I know the Bible says that "Jesus is the way, the truth, and the life, and no man comes unto the Father, but by Him." (John 14:6) I did my part; I went forward in a church service once and let Jesus forgive me for my sins, so that should be good enough for God.

I know the Bible says to "tithe" or give ten percent of my income, (Malachi 3:10) but I give what I can to the church; sometimes I give all the money I have in my wallet, so that's pretty darn good.

I know the Bible says to "be a good citizen of my country," but I stopped voting years ago, because it doesn't do a bit of good to vote. I called my representatives and they basically told me they were doing what they thought was right in their own eyes. So that's if for me.

I know Jesus said that "He came not to condemn, but to save," but I believe He has put a judgment on this country, with all the abortion, and the same-sex marriages, and the murder, and the rape, and the violence everywhere; there's just nothing anyone can do anymore, but wait for God's doom to fall, and fall it will with the 'Terrorists' running loose in the world.

I know the Bible says, "What God has joined together, let no man put asunder." But I figured I had to get a divorce, because I couldn't take it another minute. My wife and I never loved each other anyway, and we've got to get 'all' we can, while we can, what with the "Terrorists" and all. I should have a chance at 'real love and heavenly sex' when it comes along, like I have now.

I know the Bible says, "Not to lie, or bear false witness against my neighbor." But a little white lie is not the same as lying, and no one can get ahead in business today without telling some kind of untruths.

I know the Bible says, "By Jesus stripes I was healed," but I figured God gave me cancer to teach me something, and I know I've got to die sometime; so, when my number's up I'll have to go.

I know the Bible says, "God loves me." So, the best is yet to come. 'Right?' I don't believe in a personal devil, or of that configuration that's red, with horns, and a pitchfork, and a long tail; and I can't see how God would send anybody to hell when He loves everybody, no matter what, "Right?"

In John 14:6 Jesus said unto them, "I am the way, the truth, and the life, no man comes to Father, but by Me."

ALMOST PERSUADED

"Well, I'm sorta' thinkin' that Jesus could be God, and he might have helped the poor, and maybe he was crucified and then raised from the dead himself, but ya know, there are other denominations that believe that he is not God at all. The Bible may be true and the word of God, but I don't think that it is consistent with history. Most of it is only a nice story about people who were not real. Also, a baby born to a virgin is hard to swallow."

"They say that being the Son of God does not make Him God, because I, being the son of my father does not make me my father, right?"

"And ya know, it doesn't prove that Jesus was resurrected because his body was never found; back then everybody said that his disciples stole his body and hid it someplace."

"And healing people doesn't really prove anything, because I believe anything can be staged. Talking in tongues sounds like so much "humbo, jumbo," to me."

"They say Jesus raised people from the dead, but who really knows anything today."

"You might believe the Bible is God's Word, but mere men wrote it after all. And I believe that the Bible is only true for those that believe it, but for everybody else it's what they believe to be true is true for them."

"And all that talk about a devil is really just somebody's imagination. Some people do bad things, but it's only that I think it is bad, to them it seems right."

"Life after death is just one person's opinion over another, People may say they died and went to heaven, then came back to life, but it's whatever they believed in before they had this experience that dictates what they believed they saw on the other side. Also who's to say they were dead anyway."

"No, I guess there is no real "truth," and Jesus is just a crutch for people that need someone or something to lean on, Those of us that take care of ourselves, eat right, exercise, and wear a seat belt when driving, don't really believe in anything but the here and now, and what we can see and feel."

"Faith and truth is just one person's belief over another's, and no one can really know God, who he is or not, and there is no 'ONE TRUTH."

"Okay, let me ask you this one question, 'Would you say North is optional?'"

WHICH LIE, IS THE TRUTH?

"The devil made me do it!"

"I think I'm pretty good, certainly a lot better than my neighbor."

"I've gone to church approximately 26 hundred and eleven times in my lifetime, but who's counting, and that is only on Sundays. Think of all the other times I dragged myself to church, I mean attended the house of God, that should count for something."

"I drink only diet pop; that's what keeps me thin, you know?"

"I eat a lot of candy bars, but they did a study, and found out chocolate has antioxidants in it and it is really good for me, plus it gives me energy."

"They say this bottled water could have as much bacteria and chemicals in it as my tap water, but I paid $1.05 for 12 ounces, so I know it's got to be pure because it's called "Garden Water," after all."

"I've got my faith, you know, so as long as I really believe, I'm okay. I believe I'll make it to heaven okay, everything's ok."

"I tithe and I give to the handicapped, you know. I even got stuck giving to that transient family that took our church for all it was worth, but I don't believe God holds that against us, do you?"

"I eat a salad once in a while to keep healthy."

"As long as I have lots of money, I have everything; I mean if I have my health, I have everything."

"Well, I just couldn't wait, so I cut in that long line; that guy was sure mad, but I know God understands I had to get to work."

"I know I'm happy because I've got my money, my family, my job, my health and I got plenty to eat and I have a nice dog, too."

"Because God loves me, He'll let me into heaven, right"

"I'm going to heaven because I went forward 30 years ago and said I wanted to be forgiven; nothing changed in my life, but I'm sure God understood my motive."

"I believe God made man because He needs to have fellowship with somebody."

"I think I'll become a Christian today; one never knows when his number will come up."

"I know I'm going to heaven when I die, I belong to the right denomination."

"I feel separated from God, today."

"I don't know why, I just feel like I'm going to heaven when I die."

"Nobody knows if they are going to heaven when they die, it all depends on how one lived his life, good or bad."

"Boy, am I LUCKY!"

"I love Jesus, so I know I'm going to heaven when I die."

"I am dedicated to God's work, so I know I will be in heaven on the last day."

"I have "my" faith, so I know I'm going to heaven when I die."

"I believe I baked enough cookies to get me in to heaven, don't you think?"

FOOLISH STATEMENTS

All I can do now is pray."

"I've got to pray harder."

"Apparently God doesn't care."

"God must have been sleeping."

"I don't think God can hear me."

"Sometimes things happen that God doesn't know about."

"I think God wants me to be sick, so He can teach me something."

"God must have been looking the other way."

"God must have been over in China when that happened to you."

"God took her to heaven because He needed another rose in His garden."

"God needs a man to fellowship with Him."

"God needs my money."

"God is way out there in heaven someplace."

"God loves him a lot more than He loves me."

"God must have been looking the other way when He made me."

"I wanted to become a pilot but I guess God didn't want me to, because He never gave me the money to take lessons or money to buy a plane."

"I don't see why God didn't put me in a better family."

"I am a Christian, but the man I married isn't. I prayed to God, before we married to take away my love for him if He didn't want me to marry him. He didn't, so I did."

"I guess God forgot me when He was giving out gifts."

"I don't think that we should expect God to give us things, because He said He wanted to meet our needs, not our expectations."

"I prayed, but nothing happened that I can see."

"I guess the only thing left to do is to trust God."

THE RULES OF JESUS DAY

"You know, the Pharisees made up a lot of laws that they believed Jesus and all good Jews had to follow in order to be right with God, and to be able to go to Heaven someday. They constantly faulted Jesus and His Disciples for not keeping their man-made rules."

"Like what?"

"Well they had a lot of laws on what was considered work on the Sabbath Day. They didn't like it when Jesus healed people on the Sabbath Day because they considered it work. They faulted Jesus for letting His Disciples eat grain as they walked through a field, because it was on the Sabbath Day and they considered it work."

"How silly!"

"It was silly enough that they wanted to kill Jesus for not obeying their laws."

"Really?"

"We have a lot of new laws that many believe we should keep too."

"Like what?"

SOME RULES OF OUR OWN

Exercise, at least, 30 minutes a day, three days a week.

Exercise, at least, 45 minutes a day, five days a week.

Exercise, at least, one hour a day, every day of the week without fail.
Eat five raw fruits and vegetables everyday.

Eat only four ounces of meat twice a day. (The size of a deck of cards) Drink only two eight-ounce glasses of skim milk a day.

Take calcium tablets every day.

Take magnesium with your calcium tablets or it won't absorb right. Eat plenty of fiber.

Read three chapters of the Bible every day, without fail.

Laugh 100 times a day, even if you have to fake it, and you will have an aerobic workout.

Pray on your knees every day, or it isn't real prayer.

Use lots of credit cards to establish your credit.

Drink three glasses of wine a day to keep your heart healthy.

Chocolate is good for you. It has anti-oxidants in it.

Drink eight glasses of water a day.

Brush your teeth for three minutes, three times a day after meals.

No coffee.

Coffee is good for you or at least it doesn't hurt you.

Stop smoking.

Drink diet pop and it will keep you thin.

Don't drink diet pop because it has Aspartame and it will make you fat.

Eat a heavy breakfast, good lunch, and go easy on the supper.

Soy is very good so eat lots of it.

Soy has something in it that reacts to women's hormones, so, "WOMEN, DON'T EAT IT!"

Get nine hours of sleep a day.

Take a 15-minute nap in the afternoon, no longer.

Drink decaffeinated coffee.

Do not cross your legs when sitting in a chair.

Replace your toothbrush every two months.

Eat fruit one half hour before eating.

Do not cut lettuce with a steel knife.

Broil meat only.

Wash hands often, rub soap into hands for the length of time it takes to sing Happy Birthday through twice, then rinse hands.

Don't fry food.

Cook chicken well done.

Eat lots of fish, chicken, and nuts.

Drink vodka every day to prevent heart disease.

YOUR LAST DAY

WHAT WOULD YOU DO IF YOU KNEW FOR SURE, THAT THIS WAS YOUR LAST DAY?

Would you complain?

Would you take a nap?

Would you be depressed?

Would you be afraid to die?

Would you hold a grudge?

Would you deny yourself dessert?

Would you be fearful for your health?

Would your age be an issue?

Would you worry about how your hair looks?

Would you lie?

Would you go shopping?

Would you invest your money in the stock market?

Would you be glad you had made a lot of money to leave to your loved ones?

Would you be glad you didn't have all your credit cards paid off?

Would you be glad for the choices you had made in your lifetime?

Would you watch TV?

Would you go to the movies and see your favorite movie one more time?

Would you worry about time?

Would you be happy with your life?

Would you want to eat lots of your favorite dessert before the end?"

Would you 'REPENT' and ask God for more time?"

WORSHIP

What does worship mean?"

"Well, you know, we worship God?"

"Yeah, but what does it mean to worship God?"

"It is like bowing down to God and giving Him glory."

"The Bible dictionary says; 'Respect and honor shown to a person,"

"Yeah!"

"It goes on to say that man is forbidden to give his worship to any but God."

THE WORSHIP SERVICE

MARK 4: 31-32

Who's that sitting in our pew? I can't concentrate unless I sit in our own pew...Oh good they're moving back. Thank-you God.

Who's that? I never saw her before. I'll nod in her direction. Ho Hum, I didn't sleep a wink last night; I wasn't going to come, but I think I can stay awake until it's over, because I didn't want to miss the potluck dinner after, they are always so good. I just couldn't bring anything, but I am sure there will be enough, there always is.

Here we go. The pastor looks kind of peeked; he's probable doing too much again. He should slow down and take it easy or he's going to get sick.

Sounds like we've got a full schedule for the week ahead; what with the funeral on Monday, cookies for the Youth Group on Wednesday, that special choir on Thursday, and the Rest Home Service on Sunday. Next Sunday is Rally Day too. I might get through the cookies for Youth Group and Rally Day, but I see I'm on cleanup, so something has got to go. I'm sure if I don't have to stand up to sing these choruses. I am way too tired to stand all the time. These new songs may be a good change, but I personally like the old hymns; "When we all get to Heaven" and Trust and Obey;" it seems like we could sing my favorites once in a while.

The special music is nice. The guitar has its place in the church service, I'm sure. I don't like to clap in church, but everyone does it now.

Let's see...the sermon is on the "parable of the mustard seed." I used to have a mustard seed necklace; a glass ball with a mustard seed embedded in it. Everyone had one. At the time I didn't think much of it, but I would like to get one now for my granddaughter. Maybe the Christian Store has one.

What did he say? "When it is sown, it groweth up? And becometh greater than all herbs, and shooteth out great branches; so that the fowls of the air may lodge under the shadow of it." Mark 4;32

Well, I don't know, any mustard plant I ever saw was only two feet high or so. I wonder if mustard was different in Jesus day? I have seen fields of mustard plants and they are very yellow, but certainly birds couldn't lodge under it, or in it, or whatever. I guess the preacher is done so it is time for the potluck. I am sure I can struggle to the dining room, and I'm sure I will feel better after I eat.

"Hi, how are you, nice sermon wasn't it? We sure have a good turnout today. I am sure the beautiful weather has something to do with it. See you at the potluck."

ANOTHER WORSHIP SERVICE

MARK 4: 31-32

Dear Lord, what a glorious day You have made for us to enjoy together this Sunday, Your Resurrection Day, always a day to rejoice in. It is a privilege to be able to be here at church with Your lovely people to talk together and to meditate on Your Word together.

Oh, a new face at church, I will find out her needs, and see if I can be of any help to her today. I didn't get much sleep last night, but today is a new beginning with You, dear Jesus, and I have all of Your love, all of Your faith, all of Your strength, and all of Your joy, and all of Your presence in me, how sweet You are.

I see we have a busy schedule this week with the funeral tomorrow, the Youth Group, the choir coming, and the Rally Day next week. I will do whatever You tell me to do, and I will be of help as You give me the ability.

Everyone is so busy, so I want to do all I can to take part, and help others to know who You are, Lord Jesus. The Pastor looks so overworked. I ask You now to minister to him and to give him many willing hands to do his work with him too?

Oh, the text today is the 'Parable of the Mustard Seed.' Your Word, Lord, always speaks to me when I most need it. I am Your mustard seed. You make me to grow-up and to be like You, great and lovely, not of myself but because You live in my heart, mind, and soul and You bring all Your desires for me to come to pass in my life.

Thank you, thank you, for my life on this earth, in this place, and for all your people around me, even those that give me grief, because I know you, and You will give me the grace to love each one despite the differences between us.

Well, that went fast, Lord. It is already time for the potluck dinner. May all the food be blessed to us as we eat, and may we be joined together as we talk and laugh this day. This great day You have planned for me, and for all of us here, even "before the foundations of the earth." (Ephesians 1:4) You had every detail in place? May all Your plans and delights come to pass in my life. and in each one here?

AMEN

WORDS TO USE IN CONVERSATION AT CHURCH

UNTOWARD - "That is one untoward staircase to the church dinning room in the basement, but worth the trouble,"

JOB - "I can't wait to start my new job at your church, I heard the potlucks are great!"

COUNTENANCE - "You're countenance is required at the church this morning, as it is your team that is serving potluck."

MIDST - "Were standing in the midst of this table laden with potluck delicacies."

PROPITIATION - "I'll go in with propitiation and try to stop them from eating all the lasagna before you get there."

QUENCH - "You'd better quench that appetite for church cookies."

PUFFED-UP - "I'm all puffed-up after eating potluck at church."

VICTUALS - "I can't wait to get downstairs to the victuals after church. I hope someone brought blueberry pie."

GIRDLE - "I couldn't possibly wear my girdle to church on potluck day."

HAPPY - "I'm so happy you decided to come to our fellowship-get-to-know- new-people-potluck, today."

HEALED - " I'm so glad your knee was healed in time for you to go down stairs for the 'POTLUCK' today."

HEAVEN - "The Bible says we should 'salute one another with a Holy kiss.' (Romans 16:16) I could kiss the person who brought pecan pie today."

REVERENCE - "I have nothing but reverence for the cooks in this church."

SUMPTUOUSLY - "In Luke 16:19 we read that 'the rich man fared sumptuously everyday.' We must be rich, because this potlucks are sumptuous for sure!"

GIVE - "It is better to give good potlucks than to not."

GIFT - "The potlucks are a gift from God."

LOVE - "If these pot-lucks aren't a love-fest, I don't know what is."

RUN - "You better run downstairs and get in line before all the lasagna is gone."

WORK - "It is sure worth the work to have potlucks like we have at our church."

WRETCHED - "I felt wretched this morning when I got up, but after I ate that blueberry pie at the potluck, I felt MUCH better."

A CLEAN SWEEP

I woke up this morning and I figured I should become a Christian today. Yeah, I told the Lord I was sorry for everything, and that I didn't want to go to hell when I die.

Yeah, I figured it was about time I got my life in order. I thought it was time to give up a few things, ya know, like smokin' and swearin', and sleeping in all the time. I need to get a handle on my life. I need to turn over a new leaf.

Yeah, no more chasing women, no more all night parties, no more being late for work; yep, a whole new start. No more "junk food," only 'exercise, exercise, exercise,' for me. I'm sure I can be good this time. Before, I always slipped back into my old ways, but this time I'm "determined" to make it work and keep the job I have now.

I'm a whole new person. You-bet-cha, I'm a Christian now, for sure!

Matthew 12:43-45 "When the unclean spirit is gone out of a man, he walks through dry places, seeking rest, and finding none. Then he said, 'I will return unto my house from where I came out;' and when he is come he finds it empty, swept, and (put in order). Then he goes, and takes with himself seven other spirits more wicked than himself. They enter in and dwell there; and the last state of that man is worse than the first. Even so shall it be also unto this wicked generation."

LUKEWARM

"I thought you wanted to do something."

"Well, I thought somebody ought to do something."

"You said anybody could do it."

"Anybody could. But not you!"

"Well, do you want to see something happen?"

"Sure."

"Well, what are you going to do about it?"

"I'm going to let someone else do it."

"But nobody is going to do it!"

"You don't know that. Everybody is behind this and anybody can do it."

"HELP, PLEASE!"

SEX IS SEX

"What do you think about sex?"

"I like it."

"What do you think of our sex life?"

"We don't have enough."

"Do you love me?"

"It goes without saying."

"Are sex and love the same thing?"

"Don't start confusing me about sex. Nobody knows what love is."

"Isn't God love?"

"Well sure, God is love, but that's the way He is; God has nothing to do with sex."

"Didn't He invent it?"

"I suppose He did, for man's enjoyment."

"I notice you said, MAN!"

"??????"

"God loves everybody, and He wants us to express our married love in sex, so this shows us how much He loves us."

"What do you mean? SEX IS SEX!"

"For this cause shall a man leave his father and mother, and shall be joined unto his wife, and they shall be in one flesh." (Genesis 2:24)

WHY DO YOU DO WHAT YOU DO?

"MONEY, you've got to have money, you know?

"It takes money to live.

"It takes money to eat.

"It takes money to run a business.

"It takes money to get married.

"It takes money to have a house.

"It takes money to have a car.

"It takes money to raise kids.

"It takes money to buy stuff.

"It takes money to get your teeth fixed.

"It takes money to keep the church going.

"It takes money to DIE.

"It takes money to be happy.

"So that about sums it up."

"MONEY ANSWERS ALL THINGS" (Ecclesiastes 10:19)

SEVEN TIMES SEVENTY

"Have you ever forgiven anyone?"

"What kind of a crazy question is that?"

"Well, have you?"

"Well...of course. Have you?"

"Whom have you forgiven?"

"Lots of people."

"Name one."

"Well, I forgave you once."

"Oh, what for?"

"Remember the time you took the clutch out of the pickup?"

"Oh, did you forgive me for that?"

"Well, I stopped being real mad every day when I thought about it."

"OH GOOD! Because I kind-of-got a little dent in the Blazer."

"WHAATT!!"

I DID IT MY WAY

MOST DESPISED MAN

I, Judas Iscariot am the most despised man in history. My name Judas, a common name in Jesus' time, is no longer used. No one wants to use such a name as mine and rightly so.

How did I come to betray Jesus, the Son of God? It all started and ended over money. I let money come between Jesus and me, my only hope of salvation. And even after my betrayal, I could not ask Jesus for forgiveness and be saved. That is the nature of pride; it makes one separate oneself from Jesus, on the grounds of reason or denial.

A lot of small compromises caused me, a man of great promise, to be despised and hated. I was just an ordinary man with no great ambitions to be famous or remembered in history. I had friends and was trusted among the Disciples; I did not attain to anything else.

So what went so horribly wrong that I ended in despair and suicide? I took care of the money for Jesus and the Disciples. Yes, we did have money. Jesus was not "broke." People gave it to us, so we could help the needy and to supply our physical needs as we traveled around.

Jesus often told me to give $100 (denominations that you would understand in the 21st century) to a window to help her get food to care for her children, I would go to her and tell her Jesus wanted her to have $50 to help with her needs. Jesus may have told me to give $200 to a family whose father was out of work. I would give them $100 and keep the rest for myself. I was good at concealing this money from the others.

Of course, Jesus knew what I was doing, but I didn't know that He knew. I figured He would tell the others if He knew, but He realized the others would probably kill me right "then and there" if they found out. Jesus wanted me to repent and change my mind and come to Him for forgiveness. I would have none of this, because I didn't think I needed to repent, or to be forgiven. I thought I was hurting no one.

Every person in the World should take account of their life and know that it is the little things, or the daily decisions that one makes every day, that lead to life in Christ, or death, eternal death, forever separated from God's love by foolishness and greed. I will testify that it is NOT worth it.

Please hear me. I thought that Jesus would never die on the cross, Over and over again I saw Him get out of difficult situations and places that should have gotten Him killed. I knew He could disappear, and that He could change angry mobs into gentle people. He knew how to stop the Pharisees "cold in their tracks." No I had no doubt that what I did would not harm anyone.

After we had the Passover supper in the upper room, Jesus told us, His Disciples, that one of us would betray him. (Matthew 26:21) I had already made the "deal" for His life, with the chief priests for thirty pieces of silver. I went to them to get the money I needed to buy a piece of land. It was more important to me to have the money than to be faithful to Jesus to the end. To be betrayed by the one of your closest friends is the worst kind of deceit and hurt.

Jesus said, "The Son of man goeth as it is written of him; but woe unto that man by whom the Son of Man is betrayed! It had been good for that man if he had not been born." Then I said, 'Master, is it I?' (Matthew 26:23-25) I had no sense of truth in me. I could not call Him Lord, as the others had done. (McGee) I knew this was wrong, but I would not stop now. I then left the room to do my dastardly deed.

I knew that Jesus would be in the garden of Gethsemane praying, so I led the soldiers to this place and I said, "Hail, master; and I kissed him." Jesus said to me, 'Friend, wherefore art thou come?' Jesus is still calling me friend. I should have stopped then and there, but I did not. Some theologians believe that I had to betray Jesus because it was predicted. (Psalm 2:12) This is not true; God gave me choice, just as you have. I made this decision on my own and I would not change my mind.

"Jesus, knowing all things that should come upon him, "went forth, and said to them, 'Whom seek ye?' (JOHN 18:4) They answered Him, "Jesus of Nazareth." Jesus said unto them, 'I AM;' and Judas stood with them. Matthew 18:5

When Jesus said, "I AM," 'we all went backward, and fell to the ground,' (John 18:6) Then He asked them again, "Whom seek ye?" And they said, 'Jesus of Nazareth.' Jesus answered, "I have told you that I AM." (John 18:7)

Well, right here I realized that they could not touch Jesus. I was still confident that I had done no wrong. But you know the rest of the story; Jesus went to the cross and was crucified in a most excruciating death for you and for me. I did not accept His death as a substitute for my sins, but you my friend, can. I could not bare the deed I had done so I tried to undo it. I took the thirty pieces of silver back to the high priests and tried to give it to them. They would not take it back, so I threw in on the floor and went out and killed myself. Instead of going to Jesus for forgiveness, which He would have given to me most graciously, I went to man for forgiveness. Man is most unforgiving, but God is always ready to take you into His grace and mercy and forgive your every sin, no matter how bad it is.

This is the end of my story. Please heed my words. It is little things that you do each day, the choices you make, that lead you to life or death. God said, "...I have set before you life and death, blessing and cursing; therefore choose life, that both thou and thy seed may live." (Deuteronomy 30:19) Please make a decision for Jesus and 'life' today!

(Luke 22:22 And truly the Son of man goeth, as it was determined: but woe unto that man by whom he is betrayed!

JUST A BREATH AWAY

My beloved one, you keep going to the door to let Me in, but I am already in. I've been in you since you invited Me in 5 years ago.

You keep begging me to come to you and do something, but I Am always doing something for you. You plead your case, seeking help, but don't you know I am most willing to help, and I am always helping you. Listen to Me as I speak these words to you in the Bible, "And it shall come to pass, that before they (you) call, I will answer, and while they are yet speaking, I will hear." (Isaiah 65:24)

You have a plan and you present it to Me in prayer, You believe your way is the only way that I can work in your life. You're sure I haven't heard you, and you keep reviewing your plan to Me over and over again, as if I haven't heard you calling. I told you this in Isaiah 30:19, "He (I) will be very gracious unto thee at the voice of thy cry; when (I) shall hear it, (I) will answer thee."

My ways are higher than your ways and My thoughts are too, I am always working "without ceasing" in your behalf. My love for you is as great as always; I yearn to speak with you, constantly. When you feel your heart flutter, I feel it too, when your varicose veins hurt, I know all about it, and I know that you are concerned for your health.

The pain and suffering you feel, does not mean that I have left you alone, and that I am not speaking to you, or I do not care for you; it only means that I Am asking you to trust My Word, trust Me more, endless trust. ("Trust in the Lord (Me) with all thine heart; and lean not unto your own understanding. In all thy ways acknowledge (Me), and (I) shall direct your paths." Proverbs 3:5-6)

Trust Me without holding anything back; have a childlike trust in Me. I won't let you fall, I won't let you die, and I won't let go of you, EVER!

You are so afraid of dying; you need not be, because you have My life, life abundantly, life without end, "in you," and you cannot lose it, 'EVER.' Dying is not the issue, living your life in Me, that is the issue.

I am helping you to see what I have planned for your life, as it is revealed each day at a time. You are not bad or rejected, in any way, by Me, but I must test you to renew your mind to trust me, and only Me, at all times, in all situations and all circumstances.

Keep on seeking Me and I will build your life to be like Mine. You have all of My courage, all of My strength, all of My joy, all of My peace, and all of My faith, which will be revealed to you as you depend on Me.

You believe your destination is Heaven, and when you get there, everything will be different. Not so, Heaven is here and now because I am in you and I am Heaven. You are on a journey of eternal life that begins here, and continues after your life on earth is done.

I said, "I go to prepare a place for you, so that where I am, you will be also." (John 14:1) You know this place as heaven, but I prepare you on earth to live in heaven with Me, face to face. Heaven is where I am, and I am here in you. Heaven is when you trust Me and believe Me, and are cared for by Me alone. So, heaven is here because My Spirit lives in you, now and forever.

I will give you the faith you so desire, the trust of Me, and the belief in Me; I will give it to you, and you will have it as you go your way. All your prayers are answered already, because I know the end from the beginning.

Remember, "I AM THE SAME YESTERDAY, TODAY, AND FOREVER, (Hebrews 13:8) NOTHING EVER CHANGES WITH ME. 'I AM THAT I AM,' NEVER FORGET THAT!"

SOME THINGS YOU WOULD NEVER HEAR JESUS SAY

1. "Don't even think about looking at Me until I have My coffee."
2. "I didn't sleep all night, so I'm too tired to keep My appointments today."
3. "Everything hurts, My head, My bones, My back, My feet, everything."
4. "If one more person wants something, I'm out of here."
5. "What's that you're eating?"
6. "Back off, you're bugging Me."
7. "I'm broke."
8. "You look like you gained a few pounds."
9. "I love you so much, I'll overlook all your sins, come right on into Heaven."
10. "Send him away because he bothers Me."
11. "I prefer good-looking people."
12. "You're pretty good, so come right on into Heaven."
13. "Since you were baptized, confirmed and belong to a church, you will be in Heaven when You die."
14. "I can't help you."

THINGS JESUS SAYS

"Come!" (Matthew 11:28)

"It is written." (Matt. 4:4)

"You shall worship the Lord your God and Him only shall you serve." (Matt. 4:10)

"Lay up for your selves treasure in heaven." (Matt. 6:20)

"Seek God first." (Matt 7:33)

"Follow Me." (Matt. 9:9)

"For I have come to call sinners to repentance.' (Matt. 9:13)

"It is written again. Thou shall not temp the Lord thy God." (Matt. 4:7)

"Take no thought for tomorrow." (Matt. 6:34)

"Arise and be not afraid." (Matt. 17:7)

"All things are possible with Me." (Matt. 119:26)

"You shall live." (Luke 11:28)

"I give to you My power to overcome the enemy." (Luke 10:10)

"Have faith in God, speak to the mountain, 'be removed,' and have no doubt in your heart, you shall have all that you say. (Mark 11:23 - 24)

"I have overcome the wicked one." (John 16:33)

"Happy is the servant who does God's will." (Luke 12:24)

"And this is life eternal, that they might know thee the only true God, and Jesus Christ (Me) whom you have sent."(John 17:3)

"I go to prepare a place for you." (John 14:2)

"Where I Am, there you may be also." (John 14:3)

"Peace I leave with you, My peace I give unto you..."(John 14:17)

"But he shall receive an hundredfold now in this time, houses.....and lands, with persecutions...." (Mark 10:30)

"That My joy might remain in you, and that your joy might be full." (John 15:11)

"I will see you again, and your heart shall rejoice, and your joy no man takes from you." (John 16:22)

"I Am come a light into the world..." (John 12:46)

"I Am the bread of life." (John 6:35)

QUESTIONS JESUS ASKED

"BELIEVE YE THAT I AM ABLE TO DO THIS?" (Matthew 9:28)

"Which of you by taking thought can add one cubit unto his statue?" (Matthew 6:27)

"Therefore take no thought saying, 'what shall we eat, or what shall we drink or (how) shall we be clothed?" (Matthew 6:31)

"And why beholdest thou the mote (speck) that is in thy brother's eye, but considerest not the beam that is in thine own eye?" (Matthew 7:3)

"Why are ye so fearful: O ye of little faith?" (Matthew 8:26)

"O YOU OF LITTLE FAITH, WHY DID YOU DOUBT?" (Matthew 14:31)

"For what is a man profited, if he shall gain the whole world, and lose his own soul? Or what shall a man give in exchange for his soul?" (Matthew 16:26)

"If a man has 100 sheep, and one of them be gone astray, does 'HE' not leave the 99, and go into the mountains and seek that which is gone astray?" (Matthew 18:12)

"Is it lawful to do good on the Sabbath days, or to do evil? To save life or to kill?" (Mark 3:4)

"WHOM DO MEN SAY THAT I AM? BUT WHOM SAY YOU THAT I AM?" (Mark 8:27)

"What do you want Me to do for you?" (Mark 10:36)

"And why do you call Me, 'Lord, Lord,' and do not the things which I say?" (Luke 6:46)

"But God said unto him, 'Thou fool this night thy soul shall be required of thee; then whose shall these things be, which thou has provided?" (Luke 12:20)

"WHO TOUCHED ME?" (Luke 8:45)

"What king going to make war against another king, sits not down first, and counts whether he is able with ten thousand to meet him that comes against him with 20 thousand?" (Luke 14:31)

"Woman, where are your accusers? Has no man condemned thee?" (John 2:4)

"When I sent you (out) without purse, and shoes, did you lack anything?" (Luke 22:48)

"AND WHOEVER LIVES AND BELIEVES IN ME, SHALL NEVER DIE; BELIEVE THOU THIS?" (John 11:26)

"Ought not Christ to have suffered these things, and to enter into His glory?" (Luke 24:26)

"DO YOU BELIEVE ON THE SON OF GOD?" (John 9:35)

I DID IT GOD'S WAY – JESUS

GENESIS 1:1 – REVELATION 22:21

"Jesus, of course YOU would do it God's way."

"Why do you believe that I am different than you, a person?"

"You were born to a virgin, and the Holy Spirit is Your Father, and You are God. You are different than mere people."

"Why?"

"Well, You have the Holy Spirit living in You, and You have all of God's wisdom, and all of His knowledge, and You know what man is like; so this makes You different than a human man."

"Do you remember these words from the Bible: (Luke 2:52) 'And I Jesus increased in wisdom and stature, and in favor with God and man,' (Hebrew 5:8) "Though he were a Son, yet learned he obedience by the things which he suffered; And being made perfect, he became the author of eternal salvation unto all them that obey him." 'I increased in wisdom, I learned obedience, and I was made perfect.' Did I live on the earth for 33 ½ years so I could show you how different I am from you?"

"Didn't you come to die? What more is there?

"I am the God that endured all things that you endure, so I know what it is to be a man and to Identify with all that man is suffering. I did come to die in your place, but I also came to show you how to live, give you 'life more abundantly.' (John 10:10) I did not come to show you only whom "I Am," but to show you who 'you are' in Me. Do you understand this?"

"Not completely, but what do You want me to most know about You, and Your life on earth?"

"I LOVE YOU!"

"I know that You love everyone in the whole world."

"Yes, but I want you to know that I love 'YOU' with an everlasting love!"

"I know that You will love everyone forever, and that You do love me a lot, and forever too, but I can't see how 'love' is the only thing that You want me to know about You."

"Let me tell you about My life and maybe you will understand who 'I AM,' and why I came to the earth, as a baby. "I made myself of no reputation, and took upon myself the form of a servant, and I was made in the likeness of men: And being found in fashion as a man, I humble myself, and became obedient unto death, even the death of the cross." (Philippians 2:7-8) I made a way for all men to draw close to God the Father, and I lived as God's beloved son, here on the earth. In the book of John he wrote these words about Me: 'In the beginning was the Word and the Word was with God, and the Word was God. The same was in the beginning with God; All things were made by Him and without Him was not any thing made that was made. In Him was life; and the life was the light of men. And the light shineth in darkness; and the darkness comprehended it not." (John 1:1-5)

"Yes, that is what I mean, You are called the WORD; that makes you different, doesn't it?"

"Different than what, YOU? Why does being called 'the Word' make me different? You speak words don't you, so words should join us together not separate us, You know that I am a man, but you also know that I Am God; this is where you are getting mixed up, so let us "reason together," (Isaiah 1:18) so that you will understand why I came to the earth and why I am not different from you. That is the very reason I came to the earth to let you know how much God, our Father, loves you and wants you to love Him. In Matthew chapter 1:1 we have this account 'of the generation of Jesus Christ (Me), the son of David, the son of Abraham, "Why does Matthew give My genealogy as 'the generation of Jesus Christ?' In Genesis 5:1 we read, "This is the book of the generations of Adam." 'How did you get into the family of Adam? You got in it by birth. You did not perform it; in fact, you had nothing to do with it, but you are in it by birth. "But in Adam all die." (Romans 5:12) Adam's book is a book of death.' (McGee)

"Then there is the other book, the book of the generation of Jesus Christ (Me). How do you get into that family, into that genealogy? You get into it by birth, the NEW BIRTH. I told Nicodemus that, 'you must be born again to see the kingdom of God.' (John 3:3) But let us go again to the opening of Matthew. This gives an account of My genealogy leading to My father on the earth, Joseph, husband of Mary, My mother. "Genealogies are very important because they establish whether a person has a legitimate claim to a particular line." (McGee)

"We read, 'Abraham begat Isaac; and Isaac begat Jacob; and Jacob begat Judah and his brethren; and Judah begat Phares and Zara (twins) of Thamar; and Phares begat Esrom; and Esrom begat Aram; and Aram begat Aminadad; and Aminadad begat Naasson; and Naasson begat Salmon; and Salmon begat Booz of Rachab; and Booz begat Obed of Ruth; and Obed begat Jesse; and Jesse begat David the king; and David the king begat Solomon of her that had been the wife of Urias.' (Matthew 1:2-6) (McGee)

"In My genealogy there are four women's names mentioned. This is very interesting, as customarily, the names of women did not appear in Hebrew genealogies. Women and generally all women that marry, take the name of the man. (McGee)

"Tamar is the first woman mentioned. Her story is in Genesis 38, and if you read it you will see that Tamar got into the genealogy because she was a sinner. Next we have Rahab. Her story written in Joshua chapter 2, and we find there that she was a harlot in Jericho that "by faith perished not with them that believed not." Ruth is the next one mentioned. She is a lovely person, but in Ruth's time there was a Law which shut her out because she was a Moabite, and shall not enter into the congregation of the Lord (see Deut. 23:3) But Boaz fell in love with Ruth and he extended grace to her. "Bathsheba" is not mentioned by name but is called, 'her that had been the wife of Urias,' She became David's wife. (McGee)

"To go on with My genealogy: "And Ezekias begat Manasses; and Manasses begat Amon; and Amon begat Josias; and Josias begat Jechonias and his brethren, about that time they were carried away to Babylon. Now the genealogy concludes with this verse; "And Jacob begat Joseph the husband of Mary, of whom was born Jesus, who is called Christ." (Matthew 1:10-16) 'There is more that is interesting about My genealogy. If you compare this one to the one in 1 Chronicles 3, you will find that in verse eight of Matthew, the names of three men are left out. Genealogies are not necessarily complete, but they are to trace a certain line. (McGee)

"In Luke 3:23-38, the genealogy of My mother, Mary, is given." "She was also in the line of David through David's son Nathan. In this account I am revealed as the Son of Man and the Savior of the world. My line through my mother Mary does not stop with Abraham, but goes all the way to Adam, who was the first "son" of God, the created Son of God. But you know that Adam fell from that lofty position when he sinned. I, Jesus, the last Adam am the Son of God, who came to bring mankind back into that relationship with God which Adam formerly had and lost. This relationship is accomplished through faith in Me and what I did at the cross for you." (McGee)

"You know from the Biblical account in Luke 2, 'the angel Gabriel was sent from God (Our Father) unto a city of Galilee, named Nazareth, to a virgin, named Mary (My mother) who was engaged to a man named Joseph, (My earthly father) of the house of David. The angel said to her, "Hail, thou that art highly favored, the Lord is with thee: blessed art thou among women."

"My mother was troubled by his saying, and wondered what manner of salutation this should be. And the angel said unto her, Fear not, Mary: for thou has found favor with God, Behold, thou shall conceive in thy womb, and bring forth a son, and shall call his name JESUS. He shall be great, and shall be called the Son of the Highest: and the Lord God shall give unto him the throne of his father David: And he shall reign over the house of Jacob for ever; and of his kingdom there shall be no end."

"Mary then said to the angel, 'How shall this be, seeing I know not a man?'

"The angel answered and said to her, 'The Holy Ghost shall come to thee, and the power of the Highest shall over shadow thee; therefore also that Holy thing shall be born of thee and shall be called the Son of God. Behold, thy cousin Elizabeth, has also conceived a son, in her old age: and this is the sixth month with her, who was called barren."

"Mary said, 'Behold the handmaid of the Lord; be unto me according to Thy word. Then the angel departed from her. (Luke 1:28-38)

"After the visit of Gabriel, my mother Mary went to see Elisabeth, her cousin. She knew that she was six months along with John (as Gabriel had told her), whom would be later known as "John the Baptist." "When Mary entered the house of Zacharias (John's father), and saluted Elisabeth, it came to pass, that when Elisabeth heard the salutation of Mary, the babe leaped in her womb; and Elisabeth was filled with the Holy Ghost: And she spoke out with a loud voice, and said, 'Blessed art thou among women, and blessed is the fruit of thy womb. And why is this that the mother of my Lord should come to me? For as soon as the voice of thy salutation (Mary to Elisabeth) sounded in my (Elisabeth) ears, my baby (John) leaped in my womb for joy. And blessed is she that believed: for there shall be a performance of those things which were told her from the Lord." (Luke 1:40-45)

My mother Mary then prayed this prayer, "My soul doth magnify the Lord, and my spirit has rejoiced in God my Savior, for He has regarded the low estate of his handmaiden: for, behold, from henceforth all generations, shall call me blessed. For He that is mighty has done to me great things; and Holy is His name. His mercy is on them that fear him from generation to generation. He has showed strength with his arm; He has scattered the proud in the imagination of their hearts. He has put down the mighty from their seats, and exalted them of low degree. He has filled the hungry with good things; and the rich He has sent empty away. He has helped His servant Israel, in remembrance of his mercy; as He spoke to our fathers, to Abraham, and to His seed for ever." (Luke 1:46-55)

"Now, let me ask you, 'what do you know about my birth?'"

"I know that your birth was controversial because your mother, Mary, was engaged to Joseph, when he realized (before the marriage) that she was expecting a baby. Joseph was going to separate himself from her, but the Holy Spirit told him not to. ("Mary while engaged to Joseph, before they came together, she was found with the child of the Holy Ghost. Then Joseph, her husband, being a just man, was not willing to make her a public example, decided to put her away privately. While he thought on these things, behold, the angel of the Lord appeared to him in a dream, saying, 'Joseph, thou son of David, fear not to take unto thee Mary thy wife; for that which is conceived in her is of the Holy Ghost. She shall bring forth a son, and thou shall call his name JESUS: for he shall save His people from their sins. Now all this was done, that it might be fulfilled which was spoken of the Lord by the prophet, (Isaiah 7:14) saying, "Behold, a virgin shall be with child, and shall bring forth a son, and they call his name Emmanuel, which being interpreted is, "GOD WITH US." So Joseph being raised from sleep did as the angel of the Lord had bidden him, and took unto him his wife: and knew her not till she had brought forth her first born son: and he called his name JESUS.") Matthew 1:18-25

"When You were about to be born Caesar Augustus decreed that the entire world should be taxed, so Mary and Joseph had to go to Bethlehem, from Nazareth, to be taxed; they walked, but Mary rode on a donkey. When they got to Bethlehem there were no rooms anywhere, especially at the inns; so one innkeeper suggested that they go to the barn out back, where the animals were kept. They just got out there and you, Jesus, were born. Mary wrapped you in "swaddling clothes" and laid you in a manger. Then, that same night, nearby shepherds where told by an angel that You, Jesus, was born in the city of David. Then a lot of angels sang in a beautiful choir about Your birth. So they quickly went to Bethlehem to see You and worship You."

("And it came to pass in those days, that there went out a decree from Caesar Augustus, that all the world should be taxed. And this taxing was first made when Cyrenius was governor of Syria. And all went to be taxed, every one into his own city, Joseph also went up from Galilee, out of the city of Nazareth, into Judea, unto the city of David, which is called Bethlehem; because he was of the house and linage of David.) Luke 2:1-4

(And there were in the same country shepherds abiding in the field, keeping watch over their flocks by night, Lo, the angel of the Lord came upon them, and the glory of the Lord shone round about them: and they were very afraid. And the angel said to them, 'Fear not: for, behold, I bring you good tidings of great joy, which shall be to all people, for unto you is born this day in the city of David a Savior, which is Christ the Lord. And this shall be a sign unto you; you shall find the babe wrapped in swaddling clothes, lying in a manger,' and suddenly there was with the angel a multitude of the heavenly host praising God, and saying, "Glory to God in the highest and on earth peace, good will toward men." As the angels were gone away from them into heaven, the shepherds said one to another, 'Let us now go even unto Bethlehem, and see this thing which is come to pass, which the Lord hath made known unto us.' And they came with haste and found Mary, and Joseph, and the babe lying in a manger. And when they had seen Him, they made known abroad the saying which was told them concerning this child. And all they that heard it wondered at those things, which were told them by the shepherds. But Mary kept all these things, and pondered them in her heart. (Luke 2: 1-19)

"Yes, that is the account of My birth, but there is no mention of Mary, My mother, riding on a donkey, or that the angels sang."

"THERE ISN'T, THEY DIDN'T?"

"What does the Bible tell you of My life as a child, and as an adult before the time of My public ministry?"

"Well we don't know too much, but when you were two years old, "three" Kings from the East came to worship You because they had seen Your star in the sky and followed it to the place where You had been born. "When they got to Jerusalem they went to see Herod the king. They asked him where the King of the Jews was born. Herod did not know and was troubled that a king had been born, because he wanted to be the only king. So Herod told the Kings of the East to find this new king and report back to him, so he could worship him too. He didn't really want to worship You as a baby; he really wanted to kill You, because he wanted to be the only king. When the Kings of the East found You, they were told by God not to go back to Herod, but to go to their own country another way.

("Now when Jesus was born in Bethlehem of Judea in the days of Herod the king, behold, there came wise men from the east to Jerusalem, saying. 'Where is He that is born King of the Jews? For we have seen his star in the east, and are come to worship him.' When Herod the King had heard these things, he was troubled, and all Jerusalem with him. And when he had gathered all the chief priests and scribes of the people together, he demanded of them where Christ should be born. They said to him, "In Bethlehem of Judea; for it is written by the prophet, Micah," 'and thou Bethlehem, in the land of Judea, art not the least among the princes of Judah: for out of thee shall come a Governor, that shall rule my people Israel." (Matthew 2:2-7) Then Herod, when he had privately called the wise men, inquired of them diligently what time the star appeared? Then he sent them to Bethlehem, and said, Go search diligently for the young child; and when you have found him, bring me word again, that I may come and worship him also. When they had heard the king, they departed; and, lo, the star, which they saw in the east, went before them, until it came and stood over where the young child was. When they saw the star, they rejoiced with exceeding great joy. When they were come into the house, they saw the young child with Mary his mother, and fell down, and worshipped him: and when they had opened their treasures, they presented unto him gifts; gold, and frankincense, and myrrh. Being warned of God in a dream that they should not return to Herod, they departed into their own country another way.") Matthew 2:7-12

"Why do you think there were three Kings?"

"Well, the gifts they brought to You were gold, frankincense, and myrrh."

"Do you know what those gifts mean?"

"No."

"Gold speaks of My birth. Frankincense speaks of the fragrance of My life. Myrrh speaks of My death. In Isaiah 60:6 tells of My second coming and these gifts are spoken of again. 'The multitude of camels shall cover thee, the dromedaries of Midian and Ephah, all they from Sheba shall come: they shall bring gold and incense; and they shall show forth the praises of the Lord.' "As you can see myrrh is not spoken of here because there is no more death at my second coming, only life through Me as King and Lord of Lords." (McGee)

"Lord, Jesus, Your second coming is the hope of mankind when you put an end to sin and death." ('And then shall they see the Son of man coming in a cloud with power and great glory...then look up, and lift your heads; for your redemption draweth nigh.') Luke 21:27-28

"Yes that is the hope of My coming to earth again, which we will talk about again when we discuss the cross, but let's go on to what you know about My life when the Kings left?"

"Let me see, an angel came to Joseph and told him to go to Egypt with Mary and You, because Herod wanted to kill You. Herod was very mad that the wise men did not come back to talk to him. Since he could not kill You, personally, he decided to have all the children, two and under, that were in Bethlehem, and in the surrounding lands, killed; thinking You would be among them. Such a sad time for Israel, but when

Herod was dead, God, through a dream, called Joseph to take You and Mary back to Israel.

("And when they (the wise men) departed, behold, the angel of the Lord appeared to Joseph in a dream, saying, 'Arise, and take the young child and his mother, and flee into Egypt, and be thou there until I bring thee word; for Herod will seek the young child to destroy him.' When he arose, he took the young child and his mother by night, and departed into Egypt. And was there until the death of Herod: that it might be fulfilled which was spoken of the Lord by the prophet, saying, "Out of Egypt have I called my son." Then Herod, when he saw that he was mocked of the wise men, was exceeding worth, and sent forth, and slew all the children that were in Bethlehem, and in all the coast thereof, from two years old and under, according to the time which he had diligently inquired of the wise men. Then was fulfilled that which was spoken by Jeremy the prophet, saying, 'In Rama was there a voice heard, lamentation, and weeping, and great mourning, Rachel weeping for her children, and would not be comforted, because they were not. But when Herod was dead, behold, an angel of the Lord appeared in a dream to Joseph in Egypt. Saying, "Arise, and take the young child and his mother, and go into the land of Israel: for they are dead which sought the young child's life. And he (Joseph) arose, and took the young child and his mother, and came into the land of Israel. But when he heard that Archelaus did reign in Judea in the place of his father Herod, Joseph was afraid to go to thither notwithstanding, being warned of God in a dream, he turned aside into the parts of Galilee. And he came and dwelt in a city called Nazareth: that it might be fulfilled which was spoken by the prophets, 'He shall be called a Nazarene." (Matthew 2:23-25)

"We hear of You again when You were twelve years old. You and Your family went to Jerusalem for the Passover and were there for a few days. When Your parents left they realized You were not with them. They quickly returned to Jerusalem when they could not find You among the people that they were traveling with. After looking for You for three days, they found You in the temple listening and asking questions of the teachers there. Your parents were very upset with You, but You said that You were about "Your Father's business." Your parents didn't know what You were talking about, but they took You back to Nazareth with them, and You grew up there."

("Now (Jesus') parents went to Jerusalem every year at the feast of the Passover. And when (Jesus) was twelve years old, they went up to Jerusalem after the custom of the feast. And when they had fulfilled the days as they returned, the child Jesus tarried behind in Jerusalem; and Joseph and his mother knew not of it. But they supposing him to have been in the company went a day's journey; and they sought him among their kinsfolk and acquaintance. And when they found him not, they turned back again to Jerusalem, seeking him. And it came to pass, that after three days they found him in the temple, sitting in the midst of the doctors, both hearing them, and asking them questions. And all that heard him were astonished at his understanding and answers. And when they saw him they were amazed: and his mother said unto him, 'Son, why hast thou thus dealt with us? Behold, thy father and I have sought thee sorrowing. And he said unto them, "How is it that ye sought me? Did ye not know that I must be about my Father's business?' And they understood not the saying, which he spoke unto them. And he went down with them, and came to Nazareth, and was subject unto them: but his mother kept all these sayings in her heart." (Luke 2:41-51)

"After this we do not hear about You again until You go to John the Baptist to be baptized by him. He didn't want to baptize you, because 'You are God the Savior.' but You told him to go ahead because this would fulfill all righteousness. Once You were baptized and coming out of the water 'the heavens were opened, and John saw the Spirit of God descending like a dove, and lighting upon You.' A voice from heaven said, "THIS IS MY BELOVED SON, IN WHOM I AM WELL PLEASED." We realized that this is a manifestation of the Trinity; You are there and the Holy Spirit is represented by the dove, and Your Father's voice comes from heaven." (McGee)

"Let me tell you about My baptism; I identify Myself (through baptism) with sinful mankind. Isaiah prophesied that I would be numbered with the transgressors; (Isaiah 53:12) the word baptism means identification and I completely identify Myself with you and all humanity. I was not baptized to set an example for you, nor did I set a pattern for you to follow. I wanted to completely identify Myself with you and all of My subjects, which is all of humanity. Water baptism is symbolic of death; My death was a baptism because I entered into death for you. Also, at this time I was set-aside for My office of priest. The Holy Spirit came upon Me for this priestly ministry. You are saved by identifying yourself with

Me. Your sin was put on Me, at the cross; it was not put in Me, but on Me. 'For He hath made him (Me) to be sin for us, who knew no sin; that we might be made the rightousness of God in Him (Me)." (2 Corn. 5:21) Peter said that you are saved by baptism. (1 Peter 3:21) If you are saved, you are in Me. How do you get in Me? This is done by water baptism through the Holy Spirit. Baptism is God's way for you to stand for Me, to publicly proclaim that I am your Lord and Savior." (McGee)

"You are right to say John did not want to baptize Me. John said, 'I have need to be baptized of thee, and You come to me?' But I said to him, "Suffer (let) it to be so now: for thus it becomes Us to fulfill all righteousness." (Matthew 3:14-15)

"Jesus, there are so many things that I do not understand about You. Please tell me about Your temptation in the wilderness. You went there immediately after your baptism by John, and you did not eat or drink for forty days, so You were very hungry and thirsty. Did the devil tempt You or did God?"

"Let me tell you of My threefold temptation in the wilderness. This is just before My public ministry at Capernaum where I called four of My disciples by the Sea of Galilee. I was tested here to answer your questions of: Can I the King, withstand a hard test, and can I overcome the evil, or will I submit to the temptation, like all men do? (McGee)

'"Temp' means: "To entice to evil, seduce, or to test." My temptation had to be greater than all of mankind's temptations. Did God tempt Me or did the devil tempt Me? 'God does not tempt men with evil.' (James 1:13) We are told that God did tempt Abraham in Genesis 22:1, but this means that God was testing the faith of Abraham, but for Abraham's sake. God knew already what Abraham was thinking before he thought it, and He knew how it would turn out. God knows all things from the end to the beginning, Let Me tell you that I went to the wilderness to be "tested." Could I have fallen? "NO, and emphatic NO." Then was my temptation a genuine temptation? 'Yes!' My temptation was much greater than any that you have ever experienced. 'I was tempted in all ways as you are tempted, but I did not sin.' You must understand to be tempted, or to have evil thoughts is not sin. (The devil temps a man to do evil; God uses the temptation as a test for a man to, by faith, trust God to bring him through to victory) I was tested to demonstrate that I was exactly who I claimed to be. (McGee)

"Let me illustrate with a story of a boy who lived in West Texas. The Santa Fe railroad came through his town. One year there was a flood and it washed out the Santa Fe Bridge. Men worked a very long time to restore the bridge, but finally the day came to test it. They brought two engines and stopped both of them on the bridge and then tied down the whistles, so that the whistling blew long and strong through the town. Everyone came to see what was happening. Someone asked, 'what are you doing? Are you trying to break down the bridge?' The engineer laughed and said, "Of course not! We are testing the bridge to prove that it can't be broken down, ever!" (McGee)

"May I say to you, that is exactly the reason I, Jesus, was tested to prove that I could not be broken down, EVER! Even though the temptation grew and the pressure increased, I never gave in, and I never broke down. I wanted you to know, then, and I want you to know now, that I am your SURE Savior; you are safe in Me. I will never let you down, I will always be right with you to give you My courage to endure your test, So you will have a victory in your life, because I AM, "THE SAME YESTERDAY, TODAY, AND FOREVER," and I died on the cross so that you could have an abundant, joyous, life, here on earth and forever." (McGee)

"Now, Let's talk about My wilderness experience. In Matthew 4:1 we read, 'Then was Jesus (Me) led up of the Spirit into the wilderness to be tempted of the devil.' I was to be tested by the devil, and please note that the Spirit led Me into the wilderness. I was filled with the Holy Spirit) Then I fasted forty days and forty nights and was very hungry. That is when the tempter came to Me and said, "'IF,' thou be the Son of God, command that these stones be made bread." (Matthew 4:2-3) This was a physical temptation as was the one that came to Eve. ("She saw that the tree was good for food." Genesis 3:6) The devil told Me to turn stones to bread. He was tempting Me to act in the flesh, (act apart from My Father God)." I was quoting the Word found in Deuteronomy 8:3 that says, 'And he humbled thee, and suffered thee to hunger, and fed thee with manna, which thou knew not, neither did thy fathers know; that he might make thee know that man doth not live by bread only, but by every word that proceeds out of the mouth of the Lord does man live.' I ignored the insinuation that he wanted me to question, "if" I was the Son of God. I know who I am, and I want you to know who you are when you believe in Me, and have given your life to Me to mold into My own image. The devil wanted Me, and he wants you to question God's Word, and to cast doubt on God's ability to do what he has promised." (J. Swaggert)

"Next, the devil took Me up into the holy city, and set Me on a pinnacle of the temple, and said to Me, 'If thou be the Son of God, cast thyself down: for it is written, "HE shall give his angels charge concerning thee: and in their hands they shall bear thee up, lest at any time thou dash thy foot against a stone. (Matthew 4:5-6) The devil was attempting to quote Psalm 91:11-12. ('For he shall give his angels charge over thee, to keep thee in all thy ways. They shall bear thee up in their hands, lest thou dash thy foot against a stone.") This was a spiritual temptation. ('For Eve saw the fruit was to be desired to make one wise...'. Genesis 8:6) I again replied, 'It is written again, "Thou shall not tempt the Lord thy God,' He left out "to keep thee in all thy ways;" because he wanted Me to ignore God's way." (Deuteronomy 6:16) (Matthew 4:7) (McGee)

"The devil now took Me up into an exceeding high mountain, and showed Me all the kingdoms of the world, and the glory of them; and he said to Me, 'All these things will I give thee, if thou will fall down and worship me.' (Matthew 4:8-9) This was a psychological temptation. I said to him, "Get thee hence, Satan: for it is written, Thou shall worship the Lord thy God, and him only shalt thou serve." (Matthew 4:10) I was quoting Deuteronomy 6:13, 'Thou shall fear the Lord thy God, and serve Him, and shall swear by His name,' and Deuteronomy 10:20, "Thou shall fear the Lord thy God; Him shall thou serve, and to Him shall thou cleave, and swear by His name." (McGee)

"I always answered the devil with the Word of God, because it is 'powerful as a two edged sword.' It stopped the devil because he left Me alone. (Matthew 4:11) Next the angels came and ministered to Me. God was so very close to Me with His angels to help me. Waiting on the Lord can save you a lot of grief in your life. Sometimes a small wait, sometimes a long wait, but remember Psalm 27:9 says "Wait on the Lord: be of good courage, and He shall strengthen your heart: wait, I say, on the Lord." The devil wants you to act without thinking, to move quickly, so you will not have time to consider what God would have you to do." (McGee)

"Now do you understand what I (Jesus) did here, and how it applies to you?"

"Sort of... but how did the devil think that he had the kingdoms of the world to give to You? Didn't they belong to You?"

"I could have said to him, 'You can't offer Me the kingdoms of the world because you don't have them to give,' but I did not because he does have them to give; he is running everything on the earth, "he is the prince of this earth." You must understand this to understand what enemy you are up against. Satan is a spiritual enemy who wants to be like God to you, and all of mankind. He wants you to fall down and worship him." (Another words, he wants you to believe his negative thoughts toward you, and he does not want you to believe My Word to you, from the Bible) (McGee)

"Did he leave you, never to return?"

"The devil knew he was no match for Me, because I would always use God's word to stop him, and he knew it wasn't worth his time. He would rather go after you, so you must learn to use God's word too, or you will constantly be falling for his lies, and then you will end up doing his will and not Mine. He did come to Me in Gethsemane to stop Me from going to the Cross, if he could; he "COULD NOT," but I suffered greatly realizing God's will, and knowing that I would be separated from My Father for a time. (A great time of great suffering for Me.) The devil thought that because of this, he would be able to offer Me an alternative.

"Now, do you know what I did after this encounter with the devil?"

"You started Your ministry on the earth, by calling men (Your Disciples) to follow You"

"I began to preach, and to say, "Repent:" for the kingdom of heaven is at hand.' I began to gather Disciples to be with me as I went about God's business. I called Andrew, his brother Simon, called Peter, and said to them, "Follow Me, and I will make you fishers of men." I called James, the son of Zebedee, and his brother John. Later I called more Disciples: 'Philip and Bartholomew, Matthew and Thomas, James the son of Alphaeus, and Simon called Zelotes, and Judas the brother of James, and Judas Iscariot, which betrayed Me.' (Luke 6:14-16) They immediately left their fishermen nets and followed Me. I then went about all Galilee, teaching in their synagogues, and preaching the gospel of the kingdom, and healing all manner of sickness and all manner of diseases among the people." (Matthew 4:12-23)

"Do you know what happened next?"

"Let me ask You (Jesus) first, why did You let Judas do what he did, selling you out to the chief priests, which led them to put You on the cross?"

"I will explain to you why I did not exclude Judas as my Disciple. This may also explain why bad things happen on the earth, and people wonder why I let these things happen? We must go back to Genesis when Adam was "formed of the dust of the ground, and God breathed into his nostrils the breath of life; and man (Adam) became a living soul." (Genesis 2:7)

As you know, God said; "LET US MAKE MAN IN OUR IMAGE AFTER OUR LIKENESS: AND LET THEM HAVE DOMINION OVER THE FISH OF THE SEA, AND OVER THE FOWL OF THE AIR, AND OVER THE CATTLE, AND OVER ALL THE EARTH, AND OVER EVERY CREEPING THING THAT CREEPS UPON THE EARTH." (Genesis 1:26)

"What do you mean, "Let us?"

"This is the first reference to God as the "Triune God." The three in one God: 'God as the Father, God as the Son, Me (Jesus), and God as the Holy Spirit." (Steven Heppner)

"Can anyone really understand You as three persons in one?"

"I am not three persons in one, but I AM the ONE GOD' that reveals Myself as a Father, as a Son, and as the Holy Spirit that lives in you, to continue to show you whom I AM."

"Can anyone understand how You can put Yourself into Your own creation?"

"You can understand enough to know that I AM GOD, the ONE AND ONLY GOD that does not give you the spirit of confusion, but I give you My life, and My truth, and My love. 'As you seek me, you will find Me, because I understand all of your imaginations and all of your thoughts.' (1 Chronicles 28:9), and I will reveal Myself to you in ways that you will be able to understand My great love for you, but let Me tell you why I allow bad things to happen on the earth."

"Yes, Jesus."

"As you read in the Bible the account of Adam and Eve and how they ate from the tree of 'knowledge of good and evil,' when the "Lord God, commanded the man, Adam, to eat of every tree of the garden, but one.

He was not to eat of the tree of knowledge of good and evil, because in that day God told him that he shall surely die.' Adam was never supposed to know evil or death. I made him to live eternally with Me, forever and forever. (Genesis 3:6) Both had been given a free will to obey God and not eat of the fruit of the tree, or to disobey God and to eat of the fruit of the tree. It broke the Father's heart to have them eat of the tree and then lie about why they did it. Both blamed God the Father: Adam by blaming Eve, saying, 'The woman whom thou gave to be with me, she gave me of the tree, and I did eat.' (Genesis 3:12) And Eve blamed the serpent that God had made, by saying, "The serpent beguiled me, and I did eat." (Genesis 3:13)

"When man disobeyed God, he became afraid, and tried to hide himself. (Genesis 3:10) God became his enemy instead of his loving Father: Man would blame God forevermore for his disobedience. Satan's lies had entered man; doubt now filled man's soul, so that he no longer believed that God, was only good. Man decided that God was impossible to please; that He had put demands on him that no one could fulfill; man continues to do bad things and blame God for them, because, now, in the mind of man, he is human and God is supernatural, so if God wanted to change man, He could, and He would. God would make man stop doing all bad things, and the world could live in peace."

"What about that? Why doesn't God change things?"

"When God put man on the earth, He said: 'LET HIM HAVE DOMINION OVER THE FISH OF THE SEA, AND OVER THE FOWL OF THE AIR, AND OVER THE CATTLE, AND OVER ALL THE EARTH, AND OVER EVERY CREEPING THING THAT CREEPETH UPON THE EARTH.'

(Genesis 2:26) **God could not change His mind even if man decided not to obey Him.**

"This brings us to the heartbreaking plight of man today, with all of his wickedness seemingly to be in control in the world. I will put an end to evil at the end of the age, but this explains to you why Judas was allowed to be My Disciple, and why God lets bad things happen on the earth today. The people that honor God and accept Me, Jesus, as their Savior and Lord, will take My Word and use it to expose evil on the earth, and to hold those who are destroying man, accountable for their actions."

"Will all evil be stopped?"

"Not until I return to the earth and put down Satan forever, but believers must be aware of their power to speak in My authority from My Word in the Bible, and in the confidence of My Holy Spirit. My believers hesitate to 'speak' and to do My will. They continue to look at the situation and listen to the doctor's report, instead of taking My Word, by faith, and acting upon that. Believers pray for the cancer to be gone and at the next visit to the Doctor, he says, "Nothing has changed." They say, 'No, I didn't think it would be,' Without faith it is impossible to please God (Hebrews 11:6). But faith is a gift to be received by My people (Ephesians 2:8). They too quickly say, "My faith is too small, so I cannot believe God will answer." All of the promises of God are 'YES AND AMEN.' I have spoken in My Word many promises that assure you that I will answer your prayers. "And 'ALL' things whatsoever you ask in prayer, believing, you shall receive." (Matthew 21:22)

"Even though You have saved me from my sins, I still have much fear in my life, please tell me why I am so fearful?"

"You feel afraid because you don't really know Me. You don't understand what My perfect love for you is like. You think you are going to do something that will make me mad, and I will leave you, even though I have told you that ' I WILL NEVER LEAVE YOU AND I WILL NEVER FORSAKE YOU.' (Hebrews 13:5) You also believe that when I tell you that "I will never leave you or forsake you," that I am speaking to you like a man, in that I will hold your hand, and stroke your forehead, and tell you how sad I am that you have such a bad sickness, or that your marriage fell apart, or that you are broke, but I will just stay with you until you die, or until things get a little better. Nothing could be further from the truth about what I am saying to you. I am your protection; I am your answer; I can do everything that will turn your situation to victory in Me. I told you that I have not given you a "spirit of fear; but the Spirit of My power, and the Spirit of My love, and the Spirit of My sound mind, I am giving you Myself, all that I AM is inside of you, so that you can draw upon Me 24/7." (2 Timothy 1:7) I want you to learn to choose Me over the feeling of fear."

"Fear doesn't seem like a choice to me. I feel so afraid. Can I make myself not to be afraid?"

"No, you can do nothing by will power. You can only come to our Father and overcome the devil by faith. Trying to make yourself feel unafraid is not what I am talking about. Anything that I command you to do means: I will overcome for you. I have already said that 'without faith, it is impossible to please God.' (1 Corn. 5:7) Remember I told the devil that "man does not live by bread alone;" bread could be interpreted as feelings. I went on to say that you must live by every word that proceeds out of the mouth of God. 'There is no fear in love. My perfect love casts out fear (1 John 4:18). When you look fear in the face and use My words against it, you will see that no evil can overtake you ; 'if you abide in Me, and My words abide in you, you shall ask what will, and it shall be done unto you." (John 15:7)

"But Jesus, I always want to feel healthy, feel at peace, feel happy, feel Your strength, feel Your love."

"Knowing by faith that I am with you, will give you much more peace than putting your feelings first. You must be determined to not let your feelings, or the suggestions of the devil to direct your life over and above My words to you?"

"Yes Lord, 'I believe, help my unbelief.' (Mark 9:24) This is what the man that brought his son to you to be healed said; You told him that all things were possible to them that believed, and he said that he did believe, but help his unbelief."

"Unbelief is the core of all sin, but what do you think sin is, and how do you think I can help you to believe?"

"Sin is what I do that is not pleasing to You, and because You can do all things, you can strengthen me to believe more."

"What things do you do that are not pleasing to Me?"

"Well...I am overweight; I don't exercise much, and I don't eat a lot of fruits and vegetables, and I eat a lot of beef and pork, and I like peanut butter cups a lot.

"Is there anything else?"

"Well yes, I don't go to church every Sunday; I don't read the Bible everyday; I don't pray on my knees much, and my prayers are often on the run; and I watch a lot of old movies, and Jeopardy and Wheel of Fortune, and the news, and I don't go to see my Mom, at the rest home, every time I am in town.

"That is not sin, those are religious rules that you believe you should be fulfilling, but aren't. These man-made laws have nothing to do with Me."

"IT ISN'T, THEY DON'T, then what are You talking about?"

"You believe that sin is something that you do or don't do that does not follow my commandments; that do not live up to a set of religious rules. You believe that you must be constantly gauging your life to determine if you are causing Me to have to judge you, and reprimand you, for your actions."

"Well, I know that You have forgiven me when you went to the Cross. But still I seem to have a focus on sin. Please tell me what to do?"

"Being right with our Father God has nothing to do with your actions to be good, it is what I accomplished for you at the Cross. You can do nothing to make yourself better or good before the Father who is Holy and can allow no sin in His presence. You must be perfect before God. No sin can be accounted to you at all. Even one sin or even one bad thing that you have ever done in your life would be enough to separate you from the Father, in Hell, forever. Sin is the most hideous act that man can perpetrate on himself and others, because it does separate you from Me Forever, and this separation is what breaks the heart of our Father. In (James 1:14-15) I said, 'But every man is tempted when he is drawn away of his own lust, and enticed. Then when lust has conceived, it brings forth sin: and sin, when it is finished, brings forth death.' Sin always ends in death and that is why man must physically die, and if a man does not REPENT (turn away from sin completely) of his sin, his spirit will also die. But let Me explain how sin was started on the earth.

"In order for man to sin he must know the difference between right and wrong; then knowing what is right, that man, decides by his own free will to do what he knows to be wrong."

"So doing what is wrong, is sin?"

"There is more: Sin is charged to a person when he knows he has done wrong, but denies that he has done anything wrong; He will not take any blame unto himself for his bad deed. A man may recognize that he has done some wrong things in his life, but he may believe that the good things that he does will offset the bad; he wrongly believes that because he looks to Me, to be an example to him, he can then exercise his free will to do the good that he saw Me do; this is what will make him right before God, our Father. In Isaiah 64:6 I told you that 'all men are as an unclean thing, and all of his righteousness is as filthy rags…and that "all men have sinned and come short of the glory of God." (Romans 3:23) 'For the wages of sin is death; but the gift of God is eternal life through Jesus Christ (Me) your Lord.' There is nothing that a man can do to make himself good enough to be in heaven with God our Father, forever. If he could, then I would not have had to go to the Cross, and shed My blood as a sacrifice for sin. God, My Father, put all of man's sin onto Me, and then he forgave individuals their sin, as if they had not sinned at all, and therefore you and all of mankind can be 'right' before God, the Father, forever."

"So, who does sin hurt, man, or just God?"

"All sin is against God, but man hurts himself also, often for generations. God is grieved when his creation is broken, and bleeding, because of his sin. David is an example of realizing that he had sinned against God, alone, when he said, 'I have sinned against the Lord.' (11 Samuel 12:13) But you know that his sin hurt his family and all of Israel. We are still talking of his adultery with Bathsheba, and his murder of her husband, Uriah. So we know that there are consequences to sin, even though a man is forgiven by God our father. (11 Samuel 11)

"When a man does not admit his sin, he cannot be forgiven because God cannot forgive him unless he admits he has sin and wants it to be forgiven by the Father. (Matthew 6:14-15) He continues trying to cover up his wrong doing and the pain of his sin, which is where most of mankind is today. Unless a person understands that there is forgiveness, and that he needs to be forgiven by My death on the Cross, and turns away from wanting to sin and to hide it, or justify it, there is no solution; except My judgment on mankind at the 'Great White Throne Judgment' as revealed in Revelation. (Revelation 20:11)

"Sin can only be atoned for by the shedding of blood. But, you know that when you asked Me for forgiveness of your sins you were then saved, and your soul will never die but live forever with Me in heaven. This salvation is available to all living souls on the earth today: My Holy Spirit will call each person through the preaching of the Gospel, in faith. The Gospel means Good News about Me (Jesus.)

"You have said that you still have fear over your sin, even though you know I have forgiven you. Do not continue to carry your sin around with you as if you are not forgiven; this is a great grievance to My Holy Spirit living in you. (Ephesians 4:30) I want you to move forward in faith to the great future, and hope, I have planned for you, from the foundations of the earth." (Jeremiah 29:11)

"Yes, Lord, but what is faith, and what should people put their faith in?"

'Faith is the means to be saved from the wrath of God that would have come to you because of your sin, but My Father put all of your sin, all of your wrongdoing, all of your addictions, all of your evil thinking, all of your evil actions onto Me; a person cannot save himself by any means. A person is only saved by My finished work at the Cross. When a person has My faith, blessings from Me will come to him in everything he does, because it is My life that lives in the believer now. Choose to believe Me by faith. Thinking of My life as an inheritance that I gave to you when I died. When a person dies his last will and testament' will give to his heirs whatever he left to them by his own desire. I left you My life that I live in you through My Holy Spirit. "It is no longer you that lives, but Me that lives in you.' (Galatians 2:20)

"Think of faith as a checking account; you put money into it, and then you write a check, or use your debit card, to make a withdrawal. The bank will not give you your own money unless you make a demand on them through your check. You can go to the bank and yell at them all day long to give you your money, but they will not give you any of your own money until you write a check on the blanks the bank gave to you to use. (Charles Capps) Now understand I have put the "money" into your account, I put all that I AM into your life, but you must make a demand on Me, by faith, claiming what I have promised you in My Word, is now yours, FREE of charge. You don't have to scream at Me to do something, you don't have to cry all day until I hear you, and act, you don't have to be really, really good so I will say, "OKAY, I've heard you, so I guess you can have what you desire." In Psalm 37:4 I commanded you to 'Delight yourself in Me, and I shall give you the desires of your heart.' Your "desires" are all I can do and give to you: 'All things are possible to him that believes.'" (Matthew 21:22)

"You read these words written to you in the Bible: 'Now faith is the substance of things hoped for, the evidence of things not seen' (Hebrews 11:1), regardless of how you feel, or by what your emotions are telling you to do. "Faith, enables the believing soul to treat the future as present, and the invisible as seen." (Dr. J. Oswald: missionary to China) Faith is not the absence of any problems, doubts, or fears. Faith is learning to reject those things, and not let them control you as you take a stand on My Word. (Wommack)" Knowing My Word is absolutely necessary before you will have faith in Me. (John 1:1) tells you that I am the Word. "In the beginning was the Word, and the Word was with God, and the Word was God."

"Faith is not a leap in the dark, a hope-so kind of belief, a good luck charm, which you hang around your neck, or carry with you. Faith is 'substance for the scientific mind, and evidence for the legal mind.' God, our Father, wants your faith to rest upon Me, Jesus, because you can believe in a whole lot of foolish things and have faith in them." (McGee) Faith is not something that is added on to good works, or even good sounding words that put the emphasis on your faith in Me.

"Do not put your faith in the fact that you believe that I am the Son of God, the One and Only God; 'Even demons believe in Me, and tremble' (James 2:19). Do not put your faith in the joy that you know Me; do not put your faith in the fact that you went forward in a church meeting once and said that you believe in Me; do not put your faith in the works that you do at your church; do not put your faith in the money or the tithe that you give at your church, or the money that you send to other ministries that do My work around the world. In fact, it is not anything you do apart from Me; it is Me, Myself, and My death and the shedding of My shed blood that you rely upon for your daily breath and life. It is Me, the living God, that now lives inside of you to accomplish My will for you. 'I AM' what you put your faith in." (McGee)

"In Matthew 17:20 I said, 'If you have faith as a grain of a mustard seed, you shall say unto this mountain, "Remove hence to yonder place;" and it shall remove; and nothing shall be impossible unto you. I used the mustard seed to explain faith to you because this seed cannot be crossed with any other seed; I also wanted you to realize that faith is something that must grow in your spirit. It starts small, but as you believe in Me for all things your faith will grow into a big faith that cannot be shaken." (Charles Capps)

"Thank you, Lord Jesus, that you give me Your faith to change my life into Yours as I go my way every day. Lord, many people may believe that they are heading to heaven to live with You, but they may be headed to Hell instead. Please tell me about Hell and who goes there. So many people do not believe in the devil, or Hell, or they believe that hell is a good place because all their friends will be there. They believe Heaven will be a boring place because people there will not want to have any fun. Some believe that really, really evil people, like Hitler, and Stalin, will be in hell, but people who do 'good' will not. They also have a problem because they believe that You would not send innocent children and those people around the world that have not heard of You, to Hell."

"Hell is a real place 'made for the devil and his angels,' (Matthew 25:41) but people will be there because they do not believe in what I did for them at the Cross. They have not surrendered their life to Me to 'make them into a new creation.' The questions that people have about children going to hell are answered by understanding that our Father is a merciful God, that will do anything to bring people to Himself. "God, who is rich in mercy, for in His great love He loves us… (by grace you are saved;) and has raised us up together, and MADE us sit together in heavenly places in Christ Jesus (Me): that in the ages to come he might show the exceeding riches of his grace in his kindness towards us through Christ Jesus (Me)." (Ephesians 2:4-7) A child is not held accountable for his eternity until he has understanding of sin and good. When I was on the earth I wanted the "little children to come unto Me, and did not forbid them, for they are like the Kingdom of God. I took them up in my arms, put My hands on them, and blessed them." I also said that if a person led one of these little ones astray, it would be better for them if a mill stone were hung around his neck and he was flung into the deepest sea. So it doesn't make any sense that I am letting little children go into hell.

"As far as people around the world that have not heard about Me, and therefore are condemned to hell: I have commanded those that do know Me, as their Lord and Savior, to tell others what they know about Me, all missionaries are sent to go into all the world to tell everyone everywhere the Good News of My salvation. "Go ye therefore, and teach all nations, baptizing them in the name of the Father, and of the Son, and of the Holy Ghost; teaching them to observe all thing that I have commanded you… (Matthew 28:29-20) And lastly God, our Father, sends no one to hell; it is a choice of a man to choose life or death. 'I have set before you life and death, blessing and cursing: therefore choose life that both you and your seed may live.' (Deuteronomy 30:19)

"Hell is such a hideous place of torment, that is more horrible than the human mind can comprehend, because I am not there; there is no sun or light of any kind, no friendship, no peace, no love. I will do anything to keep man from choosing hell, instead of Me; but let me tell you about the devil; 'He was a murderer from the beginning, and abode not in truth, because there is no truth in him. When he speaks a lie, he speaks of his own (on his own): for he is a liar, and the father of it (John 8:44)' He is the thief that wants to steal the way that I have set before you; he wants to kill the truth of who I am, and he wants to destroy the life I gave you. (John 10:10)

"This is not a trivial matter, a little skirmish with the enemy, or something or someone you can defeat on any level. He will ruin you in everyway he can: your marriage, your children, your health, your finances, your friendships, and your whole life. He wants to convince you that there is no Hell, or that everyone is going to Heaven so you don't have to worry about hell, You must be aware of what he is doing, but not obsessed with him. I have defeated his power. I spoke of hell more than I spoke of heaven when I was on the earth. We must talk of hell because I want no man to go there, 'I want all men to be saved, and to come unto the knowledge of the truth.' (1 Timothy 2:4) You may be able to understand hell better if you think of the young woman that you saw on the 700 Club that shot herself at the age of fifteen years old, and went to hell. What do you remember of her account, and of her experience?"

"Because of a divorce in her family this young teenager was very sad, and did not want to live unless she could live happy. She believed that she could never be happy again, and this drove her to despair. She felt rejected, and guilty, because she believed that she was the cause of the divorce, so this led her to her mother's room where she found a gun, and put it to her head to end her life on earth. Immediately a voice said to her to remove the gun from her head and point it at her heart. She wrestled with the voice explaining that she was not going to miss, and that she wanted to be sure that she was going into eternity. But in the end she decided to point the gun at her heart, because she envisioned what she would look like if she shot herself in the head. She thought of her family and the toll it would take on them. Before she pulled the trigger she asked God to forgive her. She heard the bang of the gun, and knew that she was dying. She felt the blood in her lungs, and then she felt her soul leave her body where she started falling, falling, falling downward at the speed of light through a long passage. She felt an acid burn and much pain in her body, and she knew that she was in hell.

"Pat Robertson asked her if she was afraid? She said that she was now, death and fear. She knew everything about herself and why she was there. She saw a sea of people in different chambers, all screaming in agony. She knew all about them, their thoughts, their sins, everything they had done wrong, and their emotions, but she did not care about them. All that mattered to her was the knowledge that (You) Jesus Christ was Lord. She understood that she had never surrendered to Your Lordship. She told Pat that she had much regret, shame and guilt, in that she had believed a lie. She could see the whole universe, and she could look across a fixed gulf and see heaven full of light, peace, and joy. She also knew that hell was forever and that the screaming would never stop.

"Because she had asked, You, for forgiveness before she pulled the trigger, You came across the fixed gulf, from Heaven, and scooped her up into Your arms, where she experienced Your presence and wholeness. Her torment was gone, she now was full of Your life and peace. Death and fear was no longer her eternity. You did not want her to stay in Heaven, though, so You sent her back into her body, still lying in her mother's room. She called to her mother, who then called the paramedics. They did not think that they should take her to the hospital because she looked like she was dying, however, she was really just returning from the dead. You did a marvelous miracle and healed her in a few hours. The bullet should have shattered her heart, but it missed it by ¼ inch.

"This is a marvelous account of Your Love, and forgiveness for this woman, and for everyone that will call upon You in faith. But let me ask You, how could she have a second chance to live and then die again someday? You told us in Hebrew 9:27 that 'It is appointed unto man once to die, and then the judgment.' In John chapter 11 of the Bible, You give us the story of how You raised Lazarus (brother of Mary and Martha) from the dead, after he had been in the tomb for four days. You thanked Your Father God for hearing You, and then You cried in a loud voice, "Lazarus, come forth," and he walked out of the grave to live on this earth again, until he died at a later date."

"When I said, that it is 'appointed unto man once to die, but after this the judgment.' (Hebrew 9:27) I was making it plain that a man does not come back to life as someone else, or some animal, or tree, or some other created thing, as some believe they do in reincarnation.

"Man was created as a man, he lives as a man, and he dies as a man, and if his heart stops beating and he dies for a period of time, and then comes back into his body he will be the same person as before he died. I told my Disciples that Lazarus was asleep, but they did not understand, so I told them that he was dead. To Me death means, the body is dead and will decay in the grave, but My Spirit in a man is eternal, and will never die. My Holy Spirit living in you today is the same as it will be a million years from now."

"When this young woman came back to the earth what did You want her to know as she continued to live her life?"

"She realized that she was a sinner, and that she deserved to go to Hell because she had never asked for forgiveness for her sins and submitted her life to My Lordship. 'If a man was able to keep the whole law, but break it in one point he is guilty of breaking them all.' (James 2:10) "All have sinned and come short of the glory of God;" (Romans 3:23) 'For the wages of sin is death; but, the gift of God is eternal life through Me, Jesus Christ your Lord.' (Romans 6:23) At the Cross I paid the price of sin and sickness, so when a person gives his life to Me, to make out of it what I will, he is made right with our Father. His inheritance is My life living in him, but each believer has to realize, as this young woman did, that you are in a daily war with the enemy. He fights against Me in your thoughts, telling you lies about Me, that many will believe. She said that each day she learned to crucify the flesh; "Likewise reckon yourself to be dead unto sin, but know that you are alive to God through Me, Jesus Christ your Lord." (Romans 6:11) She listened to My Holy Spirit to give her My wisdom. She also understood what she had done, and that she was there because she had not given her life to Me (Jesus) to make her into a new creation.

"When you 'submit yourself therefore to Me (God), resist the devil, and he will flee from you." (James 4:7).

"Yes Lord, I understand that the devil and hell are real, and that I need to submit to You daily to resist the devil, but how do I do that? resist the devil and submit to You?"

"You must know My Word, and believe it, before you can summit to it: My Word is Me. Most of the time you are trying to follow a formula, by saying My words, and then praying, and then waiting a while, to see if what you asked for will be granted; kind of like a wish to a Genie. You are hoping that your own will, will be granted, but if it isn't then you are perplexed, because you believe that your plan is also My plan. It may be My plan for you, but I must bring it to pass in My own way and time. Remember Jacob who was always thinking up ways to do My will by his own devices. I often ask you to wait on Me: 'Wait on the Lord: Be of good courage, and God shall strengthen your heart: wait , I say, on the Lord.' (Psalm 27:14) I ask you to wait until I can build faith into your belief system (heart)."

"You told me that fear is a choice; is all sin a choice?"

"When a person reaches the age of accountability, sin is a choice, but understand that your choice is to let Me take care of your sin for you as you admit that you are unable to do anything about 'trying' to be better. Please get the word "try" out of your vocabulary. My forgiveness of sin for you is a one time thing, but sin will continue to overtake you if you do not admit that you still have sinful ways, and you need to let Me work it out of your life day by day. You take My Word and believe what I say to you by faith. Remember My Words from Numbers 14:28, 'As truly as I live, AS YOU HAVE SPOKEN IN MY EARS, SO WILL I DO TO YOU.'

"Thank you , Lord Jesus."

"I will never leave you or forsake you (Hebrew 13:5);' I speak to you every minute of every day. I tell you how much I love you and I remind you of "My Word," too."

"Jesus, I want to ask you so many things, but please explain to me about the first miracle that You did at the wedding feast in Cana, when You turned water into wine. People question if this was real wine as we know it today, and Your response to Your mother, calling her a woman and stating, 'What have I to do with thee? Saying, that "Your hour," is not yet come.' (John 2:3-4) It seemed like You were telling Your mother that it was not time for You to be doing a miracle, and that she should not be asking You to do so."

"First, let's talk about the wine. 'I would not provide an intoxicating drink for this wedding or for any occasion. In John 2:10 it was stated that "every man at the beginning doth set forth good wine; and when men have well drunk, then that which is worse: but thou hast kept the good wine until now," When I used the word "good" I meant 'intrinsically good.' Literally this means the pure and sweet juice from the grape, not the rotted, fermented, decayed, intoxicating kind of wine. I would never make anything that would make a person drunk and call it good.' (Jimmy Swaggart Expositor's Study Bible; Crossfire Edition) There was no thought of drunkenness at this wedding, because this was a religious occasion: a time to celebrate the union in marriage of a man and a woman. But this whole wedding was a picture of another wedding that is coming: When the church is presented to Me as a bride at the marriage supper of the Lamb.' My mother said, "They have no wine." (John 2:3) 'Mary had lived her life with people questioning her virginity, and whether I was the One she claimed I was; she hoped that now was the time to do a miracle and make it clear that I was the Savior of the world as she had been saying all along.' (McGee)

"This was not the time for Me to clear My mother's name. I would do this while hanging on the cross when I spoke directly to My mother, saying, 'Woman, behold Thy Son.' (John 19:26) At that time My hour had come; in three days after My death, I was resurrected from the dead. My resurrection proved who I am, and that I was virgin born, and that I Am who I claimed to be." (McGee)

"But You did turn water into wine for the wedding."

"I did, because it was My time to do miracles; it was just not the time to clear My mother of all the gossip that had plagued her for all the years of My life. This miracle holds a great spiritual lesson for you. My mother said to the servants, "Whatsoever He saith unto you, do it!" (John 2:5) This shows her great faith in Me, and it shows that the servants were willing to do as they were told. Let's focus on the water pots. They were beaten and battered vessels and not attractive, only to be pushed aside and covered up. The water was not wine until it was ladled out into a glass and served to the governor of the feast. He noted to the bridegroom that the best wine had been saved until last. (John 2:8-10)

"You represent a water pot as you have been beaten and battered by things and pushed aside by the circumstances of your life. But as my servant I want to use you as you are. I want to fill you with the water of My Word and then I want you to ladle it out to other people that do not know

Me. When My Word gets into their Spirit it will become the wine of joy to them, because it is My life. My Holy Spirit takes that water and performs a miracle in the life of an individual." (McGee)

"Jesus, how do I become a victorious Christian? It seems that I want to live as You would have me live, but the more I try the more I fail."

"What are you trying to overcome?"

"Lots of things, I want to lose weight, but can't, I want to stop worrying, but can't, and I want to believe that the future is going to be good, but I can't, I want to be at peace, but I'm not, I want to be happy, but I am not."

"How are you trying to change these things?"

"Well, I'm not sure, now that You ask me that. I know that You are the one I need to trust, so I try to believe You, but I seem to be striving and pushing myself which doesn't seem right."

"Do you remember Paul said, 'For that which I do, I allow not; for what I would, that do I not; but what I hate, that do I.' (Romans 7:15) Paul was saying that what he wanted to do for Me, he did not, but what he knew was wrong and did not want to do, he did it anyway. Why couldn't he do the things that were right? After all he was Paul, My man."

"If Paul couldn't do the things that he wanted to do, how can I?"

"All of my followers, at one time or another try to do My will in the 'flesh,' or by their own power and might. Remember what I said, "Not by your power, not by your strength, but by My Holy Spirit," When the flesh is at work the object of the Christians' faith is something other than Me, and what I did for them at the Cross. Most believe that some part of the law needs to be added to the circumstances, so the right results will come. Christians try to pray harder, beg Me to do something, work busily in their church, read the Bible more, get others to pray for them, get a person that they can be accountable to, go to church more, and a multitude of other ideas that they have heard of from self-help books or well meaning friends." (McGee)

"My question to you is this: Did your pastor or church members die on the Cross of Calvary for you? Did I ask you to clean up your life, and do every kind of good work so that I may find you acceptable to be saved? I only ask one thing of you; Faith in Me (Jesus) and what I did for you on the Cross. 'Believe on the Lord Jesus Christ and thou shall be saved, and thy house.' (Acts 16:31) I also said, 'He that believes on me has everlasting life.'" (John 6:47

"Did you do everything I need at the Cross?"

"What do you need that maybe I didn't accomplish?"

"Healing; You healed many people when you were on the earth, but many in the church today believe that Your healing was only for back then, or it is for people who don't know You (Jesus) who need a means to believe."

"Nothing could be more of a lie than that My healing does not happen today for anyone who needs it. Do you know this verse from Isaiah 53:4-5; 'Surely He hath born our grief's and carried our sorrows: yet we did esteem Him stricken, smitten of God, and afflicted, but He was wounded for our transgressions, he was bruised for our iniquities; the chastisement of our peace was upon him; and with His stripes we are healed.' Or do you know what I said from 1 Peter 2:24, "Who His own self bare our sins in His own body on the tree, that we, being dead to sins, should live unto righteousness by whose stripes ye were healed." Or these words from Jeremiah 30:17; 'for I will restore health unto thee, and I will heal thee of thy wounds, saith the Lord. Or another verse, ...He Himself took our infirmities, and bore our sicknesses. (Matthew 8:17) These words are about Me and what I did at the Cross. I have already accomplished your salvation, and your HEALING."

"Please explain these verses to me. I know You are the 'Him' and the 'He' in them."

"I bore all of your sicknesses, all of your grief of loss, all of your fears, all of your doubts, all the troubles you have endured in your lifetime, and I carried all of the things that you see and are sorry about; I carried these sorrows for you in My own body, at the Cross. God our Father afflicted Me (Isaiah 53:10 'Yet it pleased the Lord, to bruise Him (Me); He (the Father) hath put Him (Me) to grief...), so that you could go free and not be held accountable for your sins, or sicknesses. I made peace between you and God our Father, so that what you and all of mankind lost when Adam sinned was now restored. You are physically healed, but much more you are healed of the terrible malady of sin. Sickness is the result of sin."

"I think Lord, that I have been focused on the physical, but You have done so much more for me than I can ever comprehend. Still, I need to receive this healing by faith. Please tell me how to do this."

"Remember, you wrote Bible verses down that Charles Capps told you to 'take as medicine three times a day until faith comes, and once a day to maintain. If conditions worsen, double the dosage. Repeat over and over until you believe My words."

"Yes, I have them here, but some how they don't seem to be effecting me too much. All of my symptoms are still with me."

"Please let me show you how to personalize My Word, so you will know it is 'Me' speaking to you:

"Psalm 91:9-10 Because I (Your beloved person) have made You my Lord, and my refuge, and because it is my habit to believe You as my Lord and my refuge; no evil shall overcome me, neither shall any plague come anywhere near my home, or my body, or the place where I live.

"Body, you are the temple of Holy Ghost: I make a demand on you to release right nutrients, so that you are in perfect balance and harmony that Jesus has put into you.

"Pancreas, you secrete the proper amount of insulin to give me life, and health.

Mark 11:22-23 "Because I have faith in You Jesus, You have said to me, 'If I shall say to the mountain of my problem, be thou cast into the sea; and I shall not doubt You, my Lord, in my heart, but I shall believe that what I have just said will come to pass; You Lord, will give me whatsoever I have said.

"My body obeys the commands I make on it: My blood pressure is 120/70; every cell is restored to my body.

1 Peter 2:24 "You Jesus bore my sins in Your own body on the tree (cross), so that I being dead to sin now, will live unto righteousness: and by Your stripes (the beating You endured) I was healed.

"Every organ and tissue in my body functions in the perfection in which You, Jesus, created it to function, and I forbid any malfunction in my body, because I speak to my body by Your authority, Jesus.

Genesis 1:27-28 "You, Jesus, created man (me) in Your own image, in the image of You Lord, You created man: male and female. You blessed man (me) and you said to be fruitful and multiply, and replenish the earth, and subdue it: and have dominion over the fish, the birds, and over every living thing that moves upon the earth.

I speak out loud; "Heart, you beat with the rhythm of life, carrying the life of Jesus through my whole body, restoring life and health to me, so now I have a strong heart, and I command every blood cell to be normal.

"My immune system grows stronger day by day. I speak life into my immune system, and I forbid any confusion in it. Holy Spirit You raised Jesus from the dead and now you dwell in me, and You quicken my immune system with the life and wisdom that guards my health day by day.

Proverbs 16:24 "Pleasant words are as an honeycomb, sweet to the soul. As I speak them they bring health to my bones. In the authority of Your name Jesus, I make a demand on my bones to produce perfect marrow. My bones are dense and strong. I make a demand on my joints to function perfectly.

Proverbs 17:22 "A merry heart does me good like a medicine, so I laugh out loud, Jesus, and I receive health and healing to all my flesh.

"Lord, I resist the enemy in every form that he comes against me; I speak by Your authority to my body to be strong and healthy. I reject the curse of sickness, and I force Your life into my body.

"Lord, my kidneys are pristine and healthy and they function in the capacity You made them to function in. My urinary tract is pure and healthy, and My liver filters My blood perfectly.

"Lord, my intestines are clear of polyps or obstruction of any kind, and my elimination functions well. The flora in my colon is in perfect harmony with good health.

"Jesus, You are Lord of my life: I am redeemed from the curse of the law, so every disease germ and every virus that touches my body dies instantly.

"I refuse to allow sickness and disease to operate in my body, because this body is redeemed, by You Jesus, and You have already paid the price for me."

Psalm 119:164 "Seven times a day, and all day long, I will praise You Jesus, because Your judgment is right for me."

"Now do you understand how I operate in your soul and Spirit by My Word?"

"Yes, Lord, You have taught me how to make Yourself real in my life, but please speak to me daily about all of these things that I am learning about You?"

"I will never stop speaking to you and helping you in all that you think and do, because I have told you in Philippians 4:6, 'Be careful for nothing; but in everything by prayer and supplication with thanksgiving let your requests be made known unto God (Me).' To put these words into a more understandable meaning for you I would say this; "Don't worry about anything, but believe your prayer to Me, and thank Me for everything I have done, and Am doing and will do in the future, and speak to Me about everything that you are concerned about; material, physical, and spiritual." In Philippians 4:7 I tell you that My satisfying Peace will go beyond the realm of your human comprehension, and I shall keep your heart and your mind stayed on Me and My work at the Cross."

"However, I still see a problem with healing. Many people believe they will be healed, but they are not. A woman called into the 700 Club and asked Pat how she could get You, Lord, to heal her? What would You tell her?"

I AM GOD, the all seeing God, the all knowing God, the everywhere present God, and the all loving God; I am Alpha and Omega, the beginning and the ending (Revelation 1:8); I am the first and the last (Revelation 1:17): I am He that liveth, and was dead; and, behold, I am alive for evermore, Amen; and (I) have the keys of hell and of death, (Revelation 1:18).

"I want all people to be healed; I do not put sickness on people so I can teach them something, nor do I make them sick so they can be a light in the darkness to the lost. Both of these ideas are a lie; I have no sickness to give; that is the devil's realm, he is the author of sickness. I am the God of life and 'life more abundantly,' However, because I see the end from the beginning, I know the way a life should go to glorify My Name. I know how to build a life into a beautiful "mansion" that will last for all eternity, and what will make a man rejoice forevermore. I only want my beloved ones to know that there is nothing but peace and joy in their souls when I am trusted, and loved, and believed. I have said that, above all things I want man to prosper as his soul prospers, and to be in health. Remember, I have already healed everyone by My stripes. One needs to walk out this healing in their own bodies, by believing Me, that everything is done for them. Continue to speak My word as Capps suggested, until faith and healing comes.

"Lord, death is such an evil on the earth. How can people deal with death? So many today are suffering around the world because of famine, lack of medical help, bad weather that causes all sort of loss of material things, but mostly loss of life. You broke the bondage of death, but still we all have to go through the pain of the loss of a loved one; some are babies, some are children, some lose their parents when they are young, but no matter the age of the person who dies, people are very sad, and feel that You have deserted them in some way. How can I deal with death, and how can I help someone else that has just suffered a loss in their life?"

"Death was never supposed to come to My beloved people. Because man sinned against the Father he had to physically die, so that sin would not go on forever on the earth. Adam knew that if he ate of the 'tree of good and evil' he would die. Of course, he did not know what death was, but he found out when the "Lord God made coats of skins to clothe him and Eve." (Genesis 3:21) The first death came when 'Cain rose up against Abel his brother and slew (killed) him. (Genesis 4:8) He understood that blood had to be shed, so that sin would be atoned for, but he did not totally understand that. God our Father, would send His Son, Jesus (ME) to be the sacrifice for sin. Adam believed that his son would somehow atone for man's sin.

"Because I was born of a woman onto the earth, lived, and then died on a cross, I understand the woes of man, and I understand death and how it affects a person to their very soul in sorrow. My Father chose to let Me die as a common criminal while He watched. He too suffered in grief, but He put aside His sorrow so that you could be set free of sin and be restored to Him by My (Jesus) death. He considered this to be joy to Him, for Me to fulfill His purpose and will on the earth. The Holy Spirit raised Me from the dead so that now I live for evermore. You too have this hope of life eternal, and all of mankind has this hope to live on forever in eternity in peace and joy with Me.

"You believe that a life which is very brief must have been in vain, and that God has mocked mankind by giving him a little one, and then letting him die immediately or after a few years of his birth. With eternity as a measuring rod, the long life of Methuselah was merely a pinpoint on the calendar of time. Although the span of life of your little one, was brief, it completed a mission, served a purpose, and performed a God-appointed task in this world. Its presence turned your thoughts to the best, its helplessness brought out your strength and protection, and its loveliness roused your tenderness and love. Its influence will linger in your heart as long as you live. If anything can bring a man to God, it is a child.' "A little child shall lead them" is not idle rhetoric. Your little one served its purpose. A brief life is not an incomplete life." (McGee)

"You can be assured that all is well with a child, and that he is safe in My arms, and that a believing parent will see this one again, in heaven, some day." (McGee)

"But Lord, I ask you about a child that loses its mother or father in death, when this child so needs this parent to comfort and encourage them, in their journey of life?"

"I too understand this great loss to children; I 'wept' (John 11:35) at the tomb of Lazarus before I raised him from the dead. Because I can understand the broken heart of people, I can help to comfort them in their loss. Even though it may seem impossible at the time of death, to trust Me, to help and encourage, 'I CAN.' "I give power to the faint; and to them that have no might I increase strength." (Isaiah 40:29) I have a plan for every life, and I can make something good come to a person if they will make a choice to trust Me, with their spirit, and 'choose to live and not to die and declare the works of the Lord.' (Psalm 118:17) Life very often seems hard to live, death seems easier, but I can show you life is worth living. Many children that have parents all of their lives, but have not been given love, feel the great loss, also. I must become everything to a person when they give their life to Me in salvation; no matter their age: I will be a parent, I will be a friend, I will be a husband, I will be a wife, I will be a lover, and I will be the relationship each one is seeking for. No man can take My place in a person's life. "I Am the Good Shepherd of the sheep, and I know My sheep by name, and I lead them to 'green pastures, If they will follow Me. (Psalm 23) Please follow and trust 'Me' with all of your heart, mind and soul, when you have lost a loved one, or, you have the loss of "love," in your life; I will supply."

"Thank you, Lord Jesus for helping and healing those who have lost loved ones, but please tell me what to do about abortion; it is such a scourge in America and in the world, It is the taking of a life before it can have a chance to live on the earth."

"Abortion is the heart break of our Father in Heaven, because it is such a great 'LIE' that ends in death every time it is preformed. Young girls, teenagers, young women and women of all ages have believed this 'LIE' and have had an abortion only to realize too late, that it was a 'LIE' after all: they believed that their child was only a clump of cells, or it has no feeling during the abortion, or that they, as a woman, will be better off without the child, or it is better to end the child's life, than for people to know that they were pregnant out of wedlock, or it is better to hang on to their boyfriend than to keep the baby.

"What can people do to stop abortion? They can get the truth out in every way possible, by telling people about Me and LIFE, and that 'I AM' the giver of life, no matter the circumstances. There is no reason to end a life after it is started, because "you know" I can bring good out of sorrow and grief. (Romans 8:28)

"I want to speak to men, and boys in this matter of abortion. The man is the cause of abortion when he takes the gift of sex that I have given to him, and uses it to satisfy himself physically at the expense of a girl. I made man in My own image, with My life poured into him. I told man that it was "not good that the man should be alone; so I made woman as a 'helpmeet' for him." (Genesis 2:18) Since the fall of Adam, man in 'his' fallen state has used women to meet his own physical needs.

"In Proverbs I tell the young man to seek for My wisdom and understanding. 'My son, if thou will receive My words, and hide My commandments with thee; so that thou incline thine ear unto wisdom, and apply thine heart to understanding.' (Proverbs 2:1-2) If a man turns away from Me and turns to his own way, he will be destroyed. Proverbs 14:12 says "There is a way which seems right unto man, but the end thereof are the ways of death." We know abortion ends in death, even though it has been explained as a 'way of life'. Abortion is not something that girls use to correct a problem that "they" have created, or a 'right' that they have to end a life because their body belongs to them, and women can do with it as they please. It takes a boy and a girl to create a baby, so this is not a girl's problem that man has no part in. Men, "listen" to Me, and start to turn the tide of abortion that is destroying America, as now 62 million (or maybe 70 million, as records are not always accurate) lives have been cut short, (In the United States alone) (Many billions across the World); LIVES that I started, to bring glory to Myself and joy to you.

"Let Me tell you the value of a LIFE: I the Lord have examined your heart, and I know everything about you. I know you when you sit down and when you stand up and I understand your every thought. I chart your path ahead of you, and I tell you where to stop and rest. Every moment I know where you are. I know what you are going to say before you even say it. I both precede and follow you, and I place My hand of blessing on your hand. (Psalm 139:2)

"You can never be lost to My Spirit, and you can never get away from Me. When you go to heaven, I AM there; if you should go to the place of the dead, I AM there. If you follow the winds of the sea I AM there to lead you by My right hand that holds you up. If you try to hide in the darkness, the night will turn to light, because My darkness shines as bright as the day. Darkness and light are both alike to Me. (Psalm 139: 7-11)

"I made all of the delicate, inner parts of your body, and I knit them together in your mother's womb. I was there while you were being formed in utter seclusion! I saw you before you were born, and I scheduled each day of your life before you began to breathe, and I recorded everyday of your life in My Book! (Psalm 139:15-16)

"I think about you constantly, in the morning when you awaken, all day long, and when you lie down at night, and all through the night. I search your heart, and I test your thoughts toward Me. I point out anything that will take you away from Me, because I only lead you on the path to everlasting life. (Psalm 139:17-18)

"I slay the wicked that want to hurt and kill you, and I always preserve you from their violence because you belong to Me; no man can pluck you out of My hand, and separate you from My great love for you. (Psalm 139:19-20 LB)

"Lord, my life is so glorious and so wonderful as I contemplate it form your point of view. I realize how precious my life is, and how precious ALL life is to You that you would think about every person and me, constantly. I can never get away from You, and I do not want to. You told me that

Your love for me is all that I need to know about You. Now I see." (Psalm 139)

"Let Me tell you more of My love for you: In (John 3:16-17) I wrote this just for you, My beloved: 'I am so in love with you that I considered it a privilege and a joy to be sent by My Father to be born, of a woman, into My creation, so that you would know Me as "I AM" and believe Me that I died in your place so that you would never be separated from Me and our Father by your sin. I want you to know that you are not condemned, but saved, to be with Me and our Father now and forevermore in everlasting life and perfect love."

"In 1 Corinthians 13 I tell you this about yourself, and of My great love for you:

'Even though you speak the wonderful, flowing, words of men and angels and even though you have the gift of prophecy and even though you understand mysteries from My word, and you have all knowledge and all faith so that you can move mountains, but you forget Me and do not believe I really care for you, I still love you beyond your wildest imagination.

"Even though you are willing to give all your goods to the poor, and you are willing to sacrifice your body in My name, but you take the glory for yourself, I still yearn for you; I look for your smallest gesture of seeking Me.

"Even when your language is a sounding brass or a tinkling cymbal, I long to hear your voice in My ear, calling me.

"Even though you envy others, and believe you need to promote yourself; I am with you and I long for you to accept My kindness toward you. Even though you attack your loved ones and the church body, and you are so easily provoked to anger against your family and friends and to think evil of them, while all the time you are seeking man's acceptance at all cost to your own integrity: I rejoice in your slightest effort to turn from your sin and seek My truth.

"I will always bear with you and believe in you, and I will always hope you will learn to love Me, and I will always endure all things that you endure. My love will never fail you, even though prophecies will fail, speaking in tongues will cease, knowledge will vanish away, because you only know a small portion of My knowledge and my prophecy; but when

I come in all My glory, everything that is known in part must be done away with.

"When you were a child, I spoke to you as a child, you understood Me in your childlike understanding, but now that you are grown up, I long to give you the understanding that you have all of My love. The future is hidden to you now, but as you seek Me face-to-face you will know Me as I am.

"You now have all of My faith, you have all of My hope, you have all of My love; but remember; "THE GRETAEST OF ALL THINGS IS THE GIFT OF MY ENDLESS LOVE FOR YOU…NEVER FORGET THIS!"

"Hallelujah, Amen!"

"Lord, please tell me about America. Are we finished as a country because we have left You, our first love, and gone into the abyss of federal laws that go directly against You? Have our churches become complacent to the point that we do not have the will or the knowledge to pray and come back to You for our direction? You have said: Will Your people turn to You again? Can I do something to make a difference in this wonderful and great country that You put together 255 years ago when our Founding Fathers looked to You and signed the Declaration of Independence? Will You bless us again?" (Rebirth of America 1996)

"Indeed, I have blessed America because you (as a nation) looked to Me for your direction and safety, and for your invention and security. America believes they, as a people, could accomplish anything with hard work and endurance, and they believed in freedom to do well, and to do what is right was worth fighting for and dying for. Freedom is the basis of all people's initiative and ingenuity, and his endless imagination, because it reaps such great rewards for the individual who cherishes it as life itself. (Rebirth of America 1996)

"America will not be destroyed because of the Taliban, or because of abortion, or because of gay marriage, or because of its enemies; America will be destroyed because it no longer honors Me as its God." (Mike Murdock)

"When those who want to destroy freedom and enslave people, take power for themselves, they set out to teach children to be dependent and needy instead of self reliant and tough. They immediately teach that

I, Jesus, am dead and do not have any influence in the world. They teach that there are many ways to heaven and that all gods are equal.

"It is true that aborting the children of a nation means the future of that nation is facing death and destruction instead of hope and love. (America has been grieving for the 3000 lives lost on '9/11, but 3000 unseen and unnamed children are aborted "EVERY DAY" in America) The citizens will struggle with all sorts of problems not realizing they come from the destruction of life, and thus liberty (true freedom of pride from being rewarded for a job well done) is lost. Happiness and joy are gone and only 'self' becomes all important; people do not look upon their neighbor as an ally and someone to trust and care for, instead they pull away from each other in grief and fear, hoping no one will find out their secrets.

Thankfully, Row vs. Wade was overturned, and the issue of abortion was given to each state to decide what their abortion laws would be. May this law help those seeking abortions to have time to think about what stopping a life would mean to them.

"Turing to me with every need, in prayer, is where your nation can be redeemed (set free) again. 'If My people, which are called by My name, shall humble themselves, and pray, and seek My face, and turn from their wicked ways; then will I hear from heaven, and will forgive their sin, and will heal their land.' (11 Chronicles 7:14)

"How do I pray for my nation?"

"Action follows prayer. I will teach you how to 'stand' in Me and on My Word, so that evil will be stopped and righteousness will prevail. In Ephesians 6:11-14 I said to you to put on all of My armor so that you may be able to stand against the wiles of the devil. For you do not wrestle against flesh and blood, but against principalities, against powers, against the rulers of darkness of this world, against spiritual wicked-ness in high places. Therefore take unto yourself all of My armor, so that you may be able to withstand in the evil day, and having done all, to stand, "stand."

"You will have hope as a Christian as you become involved in your culture and society in a meaningful way. Proclaim My principles that human life, the family, the church, and the freedoms of America are sacred; they are endowed by God; all men are created in the image of

God (the Father, the Son, and the Holy Spirit). remember the Declaration of Independence set forth by the Congress of the United States in 1776, which started with this proclamation: 'We hold these truths to be self-evident, that all men are created equal, that they are endowed by their Creator (God) with certain unalienable Rights, that among these are: Life, Liberty and the pursuit of Happiness.' Seek to love your neighbor as stated in this "Declaration of Rights."

"Know your history and what the Founding Fathers did and sacrificed to bring your country into existence. Know your Constitution and what it means to you and all citizens of your country. You have rights as a citizen and you need to demand they be given to you and each one. Do not tolerate invasions of your sacred freedoms. (John Whitehead) I will always be with you so that you will be able to 'stand.' (2 Corinthians 1:24) "For by My (Jesus) faith you stand."

"Separation of church and state" is a slogan to try and stop a Christian from influencing public policy. The Forefathers of America wrote in the First Amendment of the Constitution; "the state will not be permitted to: (1) establish a federal, 'state' religion, or (2) prohibit the free exercise of religion (according to the dictates of the individual conscience). Those in power in America today support all religions but Christianity.

"The phrase 'wall of separation,' or the term "church and state," is not found in the Constitution of the United States. Thomas Jefferson used this phrase in a letter he wrote in 1802 which clarified this statement in 1805 to mean the separation 'between' the church and the Federal government. This statement did not mean separation of God from government. This is the kind of understanding you need to stop the lies that will destroy your country." (The Rebirth Of America 1986)

"Should a Christian vote? Many believe that one vote is worthless and that all politicians are the same, so one in office or another means only higher taxes and more regulation."

"All of the laws of America, until recently, were base on My Biblical law, but because many Christians have remained silent they have allowed corrupt legislators to make immoral judgments and statues that blaspheme My name and scorn My laws. All 50 states in the United States refer to God in their constitutions. Some elected officials have remained true to Me and want to help make America great again. Pray for your nation and those of your nation that are in authority; pray for all

Americans to be united in the truth of who I Am, and what America stands for, and why America was started by those who wanted to proclaim My name throughout the world. (The Rebirth of America 1986) 'One vote in an election' is the way to put corrupt leaders out of office, and to put moral leaders in their place. One vote combined with those who agree with righteousness will accomplish much So realize the vote is a right that will guarantee your freedom.

WHEN YOU PRAY:

(1) "Acknowledge Me as being Your God and the God of America. Without My mercy your nation would be consumed by My judgment.

(2) "Search your own heart and confess and turn away from any personal sin that I will reveal to you.

(3) "Pray for the key men in government who influence your life and your nation.

(4) "Seek My direction, for yourself, as to how you should personally be involved in turning the United States back to Me.

(5) "Pray for the current crisis situations in your nation. In these circumstances I will 'pressure' My people to return to their humble dependence on Me. (The Rebirth of America 1986)

PRAY FOR YOUR LEADERS THIS WAY:

(1) "Pray that they would realize their need for Me (Jesus Christ) to fulfill their tasks and that they would depend upon Me for their knowledge, wisdom, and the courage to do what is right.

(2) "Pray that they would reject all counsel that violates My spiritual principles.

(3) "Pray that they resist those who would pressure them to violate their conscience.

(4) "Pray that they would be ready to sacrifice their personal ambitions and political careers for the sake of this nation.

(5) "Pray they would rely on Me (Jesus) as their source of strength, wisdom and courage.

(6) "Pray they would restore dignity, honor, trustworthiness, and righteousness to the office they hold.

(7) "Pray that they would be reminded daily that they are accountable to Almighty God for the decisions they make." (Charles Stanley)

"America is the country that I choose to allow you to be born in and to live in. Work hard to understand her faults and the mistakes that have been made in her past. You must work to bring your country closer to the ideal that is the real America. Do not stand by silently while a few rule and make it their business to put her people in bondage, while they profit in power and in monetary return from the taxpayers, which seemingly have no voice in the matter. Learn to love your country through Me (Jesus). I have given this great country to you.' (Salesian Inspirational Books; God Bless America)

"Lord, Oliver Wendell Holmes wrote this hymn to You as a prayer, and again I pray it to You: Lord, God of grace, hear our call; Bless our gifts, Giver of all; the wounded healed, the captives restored, and make us a nation evermore Faithful to freedom and Thee." (Salesian Inspirational Books)

"Lord, I know that the Jews and Israel are Your chosen people, (1 Chronicles 16:13) so I ask You how does Israel fit into the United States, and how should I believe concerning Israel?"

"I blessed Abraham and told him that 'I will bless them that bless thee, and curse him that curse thee: and in thee shall all families of the earth be blessed.' (Genesis 12:3) Anyone who tries to separate the Jews from their country or Jerusalem will be cursed. History will tell you what happens to nations or individuals who have gone against Israel, and to those nations who support Israel. I directly connect the United States and Israel, and the people who hate Jews and Israel, also hate America. Hate for Jews and for Christians is directly connected to the Cross-and Me.

"I have told you that America needs 'My mercy or she would be consumed by My judgment.' The United States received a warning from Me on 9/11/2001 when the "twin towers" in New York City were attacked by terrorists. The book, THE HARBINGER, by Jonathan Cahn was inspired by Me to explain the events that took place on September 11, and what the events since that day mean to you and everyone living in the United States. I am calling My people to turn away from their distractions and their busyness so that they can 'come unto Me,' that I may direct their paths.' (Proverbs 3:6) Please read THE HARBINGER and know that "I Am not mocked: for whatsoever a man soweth, that shall he also reap." (Galatians 6:7) 'Seek Me (in prayer) while I may be found, call upon Me while I am near,' (Isaiah 55:6) and don't allow My judgment (justice) to come upon you or "My" Great Nation, the United States of America."

"I did not realize that the events of 9/11/2001 were a warning from You, Lord, until I read the book, THE HARBINGER. You are telling me to seek You everyday and to pray for my country and for my leaders. Please tell me how to pray for my family, my love ones, and for my friends, missionaries, our pastors, and all I am concerned about?"

"Always personalize your prayers to Me by reading My word and using these words to directly apply them to yourself and to the one you are praying for. Always remember that I will work as you ask Me and are specific in your requests. 'I live in the praises of My people,' so your gratitude and your 'fear' (reverence) for Me is part of your prayer time with Me.

"Turn to My Word and choose those passages in the Bible that apply to the person that you want to pray for. Let Me show you how I would pray for you:

"I pray that you, My beloved, would love Me with all of your heart, all of your soul, and all of your mind. (Matthew 22:37) As you choose to come after Me, I will help you to deny yourself and look to the Cross and know My ways, so you can follow Me. (Luke 9:23) I give unto you My peace, not as the world would give you peace, but My peace will keep your heart calm in the times that you would usually be troubled or afraid. You do not need to be afraid, because I am always with you and I will never forsake you in hard times or in good times. (John 14:27) May you always understand that you are not condemned in any way because you are in Me: you can walk everyday in My Spirit, and you no longer need to figure out how you are going to satisfy the flesh. (Romans 8:1) You have all of My faith, so I ask you to choose faith in Me over what you see, or what you hear, of what you feel, or what you taste, or what you smell, if it is contrary to My Words. (2 Corinthians 5:7) Using your faith in Me is where your life is, because it is the evidence of all the things that you are praying for, that you do not see, 'YET.' (Hebrew 11:1)

"As you trust Me in faith I will make your spirit whole, and the joy of knowing Me will give you great strength. (Nehemiah 8:10) Prayer is not for Me so that I will act in your behalf; prayer is the way you and I connect to each other. Prayer is for you to acknowledge your need for Me. You are speaking to Me as you pray, and please listen to Me as I speak to you in your spirit. Sometimes I may wake you up at night to pray for someone or something that is on My Mind. We are joined together in prayer so always remember you can: 'Pray (to Me) without ceasing." (1 Thessalonians 5:17)

"Oh Lord, You are so great to love me and to help me to do all things, but Lord, what about the Holy Spirit? How do I listen for Your Spirit? Once I am saved and the Holy Spirit comes into my heart and life to abide with me forever, (John 14:16-17) will I automatically have victory over the devil?"

"No! Because you and most believers have been in bondage to the devil and to sin for many years before you come to Me for salvation. You have been steeped in unbelief; and to all of a sudden start believing in all that I have done and said would be an impossibility. A walk with Me is a 'process' that My Holy Spirit guides each believer in everyday."

"Tell me Lord more about the Holy Spirit; how do I relate to Your Spirit that lives in me now?"

"My Holy Spirit was given to you to comfort you, and to speak of Me, Jesus. (John 16:13-14) The Holy Spirit convinces the world of its unbelief in Me, and He tells you that there is righteousness available because I Am with My Father and no one can see Me now, and He tells you that there is deliverance from judgment because the prince of this world has already been judged." (John 16:9)

"The Holy Spirit works in your life, and in all believers, by displaying God's power through you as a means to help others in the church. The gifts that are displayed are: 'the word of wisdom, the word of knowledge, faith, gifts of healing, the working of miracles, prophecy, discerning of spirits, speaking in other languages, and the ability of one to interpret these languages." (1 Corinthians 12:7)

"My Holy Spirit will produce fruit in your life. This fruit is: 'love, joy, peace, patience, kindness, goodness, faithfulness, gentleness, and self-control. This fruit is not produced because you keep the religious law, it is produced because you love Me and want to do My will." (Galatians 5:22)

"Lord, help me to have my mind renewed by studying your Word so I can live with Your gifts. Lord, what about baptism? Do we, as believers need to be immersed in water to be truly baptized?"

"Baptism is for the believer to do in obedience to Me; it is for you to proclaim to others that you have given your life to Me, and that you are turning away from your sins. The water is symbolic of cleansing from sin, and that you are now dead to 'all' sin, because I defeated sin for you at the Cross, Please do not be overly concerned how the water is applied to the believer. As long as the believer is proclaiming Me as their Messiah (Savior) and Lord; as long as the believer has repented of all his sins, and turned to Me to forgive them, and guide them in all truth through My Word, he is saved forevermore."

"Lord, I love to hear about the salvation I have received from You. But Lord, what about idols? Are they a part of the believers life any more? The Israelites had Aaron make a golden calf for them to worship, but no one believes in golden calves anymore, do they?"

"A golden calf is not the problem. Many things are idols in a believer's life, but they are not aware of them. The individual himself can become an idol. An idol is anything that you look to solve your problem other than Me; it is anything that you love more than Me; it is anything that you want to be around more than being around My Word or Me; and you know that I AM the WORD! Idols are very seductive because they are physical, and they satisfy the 'flesh' so easily.

"An idol can be your concern for your own feelings of self pity, put before your concern for Me, and how I would have you treat others with care even though you don't feel like it. An idol can be your love for the gifts I give you, more than your love for Me: for instance, you may put your children, your spouse, your parents, your friends, your 'stuff, your house, your yard, your car, your clothes, or your food above wanting to be with Me, in prayer or in My Word, the Bible, or wanting to find out My will for your life."

"Immediately a person would question whether You are saying that we should neglect our families in some way."

"You know that this is not true. In the 10 Commandments I say to 'honor your father and mother: that thy days may be long upon the land which the Lord thy God gives thee.' (Exodus 20:12) In Luke 8:19-22 I was teaching many people when My mother and My brethren came to the door and wanted to speak to Me. I said to those listening to Me that 'My mother and My brethren are these which hear the word of God, and do it.' Was I shunning them? I was declaring a new relationship here. I was saying that you have an infinitely deeper, higher, and more permanent, relationship with Me, which transcends the blood relationship that you have with your family and friends. This brings you as a believer mighty close to Me, and this is what I am wanting you to understand, so that no one or nothing will come between us."(McGee)

"Lord, what part does shame and guilt play in the believer's life?"

"Shame and guilt are enemies to you and to all believers because they become bondage to you, and you will make wrong decisions because of them. My death on the cross broke all bondage to sin; you do not need to hang on to a 'little' sin because you 'were' a sinner. You now have chosen to turn away from sin, and to look to Me for your life; it may seem necessary to be guilty about wrong things that you have done, but this is a trap of the devil. When you give your life to Me, you have all of Me; everything that I Am is now yours. I made you "righteousness" because I Am righteous. 'If you confess your sins, I am faithful and just to forgive you your sins, and to cleanse you from all unrighteousness,' (1 John 1:9)

"Lord, what about the things I have done in the past that were against You?"

"Do not let a person put guilt on you for things you have done in the past. Do not believe the devil's lies that you live in America so you should not have material things because the rest of the world is living in poverty. I have given you all of your material things to be used for My glory. My people want to share what I have given them so My Word will go throughout the World when you support ministries like Samaritans Purse, The 700 Club, and J. Vernon McGee's Thru the Bible teaching, and your local Church. Do not let a person put shame on you for what you have done in the past that you may believe that you deserve. If you are truly guilty then ask the hurt one for forgiveness and turn to Me for total cleansing, so that the devil can no longer plague you. Do not continue to think, and worry, and speak about your guilt and shame, and do not hide it any longer from Me; I already know all about it, and I have immediately forgiven you, and I no longer remember what you did. (Hebrews 8:12) 'For I will be merciful to their unrighteousness, and their sins and their iniquities will I remember no more.' (Jeremiah 31:34) (...for I will remember their sin no more.) If I have forgotten your sins, then why do you feel obligated to hang on to them? Move on to the work I have for you."

"Lord, You just mentioned that we as American have guilt over having material things that others do not have, but should Christians have much money? Most seem to believe that money is bad because You said the 'love of money is the root of all evil, but most believe You and Your family were "broke" when You lived on the earth. In Proverbs 23:4 You said 'Labor not to be rich...for riches can fly away;' In James 2:5 You said "Has not God chosen the poor of this world rich in faith, and heirs of the kingdom which He has promised to them that love Him?" in Proverbs 13:7 You said, 'There is (he) that makes himself poor, yet has great riches.'"

"There is much misunderstanding about money, who should have it and who shouldn't First of all, how could I, Jesus, when I walked on the earth, have walked in 'poverty?' Think on these things that are written in the Bible: "there came Wise Men from the East to Jerusalem, saying, where is He that is born King of the Jews...and when they were come into the house, they saw the young child with Mary his mother...they presented unto Him gifts; gold, and frankincense, and myrrh." These gifts were for My parents to use to take care of My family and Me, as I grew up. (Matthew 2:1-11) Psalm 50:10 says, 'For every beast of the forest is mine, and the cattle upon a thousand hills. I know all the fowls of the mountains: and the wild beasts of the field are mine, if I were hungry, I would not tell thee: for the world is mine, and the fullness thereof.' Psalm 89:11 "The heavens are Thine (God's), the earth also is Thine (God's): as far the world and the fullness thereof, thou has founded them." I made the earth and everything in it, and I own everything in it, so tell Me how could 'I' be "poor" in material goods, while I walked on the earth?"

"Now the next question is; do I want My people to have money? We just discussed that money is necessary to support the church, and ministries that get My word out to those who have never heard. I have said to: 'Bring ye all the tithes into the storehouse so that there will be food enough in My Temple; if you do, I will open up the windows of heaven for you and pour out a blessing so great you won't have room enough to take it in! Try it! Let Me prove it to you! Your crops will be large, for I will guard them from insects and plagues. Your grapes won't shrivel away before they ripen,' says the Lord of Hosts. "And all the nations will call you blessed, for you will be a land sparkling with happiness. These are the promises of the Lord of Host." (Malachi 3:10-12) In Luke 6:38 I said, 'Give and it shall be given unto you; good measure pressed down, and shaken together, and running over, shall men give unto your bosom. Whatever measure you use to give – large or small – will be used to measure what is given back to you.' Now, do you think that I would withhold anything from you, the one that loves Me, and are called according to My purpose?' (Romans 8:28) Remember, "Money answereth all things." (Ecclesiastes 10:19)

"Yes, thank you, Lord Jesus, for 'meeting all My needs according to Your riches in Heaven,' (Philippians 4:19) Thank you for giving me money for my family's needs, and for others, But tell me about forgiveness. How big a deal is it for me to forgive others?"

"Victory in your life will be completely stopped by unforgiveness in your heart toward another person. If you do not learn to forgive, 'an unforgiving heart is poison to your spirit, body, and soul. In Hebrews 12:15 I call unforgiveness the root of all bitterness that springs up and defiles many. It defiles many people, but it also defiles many areas of your life." (Gregory Dickow)

"Is forgiveness something that I need to learn?"

"Yes, it is a choice, but you can only forgive by faith. (2 Corinthians 5:7) I tell you in Mark 11:24 that 'All things for which you pray and ask, believe that you have received them, and you shall have them.' In Mark 11:25 I tell you that "as you stand praying, and you remember that you are holding a grudge against anyone, forgive them. If you do not, then our Father in Heaven cannot forgive you." Forgiveness is the gateway to answered prayer. How big a deal is that?"

"Lord, if the Father does not forgive me, it sounds like I am not saved, and yet I have tried to forgive, but the feeling of resentment and bitterness comes back to me when I remember what someone did to me."

"I have mentioned that forgiveness is a decision that you make by faith, so don't be fooled by your feelings of resentment, or anger when they come back to you. How another person has treated you has nothing to do with the forgiveness that you offer to them; it is because you are forgiven by our Heavenly Father through My shed blood for you, while you were yet a sinner . Because you are for given by God for no reason other than Our Father loves you so much, should be reason enough for you to want to forgive another that has hurt you. (Ephesians 1:7) Forgiveness offered to another person is really healing to your own soul, and it will bring you the answer to all your prayers, and you will see miracles. It is the way to joy and to My 'abundant life."

"Lord it seems nearly impossible to forgive someone who has hurt me to my core, but I remember a story that I heard on TV about a woman that was dying of cancer ; the doctors had given her three days to live. A friend of the family, asked a pastor friend of his, to go to the hospital and pray for this woman's healing. The pastor was reluctant because he did not know her and he knew nothing of the circumstances. So on the way to the hospital he called upon the Holy Spirit to tell him how to pray for this woman. God said to him, in his spirit, "Tell her if she will forgive her husband she will live.' The pastor said he didn't know how he could say this to a stranger, but he decided that if the Holy Spirit told him to say it, he must.. Upon arriving at the hospital the pastor went to the woman's bedside and said to her, "God has told me that If you will forgive your husband you will `live, and not die." She immediately said,` I will never, never forgive that man for what he did to me 27 years ago.' Her husband started crying, and fell to his knees at the woman's bedside, and "begged" her to forgive him. She said that she could never forgive a man that would have an affair with another woman, even if it were only a one-night stand. Her husband continued to beg her for forgiveness. She said she would rather `die' than forgive that man. So the pastor left, and the woman died in three days as the doctors had predicted. At the funeral for this woman, the family members wondered how God could let this lovely woman die. The pastor that had spoken to her at the hospital, told her family that she died because God had asked her to forgive, and she would not." (Andrew Wommack)

"Yes Lord, now that I have recounted this story in my mind, and because You have told me to: 'Love my enemies, bless them that curse me, do good to them that hate me, and pray for them which despitefully use me, and persecute me, I will forgive those that have used me and hurt me, I am a child of our Father, which is in Heaven: for God makes his sun to rise on the evil and on the good, and sends rain on the just and on the unjust.' (Matthew 5:44-45) I shall be the victor here, no matter what I believe has been done to me, wrongfully."

"It is impossible to forgive without My Holy Spirit within you, to give you strength to do it. As you move forward to live your life in forgiveness, you will wonder how you could have lived so long with a hard heart toward others, when all of My blessings now flow in you, to give you a life so satisfying that My joy will well up in you, forever. Seeking Me with all of your heart is the essence of the Christian walk, and you will love it."

"Thank you Lord for Your great forgiveness toward me, but what about envy, is that something I need to be as concerned about as forgiveness? Is envy the same as jealousy?"

"In Proverbs 27:4 you read, 'Wrath is cruel, and anger is outrageous but who is able to stand before envy?' Envy and jealousy are the same, both mean, 'discontentment or resentment because of another's success, advantages, or superiority.' (McGee) Do you realize that Cain killed Abel because of jealousy; I was put on the Cross-because men did not want people following Me, and believing Me, over themselves. Just about every sin starts with one person being jealous because another person has something they want, and believe they cannot get.

"I am so willing to give you all that you desire and more: 'Delight yourself in Me, and I will give you the desires of your heart.' (Psalm37:4) "Now glory be to God who by His mighty power at work within (you) is able to do far more than (you) would ever dare to ask or even dream of-infinitely beyond (your) highest prayers, desires, thoughts, or hopes." (Ephesians3:20LB) Can you understand that any sin will destroy you; your joy, your peace and your happiness; the very things that your desire above all else. Please turn to Me always, and I will meet all of your needs."

"I see that forgiveness and envy go hand and hand, and I want to give them up before they get a hold on me. Tell me about the Communion Services. Does this represent Your forgiveness for Me? Why do we, as

Christians, take the bread and wine together, in Communion? Should this be done only at a church service?"

"In Luke 22:19-20 during the Passover celebration with My Disciples, I took bread, gave thanks for it, broke it, and gave it to them saying: 'This is My body which is given for you: this do in remembrance of Me.' Then I took the cup saying: "This cup is the New Testament in My blood, which is shed for you." "In John 6 I spoke of Myself as the living 'bread' which came down from heaven: a man may eat of it and not die, but he shall live forever: the bread that I will give is My flesh, which I give for the life of the world. I also said that you must eat the flesh of the Son of man, and drink His blood, or you have no life in you. If you eat My flesh, and drink My blood, you have eternal life: and I will raise you up on the last day. My flesh is meat indeed, and my blood is drink indeed. He that eats My flesh, and drinks My blood, dwells in Me, and I in him. As the living Father has sent Me, and I live by the Father: so He that eats Me, even he shall live by Me. This is that bread which came down from heaven: not as your fathers did eat manna, and are dead: he that eats of this bread shall live forever." (53-58)

"Jesus, I am even more confused now; please explain what you mean that I should eat Your flesh and drink Your blood, this sounds like cannibalism."

"I came down to this earth: 'the Word was made flesh.'(John1:14) When I came in the flesh I was going to go to the cross to lay My human life down there as a sacrifice to pay for your sins and all man's sins; I was the "innocent lamb," but I was tempted in all ways as are you but I did not sin, (Hebrews4:15) I was the 'perfect' sacrifice. When you partake of the bread now you do it as a saved person. When I first said this, those around Me thought I was speaking of literal flesh, but I was speaking of the spiritual realm in which you receive My life by faith. My blood is the symbol of life; the life of the flesh is in the blood. When you go to the doctors, he often takes a blood test to find out how your body is doing. I minister to you spiritually through your obedience in observing the Lord's Supper (Communion Service). This is not a ritual that the church goes through as a way of proving one is a member of a church. This is an expression of our intimate relationship together that joins your life to Mine forever.'"(McGee)

"Communion with Me, though the bread and wine, is not only done in a church setting; I want you to come to Me anytime, and at all times, to dedicate yourself to Me. When you take of the bread and wine you are saying that you cannot do anything apart from Me, and you are saying that you believe that I came in the flesh, was crucified, dead and buried, and on the third day I rose from the dead. Kenneth Copeland helped you to understand how the taking of bread, and wine, will bring you closer to Me. He wrote these words:

"I dedicate my body, all day long, to the service of you, my Lord Jesus Christ. I take Your Pure Blood shed for me, dear Jesus, into my body.

"I put the devil in his place with these words: 'Devil, you are not going to put any sickness or disease on me today, regardless of my symptoms or how I feel, because 'I am healed by your stripes, Jesus.' The devil has tried to put a serious attack on my mind, but I only receive thoughts of health and hope through Your Words, Jesus.

'If I wake up at night, I read or recite scriptures of healing and health for my mind and body: Proverbs 4:20-22, 'Your word, Lord, is life to me and as I speak it, I receive health to all my flesh.' 2 Kings 20:5 Lord, You have heard my prayer and seen my tears, and you will heal me. "Psalm 103:3 'I am the Lord who forgives all your sins and heals all your diseases. Isaiah 53:5 "I your Lord, by My Stripes healed you (forevermore)."

"Lord, a missionary came to our church and related a story about her experience in a country where you, Jesus, had never been heard of. She told them that Christmas was the time of year, that she and other believes, in You, celebrated Your birth. The people were incredulous that her 'God' was born. We know that this is the Gospel: Your birth, Your death, Your burial, and Your resurrection? How do we as believers tell others about You?"

"Do you remember the story that Paul Harvey told every year, at Christmas, about the birds?"

"Yes, that is a wonderful story about a man who lived in the United States. Who could not believe in You, Jesus; he could not believe that You, as God, were born onto the earth as a baby, to grow up as a child, and become a man. His wife and children went to church every Christmas Eve to celebrate Your birth, but he always stayed at home because he could not see the point of this celebration. As he sat in his chair in his living room it began to snow; because it was dark outside he had his light on by his chair, and he had a fire lit in his fire place; because the light was on in the room birds started flying against his picture window, trying to get into the warm house for shelter.

"He being concerned about them freezing to death or killing themselves against the window, he put on his coat and went outside to his barn. He opened the doors wide, turned on the lights, and tried to shoo the birds into the barn for their safety. They continued to fly away from him, but they still continued to fling themselves against the window of his house. He took off his jacket and tried to use it to swish them toward the light into the warm barn for their safety. Still, they could not be convinced to go to a place where they could be protected from the cold night.

"In his frustration he said to himself, if I could only be a bird for a short time I could lead the birds to the light and to protection from the snow and the wind, and they would be saved from certain death. When these words left his lips, he immediately realized that he had just understood why God became a man on the earth.

"This story is a good one to explain, why You, Jesus, became a man to save us from the certain' eternal death' of sin. Is there anything else I should know about Your birth?"

"I had to be born' of a woman to have the legal right to heal the sick, cast out demons, and raise the dead. Because God told man to "be fruitful, and multiply, and replenish the earth, and subdue it: and have dominion over the fish of the sea, and over the fowl of the air, and over every living thing that moves upon the earth;" (Genesis 1:28) only a living person can have authority to do these things.

"In Matthew 8:28-34 you read the account of a 'man who lived in the tombs (cemetery) with an unclean spirit; no man could bind him with chains, as he would break them to pieces: neither could any man tame (stop) him. Night and day, he was in the tombs crying and cutting himself with stones when he saw Me he ran and worshipped Me.' The devils in him cried out with a loud voice, "what do we have to do with You, Jesus, thou Son of the most high God, that thou torment us before the time?" The devils asked Me to cast them into the herd of swine that were nearby. I said to them, 'Go' and the swine ran violently down a steep place into the sea, and perished in the waters. '

"The demons in this man knew that I was God, but they mistakenly believed that I had no authority over them because 'I Am God. 'I tell you because I was born onto the earth I had the authority to cast them out of this man into the swine. Please understand that you have all the authority of a man, given to you by God, and by what I did for you at the Cross. I want you, as my beloved, to take authority in My Name."

"Lord, what should I know about the Cross, and what You did there?" This is where my life lies, so please tell me what the Cross is all about."

"You know that I was put to death on a cross, and then I was Resurrected on the third day; this is the basis of what you, as a Christian, have put your faith in. Over time the account of the cross may have become 'trite' to you because you have heard it so many times before. Yet, "My crucifixion is one of the most dastardly deeds in history." (McGee) I want to tell you again of My death, so you will never take it for granted again.

"You know that My Disciple, Judas, betrayed Me to the religious rulers of the Jews. Judas came to the Garden of Gethsemane with a 'great multitude with swords and staves from the chief priests, and the scribes, and the elders.' (Mark 14:43) I was there praying to the Father about "My soul which was exceeding sorrowful unto death." (Mark 14:32) Judas 'kissed me,' identifying Me to the multitude so they could lead Me away to the high priest. I was led to Annas first, as he was the father in law to Caiaphas, the high priest. Annas had been high priest and he probably was behind the whole plot to kill Me. My trial was a mockery. "I did not defend Myself against such obvious falsehood; this fulfilled the prophecy, 'as a sheep before her shearer's is dumb, so He opened not his mouth.'(Isaiah53:7) None of it was legal under Jewish law, but My enemies were determined to put Me to death. "You may believe that the Jews put Me to death, but actually all of mankind put Me on the cross, because I willingly died for the sins of the whole world."(McGee)

"At the garden of Gethsemane I asked 'My Father if it was possible, to let this cup pass from Me.' (Matthew 26:39) "This cup was of judgment that I bore for you on the cross. Everyone who turns his back on Me, Jesus, will have to drink that cup of judgment himself. I did drink the hated cup because it was the cup of your sin." (McGee)

"Do not get the idea that I went to the cross reluctantly; it is written, 'That for the joy that was set before Me, I endured the cross, despising the shame, and is set down at the right hand of the throne of God.' (Hebrews12:2)

"The religious leaders wanted Rome to give Me the death penalty, but they had no charge against Me, so they found two false witnesses (under) Jewish law, two witnesses had to agreed that I said that I was able to destroy the temple of God, and then would rebuild it in three days. Actually I said, 'Destroy this temple, and in three days I will raise it up.' (John2:19) I was speaking of My human body that would die on the cross, be buried, and then be resurrected on the third day.

"The high priest then asked Me, 'Are you the Christ, the Son of God?' I said to him, 'Hereafter shall ye see the Son of man sitting on the right hand of power, and coming in the clouds of heaven.' (Matthew 26:63-64) The high priest knew I was claiming Daniel 7:13-14: 'I saw in the night visions, and, behold, one like the Son of man came with the clouds of heaven, and came to the Ancient of days, and they brought Him near before him. And there was given Him dominion, and glory, and a kingdom, that all people, nations, and languages, should serve Him: His dominion is an everlasting dominion, which shall not pass away, and His kingdom is that which shall not be destroyed.'

"The high priest rent his clothes, saying, 'He has spoken blasphemy; what further need have we of witnesses? Behold, now ye have heard his blasphemy. He is guilty of death,' "The high priest understood what I had said, so he tore his garment and in doing so he broke the Mosaic Law, as the garment of the high priest was not to be torn." (Matthew 26:65-66) (McGee)

"The Sanhedrin believed they had a case against Me that would stand up before the Roman court, so I was bound and delivered to Pontius Pilate, the governor. (Matthew 27:2) 'I was led to the hall of judgment by the religious leaders, but they would not go into the judgment hall themselves lest they should be defiled; later they intended to eat the Passover Supper.' (John 18:28) "This is a very interesting byplay here; the Jews absolutely would not go into the judgment hall because they did not want to contaminate themselves. They are plotting the death of Me, the very One who is the fulfillment of the Passover, yet they do not want to defile themselves so they can partake of the Passover Supper. Please understand this, so that you will search your own heart concerning Me; take account of your life, and ask yourself if you are merely religious or are you truly joined to Me?" (McGee) I have told you that you will give an account of your life to Me (Jesus). (Romans 14:12)

"As Pilate questions Me and speaks with the Jews concerning Me, he begins to sense that something is wrong. He wants to get out of making a decision to have Me crucified, because he says, 'I find no fault at all.' (John 18:38) He tells the Jews to judge Me themselves, but they were determined to have Me put to death, and only Rome could do that. (McGee)

"Pilate had Me scourged, and then a crown of thorns was put on My head; a purple robe was put on Me in mockery, as I was hailed, 'King of the Jews.' (John 19:1-2) I was blindfolded, beaten and spit upon, over and over, until I no longer looked like a man. Isaiah wrote this of Me "As many were astonished at thee; His visage was so marred more than any man, and His form more than the sons of men." (Isaiah 52:14) This 'beating was more than ordinary human hatred.' (McGee) All of man's sins and diseases were put upon Me, and for this reason I no longer looked human.

"Pilate let Barabbas, a known robber, go free because it was the custom to release one prisoner at the time of the Passover. Pilate wanted the people to say I, Jesus, should be set free, but they continued to "cry out all the more, saying, "Let him be crucified."(John 18:39-40) (Matthew 27:22)

"Pilate wanted Me to tell him why I shouldn't be crucified, but I gave him no answer; he then said to Me, 'I have the power to crucify You, and I have the power to release You. 'I answered him and said, "Thou could have no power at all against Me, except it were given to thee from above: therefore he that delivered Me unto thee has the greater sin."(John19:10-11)

"Pilate continued to ask the people what I had done? 'They cried out the more, saying, "Let him be crucified."' (Matthew 27:23) 'When Pilate saw that he could prevail nothing (not) but rather a tumult (riot) was made, he took water, and washed his hands before the multitude, saying, "I am innocent of the blood of this Just person: see ye to it."' "'Then the people said, 'His blood be on us, and on our children.' (Matthew 27:24-25) Unfortunately, that has been the case over the centuries, and it can be demonstrated. (McGee) Pilate, however, was not exonerated from guilt because he washed his hands; he had to make a decision about Me, as every man does. "The bitter irony of Pilate's action is that in the oldest creed of the church stand these words...'crucified under Pontius Pilate.'(McGee)

"My body was in a weakened condition because I had suffered much, so on the way to Golgotha (the place of the scull) the soldiers found a 'man of Cyrene, Simon by name,' and compelled him to bear the cross for Me. (Matthew 27:31-33) This fulfilled what I had said to My Disciples, "If any man will come after Me, let him deny himself, and take up his cross, and follow Me." (Matthew16:24)

"I was stripped of "ALL" of My clothes, and put on the cross; the soldiers cast lots to divide My garments among themselves. This was prophesied in Psalm 22:18: 'They part My garments among them and cast lots upon My vesture.'"

"Pilate wrote this title over My head which said, 'JESUS OF NAZARETH THE KING OF THE JEWS.' (John 19:19) It was written in Hebrew, Greek, and Latin, but the chief priests said to Pilate that he had written amiss; he should write, "He said that I am King of the Jews." Pilate would not change what he had written. You know that Pilate had written rightly. (John19:20-22)

"My mother Mary, her sister, and Mary the wife of Cleophas, and Mary Magdalene were all standing at the cross. I saw My mother there and said to her, 'Woman, behold thy Son!' I was referring to Myself. When we go back to the first miracle that I did at the wedding feast, My mother came to me and told me they had no wine. I said to her, "Woman, what do I have to do with thee? Mine hour has not yet come. My mother said to the servants, "Whatever He saith unto you, do it." I then turned the water into wine. Why did I tell her at the wedding feast that Mine hour has not yet come? At that time I was just starting My Ministry and It was not time to show the world who I was and clear her reputation as a woman who was with child before she was married to Joseph. Now, My hour had come, and in My resurrection My mothers name would be cleared forever. Her reputation would be vindicated, because everyone would know that I am the Glorified Christ, the Son of God." (McGee)

"I then said to John, My Disciple, "Behold thy mother!" At that same hour John took her to his home, because she was grieving so much over what was happening to Me. (John 19:25-27) I wanted her to go with John because her heart was broken watching Me dying on the cross. It seems that John took her to his home so she could be comforted, and it seems he was gone for about an hour and then returned to the cross." (McGee)

"There were twenty-eight prophecies fulfilled while I was hanging on the cross. "I thirst" is the fulfillment of Psalm 69:21. 'It is finished!'(John 17:4) Psalm 34:20 says, "He keepeth all his bones: not one of them is broken. "Zechariah 12:10 says…'they shall look upon Me who they have pierced, and they shall mourn for Him, as one mourneth for his only son…' I have been pierced, has been fulfilled, but people will not mourn for Me until I return again. Psalm 22, Genesis 22, Isaiah 53, and Leviticus 16 are places in the Old Testament that are especially concerned with My Crucifixion. (McGee)

"When I Jesus) said. 'It is finished,' I was referring to your redemption (freedom from sin)." (McGee) "And it was about the sixth hour, and there was a darkness over all the earth until the ninth hour. At the ninth hour I 'cried with a LOUD voice,' saying, "Eloi, Eloi, lama sabachthani?" (Mark 15:32-34) I was saying, 'My God, My God, why has Thou forsaken Me?' And the sun was darkened, and the veil of the temple was rent (torn) in the midst (middle). I then cried with a LOUD voice and said, "Father, into thy hands I commend My Spirit:" and having said this, I gave up the Ghost, and there was a great earthquake. The veil symbolized man being shut out from God, but at My death it was torn in two pieces from top to bottom. So, at My death, the way for man was now open so that he is able to approach God without fear." (Luke 23:44-46) 'I did not die because My bodily organs refused to function. I surrendered up My Spirit; My life did not ebb away, or I could not have "cried with a LOUD voice." 'I could not die until I freely had given up My Spirit.' (McGee)

"When I was dead, Joseph of Arimathaea, went to Pilate, and begged for My body: He took My body down from the cross, and wrapped it in linen, and laid it in a sepulcher (tomb) that was hewn in stone.' (Mark 15:42) "The women that came with Me from Galilee; Mary Magdalene, Mary the mother of James the less and of Joses, and Salome, and other women that came with Me, watched from afar off so they would know where I was laid." (Mark: 40-41)

"The next day, the chief priests and Pharisees came together unto Pilate, saying that they remembered Me saying that after three days I would rise again. They asked Pilate to seal the tomb, so that My Disciples could not come in the night and steal My body away and then say I had risen from the dead. (These enemies believed My words more than My followers) Pilate agreed and placed a sealed stone over the entrance of the sepulcher, and placed soldiers to watch over the tomb." (Matthew 27:62-66)

"At the end of the Sabbath (Saturday), as it began to dawn toward the first day of the week (Sunday), Mary Magdalene, and the other Mary came to where I (Jesus) had been placed in the sepulcher. They were bringing sweet spices to anoint My body. There was a great earthquake: the angel of the Lord descended from heaven and came and rolled back the stone from the door, and sat upon it. His countenance was like lightning, and his raiment white as snow. The guards that were at the tomb did shake, and became as dead men. The angel said to the women, "Fear not: for I know that you seek Jesus, which was crucified. He is not here: for he is risen, as He said. " Come see the place where the Lord lay. He told them to go quickly and tell My Disciples that 'I Am' risen from the dead. He also told them that I would go before them into Galilee, and that I would see them there.' (Matthew 28:1-10)

"The woman ran to Simon Peter, and to John, My Disciples, and said to them, 'they have taken away the Lord out of the sepulcher, and we know not where they have laid Him.' Peter and John ran forth to the sepulcher; John ran faster than Peter and stooped down and looked into the tomb and saw the linen clothes lying there. Peter then arrived and went into the sepulcher and saw the linen clothes. John went into the sepulcher too, and he realized that the linen clothes were not touched, but still in the shape of My body. The napkin around My head was folded and lying separate from the linen clothes. This convinced John that I had "RISEN INDEED!" (John 20:1-8)

"My Disciples did not remember that I had said that 'I must rise again from the dead,' so they went away again to their own home. (John 20:9-10) "Mary Magdalene came back to the sepulcher and stood weeping outside; she then looked into the tomb and saw two angels in white sitting, one at the head, and the other at the feet, where I (Jesus) had lain. They asked her why she was weeping, and she said because she did not know where 'they' had taken My body. Then she turned away from them and saw Me, Jesus standing beside her, but she did not know it was Me." (John 20:11-14)

"I said to her, 'Woman, why are you weeping? Whom do you seek?' Mary thinking that I am the gardener, said, "Sir, if you have taken Him away, tell me where you have laid him, and I will go and take Him away." (John 20:15)

"I said to her, 'Mary.' She turned to Me and said, "Rabboni;" which means Master. I then said to her, 'Touch me not, for I am not yet ascended to My Father: but go to My Disciples and tell them, "I ascend unto My Father, and your father; and to My God, and your God." (John 20:17) I told her not to touch Me, meaning that I did not want her to detain Me as if she would not see Me again. I was going to be on the earth for forty more days. When I spoke of going to 'My Father, and her father, and to My God and her God,' I was portraying the great relationship between the Believer and the Heavenly Father; actually, I was telling her that what I did at Calvary, and now in My Resurrection, opened the way for her and all of mankind, to go to the Father, through Me, in prayer." (Jimmy Swaggart, the Expositor's Study Bible)

"Mary Magdalene left Me, and ran to tell the Disciples that she had seen Me, and told them what I has spoken to her. Later that evening, Sunday, I appeared to My Disciples that were assembled together, behind locked doors, and greeted them with, "Peace be with you." The peace that I was speaking of here is the peace with God through justification by faith that I accomplished at the cross, for them." (John 20:18-19) (McGee)

"I showed them My hands and My side, and the Disciples were very glad to see Me alive. I breathed on them, and said to them, 'Receive the Holy Ghost.' "The Holy Spirit now indwelt them, and they received eternal life. This power would sustain them for the interval between My ascension and the coming of the Holy Spirit on Pentecost." (John 20:20-22) (McGee)

"During the forty days that I was on the earth, after the Resurrection, I appeared to My Disciples and to other believers, 'speaking of the things pertaining to the kingdom of God.' At the end of this period I told them "not to depart from Jerusalem, but to wait for the promise of the Father, the Holy Spirit.' (Acts 1:4) I told them that they shall 'receive power from the Holy Ghost; and they shall be witnesses unto Me both in Jerusalem, and in all Judea, and in Samaria, and to the uttermost parts of the earth.' (Acts 1:8) This is the great commission given to all believers in Me, for them and for you today, to continually get My Word out to all people. I told My Disciples in Mark 16:15-18 to "Go into all the world, and preach the Gospel to every creature. He that believes and is baptized shall be saved; but he that believes not shall be dammed. And these signs shall follow them that believe; in My name shall they cast out devils; they shall speak with new tongues. They shall take up serpents; and if they drink any deadly thing, it shall not hurt them; they shall lay hands on the sick, and they shall recover.'

"When I had spoken these things, and while My believers watched, I was taken up; and a cloud received Me out of their sight.' (Acts 1:9) "While they looked steadfastly toward heaven as I went up, two men stood by them in white apparel and said; 'Ye man of Galilee, why stand you gazing up into heaven this same Jesus, which is taken up from you into heaven, shall so come in like manner as you have seen him go into heaven." (Acts 1:10-11) In Zechariah 14:4 I tell you: 'And My feet shall stand in that day upon the mount of Olives, which is before Jerusalem on the east, and mount of Olives shall cleave in the midst thereof, toward the east and toward the west, and there shall be a very great valley; and half of the mountain shall remove toward the north, and half of it toward the south.' I left the earth at this place and I will return to this place. I speak of a great splitting of the mountain, as a means of escape for Israel." (McGee)

"Lord, I understand here that we know that when You left the earth You promised to return; is this what Revelation, the last book of the Bible, is all about? It seems like we are living in the days of Revelation with all the weather events taking place now. Are we suppose to understand this book of the Bible; many Christians believe that Your people will be taken off the earth before really, really, really bad things take place on the earth, but, already we are seeing so many powerful earthquakes , tornadoes, flooding in many places, and electricity off for a length of time, people uprooted from their homes and more is predicted to come. It seems like it is very hard to understand Revelation, with all the symbols, so how can we understand what You are saying here?"

"All the books of the Bible are impossible to understand without My Holy Spirit to explain them to you. No book should be ignored because I speak through all My books. Revelation means; unveiling or pulling back a curtain so something else can be seen. Revelation shows Me as 'KING OF KINGS AND LORDS OF LORDS' (Revelation 19:16) and reveals

Me in all My "beauty, power, and glory." Before Revelation 19:16, these words are written: `And He was clothed with a vesture dipped in blood; and His name is called, "The Word of God." And the armies, which were in heaven, followed Him upon white horses, clothed in fine linen, white and clean. And out of His mouth goeth a sharp sword, that with it He should smite the nations: and He shall rule them with a rod of iron: and He treadeth the winepresses of the fierceness and wrath of Almighty God.

"Notice that My garment is sprinkled with blood, and that I am treading the winepress of the fierceness, and wrath of God. This picture takes us back to Isaiah 63:1-6, so we are referring to My second coming here,' Next I say, `I will rule them with a rod of iron,' You can read this in Psalm 2, also: "Yet have I set My king upon My holy hill of Zion. I will declare the decree: the Lord has said to Me, `Thou are the Son; this day I have begotten thee (from the dead). Ask of Me and I shall give thee the heathen for thine inheritance, and the uttermost parts of the earth for thy possession." (I didn't get them at My first coming, so how will I get them now?) `Thou shall break them with a rod of iron: Thou shall dash them in pieces like a potter's vessel.' (Psalm 2:6-9) You can see the fury of My wrath at My second coming, is in sharp contrast to My gentleness at My first coming. However, in both I am revealed as the, "wrath of the Lamb." The armies that come with Me are the legions of angels that do My bidding.' (McGee)

"I gave man this book to show him the events that would take place before My return to the earth to set up My Kingdom. 'The Rapture' of My believers has been taught and studied through the centuries, but I have said that you as a believer should look for My return every day, and you should live each day as if it is your last."

"Revelation 1: 1 says: `The Revelation of Jesus Christ, which God gave unto Him, to show unto his servants things which must shortly come to pass; and he sent and signified it by his angel unto his servant John.' (KJV) J. Vernon McGee translated this verse like this: "The unveiling of Jesus Christ which God gave Him to show unto His bond servants things which must shortly come to pass completely, and He sent and signified it (gave a sign) by His angel (messenger) to His servant John.

"This first verse tells me that You gave us this book so that we could understand the mysteries of the kingdom of God."

"To 'show,' means: by word pictures, by symbols, by direct and Indirect representations. The symbols used here are symbolic of reality. Peter gave you a great rule for the interpretation of prophecy in 2 Peter 1:20: "Knowing this first, that no prophecy of the scripture is of any private interpretation.' You do not interpret a single text by itself; you interpret it in the light of the entire Word of God." When it was written that things which must shortly come to pass' I was not "implying that I was coming soon, but when My return is imminent these things will happen with certainly, and they will happen quickly and with great speed. My vengeance will take place in a brief period of time." (McGee)

"Lord, you mentioned 'Your angel,' and this is interpreted as a messenger. What about the angels that are written about many times in the Bible? People have angel pictures, and angel statues in their homes, and some people claim to see angels. I would like to know what part angels play in my life today."

"Because 'My Word does not return unto Me void.' (Isaiah 55:11) the words that are spoken by My people, that are in direct connection to My Word, have life in them. I said that My Word would go on forever. So you can understand that angels are the ones that surround you with My protection because My Word is life. They cannot heal you or forgive you, only I can do that, but they do My bidding at all times to help you. You can "provoke them" (Exodus 23:31) by not speaking any words that have life in them." (Charles Capps)

"It seems like the things that you told us about in prophecy, 'are' happening with great speed. In Revelation 6 we read of four horses, each with its own rider. We have the 'white horse;' it's rider has a bow and a crown, and he goes forth conquering, and to conquer.' The second horse is 'red:' the rider has the ability to take peace from the earth and he carries a great sword. The third horse is 'black:' its rider has a pair of balances in his hand, and a voice says a measure of wheat for a penny, and three measures of barley for a penny. The fourth horse is 'pale:' it's rider was called Death and Hell and he had power to kill with the sword, and with famine, and with death, and by the wild beasts of the earth, up to a fourth part of the earth. (Revelation 6:1-8) The four horses seem to be riding on the earth now. Please tell me what these horses represent."

"The white horse represents lawlessness and unrest in all nations, and because of this the world will scream for someone to bring unity and peace, at all costs, to the earth. The red horse represents blood and war, and his rider has a bow to make war, the opposite of peace. The black horse represents mourning and famine. The scales tells us that the "working man will be unable to support his family in that day." The pale horse represents 'plague and pestilence that is going to take out one-fourth of the population of the earth." (McGee)

"Lord, You mentioned when we see these things, 'we are in the beginning of sorrows.' (Matthew 24:8) What would you have me to do as I see these things happening?"

"I want you to be prepared to "preach My word in all the world, and to be a witness unto all nations,' and to support those ministries that are getting My word out to the world. (Matthew 24:14) I also want you to be prepared to help others with their physical needs in any emergency, because I do not want you to "take the mark of the beast," (Revelation 13:16-17) for any reason. I ask you to prepare now with physical things, to help yourself, and others, in an emergency, such as: have on hand "extra food (some freeze-dried food will last on the shelf of your home for 20-25 years) blankets, some cash money, hand- crank radio, flashlights and extra batteries, or hand crank flashlights, candles or oil lamps, Bible, pet food, seeds to plant a garden, work gloves, tools, dust masks, and prepare your own important documents to be carried away in an emergency, and encourage others to prepare also." (CBN: Preparing for a weather emergency)

"Dear Jesus, You have spoken to me about many things. What do you want from me as I go forth in these days ahead?"

"I always want you to know that I love you with an everlasting love, and I want you to 'love Me because I have first loved you.' in Micah 6:8 it says; "what does the Lord require of thee, BUT TO DO JUSTLY, AND TO LOVE MERCY, AND TO WALK HUMBLY WITH THY GOD?" You can see this is all I want from you as you go about your life day to day. You must realize now that 'you can do nothing apart from Me.'

"But I must tell you that My love is not enough for you."

"Lord, what are you saying? You told me that what you wanted me to know 'most' about You, was Your great "love" for me! What are You telling me now; what else do I need to know about You?"

"It is not what you need to know about Me, but what you need to do."

"I thought Lord, that I didn't need to do anything, because You have done everything for me."

"I did do everything for you at the Cross, but still My love is not enough. Let us remember the two thieves, that died on crosses on either side of Me when I was crucified at the place of the scull. One scoffed at Me and said, "If thou be the Christ save thyself and us.' (Luke 23:39) The other thief "rebuked him, saying, `Do not thou fear God, seeing thou are in the same condemnation? We indeed justly; for we receive the due reward of our deeds: but this man has done nothing amiss. He then said to Me, "Remember me when you come into thy kingdom." I said unto him, `Today you shall be with Me in paradise.' (Luke 23"39-43) Do you believe that I loved both of these men?" "Yes, I know that You loved them both."

"My love could only save one of them. You must believe Me, and trust Me and `EXPECT' Me to answer all your prayers, before you will have victory over sin, and receive the "abundant life" that I have promised you. All of my promises are `yes and amen.' I could say that you must love Me back, before you will see My love for you manifested in your life. I want you to have victory over the devil, whom will continually harass you if you do not face up to him, with the authority of My Word. I want you to do, all that you do, out of your great love for Me. I do not want you to see Me as a magician, or a doting father that will indulge you in all of your "wants." I will do anything for you, but you must come to Me in `faith;' I can only answer your prayer of faith. "I am God the Spirit, you must worship ME in spirit and in truth." (John 4:24) Always seek the truth about yourself, and Me. Do not run away from Me, or the life that I have given you. This is a letter I want to read to you:

"Dear Beloved,

I LOVE YOU! I shed My own blood for you to make you clean. You are new, so believe it is true. You are lovely in My eyes, and I created you to be just as you are. Do not criticize yourself or get down on yourself for not being perfect in your own eyes. This leads only to frustration. I want you to trust Me, Beloved one, and take one day at a time. Dwell in My power, and My love, and you will be free. Be yourself. Don't allow other people to run you.

"I will guide you if you will let Me. Be aware of My presence in everything. I give you patience, love, joy, and peace. Look to Me for answers. I am your Shepherd and I will lead you. Follow Me only. Do not ever forget this. Listen and I will tell you My will. I LOVE YOU, Beloved one. I LOVE YOU! Let it flow from you, spilling over to all you touch.

"Be not overly concerned with yourself; you are My responsibility. I will change you without you hardly knowing it. You are to love yourself and to love others simply because I LOVE YOU. Take your eyes off yourself; look only to and at Me. I lead, I change, I make, but not when you are 'trying;' I will not fight your efforts.

"You are mine, Beloved one, so let Me have the joy of making you like Me. Let Me give you joy, peace, and kindness. No one else can. You are not your own. You have been bought with My blood and you now belong to Me. Your only command is to look to Me and only Me, never to yourself and never to others. Don't struggle. Relax in My love. Stop 'trying.' Let me make you what I want. My will is perfect; My love is sufficient. Look to Me. I LOVE YOU, my beloved one.

"I give you these words to comfort you, from the book, Twice Pardoned, by Harold Morris."

"Lord, we have spoken of many things, but Your LOVE for me is the most powerful thing You have given me."

"Remember, you can come to Me any time, or any place, because I Am always with you, listening to your every need; I live in your praise for Me, and you know that we are one now. (John 14:20 'At that day ye shall know that I am in My Father, and ye in Me, and I in you.') Please meditate on what we have been saying to each other, so that My Spirit will prevail in you. When you became born-again you received My Spirit; you are identical to Me now, in your Spirit. We are one in Spirit. Your Spirit is now Me, so acknowledge Me every moment of every day.

In Acts 2:17 I wrote: 'And it shall come to pass in the last days, I will pour out of my Spirit upon all flesh: and your sons and your daughters shall prophesy, and your young men shall see visions, and your old men shall dream dreams: (18) And on my servants and on my handmaidens I will pour out in those days of My spirit; and they shall prophecy: (19) And I will show wonders in heaven above, and signs in the earth beneath; blood, and fire and vapor of smoke: (20) The sun shall be turned into darkness, and the moon into blood, before that great and notable day of the Lord. (21) And it shall come to pass; that whosoever shall call on the name of the Lord shall be saved.'

"Look forward to this, and rejoice that I am closer to you than ever before in your life. Worship Me saying: 'We give Thee Thanks, O Lord God Almighty, which art, and was, and art to come, because Thou has taken to Thee Thy great power, and has reigned.' (Revelation 11:17)

"EVEN SO, COME, LORD JESUS, YOUR GRACE IS WITH US ALL!" (Revelation 22:20-21)

BIBLE STUDY SO FAR

"So what do you think of Bible Study so far?"

"It's like riding a good horse."

"How's that?"

"At first a colt needs to learn to follow my lead. He wants to do what seems natural to him, like bucking, and playing, and pulling away, and throwing his head, and not loading in the horse trailer."

"Then what?"

"Well, I have to work with him over, and over, and over, and teach him that he can't do anything unless I tell him to do it. He has to learn to go when I say 'GO,' stop when I say "STOP." I have to cure him of all his fears and help him to like the bit, and the bridle, and the saddle. He has to be taught how to work so I can rope a calf during branding, push cows during roundup, or stay put when I put hobbles on him, and lope when I need to ride for pleasure to see how high the water is in the reservoir after a rain. Once he learns what I want, we are inseparable, and he likes to see me coming because he wants to please me above all others.

"AMEN!"

www.ingramcontent.com/pod-product-compliance
Lightning Source LLC
Chambersburg PA
CBHW070044080526
44586CB00013B/907